ASTER FAMILY FLOWER

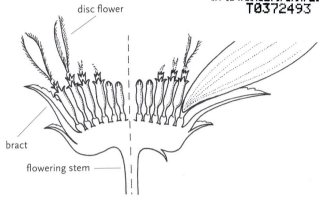

disc flower

bract

flowering stem

INFLORESCENCES

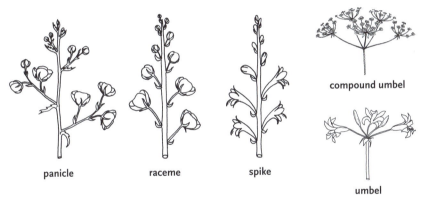

panicle

raceme

spike

compound umbel

umbel

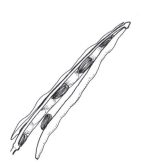

legume

silicle

silique

WILDFLOWERS
OF CALIFORNIA

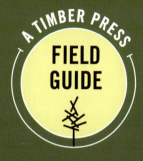

This book is dedicated to California's native plant enthusiasts and to the people who make the California Native Plant Society a special organization. We specifically honor the memories of Don Mayall, Jessica Mae Orozco, Wayne Roderick, and Dean William Taylor, who cared deeply for the flora of California.

Authors: Sandra Namoff, John Game, Bruce Homer-Smith, Nick Jensen, Julie Kierstead, Shawna Martinez, and Dylan Neubauer

Title Page: *Triteleia ixioides*
Photo credits appear on page 584.
Illustrations by Joe Medeiros
Published in 2024 by Timber Press, Inc., a subsidiary of Workman Publishing Co., Inc.,
a subsidiary of Hachette Book Group, Inc.

1290 Avenue of the Americas
New York, New York 10104
timberpress.com

Printed in China on responsibly sourced paper
Text and cover design based on series design by Adrianna Sutton
The publisher is not responsible for websites (or their content) that are not owned
by the publisher.

The Hachette Speakers Bureau provides a wide range of authors for speaking events.
To find out more, go to hachettespeakersbureau.com or email HachetteSpeakers@hbgusa.com.

ISBN 978-1-64326-059-4
A catalog record for this book is available from the Library of Congress.

California Native
Plant Society

WILDFLOWERS
OF CALIFORNIA

CONTENTS

Photo Key   6
Acknowledgments   36
Introduction   39
How to Use This Book   42
Biogeography   52
California Vegetation   60
Threats to the Flora   70
Wildflower Viewing Areas   74
Botany 101   76
Plant Families   84
Rare Species   98

GREEN FLOWERS   109

ORANGE FLOWERS   457

PINK TO RED FLOWERS   349

WHITE FLOWERS 132

PURPLE TO BLUE FLOWERS 274

Glossary	571
Sources and Resources	579
Photo Credits	584
Index	589

YELLOW FLOWERS 469

PHOTO KEY

Welcome! The goal of this book is to help you identify California's wildflowers. If you are curious about a wildflower you've found growing in California, use this Photo Key to match your unknown flower to a photo. The photos are arranged by color and then by flower similarity. As you examine your wildflower, pay special attention to the number of petals and the flower's general shape. Then use the key as a guide to locate the place in the book where you are most likely to identify and find information about the species you've found. Have fun botanizing!

GREEN FLOWERS

Prostrate Pigweed, p. 126

Great Valley Coyote Thistle, p. 110

Biscuitroots and umbrellaworts, p. 111

Small-head Aster family, p. 112–115

Rough Cocklebur, p. 115

Longbeak Streptanthella, p. 116

Chollas, p. 116–117

Chenopods, p. 117–120

Doveweed, p. 121

Chinese Caps, p. 121

Castor Bean, p. 122

Mission Bells, p. 122

Spotted Fritillary, p. 123

Brown Bells, p. 123

Orchids, p. 124

Paintbrushes,
p. 125

Fendler's Meadow-
rue, p. 126

California
Coffeeberry, p. 126

Hollyleaf Redberry,
p. 127

Bedstraws,
p. 127–128

Mountain Maple,
p. 129

Brewer's Mitrewort,
p. 129

Jojoba,
p. 130

Stinging Nettle,
p. 130

California Grape,
p. 131

WHITE FLOWERS

Soap plants,
p. 133

Desert Lily,
p. 134

Yuccas,
p. 134–135

Ice Plant,
p. 136

Water-plantains,
p. 136–137

Narrowleaf Onion,
p. 138

Laurel Sumac,
p. 138

Sumacs,
p. 139–140

Poison-oak,
p. 140

Ranger's Buttons,
p. 141

Compound umbels,
carrot family
p. 143–145

Small-cluster
carrot family
p. 142

Biscuitroots,
p. 145–146

Hemp Dogbane,
p. 148

Woolypod
Milkweed,
p. 148

Calla Lily,
p. 149

California
Spikenard,
p. 149

Yarrow,
p. 150

Sunflower-like
heads,
p. 150–151

Dandelion-like
heads,
p. 151–152

Arctic Sweet
Coltsfoot,
p. 152

American
Trailplant,
p. 153

Papery-headed
sunflower family,
p. 154

Baccharises,
p. 154–155

Pincushions,
p. 155–156

Small-headed
sunflower family,
p. 157–158

Inside-out flowers,
p. 158–159

Western Hazelnut,
p. 159

Cat's Eyes and
popcorn flowers,
p. 160–161

Combseeds,
p. 161–162

Small-flowered
mustard family,
p. 164

Mustard family,
p. 165–169

Biradial mustards,
p. 166

Scouler's Harebell,
p. 172

Threadplants,
p. 172–173

Small-flowered
pink family,
p. 173–174

Lobe-petaled pink
family,
p. 175–176

Winter Fat,
p. 177

Bastard Toadflax,
p. 177

Bindweeds,
p. 178–179

Alkaliweed,
p. 179

Chaparral Dodder,
p. 180

Pacific Dogwood,
p. 180

Red Osier
Dogwood,
p. 181

Ragged Rockflower,
p. 181

Wild cucumbers,
p. 182

Sugarstick,
p. 183

Manzanitas and
heaths,
p. 183–186

Woodland
Pinedrops,
p. 187

White-veined
Wintergreen,
p. 187

Western Azalea,
p. 188

Spurges,
p. 188–189

Spanish Lotus,
p. 189

White legumes,
p. 190

Mesquite and
acacias,
p. 191

Mountain Carpet
Clover,
p. 192

Coast Silktassel,
p. 192

Monument Plant,
p. 193

Alpine Gentian,
p. 194

Salt Heliotrope,
p. 194

Mock Orange,
p. 195

Modesty,
p. 195

Small-flowered
waterleaf family,
p. 196

Fivespot,
p. 197

Phacelias,
p. 197–198

Yerba Buena,
p. 199

White Horehound,
p. 199

White Sage,
p. 200

California
Skullcap,
p. 200

Whitestem Hedge-
nettle,
p. 201

White Globe Lily,
p. 201

Mariposa lilies,
p. 202–204

Bead Lily,
p. 204

Fawn lilies,
p. 205

Washington Lily,
p. 206

Twisted Stalk,
p. 206

White
Meadowfoam,
p. 207

Desert Stingbush,
p. 207

Rose Mallow,
p. 208

Cheese Weed,
p. 208

Death Camas and
Corn Lily,
p. 209–210

Western Trillium,
p. 209

Beargrass,
p. 210

Buckbean,
p. 211

Spring beauties,
p. 211–212

Lewisias,
p. 213–214

Hairy Yerba Santa,
p. 215

Transmontane
Sand Verbena,
p. 215

Fragrant Water-lily,
p. 216

Small-flowered
evening primroses,
p. 216–217

Enchanter's Nightshade, p. 217

Spreading Groundsmoke, p. 218

Evening primroses, p. 218–219

Phantom Orchid, p. 219

Mountain Lady's Slipper, p. 220

Small-flowered orchids, p. 220–221

White Bog Orchid, p. 221

Salt Marsh Bird's Beak, p. 222

Bird's beaks, p. 222–223

Poppies, p. 223–224

Pygmy Poppy, p. 224

Marsh Grass-of-Parnassus, p. 225

American Pokeweed, p. 225

Ghost Flower, p. 226

Coulter's Snapdragon, p. 226

Bush Beardtongue, p. 227

Dot-seed Plantain, p. 227

Small-flowered phlox family, p. 228–229

Leptosiphon species, p. 230

Large-flowered Phlox, p. 231–233

Red Triangles,
p. 233

Small-headed
buckwheats,
p. 234–235

Robust-headed
buckwheats,
p. 236–237

Spurry Buckwheat,
p. 238

Prostrate Knot-
weed,
p. 239

Red Baneberry,
p. 240

White buttercups,
p. 240–241

Sierra Columbine,
p. 241

Western White
Clematis,
p. 242

Eldorado Larkspur,
p. 242

Western Rue-
anemone,
p. 243

Mousetail,
p. 243

Buckthorns,
p. 244–245

Chamise and
Redshanks,
p. 245–246

Serviceberries,
p. 246–247

Mountain
mahoganies,
p. 247–248

Medium-flowered
rose family,
p. 248–251

Silverleaf
Cotoneaster,
p. 249

Toyon and
California
Mountain Ash,
p. 251

Small-flowered rose
family,
p. 252–253

Rose family, p.252–253

Pacific Ninebark, p. 254

Bitter Cherry, p. 254

Prunus and *Purshia* spp., p. 255–256

Western Chokecherry, p. 255

Blackberries and Thimbleberry, p. 256–257

Button-willow, p. 258

Stickywilly, p. 259

Starry False Lily of the Valley, p. 259

Parry's Beargrass, p. 260

California Buckeye, p. 260

Yerba Mansa, p. 261

Plain-flowered saxifrages, p. 262–264

Crevice Alumroot, p. 262

Common Woodland Star, p. 263

Tolmie's Saxifrage, p. 264

Ngaio Tree, p. 265

Sacred Datura, p. 265

Water Jacket and Peach Thorn, p. 266

Tobaccos, p. 267

American Black Nightshade, p. 268

Snowdrop Bush, p. 268

Hartweg's Doll's-lily, p. 269

Sea Muilla and Wild Hyacinth, p. 269–270

Western False Asphodel, p. 270

California Valerian, p. 271

Turkey Tangle Fogfruit, p. 271

Elderberries, p. 272

Macloskey's Violet, p. 273

PURPLE TO BLUE FLOWERS

Great Camas, p. 275

Wild onions, p. 275–276

Purple Sanicle, p. 276

Big-leaf Periwinkle, p. 277

Sunflower-like inflorescences, p. 277–281

Chicory,
p. 281

Cardoon,
p. 282

Small-flowered
borages,
p. 282–284

Pride of Madeira,
p. 283

Streamside
Bluebells,
p. 284

Rockcresses,
p. 285–286

Jewelflowers,
p. 286–289

Dagger Pod,
p. 287

California
Harebell,
p. 290

Calico flowers,
p. 290–292

Bluecups,
p. 291–292

California False
Indigo,
p. 293

Vetches and peas,
p. 293–295

Lupines,
p. 296–299

Mojave Indigobush,
p. 300

Clovers,
p. 300–301

Vetches,
p. 302–303

Gentians,
p. 303–304

Baby Blue Eyes,
p. 304

Phacelias,
p. 305–306

Blue Fiesta-flower,
p. 306

Three Hearts,
p. 307

Irises,
p. 307–308

Western Blue Flag,
p. 309

Western Blue-eyed
Grass,
p. 309

Desert Lavender,
p. 310

Woodbalm,
p. 310

Spearmint,
p. 311

Monardellas,
p. 311–312

Douglas' Mesamint
and Self-heal,
p. 313

Thistle Sage,
p. 314

Sages,
p. 314–317

Paperbag Bush,
p. 318

Common Skullcap,
p. 318

Wooly Bluecurls
and Vinegar Weed,
p. 319

Desert Christmas
Tree,
p. 320

Mariposa lilies,
p. 320–321

Flaxes,
p. 322

Yerba Santas,
p. 323

Parasitic orobanch
family,
p. 324

Paintbrushes,
p. 324–325

Redwood Sorrel,
p. 326

Snapdragons,
p. 327–328

Innocence,
p. 328

Collinsias,
p. 329

Blue Toadflax,
p. 330

Beardtongues,
p. 330–332

Penstemons,
p. 331–332

American
Speedwell,
p. 333

Marsh Rosemary,
p. 333

Dense False
Gillyflower,
p. 334

Woolystars,
p. 334–336

Bluehead Gilia,
p. 336

Bird's-eye Gilia,
p. 337

Parry's Linanthus,
p. 337

Downy Pincushion
Plant,
p. 338

Polemonium species,
p. 338–339

Monkshood,
p. 340

Larkspurs,
p. 340–341

Buckthorns,
p. 342

Turpentine Broom,
p. 343

Nightshades,
p. 343–344

Brodiaeas,
p. 344–345

Blue Dicks,
p. 346

Wally Basket,
p. 346

Verbenas,
p. 347

Beckwith's Violet,
p. 348

PINK TO RED FLOWERS

Chuparosa,
p. 350

Freeway Iceplant,
p. 350

Wild onions,
p. 351–353

Milkweeds,
p. 353–355

California
Pipevine,
p. 355

Creeping Wild Ginger,
p. 356

Redray Alpinegold,
p. 356

Sacapellote,
p. 357

Ray-flower sunflower family,
p. 357–358

Thistles,
p. 358–361

Desert Palafox,
p. 360

Arrowweed,
p. 360

Desert Willow,
p. 361

Western Hound's Tongue,
p. 362

Horned Sea Rocket,
p. 362

Jewelflowers,
p. 363–364

Wild Radish,
p. 364

Cacti,
p. 365–367

Mojave Kingcup Cactus,
p. 366

Common Fishhook Cactus,
p. 366

Spice Bush,
p. 367

Orange Honeysuckle,
p. 368

Pink Honeysuckle,
p. 368

Twinberry Honeysuckle,
p. 369

Snowberries,
p. 369–370

Hairy Pink,
p. 371

Catchflies,
p. 371–372

Cardinal Catchfly,
p. 372

Sandspurries,
p. 373

Pacific Bindweed,
p. 374

Lanceleaf Dudleya,
p. 374

Chalk Dudleya,
p. 375

Western Roseroot,
p. 375

Round-leaved
Sundew,
p. 376

Fanleaf
Crinklemat,
p. 376

Pipsissewa,
p. 377

Bog Laurel and
Mountain Heather,
p. 377–378

Pacific
Rhododendron,
p. 378

Snow plant,
p. 379

Huckleberry and
Mission Manzanita,
p. 379–380

Scarlet Milkvetch,
p. 380

Pink Fairy Duster,
p. 381

Western Redbud,
p. 381

Wild peas,
p. 382

Chick Lupine,
p. 382

Clovers,
p. 383–385

Ocotillo,
p. 386

Alkali Seaheath,
p. 387

Charming
Centaury,
p. 387

Stork's bills,
p. 388–389

Cutleaf Geranium,
p. 389

Currants,
p. 390–392

Sierra Gooseberry,
p. 391

Two-color
Phacelias,
p. 393

White Rhatany,
p. 393

Nettle-leaf Giant
Hyssop,
p. 394

Giraffe Head,
p. 394

Red Monardella,
p. 395

Hummingbird
Sage,
p. 395

Hedge-nettles,
p. 396

Plummer's
Mariposa Lily,
p. 397

Andrew's Clintonia,
p. 397

Scarlet Fritillary,
p. 398

Fetid Adder's
Tongue,
p. 398

Twinflower,
p. 399

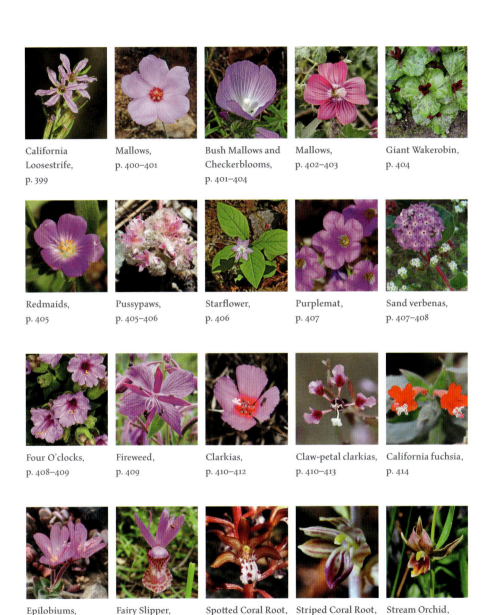

California Loosestrife, p. 399

Mallows, p. 400–401

Bush Mallows and Checkerblooms, p. 401–404

Mallows, p. 402–403

Giant Wakerobin, p. 404

Redmaids, p. 405

Pussypaws, p. 405–406

Starflower, p. 406

Purplemat, p. 407

Sand verbenas, p. 407–408

Four O'clocks, p. 408–409

Fireweed, p. 409

Clarkias, p. 410–412

Claw-petal clarkias, p. 410–413

California fuchsia, p. 414

Epilobiums, p. 414–415

Fairy Slipper, p. 416

Spotted Coral Root, p. 416

Striped Coral Root, p. 417

Stream Orchid, p. 417

Paintbrushes,
p. 418–419

Elephant's heads,
p. 419–420

Warrior's Plume,
p. 420

Dwarf Owl's Clover,
p. 421

California Peony,
p. 421

Pacific Bleeding
Heart,
p. 422

Steer's Head,
p. 422

Monkeyflowers,
p. 423–425

Monkeyflowers
(side view)

Purple Mouse Ears,
p. 423

Scarlet
Monkeyflower,
p. 426

Lewis'
Monkeyflower,
p. 426

Tincture plant,
p. 427

Foxglove,
p. 427

Heart-leaved
Keckiella,
p. 428

Red penstemons,
p. 428–430

Beardtongues,
p. 429–430

Sea Thrift,
p. 431

Purple False Gilia,
p. 431

Collomias,
p. 432

Scarlet Gilia,
p. 433

Whiskerbrush,
p. 433

Phloxes,
p. 434

Desert Calico,
p. 434

Slender Phlox and
Showy Phlox,
p. 435

Splendid
Woodland Gilia,
p. 436

Milkworts,
p. 437

Spineflowers,
p. 438–439

Buckwheats,
p. 439–441

Spotted Buckwheat,
p. 440

Alpine Mountain
Sorrel,
p. 441

Roundleaf
Oxytheca,
p. 442

pale Smartweed,
p. 442

Fairy Mist,
p. 443

Docks and sorrels,
p. 443–445

Shooting stars,
p. 445–446

Sierra Primrose,
p. 447

Western
Columbine,
p. 447

Larkspurs,
p. 448

Desert Peach,
p. 449

Roses,
p. 449–450

Salmonberry,
p. 450

Meadowsweets,
p. 451

Milk Kelloggia,
p. 452

California
Pitcherplant
(Flower), p. 452

California
Pitcherplant (Leaf)

Umbrella Plant,
p. 453

Pink Alumroot,
p. 453

Fringe Cups,
p. 454

California Bee
Plant,
p. 454

Saltcedar,
p. 455

Snake Lily,
p. 455

Longspur Seablush,
p. 456

ORANGE FLOWERS

Fiddlenecks
(flowers),
p. 458–459

Fiddlenecks (flower
clusters)

Wallflower,
p. 459

Prickly pears,
p. 460

Canyon Dudleya,
p. 461

Sulphur Pea,
p. 461

African Flag,
p. 462

Desert Mariposa
Lily,
p. 462

Pendant lilies,
p. 463

Leopard Lily,
p. 463

Palmer's Abutilon,
p. 464

Desert Mallow,
p. 465

Scarlet Pinpernel,
p. 465

California Poppy,
p. 466

Fire Poppy,
p. 466

Wind Poppy,
p. 467

Bush
Monkeyflower,
p. 467

Grand Collomia,
p. 468

Garden
Nasturtium,
p. 468

YELLOW FLOWERS

Desert Agave, p. 470

Turpentine Cymopterus, p. 470

Fennel, p. 471

Common Lomatium, p. 471

Sanicles, p. 472

Rush Milkweed, p. 473

Yellow Skunk Cabbage, p. 473

Desert Marigold, p. 474

Large sunflowers, p. 474–478

Yellow Carpet, p. 475

Rosin Weed, p. 476

Common Spikeweed, p. 476

Small sunflowers, p. 476–477

Narrow-leaf Goldenbush, p. 479

Clusters of sunflower-like flowerheads, p. 479–480

Medium sunflowers, p. 480–481

Gumweed, p. 482

Bigelow's Sneezeweed, p. 482

Sunflowers, p. 483–484

Hayfield Tarweed, p. 484

Golden asters,
p. 485

Pumice Alpinegold,
p. 486

Tidy Tips,
p. 488

Common Madia,
p. 489

Ragworts,
p. 490–492

California
Coneflower,
p. 491

Velvety Goldenrod,
p. 493

Mule's Ears,
p. 494–495

Blow Wives,
p. 495

Giant Mountain
Dandelion,
p. 496

Scale Bud,
p. 496

Bristly Ox-tongue,
p. 497

Smooth Cat's Ear,
p. 497

Prickly Lettuce,
p. 498

Dandelions,
p. 498–499

Nodding
Microseris,
p. 499

Spiny Sowthistle,
p. 500

Common
Dandelion,
p. 500

Yellow Salsify,
p. 501

Silver Puffs,
p. 501

Sweetbush,
p. 502

Sticktight,
p. 502

California
Brickellbush,
p. 503

Yellow Star-thistle,
p. 503

Yellow Pincushion,
p. 504

Clusters of disc
flowerheads,
p. 504–507

Brass Buttons,
p. 505

Valley Lessingia,
p. 508

Pineapple Weed,
p. 508

Schott's
Pygmy Cedar,
p. 529

Velvet Turtleback,
p. 509

Common
Groundsel,
p. 510

Oregon Grape,
p. 511

Basin
Popcorn Flower,
p. 512

Mustard family,
p. 512–519

Mustard family
(side view)

Small mustard
family, p. 514–519

Jared's
Pepper Weed,
p. 517

Cacti,
p. 520

Peak Rush-rose,
p. 521

Mojave Stinkweed and Bladderpod, p. 521–522

Bluff Lettuce, p. 522

Stonecrops, p. 523–524

Gourds, p. 524–525

Sydney Golden Wattle, p. 525

Lotuses, p. 526–527

Brooms, p. 527–528

Harlequin Lotus, p. 528

Narrow-leaved Lotus, p. 529

Yellow Bush Lupine, p. 529

Harlequin Lupine, p. 530

Burclover, p. 530

Sour Clover, p. 531

Blue Palo Verde, p. 531

Desert Senna, p. 532

Little Hop Clover, p. 533

Golden Currant, p. 533

Mountain Gooseberry, p. 534

Whispering Bells, p. 534

St. Johns Wort and Tinker's Penny, p. 535

Yellow-Eyed Grass,
p. 536

Diogenes' Lantern,
p. 536

Mariposa lilies,
p. 537

Yellow Star Tulip,
p. 538

Common
Meadowfoam,
p. 538

Blazing stars,
p. 539

Giant Blazing Star,
p. 540

California
Flannelbush,
p. 540

Desert Unicorn
Plant,
p. 541

Coastal Sand
Verbena,
p. 541

Rocky Mountain
Pond-lily,
p. 542

Suncups and
primroses,
p. 542–545

Claw-petal
suncups,
p. 544–545

Marsh Purselane,
p. 546

Evening primroses,
p. 546–547

Clustered
Orobanche,
p. 548

Yellow Glandweed,
p. 548

Pinewoods
Lousewort,
p. 549

Butter-and-Eggs,
p. 549

Bermuda
Buttercup,
p. 550

Bush Poppy,
p. 550

Golden Eardrops,
p. 551

Ptoppies,
p. 551–552

Cream Cups,
p. 552

Monkeyflowers,
p. 553–555

Yellow and White
Monkeyflower,
p. 553

False
Monkeyflower,
p. 555

Tangled
Snapdragon,
p. 556

Golden Desert
Snapdragon,
p. 556

Snapdragon
Penstemon,
p. 557

Lemmon's
Keckiella,
p. 557

Fluellin,
p. 558

Golden Linanthus,
p. 558

Brewer's Navarretia,
p. 559

Desert Trumpet,
p. 559

Buckwheats,
p. 560

Buttercups,
p. 561

Blackbrush,
p. 562

Cinquefoils,
p. 562

Large-leaved Avens,
p. 563

Alpine Ivesia,
p. 563

Clubmoss Ivesia,
p. 564

Wooly Mullein,
p. 565

Tree Tobacco,
p. 565

Thick-leaved
Ground Cherry,
p. 566

Common
Goldenstar,
p. 566

Prettyface,
p. 567

Violets,
p. 567–568

Creosote Bush,
p. 569

Puncture Vine,
p. 569

ACKNOWLEDGMENTS

PRODUCING A WILDFLOWER GUIDE that covers the entire state of California is quite an undertaking. Initially, it seemed an impossible task to choose a satisfying species list and gather attractive, high-quality photos useful for field identification. The combined efforts of plant experts, photographers, and enthusiasts from around the state and beyond have helped bring *Wildflowers of California* to fruition.

First, we would like to thank the contributing authors. The book certainly would not have been possible without their hard work and dedication. Thank you to John Game, Bruce Homer-Smith, Nick Jensen, Julie Kierstead, Shawna Martinez, and Dylan Neubauer.

Obtaining and curating photographs was really a group effort; in total, more than 50 people submitted photographs. We are thankful to the dedicated photographers who donated hundreds of their photos and countless hours of their time to the project, including Matt Berger, Robert Case, John Doyen, Aaron Echols, Susan Fawcett, John Game, David Greenberger, Stephen Ingram, Laura Lovett, Steve Matson, Len Mazur, Cliff McLean, Gabi McLean, Dan Noreen, Katy Pye, Vernon Smith, Morgan Stickrod, Robert Sweatt, and Ron Vanderhoff. Also, many, many thanks to others who provided photos, including Matthew Below, Jeff Bisbee, Jane Cole, Christopher Collier, Patrick Crooks, Tawnee Dupuis, Ann Elliott, Woody Elliott, Julie Evens, Sherrie Felton, Devlin Gandy, Kean Goh, Terrence Gosliner, Ken Hickman, David Hofmann, Mary Hunter, Ira Koroleva, Neal Kramer, Tony Kurz, Belinda Lo, Maureen McHale, Jason Matthias Mills, L. Maynard Moe, Graham Montgomery, Melissa Mooney, Keir Morse, Caroline Murray, David Nelson, Gary Nored, Amy Patten, Jean Pawek, Gina Radieve, Casey Richart, Lynn Robertson, Jake Ruygt, Aaron Schusteff, Judy Schwartz, Doreen Smith, Ken-ichi Ueda, Brad Winckelmann, and Gary Zahm.

A very special thank you is due to the photo-processing duo of Laura Lovett and Katy Pye, who not only donated photos, but spent countless hours organizing the many thousands of submissions that were evaluated during the selection process.

The rare plant section was a genuine collaboration between chapters of the California Native Plant Society (CNPS) and the book team. Chapter volunteers supplied photos and information about the rare species they work to protect. Thank you to

Barbara Brydolf, Don Burk, Eva Buxton, John Chesnut, Judy Fenerty, Steve Hartman, David Imper, Stephen Ingram, Brian Le-Neve, Gabi McLean, Cliff McLean, Melissa Mooney, David Nelson, Dylan Neubauer, Katy Pye, Jake Ruygt, Judy Schwartz, Don Thomas, and Ron Vanderhoff for your important contributions.

The book team included dedicated CNPS volunteers whose long hours and expertise made the project shine. We owe a debt of gratitude to Joe Medeiros, who drew illustrations for the introduction. In addition to donating hundreds of photos, Stephen Ingram edited the introduction and was always available to provide feedback and guidance. Thank you to Gabi and Cliff McLean. Cliff contributed to the glossary and rare plant sections. Gabi McLean donated hundreds of photos, edited the manuscript, and contributed to the rare plant section. Thank you to Dan Noreen for providing photos and feedback on the manuscript. Dan also supplied a wealth of native plant poetry to make the guide more interesting from a literary perspective. Much gratitude goes to Katy Pye, whose writing expertise and enthusiasm for gardening kept the book moving forward, and to Vernon Smith, who helped with the rare plant section and was always ready to find the perfect photo upgrade.

Many thanks to all the volunteers who attended the steering committee meetings for the book. Thank you also to Cynthia Powell at CalFlora.org, who graciously made many resources available during the writing process, and to the folks at the Jepson Herbarium and the California Consortium of Herbaria, who organize and maintain a wealth of information about the flora of California.

Thank you to the staff members at Timber Press, who were thoughtful, responsive, and patient throughout the entire manuscript development and publishing process.

Like CNPS itself, this book exists because people who care about native plants work together to produce something that is greater than themselves for the benefit of California's native plants, their habitats, and the people who love them.

SANDRA NAMOFF, LEAD AUTHOR

Foothill habitats have the potential to become blanketed in an array of wildflowers.

INTRODUCTION

CALIFORNIA IS A SPECIAL PLACE.
Millions of Californians and visitors from
all over the world have long been attracted to
the state's natural beauty and diversity. Our
state has more than 800 miles of coastline,
the tallest peak in the lower 48 states (Mount
Whitney), special habitats such as vernal
pools and serpentine meadows, and nearly
40 million residents. As if the vastness and
beauty of the state were not enough, springtime often brings an irresistible profusion of
wildflowers.

Recent superblooms in foothill and desert
habitats, when massive amounts of wildflowers bloom simultaneously, have garnered
worldwide attention, with thousands of
people flocking to these areas to take in the
colorful vistas. Prior to development, much
of California's foothill landscapes would
have supported these displays. In 1890, they
were the norm in California, gracing foothill
habitats in abundance. Alice Eastwood, one
of the most important botanists of the time,
wrote, "The open country everywhere around
San Francisco was a beautiful wildflower
garden in the Spring . . . [the flowers] were
so thick that it was impossible to avoid step-
ping on them."

Although the abundance of wildflowers
and their habitats has declined since Alice's
time, California continues to boast more
plant diversity than any other place in North
America, with more than 5300 native species.
In fact, the part of California with a Mediterranean climate, the California Floristic Province, is one of Earth's 36 biodiversity hotspots,
characterized by high species richness, a large
proportion of species found nowhere else, and
a high potential for habitat loss.

Why is California so diverse? Biodiversity
is influenced by a variety of factors, including geologic history, climate, topography, soil
type, and latitude. For a long time, researchers
assumed that the high plant diversity here primarily resulted from the ongoing formation
of new and distinct species in special habitats;
however, more recent research suggests that low
extinction rates also contribute to high plant diversity in the region. In summary, California is
a place that has unique habitats that naturally
foster species that might have just gone extinct
elsewhere—which suggests the importance
of understanding and preserving our natural
areas for the future.

With such an extraordinary richness of
species to choose from, selecting only 900 to
include in this book was not an easy task. We
made our best effort to highlight Califorinia's
most frequently encountered wildflowers. The
archetypal wildflower is a small, non-woody
annual or perennial that produces impressive
displays of showy flowers when rainfall and
temperatures are favorable. We also include
shrubs and trees that flower copiously or are
important ecologically. Additionally, a wide
selection of summer-flowering species of montane, coastal, and wetland habitats are covered.
Our hope is that you will be able to identify the
flowering plants you encounter on a typical
hiking trail. Unfortunately, because trails and
roads are often lined with naturalized species,
many non-native species are also covered.

OPPOSITE   Munz's Tidy Tips (*Layia munzii*) is a rare species that was once more abundant in the Southern Central Valley, but it has been displaced by agriculture. Most of what remains is in the Carrizo Plain, often growing among Common Goldfields (*Lasthenia gracilis*).

ABOVE   Native landscapes can be negatively impacted by species that have been introduced from other parts of the world. California's foothills are often invaded by non-native brooms, which compete with native plants.

Rare plants are an important component of California's flora. The California Native Plant Society Rare Plant Program has classified more than 2400 plant species, subspecies, and varieties as rare. Because rare plants are important and charismatic components of the flora, rare plants and the work done to protect them are highlighted. Furthermore, rare species are sometimes quite abundant where they occur, producing substantial wildflower displays. We hope that botanists of all skill levels will be inspired to search out and learn to appreciate these special gems.

Does California need another wildflower book? To be fair, many excellent region-specific wildflower guides are available. Surprisingly, the only books that cover all of California's wildflower diversity are typically geared toward trained botanists. Most books cover a specific region of California, not the entire state. *Wildflowers of California* is the only species-level book designed to help readers identify wildflowers throughout the state. It covers the most common, abundant, and attractive flowering plant species that occur here. It is geared toward beginners and enthusiasts who are diving into the realm of botany. Plants are organized first by color, and identification simply involves matching an unknown plant to plant photos.

To begin your journey, special plant knowledge is not necessary; however, a wealth of information is provided to build up your botanical skills. If you want to understand the species that contribute to the kaleidoscope of color in California's wildflower displays, this book is for you.

HOW TO USE THIS BOOK

THE PURPOSE OF THIS BOOK is to help new botanists identify and learn about the wildflowers of California, with the hope that this understanding will deepen their appreciation for the natural world. By far the easiest method to identify flowers is to match your unknown plant to a photo. Use the book's Photo Key to find groups of plants that are similar to your unknown species and locate the pages that include information on these plants. Each chapter is arranged by flower color. Within each flower color chapter, each species is arranged alphabetically by its family name first, and then by its scientific name, so that closely related plants are grouped together.

Within the largest family, the sunflower family (Asteraceae), however, an extra layer of organization helps to organize species. Profiles for plants within the Asteraceae are grouped by their color, flowerhead type, and then by the scientific name. Aster flowerheads can comprise two flower types. Individual flowers can have very short, inconspicuous petals (disc flowers) or petals that are fused into one long, showy, straplike structure (ray or ligulate flowers). A flowerhead can have only disc flowers (sagebrushes, discoid head), only straplike flowers (dandelions, ligulate head), or both (sunflowers, radiate head).

After you use the photos to determine which plant your unknown flower most closely resembles, you can consult the plant profile to determine whether you are on the right track. In the profile description, botanical jargon is minimized so that anyone can start identifying plants. Any terms that are unfamiliar are likely included in the glossary at the back of the book. Some people are better than others at identification, but all of us have some aptitude for it. Until relatively recently in human history, all people needed to be able to identify the plants they used for food, medicine, and shelter. That said, basic knowledge of the parts of a flower is necessary to begin your botanical adventures. In its most basic and common form, a flower is made of sepals, petals, stamens, and carpels.

Organization and species identification rely heavily on flower color, which seems like a simple characteristic, but it can get complicated. A single flower can be more than one color, and a single species can have multiple flower colors. For example, Harlequin Lupine (*Lupinus stiversii*) has striking yellow and pink flowers. Other species have two different-colored flowers on different plants. Parry's Linanthus (*Linanthus parryae*) usually has white flowers. After low rainfall years, blue flowers will become more abundant in populations.

If a flower is variable, the species is placed in the color section consistent with the more common, bright, or obvious flower color. Flowers, however, are not always the most colorful and showy part of the plant. *Castilleja* species, for example, have bracts, which are leaflike structures that are often the showiest, most eye-catching part of the plant. Purple Owl's Clover (*Castilleja exserta*) has obvious purple bracts and somewhat hidden flower petals that are yellow or white. Plants are grouped based on their most obvious showy part, so Purple Owl's Clover is located in the chapter devoted to purple to blue flowers.

Within each flower color chapter, plant profiles are designed to help you confirm your identification and to provide information about the species. Each profile includes a photo, a California distribution map, basic identification information, a narrative, and a description of the plant's structure. If you are unable to find an exact match for your plant among the profiles, the species might not be included in the book. It is likely, however, that you can find a close relative that looks similar to your unknown plant among the profiles.

LEFT   Each Harlequin Lupine flower has both pink and yellow petals. Flower color seems like a simple characteristic, but variation can complicate flower color classification.

RIGHT   Parry's Linanthus can have both white and blue flowers in a single population.

ABOVE   Although petals are usually the most eye-catching part of a wildflower, sometimes other parts have evolved to attract pollinators, such as the purple bracts of Purple Owl's Clover.

PHOTOS

Photos show the natural perspective of the wildflower as you would likely encounter it in the wild. They emphasize the key diagnostic features of each species, as well as its growth form (habit) and habitat. Although all aspects of the book have been a collaborative effort, the photography included here would have been impossible without the support of California Native Plant Society members who donated thousands of photos and hundreds of hours of photo-editing effort.

MAPS

Each map shows the distribution of the species in California, where you are likely to encounter it. Location information from the places where botanists have collected a species is used to estimate its distribution. Location data is from the California Consortium of Herbaria and Global Biodiversity Information Facility (GBIF). The lines within the maps delineate county boundaries. Many species occur outside of California, and the narrative section often broadly describes species distributions outside of California based on information from GBIF and the Flora of North America website.

BASIC IDENTIFICATION INFORMATION

Certain information is very basic to every species and helps distinguish it from other species in a practical way. The scientific, family, and common names define each species. Additionally, vegetation type and elevation help characterize a species essentially by describing its neighborhood.

Scientific name. Though less approachable than common names, scientific names are important because they unite plants that are similar in form and have a shared history. Scientific names have two components. The genus name encompasses a group of species that are similar in form and occupy a small branch of the tree of life. The epithet, or specific name, describes and refers to a single species.

Family name. A plant family is a relatively large branch of the tree of life that is commonly used to organize diversity above the genus level. Whereas genera (plural of genus) usually include anywhere from 10 to 200 species, more or less, families typically include hundreds to thousands of species. The most species-rich family, Asteraceae (sunflower family), includes an estimated 32,000 species worldwide. It is intuitive to group plants by family, because all members have major morphological similarities and a shared evolutionary history.

Common name. A major goal of this book is to help beginner botanists become interested in and able to communicate about California's wildflowers. A plant's common name is usually easier to use and pronounce than its sometimes unwieldy scientific name. Common names can be fun, especially if you make up your own names based on a plant's unique characteristics. The beauty of common names is that they are unregulated. You can use the name that works for you. We bucked tradition and chose to capitalize common names. Common names are largely a function of historical and cultural influences, and because of this, some names have not aged well. Alternative common names have been substituted for those that seem pejorative or insensitive, so that offensive names are left in the past.

Vegetation type. Vegetation type is the first piece of supporting diagnostic information and is important with regard to plant ecology. It can also help you identify species. For example, if you are standing in coastal chaparral, the plant with a basal rosette of long, sharply pointed, narrow leaves is more likely to be Chaparral Yucca (*Hesperoyucca whipplei*) than Joshua Tree (*Yucca brevifolia*), which usually occurs in desert woodlands. The trick here is to learn a little about the most common vegetation types in California, classified here as alpine, chaparral, conifer forests, deserts, disturbed areas, dunes, grasslands, montane, riparian, vernal pools, wetlands, and woodlands. Some species occur in many communities.

Elevation. Elevation can easily be determined by a smartphone application with reception. The elevations reported were aggregated from the Jepson Herbarium's eFlora database and from the Calscape database.

Native vs. non-native. Whether or not a plant is considered a native requires a geographic frame of reference. Native plants are indigenous to an area and not introduced by modern human activity. In this book, the reference area is California, as defined by geopolitical boundaries. Admittedly, there are more biogeographically relevant ways we could define our region of interest, such as the California Floristic Province. However, most people do not think of the world in terms of ecoregions.

From a practical perspective, native plants have evolved in California or arrived prior to European settlement of North America. Non-natives are organisms that have been introduced into an area as the result of human activity and have established themselves in natural areas. Non-natives frequently grow along roads and hiking trails. Some are relatively innocuous, while others will displace native species and disrupt natural habitats. Non-native plants that crowd out natives are considered invasives. Some invasives are designated as noxious weeds by regulatory agencies.

NARRATIVE

Key morphological characteristics useful for species identification are described. Although jargon is minimized, this section uses some basic plant-specific terminology to describe species. Differences between closely related species are emphasized. The section may also provide information about natural history, ecology, pollinators, edibility, toxicity, uses, or other fun facts. It also includes information on flowering time and life form.

Bloom time. Plants have specific physiological requirements that determine when they will be in flower. Some species germinate and flower adjacent to melting snow; others wait until the hottest days of summer to produce reproductive displays. We provide an expected bloom time window. Also, flowering time and elevation are related: If a plant has a wide distribution across many elevations, its flowering time will likely be extended. For example, Yarrow is found from sea-level up to 11,000 ft. It flowers in early spring at lower elevations and in summer in the mountains. Alternatively, if you are trying to identify a blue-flowered plant in midsummer, you can rule out Baby Blue Eyes

(*Nemophila menziesii*), which is completely done flowering by the end of spring.

Life form. This information describes the plant's size and life cycle. Annuals are usually small and complete their life cycles in one year. Biennials take two years to complete their life cycles, with the first year often spent producing a basal rosette of leaves. Perennials live for more than two years, often for decades, and some species live thousands of years. They tend to flower each year during a particular season when conditions are favorable. Perennials can range from small and herbaceous, to large and woody.

Superblooms are usually composed of massive numbers of showy annuals that germinate and bloom in response to ideal rain and temperature conditions. Because they move through their life cycles very quickly, annuals do not usually grow very large. There are exceptions: for example, Common Sunflower (*Helianthus annuus*) is a familiar annual that regularly grows as tall as a person.

Perennials are long-lived and are further divided into categories that describe their basic growth form. Herbaceous perennials are generally not woody and tend to be pretty small. Some annuals and herbaceous perennials have noticeable, attractive wildflowers. Sometimes it can be difficult to tell the difference between annuals and herbaceous perennials. Annuals invest in aboveground growth and seed production. They usually have poorly developed roots, compared to perennials. Shrubs and subshrubs are perennials that can grow multiple woody stems, rather than a main stem, and are usually less than 20 ft. tall. Trees are large and woody, with a main axis, or trunk. Vines are perennials or, rarely, annuals that have thin stems and use other species or structures for support. The focus of this book is wildflowers, but showy shrubs, vines, and a few important flowering trees are also included.

MORPHOLOGY

Technical characteristics of a species, including plant height, leaf shape, and flower form and color will help you confirm your identification. Careful observation and some knowledge of botanical terminology will help you fully appreciate each species' characteristics. The number of showy flower parts is an important characteristic that is easy to observe.

Plant height. Typical plant height is reported, though this can be highly variable. Although most individuals' heights fall within a certain range, occasionally very small and larger forms can occur. Yarrow, for example, may grow to 6 ft. tall, but it's typically 3 ft. tall. Therefore, the plant profile for Yarrow reports that it is "to 3 ft. in height." When identifying a species, try not to focus on a single individual, especially if it seems unusual. Instead, look broadly across all the individuals you can find to try to determine what is typical of that species.

Leaf arrangement. All plants follow a typical growth pattern, with leaves arising at specific areas, or nodes, along the stem. The way leaves are arranged along a stem can be an important diagnostic feature of a species or plant group. The most typical form is alternate, where each node has one leaf. An opposite arrangement has two leaves per node. If more than two leaves are at each node, it is a whorled arrangement. It is very common for annuals and biennials to form a basal rosette, an arrangement of leaves that radiates from a very short stem before the plant enters its flowering phase. Leaf arrangement is especially important for learning to recognize plant families. For example, almost all of the species in the mint family (Lamiaceae) have opposite leaves.

Leaf type. In the plant world, leaf form is highly variable, but for the purposes of identification, you need to look for a few things.

BELOW   Plants can have alternate, opposite, or whorled leaves at nodes along the stem.

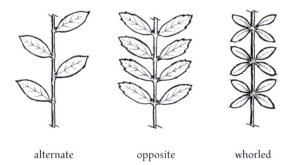

alternate   opposite   whorled

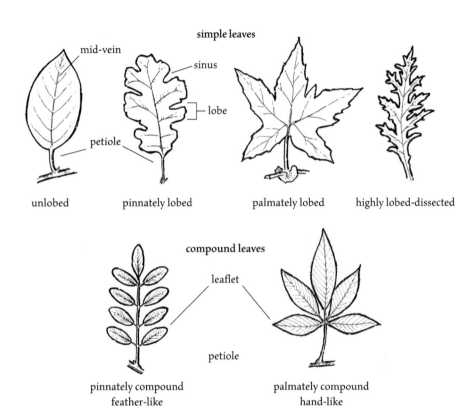

simple leaves

mid-vein

sinus

lobe

petiole

unlobed   pinnately lobed   palmately lobed   highly lobed-dissected

compound leaves

leaflet

petiole

pinnately compound
feather-like

palmately compound
hand-like

ABOVE   Leaf variation can be parsed into a few basic categories that help with plant identification. Leaves are either simple or compound. Simple leaves are further categorized as unlobed, lobed, or dissected, whereas compound leaves are pinnate or palmate.

There are two main leaf types: simple and compound. Simple leaves have a single, continuous blade that connects with the midvein (or midrib) at the base of the leaf. Simple leaves can be unlobed, lobed, or dissected. Unlobed leaves do not have sinuses (spaces between lobes) and form continuous and usually symmetric leaf blades. Leaves without any toothing or division are said to be entire. Lobed leaves have uneven blades, and the distance between the margin (leaf edge) and midvein is variable; some oaks, for example, have lobed leaves. Pinnately lobed leaves have lobes arranged on either side of a central axis, like the structure of a feather. Palmately lobed leaves have lobes that are arranged radially, like fingers on a hand. A leaf that is highly lobed, with blade sections that are too numerous to count, is dissected; ferns are a good example. Compound leaf blades are

leaf margins

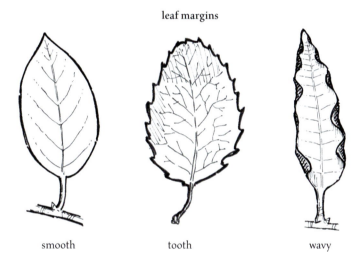

smooth   tooth   wavy

divided into independent sections, or leaf-lets, which can be attached to an extension of the petiole, called a rachis, like a feather (pin-nate) or like a hand (palmate).

The shape of the leaf blade or leaflet is not treated systematically here but is sometimes described in the narrative section. The most typical leaf shape is oval or elliptical. The monocots, such as grasses and orchids, are a group of plants that usually have long, narrow, straplike leaves.

Leaf margin. The margin is the edge of the leaf. Many terms are used to describe leaf

ABOVE   Leaf margins can be highly variable but are classified here as smooth, toothed, or wavy.

margins, but here margins are regarded as smooth, toothed, or wavy. (Beginners some-times confuse margin type and leaf shape. Keep in mind that margins refer to the edge of the leaf only.)

ABOVE Flower petals can be free/unfused, (yellow flower, top left); fused (white flower, center); or partially fused with free upper lobes and a fused tube (purple, flower right). Most flowers have radial symmetry (bottom left), but many insect-pollinated groups have evolved bilateral, or mirror, symmetry (bottom right). Note that the yellow sunflower in the bottom row is actually a radially symmetric flower cluster.

Flower form. Flower form is another important aspect to look at as you are trying to identify a plant. Because flowers are important for reproduction, they tend to reflect the evolutionary processes that shaped major plant groups. Each plant profile provides information about the number of showy parts, petal fusion, and flower symmetry.

Number of showy parts

For most flowering plants, the petals are the showy parts of the flower, but this is not always the case. Sometimes the petals are small, and the showy parts of the plant are its sepals, fruit, or some other part. Showy flower parts are important in identifying a plant. For example, all mustards (Brassicaceae) have four-petaled flowers, so if a plant's flower has five petals, you can be certain that it is not a mustard.

Fusion

Petal fusion is another important characteristic. Free (unfused) petals are separated from one another other all the way down to the receptacle, whereas fused petals are connected along their lateral margins. Fusion is not always complete. Often petals are free toward their tips but fused at the base, forming a corolla tube. Partially fused flowers often have upper and lower petal lips, most obvious from a side view. You can often tell how many petals a flower has even if they are partially fused.

Symmetry

Symmetry describes whether, and how, a flower can be divided into two or more identical or mirror-image parts. It is generally assessed by looking at the flower head-on. Flower symmetry is described using three terms: radial, mirror (bilateral), and biradial. Flowers with radial symmetry have a central axis and can be bisected into identical halves along any diameter (consider California Wild Rose, *Rosa californica*. Mirror (bilateral) symmetry describes a form in which two opposite sides are similar, such as an object and its reflection. Flowers with bilateral symmetry can be divided into two identical halves in only one plane (consider Bristly Jewelflower, *Streptanthus glandulosus*). A flower with biradial symmetry has exactly two planes of symmetry at right angles. Biradial symmetry is not common in the plant world, but it does occur in the mustard family (consider American Yellowrocket, *Barbarea orthoceras*).

Color variation. Flower color can be variable within a species or even within a single flower. The colorful flowers or other plant parts in this guide are grouped according to their predominant color, even if more than one color is present or possible. Complicated color variation patterns are described in the narrative section when necessary.

FINAL THOUGHTS

As you dive into this book, keep in mind some important caveats. Not every California wildflower is covered within these pages; only about 20 percent of the species in California are included. To identify unknown grasses, sedges, ferns, diminutive plants, and trees, you will need to consult more comprehensive botanical resources such as *The Jepson Manual*, the Jepson eFlora online database, PlantID.net, or the CalFlora online database.

The key to successful plant identification is to become a good observer. Before you try to identify an unknown species, examine it closely. Is it hairy? What type of leaf does it have, simple or compound? How many flower petals? Once you start building your observational skills, the terminology and other details will follow as your interest and expertise grows.

Any information about toxicity, medicinal and other uses, and edibility are for entertainment only. Remember that you can eat any plant once, but if you've misidentified it, it could be the last thing you do.

BIOGEOGRAPHY

THE STATE OF CALIFORNIA is a geopolitical area bounded by the Pacific Ocean to the west, Oregon to the north, Nevada and Arizona to the east, and Baja California, Mexico, to the south. Without a doubt, many of its residents and visitors may not be fully aware that California is far more than political boundaries drawn on a map.

There are many ways of perceiving and making sense of California. The state contains 840 miles of coastline and a mind-boggling variety of climatic conditions, geology, and topography. In one long day, you could drive from the Mojave Desert, one of the driest and hottest places on Earth, to the redwood forests of Northern California, which are technically rainforests. No matter where you travel in California, you are unlikely to stay in any single environment for very long. This diversity of landscapes and habitats is, in many ways, what makes California, California.

In the quest to understand California's plants, it helps to know common vegetation types. Let's start first at the broadest scale, the ecoregion, and then drill down to the vegetation communities featured in each species profile. In an attempt to make sense of variation in climate, vegetation, and topography, the world has been divided into ecoregions, areas where ecosystems are generally similar. Ecoregions tend to ignore political boundaries, such as those that separate one state from another. Ecoregions have cohesive biological (such as plant communities), physical (such as soil type), and environmental (such as weather and climate) factors that affect the biodiversity found within them. Two of the major ecoregions that occur in California are the California Floristic Province and the California Deserts (Mojave, Sonoran, and Great Basin).

CALIFORNIA FLORISTIC PROVINCE: A REGION OF MODERATION

The California Floristic Province ecoregion covers much of California, with portions extending south into Baja California, north into Oregon, and east into Nevada. About 90 percent of the California Floristic Province occurs within the state's political boundaries, but only 65 percent of California is covered by this ecoregion. Its most important feature is a Mediterranean climate, which is characterized by moderately warm, dry summers and cool, wet winters. Almost the entire western portion of the state is included in the California Floristic Province, with valleys and coastal plains flanked by prominent mountains.

The International Union for Conservation of Nature has named the region as one of Earth's 36 Biodiversity Hotspots, which highlight the most important areas for biodiversity in the world. All hotspots are characterized by high levels of species endemism (unique to a place or region), diversity, and threat. Endemism is an incredibly important component of the California flora, with about 30 percent of the entire state's native plants occurring nowhere else on the planet. About 42 percent of the native plants within the California Floristic Province are endemic.

Although this ecoregion is characterized by a Mediterranean climate, it is far from homogeneous with regard to its component regions. Variations in precipitation, temperature, and topography create major bioregions within the California Floristic Province, including the Central Valley, Sierra Nevada, Cascade Range, Klamath Mountains, Coast Ranges, and Southern California Mountains.

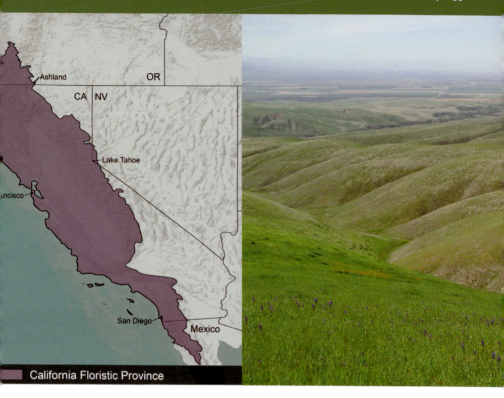

California Floristic Province

LEFT   Most of the California Floristic Province is within the state of California.

RIGHT   The Central Valley is a massive drainage surrounded by foothills and mountains. Once largely composed of wetlands, perennial grasslands, and wildflower fields, it is now heavily impacted by agriculture.

Central Valley. The Central Valley, or Great Valley, is on average 50 miles wide and extends from near Redding in the north to near Bakersfield, 450 miles to the south. This vast, nearly flat plain hovering around sea level is surrounded by mountain ranges. As one of the richest agricultural areas in the world, the Central Valley and much of its original habitat have been tilled under to grow crops. The northern portion of the Central Valley, the Sacramento Valley, was named for the Sacramento River. The southern portion, the San Joaquin Valley, was named for the San Joaquin River. These rivers collect runoff from adjacent mountain ranges converging in the Sacramento–San Joaquin Delta southwest of Sacramento. The Delta is a vast, marshy region that drains into San Francisco Bay. The flow feeding the Delta has been greatly reduced by agriculture and other human uses.

The remaining natural habitat in the Central Valley is largely dominated by non-native grasslands with a smattering of wetlands, including vernal pools and riparian forests. Summers can be very harsh in this region, with temperatures routinely exceeding 100°F. Rainfall varies substantially, with an annual average of 20 in. in the north to less than 10 in. in the south. The southern area of the San Joaquin Valley is so dry that some consider it a desert.

LEFT TO RIGHT

The iconic Yosemite Valley is framed by massive granite walls and is lined by conifer forest, typical of the Sierra Nevada, which means "snowy mountain range" in Spanish.

Mount Shasta epitomizes the rugged volcanic terrain that characterizes the Cascade Range.

The forests of the North Coast of California, with ample moisture and moderate temperatures, produce some of the largest trees in the world.

Sierra Nevada. East of the Central Valley, the Sierra Nevada is a mountain range that extends for 400 miles, from near the Feather River in the north to Tehachapi Pass in the south. The Western Sierra rises gradually from the Central Valley. From the lower foothills east of Sacramento, it takes 70 air miles to reach the 10,000-foot peaks around Lake Tahoe. On the east side of the Sierra, the rise to the crest is much more dramatic. The town of Lone Pine (4000 ft.) is just 13 air miles from the top of Mount Whitney (14,495 ft.). The tallest peaks of the Sierra are in the south, with numerous peaks exceeding 14,000 ft. In contrast, the tallest mountains around Lake Tahoe, 200 miles to the north, scarcely exceed 10,000 ft.

The climate of the Northern Sierra is cooler and wetter than that of the Southern Sierra, and habitats that occur at much higher elevations (conifer forests or alpine vegetation types) in the southern part of the range occur at lower elevations in the northern part of the range. The Sierra Nevada is characterized by picturesque alpine lake basins with vast meadows. Middle to upper elevations include extensive conifer forests, streams, and rivers. Lower elevations transition to oak woodlands, chaparral, and grasslands. The massive size of the region makes characterizing its climate challenging, but it typically consists of cold winters with much snow at higher elevations, warm summers with most precipitation falling as rain, and cooler temperatures and wetter winters to

the north. Because of a rain shadow, the Eastern Sierra is drier than the Western Sierra.

Cascade Range. The Cascade Range, which is characterized by a series of volcanic peaks, extends from British Columbia to its southern terminus in Northern California, near the Feather River. Lassen Peak (10,457 ft.) and Mount Shasta (14,179 ft.) preside over this region. The vegetation is largely similar to that of the Northern Sierra, with extensive conifer forests, montane meadows, and lower elevation woodlands. The climate is also similar to that of the Northern Sierra, with marked transitions to drier conditions in the north and east and wetter conditions to the west. Quite a few species that occur in the Sierra Nevada and Klamath ranges are absent from the Cascades.

Klamath Mountains. The Klamath Mountains region extends north into Oregon. It flanks the northern Sacramento Valley, with numerous mountain ranges including the Trinity Alps, Siskiyou, Marble, and Yolla Bolly mountains. Much of the Klamath region is higher than 6000 ft., with Mount Eddy and Thompson Peak exceeding 9000 ft.

The region is characterized by diverse conifer forests. Russian Peak in the Salmon Mountains, for example, notably boasts 18 conifer species in a single square mile, making it one of the most diverse areas of cone-bearing trees in the world. Within the matrix of conifer forest is a diversity of other habitats, including montane chaparral and wet meadows and riparian areas. This is a center of abundance for the California Pitcherplant (*Darlingtonia californica*). The climate is characterized by warm, dry summers and notably more precipitation—much of it falling as snow—than areas farther to the south.

Coastal California and Coast Ranges. The California coast extends for more than 840 miles from north to south. Inland from the immediate coast, much of the region is

The Southern Coast Ranges boast some of the most spectacular wildflower displays in the world. In years with adequate rain, the valleys and foothills of the Carrizo Plain are literally covered in annual blooms.

Deserts invoke images of wide-open spaces and barren landscapes, but the deserts of California host a wide variety of vegetation, including shrublands and gorgeous wildflower displays.

Nestled in the Western Mojave is the Antelope Valley California Poppy Reserve, a state-protected area dedicated to the preservation and enjoyment of wildflowers.

flanked by mountain ranges, some of which exceed 6000 ft. in elevation. From redwood forests in the north to chaparral in the south, Coastal California harbors many vegetation types, with good displays of wildflowers on beaches, bluffs, dunes, and coastal prairies.

This region includes much of the western portion of San Diego County, which has more plant species than any other county in the United States. Off the coast of Southern California—from Santa Barbara County south—the Channel Islands feature vegetation of mainland coastal habitats and a diverse suite of endemic species found nowhere else on Earth.

The climate is moderated by the Pacific Ocean, though this influence becomes less pronounced farther to the east. Along the coast, from the Oregon border to Santa Barbara, are the Coast Ranges, with a mixture of woodland, grassland, scrub, and chaparral vegetation. A good area to experience the grandeur of the inland Coast Ranges is Mount Diablo, east of San Francisco, with its spectacular botanical diversity. Some general trends for the California Coastal Region include cooler and wetter winters and summers to the north, moderate climates immediate to the coast, and drier and hotter conditions to the east.

Southern California Mountains. These mountain ranges form the backdrop for the most populous metropolitan area in the United

States. The San Gabriel Mountains rise precipitously from the Los Angeles Basin and include Mount San Antonio (Mount Baldy), with an elevation of more than 10,000 ft. On a clear day, it is not uncommon to see snow-capped peaks from beaches along the Southern California coast. Similarly, the Transverse and Peninsular ranges rise above communities inland and to the south into San Diego County.

Southern California mountain ranges contain a mélange of vegetation types, often transitioning from those moderated by coastal influences, to those that can tolerate the extremes of the desert. These mountains have conifer forests reminiscent of the Sierra Nevada and patches of alpine and subalpine vegetation. Lower elevation areas are covered in dense and diverse shrublands. The Big Bear area of the San Bernardino Mountains hosts a higher density of rare plants than any other location in the state. Compared to other parts of the state, Southern California mountain ranges are drier and warmer with less precipitation falling as snow.

CALIFORNIA DESERTS: A REGION OF EXTREMES

The deserts of California experience extreme conditions. A ridgeline of mountains formed by the Cascades, Sierra Nevada, and mountains of Southern California runs along the north-south axis of the state. They cause the majority of the moisture coming off of the ocean to fall as rain or snow on the California Floristic Province. Consequently, the desert regions are in an arid rain shadow. The Mojave, Sonoran, and Great Basin deserts experience dry conditions and extreme temperature fluctuations, typical of continental climates.

Mojave Desert. Transitioning to the Mojave Desert from adjacent mountain ranges (San Gabriel or Inyo mountains), temperatures increase and elevation and precipitation decrease. As you enter the Mojave Desert, Joshua Trees (*Yucca brevifolia*) pepper the landscape. The Mojave is the smallest of the deserts in Western North America and is the hottest and the driest of the California deserts.

Sonoran Desert. Just past the West Gate entrance to Joshua Tree National Park is the classic Joshua Tree Woodland characteristic of the Mojave Desert. Traveling toward the southeastern gate, you enter the Sonoran Desert, where the vegetation transitions from Joshua Trees to Ocotillo (*Fouquieria splendens*), an indicator species of the Sonoran Desert. Unlike Joshua Trees and other inhabitants of the Mojave, Ocotillo are frost-intolerant. Conditions in the Sonoran are generally wetter than the Mojave, and only a small portion of the Sonoran Desert is inside California. The most iconic species of the Sonoran Desert, Saguaro (*Carnegiea gigantea*), occurs infrequently in the state and does not tolerate freezing temperatures that occur in the California portion of the Sonoran Desert. The Sonoran gets much of its precipitation in summer in the form of monsoon rains. In all the desert regions of California, the wildflower displays can be magnificent when weather conditions coalesce to produce ideal germination and growth.

Great Basin Desert. The Great Basin region is between the Cascade-Sierran axis and the Rocky Mountains. All of the precipitation that falls in the area drains into lakes, soaks into the ground, or evaporates, with no external runoff into the ocean. There are many important species of sagebrush throughout the Great Basin. In Eastern California, Big Sagebrush (*Artemisia tridentata*) abounds. California makes up only a very small fraction of the Great Basin, which includes the Warner Mountains to the north, which rise from the Modoc Plateau, and extends south along the eastern side of the Sierra Nevada until it meets the Mojave. Technically, this is a desert, because it receives on average less than 12 in. of precipitation per year. The region is a series of basins and ranges with a relatively high average elevation of around 4500 ft. It is a land of extremes; the White Mountains include the highest peak in the Great Basin, at 14,252 ft. At 200 ft. below sea-level, Death Valley is the lowest basin, which occurs at the transition between the Great Basin and Mojave deserts.

The Sonoran Desert is a warm, comparatively wet, desert where frost-intolerant species such as Ocotillo thrive.

CALIFORNIA VEGETATION

WITHIN THE ECOREGIONS of California, broad associations of plants are classified into vegetation types, which describe a collection of species and their physical arrangement in an area. For example, a forest typically has tall trees forming a canopy, shrubs in the understory, and smaller perennial herbs and annuals on the forest floor. Chaparral is a vegetation type that lacks large trees and is dominated by dense shrubs.

When early American botanists collected a plant, they described vegetation types using broad classifications, such as oak woodlands or riparian forests. Throughout the 20th century, vegetation scientists have gone beyond generalizations to define and map the vegetation of California precisely. Decades of vegetation research, much of it conducted by the CNPS Vegetation Program, has culminated in the publication of *A Manual of California Vegetation*. Modern, precise vegetation classification attempts to describe the species and habitat conditions associated with a single dominant species in an area. For example, the *Artemisia tridentata* (Big Sagebrush) shrubland alliance is found throughout the desert regions of California and is defined by having greater than 2 percent cover of this species. The goal of this level of precision is to ensure that rare vegetation types are recognized for their importance and are not lumped into more common groups.

One of the most important abiotic factors that impacts vegetation type is soil composition. California's wide range of rock and soil types can hugely influence the plants that grow at any given place. The most typical soils in California are derived from sandstone, shale and other common sedimentary rocks, or igneous rocks such as granite. These all influence plant life, but two less common rock types, limestone and serpentinite, each have particularly strong effects.

Limestone is a sedimentary rock mostly formed under the ocean from calcium-containing minerals. Limestone contains the mineral calcium carbonate, which typically gives rise to alkaline soils with relatively high pH and calcium. California has many areas of limestone rock, especially in mountainous regions. As well as common plants, these regions typically support rare species that require high levels of calcium to survive in the wild. These are "calcicole" plants, in contrast to "calcifuge" plants that cannot tolerate high calcium levels and require more acidic soils. Calcicole plants are often localized individual species in otherwise widespread Californian genera such as *Dudleya*, *Eriogonum*, *Erythranthe*, and *Penstemon*. Examples of calcifuge plants include many members of the heath family (Ericaceae), such as rhododendrons.

Serpentine soils have an even more dramatic influence on California's plants. Serpentine is less abundant than limestone, though California is one of the most serpentine-rich places in North America. This metamorphic rock is initially formed under the ocean. Its minerals generate soils that are low in calcium but high in magnesium and rich in metals such as chromium and nickel that are toxic to most plants. Because of this, serpentine areas often look barren and rocky. However, species that are able to tolerate these heavy metals thrive on serpentine soil because they have little competition from other plants. Some of the rarest plants in California are found only on serpentine, having evolved in isolation in different serpentine areas widely separated by more typical geology. Hence, serpentine soils harbor tremendous rare species diversity in California and are of great interest to botanists.

ABOVE   Dominated by shrubs, chaparral is widely distributed throughout the California Floristic Province, from coastal regions to the mountains.

CHAPARRAL AND SHRUBLANDS

Chaparral is dominated by shrubs with leathery, drought-resistant foliage that stays green all year. Most shrubs in a chaparral are less than 10 ft. tall and usually very dense. Trees and understory herbs are mostly absent. Dominant plants includes manzanitas species, Chamise (*Adenostoma fasciculatum*), Toyon (*Heteromeles arbutifolia*), and Laurel Sumac (*Malosma laurina*). The name chaparral is derived from the Spanish word for scrub oak, *chaparro*. Common scrub oaks that dominate chaparral habitats in California include California Scrub Oak (*Quercus berberidifolia*) and Huckleberry Oak (*Q. vaccinifolia*).

Periodic fire is an important component of California's chaparral. Many herbaceous perennials and annuals germinate and grow after fire opens the shrubby canopy. Note that fire frequency has increased dramatically with human population growth. After fires that burn too hot or too frequently, chaparral often converts to non-native annual grasslands.

California sagebrush (*Artemisia californica*) is often the dominant species in coastal environments. It is drought-deciduous instead of evergreen, and the vegetation type as a whole tends to be less dense than chaparral. Northern California shrublands are most often dominated by manzanita (*Arctostaphylos* spp.) and California-lilacs (*Ceanothus* spp.), with other important woody species, including Coyote Brush (*Baccharis pilularis*), California Yerba Santa (*Eriodictyon californicum*), silk-tassels (*Garrya* spp.), and Salal (*Gaultheria shallon*). In the Great Basin, shrublands tend to be open and are often dominated by Big Sagebrush (*Artemisia tridentata*).

Woodlands are a broad class of vegetation that include an overstory of trees, often oaks, and an understory of shrubs and grasses.

Perennial grasslands are among the rarest vegetation types in California, having been mostly converted to non-native annual grasslands or destroyed by development.

Non-native annual grasslands dominate much of the Central Valley and surrounding foothills, where they have displaced native forbs and grasses.

WOODLANDS

Valley and foothill woodlands cover large areas of California from 300 to 5000 ft. Woodlands usually have a dominant overstory tree species loosely scattered across the landscape. The understory is variable and can be more open with grasses and forbs or dense with shrubs. Common dominant woodland species throughout California include oaks (*Quercus* spp.), Gray Pine (*Pinus sabiniana*), Jeffrey Pine (*P. jeffreyi*), and junipers (*Juniperus* spp.).

GRASSLANDS

California has two main types of grasslands, native perennial and non-native annual. They are found throughout the California Floristic

Province from low to middle elevations, are dominated by grass species, and lack shrubs and trees. Even before European settlement, native perennial grasslands never dominated vast areas of California, and now they are extremely rare. The most common native perennial grasses include Purple Needlegrass (*Stipa pulchra*), bluegrasses (*Poa* spp.), and Purple Three-awn (*Aristida purpurea*). Abundant populations of bunchgrasses remain in a few areas of Southern California, including Camp Pendleton and Tejon Ranch. Unfortunately, most bunchgrass-dominated areas have been lost to development and agriculture.

Non-native annual grasslands have become widespread throughout California during the last 150 years. Prior to colonization by Europeans, much of the Central Valley and lowland areas were dominated by annuals. During the spring, massive wildflower displays covered the landscape, and in winter these areas were mostly bare ground. As California was developed for agriculture, it was deemed necessary to seed these "wastelands" with non-native annual grasses that would provide forage for livestock. Thus, the non-native annual grassland was born. Non-native grasses dominate huge areas of California. Although natives are able to compete with them under certain conditions, it is common for non-native annuals to displace the native vegetation completely.

ABOVE   Vernal pool vegetation is largely composed of annual and perennial herbs that are uniquely adapted to this ephemeral, wet environment.

OPPOSITE   Riparian areas are characterized by the presence of running water, and often have an overstory of deciduous trees with a shrubby understory.

VERNAL POOLS

Vernal pool vegetation is a quintessential part of the California flora. Vernal pools occur within areas that are now largely covered by non-native annual grasslands. On land underlain with clay soils, natural depressions in the topography fill with water in the winter and spring, and then slowly dry via evaporation. As water levels lower in the pools, wildflowers germinate and bloom, often forming ring-shaped displays. The plants found in vernal pools are often rare, highly localized species that exist in nature growing only under these very specific conditions. For example, Clare's Pogogyne (*Pogogyne clareana*) is a super-rare species found only at Fort Hunter Liggett in the Santa Lucia Mountains. Vernal pools are distributed from San Diego to the Modoc Plateau. They occur in flat areas and are intrinsically threatened by agriculture and development.

RIPARIAN

The vegetation surrounding perennial streams and rivers is distinctive, because water is available even during the hot, dry summer. These areas occur throughout the state and cut through other vegetation types. Because of the available moisture, riparian areas usually have an overstory of trees. They often have a dense understory of shrubby vegetation. Maples (*Acer* spp.), cottonwoods (*Populus* spp.), and alders (*Alnus* spp.) are common overstory trees. Valley Oak (*Quercus lobata*), and California Sycamore (*Platanus racemosa*), where present, are the largest overstory trees in valley and foothill riparian areas. The understory is highly varied and often includes willows (*Salix* spp.), California Grape (*Vitis californica*), clematis (*Clematis* spp.), and blackberries (*Rubus* spp.). Sadly, only 5 to 10 percent of original riparian habitats remain in the state. Himalayan blackberry (*R. armeniacus*) has proven extremely invasive in riparian areas, crowding out native riparian shrubs and herbaceous flora.

Plants adapted to Mediterranean climates must be able to tolerate very dry, hot summers. One strategy is to be drought-deciduous, meaning they become dormant when rainfall becomes scarce in the summer months. Riparian species have no water limitations and tend to be winter-deciduous, similar to species of temperate North America.

Wetland vegetation is often dominated by a single species; in this wetland, the main species is Broadleaf Cattail *(Typha latifolia)*.

In this coastal dune system, mounded sand is stabilized by low-growing succulent species.

Forests dominated by cone-bearing species are common throughout California, especially at high elevations.

WETLANDS

Wetlands can contain salt water or fresh water. Salt marshes are narrowly distributed in coastal areas, from Humboldt to San Diego. Salt marshes tend to be dominated by perennial herbs and subshrubs that can tolerate high salinity and wet soil. Because people like to live and build homes in coastal areas, this vegetation type is highly threatened. Freshwater marshes occur in flat places where riparian runoff collects and forms shallow pools. Historically, they covered vast expanses of California. At the time of European colonization, Tulare Lake, an inland marsh in the southern Central Valley, stretched for more than 100 miles. This area was drained long ago and is now agricultural land. Remaining freshwater marshes are largely found in mountainous areas (meadows) and the Central Valley. Like salt marshes, they tend to be dominated by herbaceous perennial species. With the exception of meadow species, both saltwater and freshwater marsh species tend to have inconspicuous flowers.

Montane wet meadows are often flower-filled paradises in summer. Fens and seeps harbor a high diversity of unusual flowering plants, including carnivorous California Pitcherplant *(Darlingtonia californica)*, sundews *(Drosera* spp.), Western False Asphodel *(Triantha occidentalis)*, and California Butterwort *(Pinguicula macroceras)*.

DUNES

Dune vegetation must be able to withstand high winds and natural disturbance. Coastal dune vegetation can be found from San Diego to Oregon, where mounds of dry sand

accumulate. Plants that can tolerate salt spray and high winds stabilize the sand, creating dunes. Inland dunes occur in desert areas where high winds and extreme temperatures create harsh growing conditions. Dune species are usually low-growing with deep roots. They often have small, succulent leaves that store water. Common dune plants include saltbushes (*Atriplex* spp.) and sand verbenas (*Abronia* spp.). Coastal areas are highly impacted by recreation and invasive species, including some that were planted intentionally to stop dune movement for development purposes. In the deserts, off-highway vehicle activity threatens dune vegetation.

CONIFER FORESTS

California conifer forests include a broad range of species. Pine species have distinctive narrow, desiccation-resistant leaves, or needles, whereas redwoods and yews have more flattened leaves. In general, conifers tend to be evergreen, woody trees that tolerate freezing temperatures and drought.

In California, conifer forests occur in mountainous regions, coastal areas, and the deserts. Conifer forests tend to have a tall canopy dominated by cone-bearing species and an understory of annuals, perennials, or shrubs.

In Coastal and Northwestern California, conifer forests are dominated by Coast Redwood (*Sequoia sempervirens*), Douglas-fir (*Pseudotsuga menziesii*), Western Hemlock (*Tsuga heterophylla*) and pines (*Pinus* spp.). Understory species are usually perennial shrubs and herbs, including Thimbleberry (*Rubus parviflorus*), sword ferns (*Polystichum* spp.), and Redwood Sorrel (*Oxalis oregana*), to name a few. In some forests, dense trees shade the relatively sparse understory. In addition to conifers, these forests often have broadleaf flowering trees including oaks (*Quercus* spp.), California Laurel (*Umbellularia californica*), and Pacific Madrone (*Arbutus menziesii*).

Conifer forests in inland California occur in the mountainous portions of the state. Forests tend to be dominated by conifers from about 2000 to 8000 ft. of elevation.

ABOVE At the highest elevations, low-growing alpine vegetation can tolerate the bright, harsh conditions found above the treeline.

OPPOSITE Despite the extreme climatic conditions of desert regions, tough annuals, perennials, and shrubs form diverse communities.

Dominant species include Ponderosa Pine (*Pinus ponderosa*) and Jeffrey Pine (*P. jeffreyi*), Sugar Pine (*P. lambertiana*), Incense Cedar (*Calocedrus decurrens*), White Fir (*Abies concolor*), and Douglas-fir (*Pseudotsuga menziesii*). This vegetation type also includes the world's largest tree, Giant Sequoia (*Sequoiadendron giganteum*), which occurs in the Central and Southern Sierra Nevada. In higher mountain regions, conifer forests transition to Red Fir (*Abies magnifica*), Lodgepole Pine (*Pinus contorta*), and Mountain Hemlock (*Tsuga mertensiana*) dominance. Though the understories of these forests are variable, Huckleberry Oak (*Quercus vaccinifolia*), Mountain

Misery (*Chamaebatia* spp.), various currant species (*Ribes* spp.), blackberries (*Rubus* spp.), manzanita (*Arctostaphylos* spp.), and California-lilac (*Ceanothus* spp.) are regulars in this vegetation type.

ALPINE

In the Sierra Nevada and other high elevation ranges, alpine species begin to populate the landscape at about 9000 ft. At this elevation, temperatures and snowfall limit tree growth, as environmental conditions become too difficult for most trees. True alpine vegetation lacks trees and comprises mat-forming perennials that complete their growing season in the short window of time when snow abates. In late summer, their floriferous displays include penstemons (*Penstemon* spp.), mule's ears (*Wyethia* spp.), mustards (Brassicaceae), buckwheats (*Eriogonum* spp.), and phloxes (Polemoniaceae).

DESERTS

California's three desert regions have distinct geographic, climatic, elevation, and hydrological characteristics. Deserts are very hot during the day, cold at night, and dry most of the year. Desert vegetation is usually composed of tough, sparsely distributed shrubs interspersed with annuals, perennial herbs, and grasses. Many desert shrublands have been defined based on the dominant species, but all are similar in that they have relatively low-growing and usually sparse vegetation. Important dominant species include Big Sagebrush (*Artemisia tridentata*), Shadscale (*Atriplex confertifolia*), and Creosote Bush (*Larrea tridentata*).

Pinyon–juniper woodland is one of the few desert vegetation types defined by the presence of trees and usually occurs at higher elevations. Single-leaf Pinyon (*Pinus monophylla*) and junipers (*Juniperus* spp.) are medium-sized, cone-bearing trees that form relatively open woodlands. Pinyon–juniper woodlands are similar to shrublands, but

with an overstory of sparsely distributed small trees. Joshua Tree woodland is similar in structure, but is, of course, dominated by Joshua Tree (*Yucca brevifolia*). What is true of all desert habitats is that they have the potential for truly spectacular wildflower displays when weather and precipitation are favorable.

DISTURBED AREAS

Much of California's Central Valley and many coastal areas have been converted to agriculture or are severely altered by development or other human activities. These altered areas host a suite of species, often non-natives, that benefit from disturbance. This book uses disturbed areas as a vegetation type. It roughly encompasses areas where the ground has been altered by human activity, such that its native vegetation is not easily categorized. In addition to abandoned agricultural areas, disturbed areas included roadsides, trail edges, and abandoned lots.

THREATS TO THE FLORA

IN RECENT YEARS, visitors have flocked by the thousands to locations throughout California to view superblooms, massive and spectacular displays of wildflowers. By any standard, the vast fields of poppies near Lake Elsinore and the Antelope Valley California Poppy Preserve, the kaleidoscope of colors in the Carrizo Plain, and the carpets of blooms at North Table Mountain are worthy of international media coverage and robust visitorship. These superblooms are a part of what makes California a special place. Many books are available to help prepare you for a visit to the wildflower shows of Death Valley National Park, Anza Borrego State Park, and Bear Valley in Colusa County.

Indeed, our superblooms are to be cherished, but few visitors realize that these rare events were once much more abundant than they are today. Not too long ago, much of the state's lower elevations would have been covered in wildflowers in a year with ample, well-timed precipitation. Consider, for example, the observations of conservationist and naturalist John Muir, who in 1883 wrote, "The Great Central Plain of California, during the months of March, April, and May, was one smooth, continuous bed of honey-bloom, so marvelously rich that, in walking from one end of it to the other, a distance of more than 400 miles, your foot would press about a hundred flowers at every step. Mints, gilias, nemophilas, castillejas, and innumerable compositæ were so crowded together that, had ninety-nine per cent of them been taken away, the plain would still have seemed to any but Californians extravagantly flowery."

Today, visitors must travel to distant places, such as the Carrizo Plain, to catch even a glimpse of what was commonplace less than two centuries ago. The Central Valley and many other once superfloriferous locations are shadows of their former selves. We have traded fields of flowers for housing developments and agriculture. In addition, the California Coastal Commission has determined that more than 60 percent of our state's coastal wetlands are severely damaged. Only 10 percent of the original vernal pools in the Central Valley remain. In the foothills, only a small fraction of habitats once dominated by wildflowers are still dotted in spring ephemerals.

It's important to emphasize some of the ongoing threats to our flora and to focus on ways that we all can be a part of the solution. We must cherish the intact wild places that remain and manage these areas appropriately so that future generations will have the opportunity to experience the grandeur of California's wildflowers.

In recent years, we have witnessed numerous proposals to develop some of California's last remaining wildflower habitats in places like Tejon Ranch in Los Angeles County. When the areas around Lake Elsinore exploded into bloom with billions of California Poppies in 2019, visitors mobbed the area, but few realized that their beloved display was on private land that could be developed in the future. CNPS and other conservation-minded organizations have fought hard to ensure that these special places are conserved in perpetuity.

California's flora also faces other threats that cross ownership boundaries on both private and protected land. This book includes numerous plants that are not native to California but can grow and reproduce in wildland areas. In contrast to native species, naturalized plants did not evolve here and most have arrived within the last 200 years. However, some of these naturalized plants came from places that have a Mediterranean climate similar to

Native annuals bloom profusely in spring, bringing Table Mountain's volcanic geology into striking relief.

ABOVE   California's iconic and beautiful golden foothills get their brilliant glow from dead non-native annual grasses, originally introduced as cattle fodder.

OPPOSITE   Between Highway 1 and the Pacific Ocean, Crystal Cove State Park is a patch of coastal sage scrub–dominated habitat that has been preserved for public access.

California's. They can be naturally well suited to conditions here and, in some cases, have been able to outcompete native plants in natural areas.

You may have noticed, for example, that many lower elevation habitats statewide are cloaked in deep green grasses. These non-native annual grasses were introduced as cattle food by European settlers. Annual grasses die and turn brown in the summer, creating the famous "golden hills of California." In the not-so-distant past during wet springs, these hills would have been cloaked in brightly colored native wildflowers. Sadly,

our iconic golden hills are now filled with non-native grasses that often smother our wildflowers. In addition to noxious weeds, pervasive threats to native plants and habitats include climate change, recreational impacts, and alterations to our natural wildfire regime. This list could go on and on. So when you visit your favorite wildflower spot or hike to an alpine lake in the Sierra Nevada, know that many of these landscapes are fragile, and we all must take necessary steps to minimize our impacts.

The realization that California is a globally significant place for plant diversity whose plants are also imminently threatened has guided the work of CNPS since its inception in 1965. The organization and its partners advocate for policies and practices that seek to balance the needs of a growing population with the urgent need to conserve habitats for plants and the animals that rely upon them. We contend that it is impossible to ensure a high quality of life for humans without the natural services that intact habitats provide.

Conservation advocacy functions at a variety of levels. In its most simplistic form, community members and environmental organizations rise up to oppose a project (such as a large housing project in sensitive habitat) by influencing decision-makers who have the final say in approving or denying the project. Should a project be approved despite opposition from the community, project opponents might respond with a lawsuit. This style of advocacy, while often necessary, is risky, expensive, and time-consuming.

With the pitfalls of project-based advocacy in mind, politicians, scientists, advocates, and community members have devised a variety of mechanisms to steer necessary development away from irreplaceable habitats. Proactive planning is often incorporated in city and county general plans, which often seek to conserve vital habitats while enabling economic growth. Additionally, regionwide planning efforts continue to take shape in various areas of California. One example of a successful, collaborative planning effort is the Desert Renewable Energy Plan (DRECP). Signed into law in 2016, the DRECP identified hundreds of thousands of acres of public, federal land in the California desert where renewable energy could likely be developed with fewer environmental impacts. The plan resulted in the permanent conservation of more than 6 million acres of land, much of which is available for recreation and wildflower viewing.

In 2020, the state government embarked on an ambitious effort to ensure the permanent conservation of 30 percent of California's land and waters by 2030 (the 30×30 Iniative). This endeavor not only aims to ensure the conservation of species and habitats but also seeks to ensure that all of the state's residents have access to nature. The initiative challenges California to grow and adapt to a complicated world beset by difficulties, including climate change, the loss of species, and housing crises. The choices we make and priorities we set in these next few decades will determine what kind of environment we deed to future generations.

WILDFLOWER VIEWING AREAS

CALIFORNIA HAS HUNDREDS of wildflower viewing spots with glorious displays. For a more complete treatment of wildflower viewing areas, check out the book *California's Wild Gardens: A Guide to Favorite Botanical Sites.* Bear in mind that not every location will have a superbloom in a given year. Good wildflower years should be remembered, talked about, and cherished. A number of online resources track where wildflowers are blooming and provide regular springtime updates, including DesertUSA Wildflowers and the Theodore Payne Foundation's Wildflower Hotline. Additionally, parks and preserves often update their websites with posts about wildflowers.

When you're out on a wildflower excursion, remember to plan for your own safety. Make sure you have ample water, know how to recognize Poison Oak (*Toxicodendron diversilobum*), check yourself regularly for ticks, and avoid rattlesnakes. Also remember that wildflower trips can be about more than aesthetic enjoyment, snapping photos for social media, and basking in nature's beauty. Each wildflower you observe is part of an intricate ecological web. Learning about the interconnected relationships of California's plants and animals can become a lifelong pursuit. The iNaturalist app is a great way to document plant locations and is used by scientists and amateurs alike. Furthermore, local chapters of CNPS help with land stewardship by pulling invasive plants that compete with wildflowers, and they can always use another set of hands.

CARRIZO PLAIN NATIONAL MONUMENT

Location: San Luis Obispo County

When: Mid-March to early May

Highlights: One of the premier locations for wildflowers in California, the Temblor Range, in particular, features massive displays of Common Monolopia (*Monolopia lanceolata*), phacelia (*Phacelia* spp.), and California Poppy (*Eschscholzia californica*). Keep an eye out for rare plants, including California Jewelflower (*Caulanthus californicus*) and Jared's Pepper Weed (*Lepidium jaredii*).

SANTA MONICA MOUNTAINS

Location: Los Angeles County

When: April to June

Highlights: Portions of this mountain range burn regularly, making it a great place to view fire-following annuals.

ANZA-BORREGO DESERT STATE PARK

Location: San Diego County

When: February to May

Highlights: Unbeatable in a year with good precipitation. Enjoy the sight of Ocotillo (*Fouquieria splendens*) towering over an expanse of Smooth Desert Dandelion (*Malacothrix glabrata*).

TABLE MOUNTAIN

Location: Butte County

When: March to May

Highlights: Fairly reliable for displays of lupines (*Lupinus* spp.) and Purple Owl's Clover (*Castilleja exserta*). Look out for fields of meadowfoam (*Limnanthes* spp.) and poppies (*Eschscholzia* spp).

JEPSON PRAIRIE

Location: Solano County

When: March to May

Highlights: A great place to learn about vernal pool habitats and see what the Central Valley would have looked like prior to development and agriculture. The Solano Land Trust hosts excellent docent-led tours.

JOSHUA TREE NATIONAL PARK

Location: Riverside County

When: March to May

Highlights: It's hard to beat the majestic, boulder-strewn landscape of this national park, studded with poppies, phacelia, and Smooth Desert Dandelion. Seeing all the Joshua Trees is a treat.

BEAR VALLEY

Location: Colusa and Lake counties

When: March to May

Highlights: Stunning displays of California Poppies, lupines, tidy-tips, and Purple Owl's Clover decorate this Inner Coast Range valley. Bear Valley is considered one of the best places to see displays of the rare, fragrant Adobe Lily (*Fritillaria pluriflora*) in March.

NORTH COAST DUNES

Location: Humboldt County

When: April to June

Highlights: Home to some of California's finest sand dune habitat, Lanphere-Christensen Dunes Preserve in Humboldt County is accessible via guided tours only. Look for gems such as sand verbenas (*Abronia* spp.) and Roundhead Collinsia (*Collinsia corymbosa*).

RED HILLS

Location: Tuolumne, Sierra Nevada

When: March to April

Highlights: This is one of the finest places in California to appreciate serpentine habitats. Serpentinite, our state rock, hosts a unique array of plants endemic to California and this soil type. In years with adequate rainfall, the area is covered in carpets of Common Goldfields (*Lasthenia gracilis*).

BOTANY 101

LEARNING ABOUT PLANTS in greater detail will undoubtedly enrich your experience of the natural world. To facilitate understanding and communication, biologists employ systematics to organize living things hierarchically based on shared evolutionary history. Here we discuss basic plant morphology and how scientific names help organize diversity.

A TOUR THROUGH A FLOWER

A flower is a determinate modified shoot system that gives rise to modified leaves in whorls. What the heck does all that mean? If you understand that statement, you're probably ready to use more advanced botanical identification methods. Here, however, we'll cover the basics.

Flowers are the reproductive structures of the majority of plants on Earth. Because adult plants cannot move or migrate themselves, they produce parts that can. Flowers have to be showy or smelly to attract insects and other pollinators. Flowers have evolved to attract us too. They also produce showy, tasty, smelly, or windborne fruits that help disperse their seeds. All flowering plants evolved to disperse seeds via their fruits, making them the most dominant land plants on Earth.

Imagine you are holding a freshly picked flower between your fingertips. The part of the stem that you are holding is the pedicel, which is attached to leaflike structures, or sepals, at the bottom of the flower. Collectively, the sepals are referred to as the calyx. Moving toward the center of the flower are the petals, the showy, attractive structures that appear on most plants' flowers. The term corolla is used to describe all of the petals collectively, which is especially useful when petals are fused. For example, the corolla of Coast Range Bindweed (*Calystegia collina*) has five fused petals, which ensures that pollinators brush past the reproductive parts when trying to get to the sugary nectar reward at the base of the flower.

Moving inward toward the center of a flower are the male parts, or stamens. A single stamen has two components: a filament (or stalk) and an anther at the top. Anthers produce pollen, which are like plant sperm, but without tails. Consequently, wind or pollinators are needed to move the pollen from the anthers to the stigma. Germinated pollen then grows down the style via a pollen tube into the ovary to fertilize the ovules. Collectively, the stigma, style, and ovary is called a carpel. Fertilized ovules develop into seeds inside the ovary. As the seeds develop within, the ovary matures into a fruit. Often, beneath the flower, or group of flowers, are modified leaves, or bracts.

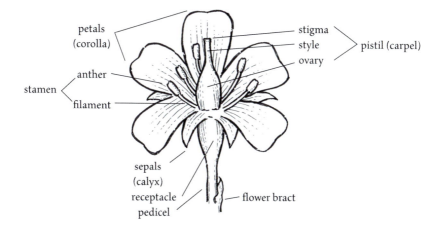

petals
(corolla)

anther

stamen

filament

stigma
style
ovary

pistil (carpel)

sepals
(calyx)
receptacle
pedicel

flower bract

ABOVE A basic understanding of flower anatomy is a prerequisite for improving your botanical skills.

Flower parts always occur in the same order, from the outer parts toward the center. Most flowers have all these parts, but flowers may lack one or more of them. For example, female flowers have only carpels and lack stamens. In addition, sepals and petals often look the same, in which case they are known as tepals. Tepals are common in monocots, a group that includes lilies, which have flower parts arranged in whorls of three with straplike leaves. A whorl is an arrangement of sepals, petals, stamens, or carpels that all radiate from a single position on the stem. Sometimes different types of flower parts are fused together. For example, filaments are often fused to petals at some level. Fusion can make understanding flower parts confusing. As you continue on your botanical education journey, determining exactly what parts of the flower you are seeing becomes part of the fun.

This book uses the showiest part of the plant to guide its color classification, even if the showy part is not the petal. For example, the showy structures of Pink Fairyduster (*Calliandra eriophylla*) flowers are actually filaments. Paintbrushes (*Castilleja* spp.) often have brightly colored bracts below their flowers. In a sunflower, what looks like a single flower is actually a group of tightly clustered flowers. The ray flowers that surround the cluster have long, straplike petals, whereas the inner flowers are very small with reduced petals. A less extreme form of this strategy is common among flowering plants. Flowers are often clustered in groups along a flowering stem in an inflorescence.

The corolla of Coast Range Bindweed includes five fused petals.

Pink Fairyduster has reduced petals and numerous showy filaments.

All plants follow a basic blueprint established by the area of cell division at the tip of the growing stem—the shoot apical meristem.

THE PLANT BLUEPRINT

Have you ever thought about how simple plants are? They have roots, stems, leaves, and flowers. The simplicity of plant form is a function of how plants grow. New plant cells are created at the shoot apical meristem (SAM) through cell division. In the SAM, cell division lays down leaves and new meristems (growth points) in succession. New lateral shoots can arise only from where lateral meristems, or buds, have been deposited by the SAM. The result is that the SAM controls the architecture of the plant.

Plants are composed of repeated sections of leaf, bud, and stem. The node is the part of the plant with a leaf and a lateral bud or shoot. Each node has one leaf (alternate), two leaves (opposite), or more than two leaves (whorled). New lateral shoots can arise only from the meristems that occur between the stem and leaf at a node. The internode is the elongated area of the stem between nodes. Leaves are determinate structures that capture light and carbon dioxide, which are converted into glucose. This process, photosynthesis, is the basis for almost all life on Earth.

But the story can be even simpler. *Alles ist blatt* is a German saying that translates as "everything is leaf." Johann Wolfgang von Goethe was an 18th-century poet and naturalist who came up with the idea that all flower parts evolved from leaves. The sepals, petals,

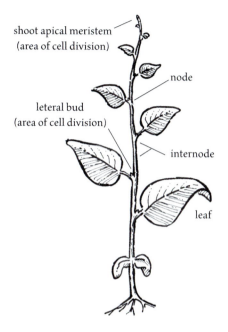

shoot apical meristem
(area of cell division)

node

leteral bud
(area of cell division)

internode

leaf

stamens, and carpels all came about as the function of leaves were modified for protection, attraction, and sexual reproduction. All plants conform to this basic plan outlined, from poppies to sycamores; modification of flower parts, however, has resulted in the tremendous diversity of form seen in nature. Variation in petal number, flower shape, and of course color all function to create this diversity. Keep in mind that the colorful, attractive parts of the plant are not always petals. Instead, bracts, sepals, or stamens can be the plant's showiest parts.

The number of flowers clustered together also influences the appearance of a wildflower. A Coulter's Matilija Poppy (*Romneya coulteri*) attracts pollinators with its few very large, showy flowers, whereas a Woolypod Milkweed (*Asclepias eriocarpa*) has many small flowers clustered together in an inflorescence. In the flowering plant world, inflorescence morphology is tremendously diverse.

Variation in leaf shape is also helpful for identification. Leaves can be simple or compound, and leaf blades can have various shapes and types of lobes. Leaf margins can be smooth, toothed, or wavy. Leaf variation can sometimes be useful in distinguishing between closely related species. For example, Lemonade Berry (*Rhus integrifolia*) has flat blades and toothed leaf margins, while Sugar Bush (*R. ovata*) has unlobed, taco-shaped leaves with smooth margins.

What's in a Name? For each species, two types of names are used: the common name and the scientific name. The easier of the two is usually the common name. Common names have their limitations, however. They can be redundant, and most often species have more than one common name. For example, Chamise and Greasewood are common names for the same plant, *Adenostoma fasciculatum*. The real

Coulter's Matilija Poppies attract pollinators with a few large flowers.

Woolypod Milkweeds have many small flowers clustered in an inflorescence.

In this book, the common names of species are capitalized, so that Joshua Tree (*Yucca brevifolia*) has the same level of specificity as the park that bears its name.

problem with common names is that they can be ambiguous. Greasewood, for example, is a common name used for at least two species: *A. fasciculatum* and *Sarcobatus vermiculatus*. So when you mention Greasewood, which plant are you referring to? To avoid such confusion, scientists use standardized scientific names when communicating about plant species.

In this book, plant common names are capitalized. Why should California be capitalized, but not California Poppy? After all, both refer to specific, individual entities. When a common name is used with the same specificity as a scientific name, then the common name is capitalized.

Demystifying scientific names. Scientific names have two components: a genus name and a specific name, or epithet. The genus name tells us which part of the tree of life the plant belongs to. For example, the genus *Calochortus* includes a group of plants known as mariposa lilies and globe lilies. The genus encompasses about 45 species in California that evolved from a common ancestral species about 23 million years ago and that are similar morphologically. They all have three sepals, three petals, six stamens, and strap-shaped leaves.

In botanical parlance, and in this book, when referring to more than one species in a particular genus, the abbreviated form for species, spp., is used. So, for example, when

referring to several mariposa lilies in the genus *Calochortus*, rather than including several particular specific names, we use *Calochortus* spp. When the specific name is included, such as *Calochortus albus*, we are referring to a particular species of globe lily that has white flowers. The specific name, *albus*, comes from Latin and means "white." The common name, White Globe Lily, is derived from the simple translation of the species' name from Latin. Although scientific names often provide useful information, it's usually in Latin or Greek! If you want to dig further into botanical Latin, consult William Stearn's *Botanical Latin* or Michael Charters's California Plant Names website.

Another major advantage of using a scientific name is that it is independent of language and geography. If you were writing about a mariposa lily in Germany, its common name would be *schmetterling lilie*, but its genus name would still be *Calochortus*. Scientific names are governed by a set of rules: the International Code of Botanical Nomenclature, which deals with algae, fungi, and plants (recorded in *Shenzhen Code*), was adopted by the Nineteenth International Botanical Congress in 2018. Any name issues are reconciled and published in this book.

In some groups, even the common names are standardized. Birds, for example, have regulated common names. The American Ornithological Society's Classification Committee manages the official common names of birds in North America. For example, it would be incorrect to call *Gymnogyps californianus* California Vulture, because the accepted common name is California Condor.

Names and biological organization. You may remember from biology classes that all life is organized hierarchically from kingdoms, all the way down to species. Many species of plants (and other organisms) are

ABOVE –. The genus name *Calochortus* indicates a very particular group of plants, no matter where you are in the world and what language you speak.

divided even further into subspecies and varieties. For simplicity's sake, this book focuses primarily on three taxonomic levels: family, genus, and species. The species within a genus are similar morphologically and have a shared common ancestor. The next commonly used hierarchical group is the plant family. A family is usually composed of numerous genera. Again, all members of a family have a shared common ancestor and morphological features that unite the group.

The plant families with the most species in California are Asteraceae (sunflower family) and Fabaceae (pea family). Species in the sunflower family often have many yellow flowers packed very closely together in a tight flowerhead (capitulum). The thousand or so species of sunflowers in California are arranged into more than 300 genera. With the exception of a few species, all members of the sunflower family have flowerheads (capitula). The first members of the sunflower family are estimated to have evolved 80 million years ago. Once you start recognizing the characteristics of a given family or genus, it can make identifying unknown plants to species much quicker.

Names and evolutionary history. What does it mean to say that a plant family evolved 80 million years ago? There are two major lines of evidence used to make that statement.

First, paleobotanists look for evidence of fossilized plants to determine when plants with a particular characteristic first appeared in the fossil record. This provides information about the latest date that the ancestor of the family could have evolved (minimum age), but it does not precisely determine the actual age of the common ancestor or group. Instead, molecular phylogeneticists use the DNA of species alive now to estimate when a particular plant family first evolved. DNA data is plugged into an algorithm with the goal of estimating how long it took to generate the variation in the species we see today. This is how we know that the sunflower family is about 80 million years old.

The real advantage of understanding plant families is that they help organize diversity. Plant families can be defined by key evolutionary innovations. For example, members of the sunflower family all have flowers arranged into tight flowerheads (capitula) and fruits called achenes. Tightly packed flowerheads tend to make large floral displays that are very attractive to pollinators, and achenes are single-seeded fruits that disperse efficiently. Scientists think that both these characteristics increase reproductive success in the family. Indeed, the sunflower family has more species than any other plant family. If you see a flowerhead that looks similar to a sunflower, it is probably a member of the Asteraceae. The neat thing about key evolutionary innovations is that they are often morphologically distinctive and can help you further your botanical skills.

Further your botanical skills. Education is an integral part of the mission of the California Native Plant Society, and we hope this book inspires readers to expand their botanical education. Once you become familiar with the plants you regularly encounter in natural areas, you may start noticing some patterns in the shape or arrangement of flowers among species. You may begin to focus on the morphological characteristics of plant families. A plant family is the main group that most advanced botanical identification resources use to organize diversity, so learning to recognize the most species-rich families is an important step toward improving your botanical education.

Next, it is important to look closely at plant parts. Do you know the difference between a pedicel and a petiole? If not, get to work by looking at plant diversity and learning more advanced terminology. Become familiar with using dichotomous identification keys, which simply involves choosing between two states of a characteristic. For example, is the calyx hairy or hairless? These simple choices are repeated for many different characteristics. Keys are the standard method used in most advanced texts, including California's most comprehensive resource for plant identification, the Jepson Herbarium's eFlora. Additionally, many organizations, including CNPS, provide plant identification workshops for both beginners and professional biologists alike. Many people benefit from drawing plant structures and taking identification workshops or classes. Online resources that aid in botanical identification include the Jepson eFlora, PlantID.net, CalFlora, iNaturalist, the California Consortium of Herbaria, and Calscape.

Once your plant vision becomes more focused, you can gain a greater appreciation for the natural world around you. You may notice that birds use certain shrubs more than others. Or you may start to differentiate between fields of native wildflowers versus non-native plants. Rare plants might tickle your fancy, or you might get involved with habitat conservation. You might even take up native gardening and convert your lawn into a wildlife habitat.

PLANT FAMILIES

You may recognize that some species have similar leaf or flower characteristics. In doing so, you are repeating what biologists have done for centuries. In an attempt to understand the biological world, organisms are grouped based on shared similarity in form. Some of the groups are very obvious. We intuitively know the differences among animals, plants, fungi, and bacteria. Within the plant world, families are a useful level of organization that groups organisms usually with regard to recognizable characteristics. For example, the distinctive flowerhead (capitulum) of a sunflower is a key characteristic of Asteraceae, the sunflower family.

Botanists have organized plant diversity into hundreds of families with hundreds, or even thousands, of species. California alone is home to almost 200 plant families. Learning to recognize plant families might seem like a daunting amount of information to process, but if you learn how to recognize even 20 families, you will be able to identify about 70 percent of California's species at the family level.

Note that in the plant profiles, plant families are the second level of organization, after flower color. Grouping plant profiles by families ensures that closely related species with similar flowers and form occur close to one another in the book. With time, you'll find that paying attention to plant families will be instrumental in helping you build your botany skills.

CALIFORNIA'S MOST DIVERSE PLANT FAMILIES

Rank	Family	Native species	Percentage*
1	Asteraceae	758	14.2
2	Fabaceae	305	5.7
3	Poaceae	265	5.0
4	Brassicaceae	232	4.3
5	Polygonaceae	215	4.0
6	Cyperaceae	204	3.8
7	Polemoniaceae	192	3.6
8	Boraginaceae	163	3.0
9	Rosaceae	149	2.8
10	Onagraceae	136	2.5
11	Apiaceae	134	2.5
12	Plantaginaceae	128	2.4
13	Hydrophyllaceae	121	2.3
14	Lamiaceae	111	2.1
15	Ericaceae	105	2.0
16	Phrymaceae	104	1.9
17	Liliaceae	98	1.8
18	Orobanchaceae	89	1.7
19	Ranunculaceae	81	1.5
20	Caryophyllaceae	73	1.4
	Top 20 familes	3663	68

* Percentage of native species (5353) in California; source: Jepson Herbarium, ucjeps.berkeley.edu/IJM_stats.html

EACH PLANT FAMILY HAS SEVERAL KEY CHARACTERISTICS.

Acanthaceae (ah-kanth-AY-see-ee), acanthus family, 2 native spp., 4300 spp. worldwide. This large, mainly tropical family is much less diverse in California and more temperate regions. Most species are herbs and shrubs, with simple, opposite, decussate leaves. Flowers are usually large, with mirror symmetry. Flower clusters sometimes have showy bracts.

Agavaceae (ah-gav-AY-see-ee), agave family, 18 native spp., 637 spp. worldwide. This family includes agaves, yuccas, and Chaparral Yucca (*Hesperoyucca whipplei*). Seeds are black because of the presence of phytomelan, a carbon-based seed coat.

Aizoaceae (ay-zoh-AY-see-ee), iceplant family, 2 native spp., 1900 spp. worldwide. Found in tropical, subtropical, and arid regions worldwide, this family comprises perennial herbs that often naturalize, becoming invasive (such as iceplant in coastal habitats). They have succulent opposite leaves and showy floral features.

Alismataceae (al-is-ma-TAY-see-ee), water plantain family, 9 native spp., 75–100 spp. worldwide. The annuals and herbaceous perennials of this family are often aquatic. Genera such as *Sagittaria* and *Damasonium* have beautiful flowers and leaves and are a delight to see in riparian and wetland habitats.

Alliaceae (al-ee-AY-see-ee), onion family, 48 native spp., 600 spp. worldwide. This family includes onions, garlic, and leeks (*Allium* spp.). The most-diverse genus, *Allium*, encompasses 200 species and is found in temperate regions worldwide. Key characteristics include bulbs, plus flower parts in threes, arranged in umbels.

Amaranthaceae (am-ah-ran-THAY-see-ee), amaranth family, 11 native spp., 900 spp. worldwide. Much of the diversity in California occurs in the genus *Amaranthus*, which is also of worldwide agricultural importance for grain production. Plants generally have small, inconspicuous flowers and can often tolerate harsh ecological conditions.

Anacardiaceae (an-a-kard-ee-AY-see-ee), cashew family, 5 native spp., 875 spp. worldwide. Some members of this family, which includes Poison-oak (*Toxicodendron diversilobum*), produce varying degrees of dermatitis in people. The family is represented by shrubs and trees, many of which are aromatic.

Apiaceae (ay-pee-AY-see-ee), carrot family, 133 native spp., 3500–3780 spp. worldwide. Although fennel, dill, coriander, parsnips, and celery are all family members, many species are very poisonous. Consider Poison Hemlock (*Conium maculatum*), which is common in wet areas of California. Ingestion of even a small amount can be lethal. Key characters include compound umbels, aromatic herbage, and small, five-parted flowers.

Apocynaceae (a-pos-ih-NAY-see-ee), dogbane family, 23 native spp., 4555 spp. worldwide. This very widespread family is represented principally in our flora by milkweeds (*Asclepias* spp.) and their close relatives. Members of this family often have remarkable and unique floral morphology. Many species have toxic milky sap.

Araceae (a-RAY-see-ee), arum family, 16 native spp., 3300 spp. worldwide. This family is part of the monocot lineage. Typically the flowers are small and arranged along a fleshy flowering stem (spadix), which is surrounded by a showy bract (spathe). It contains the subfamily Lemnoideae that has some of the smallest flowering plants on Earth. It also has economically important food crops, including Taro (*Colocasia esculenta*).

Araliaceae (uh-ray-lee-AY-see-ee), ginseng family, 4 native spp., 1450 spp. worldwide. This primarily tropical family is most well-known for Asian Ginseng (*Panax ginseng*). The family is sparsely represented in California by diminutive aquatic herbs in the genus *Hydrocotyle* and the robust perennial California Spikenard (*Aralia californica*). Members typically have small five-parted flowers arranged in spherical umbels.

Aristolochiaceae (a-ris-tuh-loe-kee-AY-see-ee), pipevine family, 5 native spp., 550 spp. worldwide. The genus *Aristolochia* includes tropical vines with spectacular floral form and diversity. California is home to California Pipevine (*Aristolochia californica*) and four species of wild ginger (*Asarum* spp).

Asteraceae (as-ter-AY-see-ee), sunflower family, 758 native spp., ~32,000 spp. worldwide. The most species-rich family in the world and in California was once called Compositae because the head is a composite of many flowers. Bright flowerheads attract pollinators, providing opportunities for reproductive success. Seeds may be dispersed by wind (think dandelions, *Taraxacum* spp.). Potent chemicals, sometimes aromatic, may protect plants from herbivores (think sagebrush, *Artemisia* spp.).

Berberidaceae (bear-ber-id-AY-see-ee), barberry family, 13 native spp., 700 spp. worldwide. In California, this family primarily consists of shrubs in the genus *Berberis* (barberries). It also includes herbaceous plants in the genera *Vancouveria* and *Achlys* in coastal forests.

Betulaceae (beh-tyoo-LAY-see-ee), birch family, 7 native spp., 145 spp. worldwide. This family contains some undeniably important species, including birches (*Betula* spp.), alders (*Alnus* spp.), and hazelnuts (*Corylus* spp.). Small, inconspicuous, wind-pollinated flowers are arranged in tight, pendant clusters (catkins).

Bignoniaceae (big-no-nih-AY-see-ee), trumpet creeper family, 1 native sp., 790 spp. worldwide. Most diverse in tropical areas, species in this family are usually trees or woody shrubs with large, bilaterally symmetric flowers and opposite leaves. The only California native is Desert Willow (*Chilopsis linearis*), which has large flowers and is often used as an ornamental.

Boraginaceae (bor-aj-in-AY-see-ee), borage family, 145 native spp., 2400–2740 spp. worldwide. Until recently, this family included five subfamilies that are now treated independently: Ehretiaceae, Heliotropiaceae, Hydrophyllaceae, Lennoaceae, and Namaceae. Key characters include coiled flower clusters and nutlet fruits that often have ornamentation (such as spikes or knobs) that aid in identification.

Brassicaceae (brass-ih-KAY-see-ee), mustard family, 234 native spp., 3400–3700 spp. worldwide. Once known as Cruciferae because of its members' cross-shaped flowers, this family includes some of the state's most widespread and problematic weeds. It also includes broccoli, kale, Brussels sprouts, and cabbage, which are all derived from Wild Cabbage (*Brassica oleracea*). Key characters include flowers with four petals and superior ovaries.

Cactaceae (kak-TAY-see-ee), cactus family, 38 native spp., 1866 spp. worldwide. This family includes succulent plants with water-filled stems and modified leaves (sharp spines). The pads and fruit of Mission Prickly-pear (*Opuntia ficus-indica*) are used culinarily. Many species are quite beautiful and have large, almost garish, flowers.

Campanulaceae (kam-pan-yew-LAY-see-ee), bellflower family, 54 native spp., 1900–2350 spp. worldwide. This diverse family includes many plants of horticultural importance, such as lobelias (*Lobelia* spp.). More than 100 endemic species in the family are found in Hawaii. Key characters include bell-shaped or two-lipped, five-parted flowers with fused petals.

Caprifoliaceae (cap-ree-foh-lee-AY-see-ee), honeysuckle family, 11 native spp., 890 spp. worldwide. Though not an exceptionally diverse family in California, the Caprifoliaceae includes the widespread and ecologically significant genera *Lonicera* (honeysuckles) and *Symphoricarpos* (snowberries). The family contains shrubs and vines, often with showy, five-parted flowers.

Caryophyllaceae (kar-ree-oh-fil-AY-see-ee), pink family, 73 native spp., 2400 spp. worldwide. Many pinks have fringed petal margins that are reminiscent of the zigzag cuts made by pinking shears. The family includes baby's breath (*Gypsophila* spp.) and carnations (*Dianthus* spp.). Key characteristics include opposite leaves, swollen nodes, and five-parted flowers.

Chenopodiaceae (ken-oh-poh-dee-AY-see-ee), goosefoot family, 70 native spp., 1500 spp. worldwide. This group comprises important food crops, including beets, Swiss chard, spinach, and quinoa. The family evolved to grow in harsh desert conditions, often in saline or alkaline soils. Flowers are small and inconspicuous, and fruit morphology is often used in identification.

Cistaceae (sis-TAY-see-ee), rock-rose family, 4 native spp., 200 spp. worldwide. Primarily a family of shrubs in the Mediterranean region of Europe, some species are important horticulturally. The California flora includes four native species of rush-rose (*Crocanthemum* spp.).

Cleomaceae (klee-oh-MAY-see-ee), spider-flower family, 13 native spp., 270 spp. worldwide. Plants in this family have flower parts in fours, and nearly all have palmately compound leaves. This is certainly the case for the most-widespread California native in the family, Bladderpod (*Peritoma arborea*). Many plants in this family have an aromatic or a fetid smell.

Comandraceae (koh-man-DRAY-see-ee), bastard toadflax family, 1 native sp., 2 spp. worldwide. Found in North America, Mexico, and Eurasia, this small family was recently separated from Santalaceae, a larger family of almost 1000 species. The single species native to California, Bastard Toadflax (*Comandra umbellata*), is common in the forests of the Sierra Nevada and northward.

Convolvulaceae (kon-volv-yoo-LAY-see-ee), morning glory family, 32 native spp., 1900 spp. worldwide. Species of vining, herbaceous plants in this family have heart-shaped leaf bases and milky sap. In California, the family is well-represented by species of *Calystegia*, often clustering, twining plants with large funnel-shaped white flowers. Also prominent in our flora is the parasitic genus *Cuscuta* (also known as dodder or chaparral spaghetti for its orange, stringy appearance).

Cornaceae (kor-NAY-see-ee), dogwood family, 5 native spp., 85 spp. worldwide. This group of trees and shrubs is represented primarily by the dogwoods (*Cornus* spp.), which are most diverse in temperate North America.

California has four species. Many species, both native and exotic, are of horticultural importance.

Crassulaceae (krass-yoo-LAY-see-ee), stonecrop family, 45 native spp., 1400 spp. worldwide. Members of this relatively large family are often found in xeric regions. They have succulent stems and leaves that store water as a hedge against drought. For many members, photosynthesis occurs during the day but gasses are exchanged at night, which helps decrease water loss.

Crossosomataceae (kros-o-so-ma-TAY-see-ee), crossosoma family, 4 native spp., 12 spp. worldwide. A third of the diversity in this family is native to California, also located in Western North America and Northern Mexico. Included in our native flora is Ragged Rockflower (*Crossosoma bigelovii*).

Cucurbitaceae (koo-ker-bih-TAY-see-ee), gourd family, 9 native spp., 1000 spp. worldwide. This family includes agriculturally important squashes, cucumbers, and melons. California natives include plants in the *Marah* and *Cucurbita* genera. Most species are vining plants with tendrils, which are modified branches in Cucurbitaceae.

Droseraceae (dross-er-AY-see-ee), sundew family, 2 native spp., 205 spp. worldwide. Most members of this fascinating family are in the genus *Drosera*. The narrow leaves have stalked glands that secrete a gluelike substance that traps and digests insects. Because they get their nutrients from insects, sundews can live in low-nutrient, boggy soils.

Ehretiaceae (eh-ret-ee-AY-see-ee), ehretia family, 4 native spp., 150 spp. worldwide. Found in subtropical and tropical areas throughout the world, this group comprises herbs and trees. Until recently it was considered part of Boraginaceae but was elevated to the family level based on DNA and morphological evidence. Four species in the genus *Tiquilia* are native to California.

Ericaceae (er-ek-AY-see-ee), blueberry or heath family, 105 native spp., 3850–3995 spp. worldwide. In California, the shrub genus *Arctostaphylos* (manzanita) is a characteristic component of chaparral communities. Their specialized flowers have evolved to be buzz-pollinated: bumble bees vibrate their wing muscles at a specific frequency, causing pollen to shoot out of cannon-shaped anthers. The family also includes other shrubs and herbaceous species, many of which are mycoheterotrophs, parasitic plants that get some or all of their carbohydrates from fungi that grow into the roots. Key characters of manzanitas include clustered, urn-shaped, fused flowers and thick, leathery leaves.

Euphorbiaceae (yoo-for-bee-AY-see-ee), spurge family, 39 native spp., 6745 spp. worldwide. The genus *Euphorbia* alone has more than 2400 species, making it one of the world's most diverse genera. Members of the family often have milky sap that is usually toxic and/or caustic. Many are succulents. Flower clusters often appear as a single flower but are actually numerous separate male and female flowers clustered together.

Fabaceae (fab-AY-see-ee), legume or pea family, 308 native spp., ~19,500 spp. worldwide. The third largest plant family has almost as many species as the orchid family. Legume roots become inoculated with bacteria that can fix atmospheric nitrogen, essentially creating their own fertilizer. Key characterics of the family include pea-shaped flowers (subfamily Faboideae) and pealike pods, or legumes.

Frankeniaceae (fran-ken-ee-AY-see-ee), frankenia family, 2 native spp., 90 spp. worldwide. Found scattered around the world in dry, warm areas, the members of this group are usually shrubby with small, opposite, unlobed leaves and flowers that have a fused calyx and clawed petals. *Frankenia* species in California are restricted to saltmarsh habitats.

Garryaceae (garr-ee-AY-see-ee), silk tassel family, 6 native spp., 17 spp. worldwide. The Garryaceae includes silk tassels (*Garry* spp.), evergreen shrubs with attractive catkin flower clusters that make wonderful garden plants. Individual plants are either male or female (dioecious), with female flowers producing attractive berries.

Gentianaceae (jen-tee-un-AY-see-ee), gentian family, 29 native spp., 1750 spp. worldwide. Many members of this widespread family of primarily herbaceous plants are beautiful and horticulturally important. In California, encountering the large-flowered montane species in genera such as *Swertia*, *Frasera*, *Gentiana*, and *Gentianopsis* is a true joy. Look for basally fused sepals and petals, often with fancy appendages between the unfused portions of the petals.

Geraniaceae (jer-ay-nee-AY-see-ee), geranium family, 8 native spp., 850 spp. worldwide. Most people are familiar with this family because of the prevalence of horticultural geraniums. Many are aromatic. In California, non-native species in the genus *Erodium* are widespread and abundant. Fruit is separated into elongated segments (mericarps).

Grossulariaceae (gros-you-lare-ee-AY-see-ee), gooseberry family, 31 native spp., 150 spp. worldwide. All members are shrubs native to temperate areas of the Northern Hemisphere. The only genus in the family is *Ribes*—currants and gooseberries, which are economically important. Plants in this genus are the alternate host of white pine blister rust, a disease that has decimated certain pine species in North America, and some states restrict the cultivation of these plants.

Heliotropiaceae (hee-lee-oh-trope-ee-AY-see-ee), heliotrope family, 2 native spp., 425 spp. worldwide. Recently segregated from Boraginaceae, plants in this family have coiled flower clusters, short styles, and unbranched stigmas. They are found in tropical and warm temperate regions worldwide.

Hydrangeaceae (hy-drain-jee-AY-see-ee), hydrangea family, 6 native spp., 270 spp. worldwide. This widespread temperate family consists primarily of shrubs, including the namesake genus, *Hydrangea*, which includes some of the most common plants found in North American gardens. In California, native species that are horticulturally important include Bush Anemone (*Carpenteria californica*) and mock orange (*Philadelphus* spp.).

Hydrophyllaceae (hy-dro-fil-AY-see-ee), waterleaf family, 125 native spp., 240–260 spp. worldwide. The morphological distinctness of this family has been recognized by botanists for a long time, but until recently it was considered part of the Boraginaceae. Boraginaceae fruits are nutlets, whereas Hydrophyllaceae have many-seeded capsules. Key characters include coiled flower clusters and abundant hairs that can cause contact dermatitis.

Hypericaceae (hy-peer-ih-KAY-see-ee), St. John's wort family, 3 native spp., 480–560 spp. worldwide. Species occur in temperate and tropical regions. Many have a multitude of stamens and glands on their petals that resemble black or orange dots. St. John's Wort (*Hypericum perforatum*) is a widely used herbal supplement.

Iridaceae (eye-rid-AY-see-ee), iris family, 23 native spp., 2120 spp. worldwide. The plants of the iris family include species of *Crocus*, *Iris*, and *Gladiolus*. All members have strap-shaped leaves, and many have showy flowers with parts in threes. In California, the *Iris* and *Sisyrinchium* genera are among our most common. Western Blue Flag (*Iris missouriensis*) can form vast spring floral displays in Eastern Sierra meadows and should be on any wildflower watcher's bucket list.

Krameriaceae (cray-mer-ee-AY-see-ee), ratany family, 2 native spp., 18 spp. worldwide. The only genus in this new world lineage of shrubs is *Krameria*. It is found in warm, dry regions and has been used locally to treat medical conditions and to dye fabric. All species are hemiparasitic and obtain a portion of their carbohydrates by tapping into the roots of nearby plants. Fruits in this family are fascinating nuts with elaborate and beautiful trichomes.

Lamiaceae (lay-mee-AY-see-ee), mint family, 111 native spp., 6500–7170 spp. worldwide. Oregano, marjoram, mint, and sage are all members of this family. Five-lipped, bilaterally symmetric flowers often occur in dense whorls. Species support insect and hummingbird pollinators, and they also have a rich medicinal history. Key characters are opposite leaves, square stems, and often small flowers with mirror symmetry. The minty smell of some species comes from trichomes, tiny glandular hairs on the leaves.

Lennoaceae (len-oh-AY-see-ee), lennoa family, 2 native spp., 5 spp. worldwide. This tiny family was recently segregated from Boraginaceae and includes fully parasitic herbaceous perennials. It can be found in the new world from California through South America. In California, look for species of *Pholisma*, which occur primarily in sandy habitats.

Liliaceae (lil-ee-AY-see-ee), lily family, 97 native spp., ~600 spp. worldwide. Molecular studies have prompted the reorganization of this family, which historically was a dumping ground for showy monocots with inferior ovaries. Monocots are a lineage of flowering plants with flower parts in sets of three that produce a single seed leaf during germination. The lily family is the most species-rich monocot family in California after the grass (Poaceae) and sedge (Cyperaceae) families. In California, look for beloved wildflowers in the genera *Lilium*, *Calochortus*, and *Fritillaria*.

Limnanthaceae (lim-nan-THAY-see-ee), meadowfoam family, 8 native spp., 10 spp. worldwide. Nearly all species in this family are native to California. The family includes 10 species of *Limnanthes* (meadowfoams) and the monotypic genus *Floerkea*. Seeds of White Meadowfoam (*Limnanthes alba*) contain high-quality oil, a potential alternative to sperm whale oil. In California, most species are showy annuals found in ephemeral wetland habitats.

Linaceae (ly-NAY-see-ee), flax family, 15 native spp., 300 spp. worldwide. Most of the species in this family are in the genus *Linum*. Common Flax (*L. usitatissimum*), the source of flax seed, is most likely native to the Middle East but has naturalized in California. The diversity of flax family plants in California is parsed between species of *Linum* and *Hesperolinon*. Capsule fruit generally contains 10 seeds.

Linnaeaceae (LIN-ee-AY-see-ee), twinflower family, 1 native spp., 35 spp. worldwide. The distribution of the family is mostly circumboreal but dips into Mexico and temperate East Asia. Most taxonomic systems include it as a subfamily within Caprifoliaceae. The flower cluster of our charming Twinflower (*Linnaea borealis*) comprises a pair of pink flowers.

Loasaceae (low-ah-SAY-see-ee), loasa family, 35 native spp., 350 spp. worldwide. This is primarily a group of herbaceous plants of the Western Hemisphere. In California, Loasaceae is well represented by blazing stars (*Mentzelia* spp.). Perhaps the most recognizable characteristic of the family is its spectacular variety of trichomes. Some South American species have stinging hairs.

Lythraceae (ly-THRAY-see-ee), loosestrife family, 4 native spp., 600 spp. worldwide. The family contains many herbaceous plants of aquatic habitats. The native species in California are appropriately herbs of wetland habitats and vernal pools in the genera *Ammania*, *Lythrum*, and *Rotala*. Pomegranate is an economically important member.

Malvaceae (mal-VAY-see-ee), mallow family, 63 native spp., 4225 spp. worldwide. The family includes the genus *Hibiscus*, which is emblematic of tropical paradise, though most species in California are shrubs and herbs that grow in dry areas. Many plants in the mallow family have star-shaped hairs that are visible with a hand lens. The family includes one of the most important food plants in the world, Cacao (*Theobroma cacao*), whose seeds are processed into chocolate.

Martyniaceae (mar-tin-ee-AY-see-ee), unicorn plant family, 1 native spp., 16 spp. worldwide. Species have large flowers with mirror symmetry and are usually covered in sticky hairs. The fruits develop two large hooks that help with dispersal. Most members of this New World family are in the genus *Proboscidea*.

Melanthiaceae (mel-an-thee-AY-see-ee), false hellebore family, 18 native spp., 177 spp. worldwide. This monocot family includes widespread and charismatic genera, including *Trillium* and *Xerophyllum*. It also includes species of *Veratrum* and *Toxicoscordion*, which are simultaneously beautiful and very toxic.

Menyanthaceae (men-ee-an-THAY-see-ee), bogbean family, 1 native spp., 60 spp. worldwide. These aquatic or marsh herbs can be found around the world except in the driest parts of Africa and Australia. Species are often used in water gardens, and many have become naturalized worldwide. The petals of our single native species, Buckbean (*Menyanthes trifoliata*), are ornate.

Montiaceae (mon-tee-AY-see-ee), miner's lettuce family, 51 native spp., 225 spp. worldwide. Once considered part of Portulacaceae, this family includes diverse and ecologically important genera, including *Claytonia* and *Lewisia*, which are of horticultural importance. Plants in this family generally have two sepals.

Myricaceae (my-ri-KAY-see-ee), bayberry family, 2 native spp., 57 spp. worldwide. This is a small family of shrubs and small trees. Most species are in the genus *Myrica*. They are often aromatic and many are able to fix atmospheric nitrogen in their roots.

Myrsinaceae (mer-sy-NAY-see-ee), myrsine family, 5 native spp., 1400 spp. worldwide. Only one genus in this family, *Lysimachia*, is represented in California. Perhaps the most widespread and recognizable native species is Starflower (*Lysimachia latifolia*). This family was once included in Primulaceae.

Namaceae (na-MAY-see-ee), nama family, 21 native spp., 76 spp. worldwide. Primarily comprising woody shrubs, this family was previously included in Boraginaceae, a lineage in which woody species are exceedingly uncommon. In California, the Namaceae is represented by pretty, herbaceous species of *Nama* and woody shrubs in the genus *Eriodictyon*.

Nyctaginaceae (nick-tahj-in-AY-see-ee or nick-tag-i-NAY-see-ee), four o'clock family, 25 native spp., 405 spp. worldwide. This family of common horticultural plants includes the genus *Bougainvillea* and common native and widespread species in the genera *Mirabilis* and *Abronia*. Encountering the bright flowers of sand verbenas (*Abronia* spp.) in sparse sand dune habitats is an unforgettable experience. Family members have opposite leaves, and many have conspicuous bracts below inflorescences.

Nymphaeaceae (nim-FAY-see-ee), waterlily family, 1 native spp., 70 spp. worldwide. This family consists of aquatic herbs that root in ponds and streams, with leaves and flowers emerging above the surface. Fossil evidence from seeds indicates that this lineage was much more diverse in the Cretaceous (145 to 66 million years ago). Plants generally have many petals and stamens.

Oleaceae (oh-lee-AY-see-ee), olive family, 8 native spp., 900 spp. worldwide. The source of many ornamental plants, this family also includes olive trees. In addition to plants of culinary importance, the family comprises some widespread native shrubs and trees, including species of *Forestiera* and *Fraxinus*. Plants generally have two stamens.

Onagraceae (on-uh-GRAY-see-ee), evening primrose family, 136 native spp., 650 spp. worldwide. This showy family includes many ornamentals, such as evening primroses (*Oenothera* spp.), fuchsias (*Fuchsia* spp.), and willowherbs (*Epilobium* spp.). The fragrant flowers of some

species open at night to attract moth pollinators, and many are larval hosts to hawk moths. Key characters of this family include four petals and inferior ovaries.

Orchidaceae (or-kid-AY-see-ee), orchid family, 33 native spp., 28,484 spp. worldwide. As the world's second-most diverse plant family, the Orchidaceae exhibits a bewildering array of floral diversity. Most plants hail from the tropics, where evolutionary time and relationships with pollinators have driven an exceptional level of speciation. In comparison to tropical areas, California has a paucity of species. However, genera such as *Cypripedium*, *Calypso*, and *Epipactis* display some of our most wonderful flowers.

Orobanchaceae (or-oh-ban-KAY-see-ee), orobanche family, 87 native spp., 2060–2100 spp. worldwide. The genus *Castilleja* (paintbrushes) is the most common and conspicuous member. They usually have brightly colored bracts hiding slender, tubular flowers. Less conspicuous members of the family are fleshy, leafless, fully parasitic perennials in the genus *Aphyllon*. These true parasites form root connections with nearby plants and get all of their food (carbohydrates) from their host species.

Oxalidaceae (oks-al-eh-DAY-see-ee), oxalis family, 5 native spp., 700 spp. worldwide. Nearly all of the diversity in this family is included in the genus *Oxalis*, which is particularly diverse in South Africa and South America. A few are native to California, and some are very widespread non-natives. Leaves are usually palmately compound.

Paeoniaceae (pee-own-ee-AY-see-ee), peony family, 2 native spp., 33 spp. worldwide. Found in north temperate Eurasia and North America, this group of perennial herbs and subshrubs has large flowers with sepals and petals that intergrade, many stamens, and free carpels. It is an important genus from a horticultural perspective, though our native species are infrequently grown.

Papaveraceae (pa-pav-er-AY-see-ee), poppy family, 33 native spp., 825 spp. worldwide. This family includes many important species, including California Poppy (*Eschscholzia californica*), California's state flower. Other species are important medicinally, such as Opium Poppy (*Papaver somniferum*), which contains alkaloids used as painkillers, including morphine. Species often have free petals, deciduous sepals, and many stamens.

Parnassiaceae (par-NAS-ee-AY-see-ee), parnassia family, 4 native spp., 70 spp. worldwide. Treated as a part of the Celastraceae elsewhere, the Parnassiaceae is represented in California by four species of *Parnassia*, all of which are beautiful herbs of moist habitats.

Phrymaceae (fry-MAY-see-ee), lopseed family, 62 native spp., 220 spp. worldwide. Though superficially similar to the mint family, species in Phrymaceae have round stems and do not smell minty. The family was once part of the Scrophulariaceae. All Californian species in the family were once in the genus *Mimulus* but are now considered species of *Erythranthe*, *Diplacus*, or *Mimetanthe* because of evolutionary relationships and nomenclatural rules.

Phytolaccaceae (fie-toe-la-KAY-see-ee), pokeweed family, 0 native spp., 32 spp. worldwide. This small family includes five genera that are mostly found in tropical and temperate regions of the Americas. American Pokeweed (*Phytolacca americana*) is a common weedy plant in many places in California and beyond.

Plantaginaceae (plan-tuh-JIN-ay-see-ee), plantain family, 128 native spp., 1900 spp. worldwide. Like plants in the mint family, those in the Plantaginaceae have partly fused corollas and flowers with mirror symmetry. However, species have round stems and do not smell minty. Most genera have relatively large flowers, though *Plantago* (plantain) species are diminutive herbs with tiny radially symmetrical flowers with four tepals.

Polemoniaceae (po-le-moh-nee-AY-see-ee), phlox family, 191 native spp., 385 spp. worldwide. Western North America is this relatively small family's center of diversity. It includes nearly 400 species, almost half of which occur in California. Some species offer spectacular floral displays in years with good rainfall. Key characters include three-parted stigmas and flowers with five partly fused petals.

Polygalaceae (pol-ee-gah-LAY-see-ee), milkwort family, 6 native spp., 1200 spp. worldwide. The flowers in this family superficially resemble the flowers of some members of the pea family (Fabacae). While the Polygalaceae has a worldwide distribution and is quite diverse, only a few species in the genus *Polygala* occur in California.

Polygonaceae (pol-ig-oh-NAY-see-ee), buckwheat family, 214 native spp., 1100 spp. worldwide. The group with the most diversity in California are species in the genus *Eriogonum* (wild buckwheats) and their close relatives, which have flower parts in multiples of 3. Slightly less diverse are *Polygonum* species (knotweeds) and their close relatives, which have 5-parted flowers. Culinary Buckwheat (*Fagopyrum esculentum*) is an Asian species and has been used as a grainlike cereal for thousands of years.

Primulaceae (prim-yew-LAY-see-ee), primrose family, 13 native spp., 2615 spp. worldwide. This extremely diverse family is represented in California by the genus *Primula*, which now includes our shooting stars, and the diminutive members of the genus *Androsace*. Many *Primula* species are horticulturally important.

Ranunculaceae (ra-nun-kew-LAY-see-ee), buttercup family, 81 native spp., 2300 spp. worldwide. This family is difficult to characterize morphologically because it is so variable. These plants' preference for wet, shady habitats can be a helpful identification clue. The name means "little frog," in reference to the aquatic habitats species often prefer. Fruits often consist of multiple free segments, and flowers often have many petals.

Rhamnaceae (ram-NAY-see-ee), buckthorn family, 59 native spp., 1050 spp. worldwide. In California, the diversity is dominated by species of *Ceanothus*, an ecologically important genus of shrubs that are abundant in chaparral and woodland habitats. The family is closely related to Rosaceae.

Rosaceae (ro-ZAY-see-ee), rose family, 149 native spp., 2500–3000 spp. worldwide. Humans get many of their favorite treats from members of this family, including strawberries, apples, raspberries, and the stone fruits. Roses are also quite diverse in California, which has several natives (*Rosa* spp.). California also showcases a diversity of herbaceous species that are especially prevalent in montane habitats. The diversity in this family makes it challenging to characterize any cohesive morphological trends, but clawed petals (with a narrowed petal base), hypanthia (the fleshy part of a rosehip), prickles, and thorns are common characteristics.

Rubiaceae (roo-bee-AY-see-ee), madder family, 41 native spp., 13,465 spp. worldwide. This is an incredibly diverse family in tropical and subtropical areas, but only a few occur in California, including species in *Galium* and *Cephalanthus*. These shrubs usually have opposite or whorled leaves with interpetiolar stipules (structures located between the stem and leaf petioles). Arguably, the family's most important member is *Coffea arabica*, whose ripened and roasted fruits are used to make coffee.

Ruscaceae (rus-KAY-see-ee), butcher's broom family, 7 native spp., 475 spp. worldwide. Sometimes treated as part of Asparagaceae, this family represents only a few species in California. Notable plants include beargrasses (*Nolina* spp.) and False Lily of the Valley (*Maianthemum* spp.).

Rutaceae (roo-TAY-see-ee), citrus family, 3 native spp., 2100 spp. worldwide. The most economically important members of the family are the various *Citrus* species, including lemons, limes, oranges, and grapefruits. Members of the Rutaceae are usually trees and shrubs that produce delicate, aromatic oils (look for tiny, oil-filled dots on vegetation and flowers). Very few native species occur in California.

Sapindaceae (sap-in-DAY-see-ee), soapberry family, 5 native spp., 1900 spp. worldwide. This diverse family of trees and shrubs contains many ornamental and culinarily important species, including lychees and maples (think maple syrup). The California flora contains several maples (*Acer* spp.) and our lovely California Buckeye (*Aesculus californica*).

Sarraceniaceae (sar-uh-sen-ee-AY-see-ee), pitcherplant family, 1 native spp., 32 spp. worldwide. Rosettes of tall pitcher-shaped leaves are the hallmark of this lineage. All members are carnivorous. With the help of bacteria, insects trapped in their vase-shaped pitchers are digested and then absorbed. Like all carnivorous plants, they grow in wet, nutrient-poor, sunny habitats. The California Pitcherplant (*Darlingtonia californica*) is beautiful and unforgettable.

Saururaceae (sore-ur-AY-see-ee), lizard's tail family, 1 native spp., 6 spp. worldwide. Found in North America and East Asia, species in this small family have aromatic, fleshy leaves and large bracts below their flower clusters. The flowers lack sepals and petals; the showy parts are actually bracts.

Saxifragaceae (saks-ih-frag-AY-see-ee), saxifrage family, 58 native spp., 600 spp. worldwide. The family name means "rock-breaking," which may indicate its medicinal use to treat kidney stones or its abililty to break rocks apart as it grows in stony crevices. Primarily found in temperate regions, plants in the family consist mostly of herbaceous perennials in diverse genera, including species of *Heuchera*. Saxifragaceae was once much more diverse but has been split up based on molecular evidence.

Scrophulariaceae (skrof-yoo-larr-ee-AY-see-ee), figwort family, 8 native spp., 1880 spp. worldwide. Many species that were once included in this family are now in other families including Plantaginaceae, Orobanchaceae, and Phrymaceae. These changes were made so that taxonomy reflects evolutionary history. In California, there are a few native genera. California Bee Plant (*Scrophularia californica*) is common and widespread.

Simmondsiaceae (sim-onds-ee-AY-see-ee), jojoba family, 1 native spp., 1 spp. worldwide. The only species in this family is *Simmondsia chinensis* (Jojoba), a shrub valued for the oil produced from its seeds. It is native to Southwestern North America, not China as the specific name would indicate. It has often been treated as part of Buxaceae.

Solanaceae (so-lan-AY-see-ee), nightshade family, 29 native spp., 2280 spp. worldwide. This family includes peppers, tomatoes, eggplants, and potatoes, making it one of the most important families in the world from a culinary perspective. That said, some species are quite toxic. In California, species of *Solanum* and *Lycium* are common.

Styracaceae (sty-ra-KAY-see-ee), storax family, 1 native spp., 160 spp. worldwide. Eleven genera of deciduous trees and shrubs are recognized within the family, with the majority of species in *Styrax*. Members have starlike or scalelike hairs, usually white, drooping flowers, and stout filaments. Our single native species, Snowdrop Bush (*Styrax redivivus*), is simply beautiful when in flower.

Tamaricaceae (Tam-ar-ee-KAY-see-ee), tamarisk family, 0 native spp., 90 spp. worldwide. This family's native distribution is throughout Eurasia and Africa. In Southwestern North America, various *Tamarix* species have become naturalized. They tolerate difficult ecological conditions, including salty soils and high temperatures, and can displace native vegetation.

Tecophilaeaceae (tek-o-fy-lee-AY-see-ee), tecophilaea family, 1 native spp., 25 spp. worldwide. This small family is found in Mediterranean climates in regions of Africa, Chile, and North America. In California, our sole representative is Hartweg's Doll's-lily (*Odontostomum hartwegii*), which is often found in serpentine habitats. It is one of the many groups segregated from the lily family based on DNA and other evidence.

Themidaceae (them-ih-DAY-see-ee), brodiaea family, 43 native spp., 70–80 spp. worldwide. This group is sometimes considered a subfamily of Asparagaceae called Brodi-aeoideae. All members of this group have corms, underground storage organs that are actually modified stem tissue. Look for wonderful, showy wildflowers in the genera *Brodiaea*, *Dipterostemon*, *Dichelostemma*, and *Triteleia*.

Tofieldiaceae (toh-feel-dee-AY-see-ee), false asphodel family, 1 native spp., 31 spp. worldwide. Historically included in the lily family, the Tof-ieldiaceae comprises small herbaceous species that are mostly native to high altitudes and/or Arctic regions.

Tropaeolaceae (trow-pee-oh-LAY-see-ee), nasturtium family, 0 native spp., 100 spp. world-wide. The family includes a single genus, *Tro-paeolum*. The genus name means "little trophy." Most species occur in South America and Cen-tral America.

Urticaceae (ur-ti-KAY-see-ee), nettle family, 4 native spp., 2600 spp. worldwide. This family is diverse in the tropics and comprises herbs, shrubs, and even trees. In California, it is repre-sented by the stinging nettles (*Urtica* spp.).

Valerianaceae (val-air-ee-an-AY-see-ee), valerian family, 7 native spp., 375 spp. world-wide. Considered part of the Caprifoliaceae in some taxonomic treatments, this family includes medically important species in the genus *Valeriana* (valerian). In California, *Plectritis* species are the most common.

Verbenaceae (ver-ben-AY-see-ee), verbena family, 10 native spp., 775 spp. worldwide. Repre-sented primarily in California by species of *Ver-bena*, this family also includes a number of hor-ticulturally important plants, including *Lantana* species. Turkey Tangle Fogfruit (*Phyla nodiflora*) is a widespread species in the family that can be used as a lawn substitute.

Viburnaceae (vie-BURN-ay-see-ee), musk-root family, 3 native spp., 200 spp. worldwide. Members of this family have opposite leaves and flowers usually with 5 petals that develop into single-seeded fruits. Some of its members have complicated taxonomic histories. For ex-ample, elderberries (*Sambucus* spp.) have been included previously in the Caprifoliaceae and Adoxaceae.

Violaceae (vy-oh-LAY-see-ee), viola family, 22 native spp., 985 spp. worldwide. In our flora, this diverse family is represented solely by the genus *Viola*, the violets. These beautiful herbaceous plants have 5 petals with the lowest one elongat-ed into a spur, which can be quite pronounced.

Vitaceae (vee-TAY-see-ee), grape family, 2 na-tive spp., 975 spp. worldwide. Most family mem-bers are vines with tendrils for climbing located opposite simple leaves. Evidence from a gene expression study indicates that the tendrils are modified inflorescences. The family has a world-wide distribution in warm temperate areas. *Vitis vinifera* (Cultivated Grape) forms the basis of the annual $340-billion wine industry.

Zygophyllaceae (zy-go-fil-AY-see-ee), caltrop family, 5 native spp., 325 spp. worldwide. This family occurs especially in xeric regions. The trees and shrubs of the Zygophyllaceae are perhaps best recognized by their characteristic 5-pointed star-shaped fruits. Creosote Bush (*Larrea tridentata*) is probably the most ecologi-cally important member of the family in California.

For more information about families, consult a helpful resource with illustrations, such as *California Plant Families* by Glenn Keator.

RARE SPECIES

RARITY IS A DEFINING ASPECT of Californian flora, but not every rare plant is created equal. Indeed, some plants are naturally rare and likely always have been. Tehachapi Buckwheat (*Eriogonum callistum*), for example, was discovered only within the last 20 years, growing on a special soil type in a handful of places in the Tehachapi Mountains. Other species have become rare because of human actions. An excellent example is California Jewelflower (*Caulanthus californicus*), a plant that was once locally abundant in scattered patches across six counties. By the early 1980s, more than half of its populations had been wiped out, primarily as a result of development and agricultural conversion. Concerns for the future of the this species resulted in its listing as endangered under the California Endangered Species Act (CESA) and the federal Endangered Species Act (ESA).

Starting in 1968, G. Ledyard Stebbins, a University of California professor and one of the leading evolutionary biologists of the mid-20th century, began keeping track of uncommon plants in California. CNPS volunteers continued his work tracking and categorizing the rare plants of California. The organization now maintains an online Rare Plant Inventory that, to date, has identified more than 35 percent of the state's flora as rare—that's 2400 species, subspecies, and varieties! Rarity is assessed based on several criteria, including how many places the plant occurs, its distribution in and outside of California, and the species's ecology.

Perhaps the most important aspect of rarity assessment is determining how many places the species occurs in the wild. The California Department of Fish and Wildlife keeps track of the locations of rare plants and animals in the California Natural Diversity Database (CNDDB). Most species classified as endangered occur in fewer than 80 areas.

Many, but not all, rare species have legal protection. A goal of the Rare Plant Inventory is to help ensure that plants in need get legal protection. Both the State of California and the federal government have rare species laws, and although nearly 300 species in California are formally protected under CESA or ESA, hundreds of our rarest and most threatened species are not protected. In California, any species that meet the criteria for listing under CESA are included in the Rare Plant Inventory. These plants are designated California Rare Plant Rank (CRPR) 1B so that impacts can be documented and mitigated when implementing projects.

Not every plant needs formal legal protection. Although rare species face many threats, some rare species occur only in remote wildland areas that are not threatened by potentially destructive activities. However, we live in an ever-changing world, where "remote" becomes "central" as human populations expand. The Rare Plant Inventory has a watchlist (CRPR 4) for rare plants that may not need legal protection now, but should be monitored for threats. There is also a list (CRPR 3) that calls attention to species that are not well studied and need more research.

Although laws, lists, and policies set the framework for rare plant conservation, the real work to protect rare plants happens because of people. CNPS has 35 local chapters that spend countless hours working for rare plant conservation. Chapter members know their local areas and act as watchdogs for rare plants and their habitats. CNPS also has a long-running community science program, The Rare Plant Treasure Hunt, that surveys historical rare plant populations, updating CNDDB records. Some of California's rare gems and the work CNPS chapters have done to protect them are highlighted here.

Tehachapi Buckwheat was discovered relatively recently on private land in an area of the Tehachapi Mountains that had been under-explored botanically.

Arctostaphylos pallida
ERICACEAE

Pallid Manzanita

Woodlands, chaparral; 660–1500 ft.; spring; shrub; CRPR 1B, CESA Endangered & ESA Threatened

The remaining populations of Pallid Manzanita grow on ridgetops between El Sobrante and Oakland in protected parks in the East Bay. Its leaves have a white coating, hence the common name. Although this species was never widely distributed, development has eliminated most of the plants outside regional parks, and a water mold can cause root rot and plant death. In addition, fire is needed for seed germination, and if fires occur too frequently, the seed bank can be depleted before plants mature. Pallid Manzanita is listed as endangered by the California Department of Fish and Wildlife. Members of the East Bay Chapter have commented on the East Bay Regional Parks Department's management plan and have worked with park staff to remove bay laurels that were encroaching upon the species. Look for this shrub along ridges in Huckleberry Botanic Regional Preserve and Sobrante Ridge Regional Park.

Astragalus brauntonii
FABACEAE

Braunton's Milkvetch

Chaparral; up to 2100 ft.; spring–summer; perennial herb; CRPR 1B, ESA Endangered

Braunton's Milkvetch is the poster child for Southern California rare plants, and it grows in fewer than 40 locations. Following the 2018 Woolsey Fire, large patches of the species germinated throughout the Santa Monica Mountains. After the Los Angeles Department of Water and Power (LADWP) began a project replacing aging wooden utility poles in the area, CNPS member David Pluenneke happened upon the project just before bulldozers plowed through a population of the plants on Temescal Ridge in Topanga State Park. A week after he informed LADWP of the rare species in their project path, he discovered that the population had been bulldozed. He contacted the CNPS Conservation Program, and after media attention and negotiation, the LADWP agreed to restore 30 acres of habitat and pay $1.9 million to the Coastal Commission Violation Remediation Fund. Temescal Ridge in Topanga State Park is still a good place to see Braunton's Milkvetch.

Brodiaea matsonii
THEMIDACEAE

Sulphur Creek Brodiaea

Woodlands; 620–770 ft.; summer; perennial herb; CRPR 1B

A few hundred Sulphur Creek Brodiaea plants exist along a mile-long stretch of Sulphur Creek near Redding in Shasta County. This pink-flowering species is restricted to areas along an ephemeral watercourse running through a Blue Oak woodland. Although it has one of the most limited distributions of any rare plant, it is not yet listed as federally endangered, though CNPS has included it in its Rare Plant Inventory. In 1993, Shasta Chapter member Gary Matson found the plant and brought it to the attention of professional botanists. Chapter members have embarked on conservation activities, including monitoring, seed collection for seed banking, and cultivation, and the chapter teamed up with the Bureau of Land Management to evaluate the population following the 2018–2019 Carr Fire. The species occurs on land owned by the BLM, the McConnell Foundation, and private owners. To visit populations of this species, contact the Shasta Chapter.

Calochortus tiburonensis
LILIACEAE

Tiburon Mariposa Lily

Grasslands; 300–500 ft.; late spring–early summer; perennial herb; CRPR 1B, CESA & ESA Threatened

This perennial is distinguished from other species in the genus by its erect, bell-shaped flowers with purple-flecked, yellow-green petals; erect capsules; and a persistent, copper-colored basal leaf. It grows in rock outcrops in serpentine soils. The species was first discovered on Ring Mountain in May 1971 by Dr. R. West, a member of the Marin Chapter. It is remarkable that such a distinctive plant had remained undiscovered for so long, given that eminent botanists had surveyed the mountain in the past. This species is restricted to Ring Mountain, a Marin County Open Space District preserve that was acquired from The Nature Conservancy in 2007. Based on monitoring results by several agencies, the population, which occurs in nine colonies on about 46 acres, appears to be stable. The Marin Chapter has been a strong advocate for its original protection in 1983 and continues to encourage the county to manage the species responsibly.

Calystegia stebbinsii
CONVOLVULACEAE

Stebbins' Morning Glory

Chaparral; up to 1000 ft.; late spring–early summer; perennial vine; CRPR 1B, CESA & ESA Endangered

This morphologically distinctive species occurs only in El Dorado and Nevada counties. It requires an open habitat with full sun and low competition. After a fire burns through dense chaparral, this species germinates from its seed bank and thrives. As the chaparral regrows, the species becomes shaded and returns to the seed bank. It can grow in soils derived from gabbro parent rock, which have high concentrations of minerals that are toxic to most plants. Redbud Chapter members obtained a grant to conduct a prescribed burn, which opened up habitat and enabled a population of the species to thrive. To visit this species, travel to the Pine Hill State Ecological Preserve. Take Highway 50 to the Shingle Springs exit and travel north on Ponderosa Road. Immediately turn left onto Wild Chaparral Drive and park at the end of the road. Look for plants under the transmission lines and in open areas on the north side of the parcel.

Cirsium fontinale var. *fontinale*
ASTERACEAE

Fountain Thistle

Chaparral, grasslands, wetlands; 400–500 ft.; spring–summer; biennial, perennial herb; CRPR 1B, CESA & ESA Endangered

Found in three areas in San Mateo County, Fountain Thistle can grow upwards of 3 ft. tall, with red stems and thin leaves usually covered in hairs. The flowerheads on this spiny plant range in color from white to pink. Competition from invasive Giant Reed (*Arundo donax*) has negatively impacted populations. Another threat is the invasive Argentine Ant (*Linepithema humile*), which eat the seeds' elaiosomes in place, limiting seed dispersal. Native ant species transfer seeds to their burrows and eat the elaiosomes there, thus dispersing the seeds. Since 1995, the Santa Clara Valley Chapter has supported habitat restoration by removing invasive species, which has led to an increased density of Fountain Thistle in treated areas. The most accessible population of Fountain Thistle is located in Stulsaft Park in Redwood City. Other populations are in Crystal Springs Reservoir and near Woodside Glens.

Clarkia springvillensis
ONAGRACEAE

Springville Clarkia

Woodlands, chaparral, grasslands; 800–4000 ft.; late spring–summer; annual; CRPR 1B, CESA Endangered & ESA Threatened

Each of the four petals of Springville Clarkia is pinkish lavender with a dark purple spot. It occurs only in Tulare County, in the foothills of the Tule, Kaweah, and Deer Creek drainages, in about 27 locations. The species' greatest threats are road maintenance activities, overgrazing, and competition from non-native species. Federal agencies have made efforts to protect the plant by modifying cattle grazing schedules that affect the species. Road maintenance activities through populations now occur after the annual has set seed but before germination begins. Alta Peak Chapter members Barbara Brydolf and Gary Adest own River Ridge Ranch, which includes populations of Springville Clarkia. They placed a conservation easement on their land so that it cannot be developed in the future. To view the species, visit the Springville Clarkia Ecological Reserve or the River Ridge Ranch during open days in late spring.

Collinsia corymbosa
PLANTAGINACEAE

Roundhead Collinsia

Dunes; up to 65 ft.; late spring–early summer; annual; CRPR 1B

This low-growing species occurs only in the Ten Mile River Dunes Preserve north of Fort Bragg, Mendocino County, mostly in MacKerricher State Park. Despite its narrow distribution, it is not listed as endangered by the state—though, occurring at fewer than 11 sites according to the Rare Plant Inventory, it meets the state's criteria for listing. The Dorothy King Young Chapter, in collaboration with government and environmental organizations, has restored 10 acres of habitat in the park. The project involved ripping out acres of Freeway Icepant (*Carpobrotus* "edulis") by hand. Roundhead Collinsia responded well and populations are increasing in the area. Chapter plant experts continue to increase public awareness of the species and lead public field trips at the site. Along with a suite of other rare dune plants, Roundhead Collinsia can be seen at MacKerricher State Park near Ward Avenue. From the parking area, look for the species to the south and north along the bike trail, for a quarter mile in each direction.

Dudleya densiflora
CRASSULACEAE

San Gabriel Mountains Live-forever

Chaparral; 650–1500 ft.; late spring–early
summer; perennial herb; CRPR 1B

This species' dense flower clusters emerge
from a rosette. In the dry summer months, its
succulent leaves may become flattened, limp,
and gray. With the return of rainfall, they
quickly absorb water and become fleshy and
green. The species is endemic to three canyons
within the San Gabriel Mountains. All populations grow within a radius of about 5 miles,
with the majority located near the mouth of
San Gabriel Canyon. It is vulnerable to being
crowded by invasive species, especially Red
Valerian (*Centranthus ruber*). It is also threatened by road-widening projects and expand-
ing rock-mining operations, and more recently
by poaching. San Gabriel Mountains Chapter
members watch for threats to the species and
alert the appropriate Angeles National Forest
staff and other land managers when necessary.
The chapter plans to petition for federal and
state protection. Plants can be viewed at the
mouth of San Gabriel Canyon where the river
enters the San Gabriel Valley.

Dudleya stolonifera
CRASSULACEAE

Laguna Beach Dudleya

Coastal sage scrub; up to 820 ft.; late spring–
summer; perennial herb; CRPR 1B, CESA &
ESA Threatened

Growing on cliffs and rocky outcrops, this
perennial is the only plant species endemic to
Orange County. A handful of colonies grow
exclusively on vertical, north-facing rock walls
within a few miles of the ocean. The species
spreads via stolons, which enable the plants to
colonize sheer rock. For decades, Orange County Chapter members have monitored, mapped,
and documented threats to the species. In the
1990s, a chapter member worked on the original listing petition that led to its federal protection. Fish and Wildlife Service botanists rely
heavily on chapter members' work to carry out
the recovery plan for Laguna Beach Dudleya.
Poachers remove whole plants from natural
areas, and populations of rare dudelya are at
risk of being wiped out. For this reason, the
exact locations of populations are not widely
published. Location information is made available on an individual basis to the research and
conservation communities.

Erysimum teretifolium
BRASSICACEAE

Ben Lomond Wallflower

Woodlands, chaparral; 330–1300 ft.; spring; annual or perennial herb; CRPR 1B, CESA & ESA Endangered

Endemic to Santa Cruz County, Ben Lomond Wallflower grows only in soils from the Zayante Sands geologic formation, in sand spits and sunny openings in the chaparral. The species currently is limited to 20 populations. Documented threats include impacts from sand mining, residential development, and fire suppression. Extensive management and conservation work, including outplanting, has helped stabilize populations. Santa Cruz Chapter members have worked to protect the special habitat that the species requires. The best place to see this species is the Bonny Doon Ecological Reserve, where flowering plants grow along the loop trail south of the parking area. Plant numbers have declined dramatically, from about 1000 plants in 1986 to a few dozen or less annually. Plans to increase the population by outplanting are underway.

Hooveria purpurea **var.** *reducta*
AGAVACEAE

Camatta Canyon Amole

Woodlands; around 2000 ft.; late spring–early summer; perennial herb; CRPR 1B, CESA Rare & ESA Threatened

This species grows on Red Hill Mesa in the La Panza Range of central San Luis Obispo County. Plants occur on four adjacent locations in an area of about 1 square mile—three locations on public land and a separate area on private property. Monitoring efforts indicate that numbers are declining. Non-native annual grasses are thought to outcompete this diminutive plant. The San Luis Obispo Chapter has played a major role in protecting the species throughout the years. The population on Red Hill occurs in an area that off-highway vehicle enthusiasts were using as a staging area. With permission from the U.S. Forest Service, chapter members fenced off the population to prevent it from getting trampled. The plants at Red Hill are accessible via Highway 58 in San Luis Obispo County. Flowering time is late spring through early summer.

Lasthenia conjugens
ASTERACEAE

Contra Costa Goldfields

Vernal pools; 30–500 ft.; spring–summer;
annual; CRPR 1B, CESA & ESA Endangered

Contra Costa Goldfields occurs in vernal pools,
which are seasonally flooded depressions in
grasslands that offer micro-niches to many California endemic species. The species' range has
diminished dramatically. A population south
of the city of Napa was protected from land
conversion in 1998, but the grassland lay fallow
for several years and the population eventually
disappeared among invasive grasses. Grants
and a cooperative agreement that included
the Napa Valley Chapter helped fund fencing
and controlled grazing, which has helped res-
urrect this population. The chapter continues
to monitor the grazing and population health
annually. Land ownership and habitat fragility
limit access to Contra Costa Goldfields. Currently, there is no publically accessible place in
Napa County to see this species. In the future,
with landowner permission, the Napa Chapter
may organize small outings to the site at Suscol
Creek. Vernal pools, when filled with water, are
delicate habitats that can easily be degraded by
foot traffic.

Lilium occidentale
LILIACEAE

Western Lily

Shrublands, wetlands; up to 330 ft.; summer;
perennial herb; CRPR 1B, CESA & ESA
Endangered

Western Lily plants can grow to 7 ft. tall, with
attractive whorled leaves and large, pendant,
three-toned flowers with recurved petals that
produce copious nectar to attract hummingbirds. Fire and grazing by large ungulates (such
as elk) have helped maintain its preferred open
habitats, but as these natural processes have
been disrupted, trees and other natives shade
out the species. Its total distribution includes
a 200-mile stretch of coast between Southern
Oregon and Northern California, where only 16
locations are known on private and state lands.
For 40 years, North Coast Chapter members
have contributed thousands of hours of work to
protect this species by monitoring populations,
erecting fencing, propagating and planting
bulbs, restoring habitat, educating the public,
and facilitating seasonal grazing to offset natural vegetation encroachment. Because access
to populations of Western Lily is limited, the
best way to see them is to join the North Coast
Chapter on a group field trip.

Malacothamnus davidsonii
MALVACEAE

Davidson's Bush-mallow

Chaparral; 1600–2300 ft.; summer–winter; perennial herb; CRPR 1B

Growing to 12 ft. tall, this shrub has large, lobed leaves of up to 8 in. wide and is covered in star-shaped, yellow hairs. It grows on open slopes and has an unusual and relatively wide distribution for a rare species, mostly in the Transverse Ranges. Other populations exist near Monterey County and near San Mateo. Threats to the species include urbanization, road maintenance activities, and erosion. The species is also known to hybridize with other *Malacothamnus* species, which threatens its genetic integrity. Los Angeles/Santa Monica Mountains Chapter members have participated in the Rare Plant Treasure Hunt, a CNPS community science program, to document the species. Populations are easily accessible throughout the San Gabriel Mountains and can be found growing east of Hansen Dam along the banks of Big Tujunga Wash.

Oenothera californica subsp. eurekensis
ONAGRACEAE

Eureka Dunes Evening Primrose

Deserts; 2800–3900 ft.; late spring–early summer; perennial herb; CRPR 1B, CESA Rare

This perennial herb has smooth to slightly toothed leaves and new rosettes that can sprout from the stem tips. It is endemic to Eureka Valley in Inyo County, where it grows on the sandy flats around the Eureka Dunes and in other sandy areas. In wet years, it puts on a spectacular display of flowers that are visited by hawk moths and other insects. It was listed as federally endangered in 1978 after populations were threatened by recreational activities. When Eureka Valley became part of Death Valley National Park in 1994, restrictions were enacted to protect sensitive plant habitats, eventually leading to the federal delisting of the species in 2018. In addition to climate considerations, invasive Russian Thistle is a major threat. National Park Service employees and Bristlecone Chapter volunteers monitor the thistle annually and help to control it. The only place to see this rare species is at the Eureka Dunes in Death Valley National Park. It usually blooms in May, except in dry years.

Piperia yadonii
ORCHIDACEAE

Yadon's Piperia

Chaparral, conifer forests; up to 490 ft.; summer; perennial herb; CRPR 1B, ESA Endangered

One of the rarest terrestrial orchids in North America, the flowers of Yadon's Piperia have sickle-shaped upper petals and a short nectar spur. It is dormant for much of the dry season, existing as an underground stem. Every year, only about 20 percent of the plants in a given population break dormancy to produce leaves and flowers. The species is currently found in 25 locations throughout the Monterey Bay Region, where it grows among fragmented maritime chaparral and Monterey Pine forests. Threats to the species include development and road maintenance, competition from non-native plants, and consumption by herbivores. Monterey Bay Chapter members provided support for a genetic study and also provided public comments related to projects that impact its habitat. Yadon's Piperia is named after Vern Yadon, a longtime Monterey Bay Chapter member and CNPS fellow. Look for plants at the SFB Morse Botanical Reserve in Del Monte Forest on the Monterey Peninsula.

Silene verecunda subsp. *verecunda*
CARYOPHYLLACEAE

San Francisco Campion

Chaparral; 100–2100 ft.; summer; perennial herb; CRPR 1B

San Francisco Campion is recognized as a distinct, endangered subspecies in the CNPS Rare Plant Inventory. It occurs in only 13 areas along the Central Coast, from Santa Cruz through San Francisco. Threats include development, recreational activities, and competition from non-native plants. Several populations in and around San Francisco have been destroyed. In collaboration with the San Francisco Natural Resources Division, Yerba Buena Chapter members have raised funds and are working to augment the population with nursery-grown individuals on Mount Davidson, where the plant was first collected. As a result, by 2022, more than 300 plants existed. Visitors to remaining populations in the Presidio and on San Bruno Mountain should proceed with care. A goal of the Yerba Buena Chapter is to promote and protect rare species. Contact the chapter if you are interested in helping to conserve this rare species, which needs greater protection.

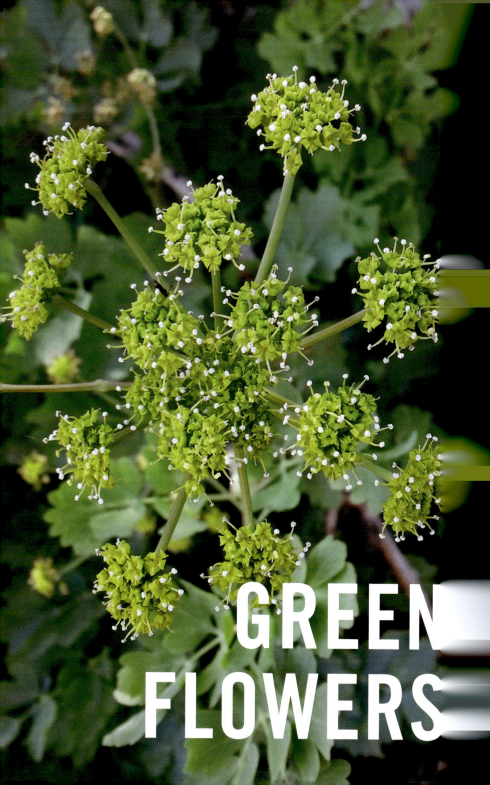

GREEN
FLOWERS

Amaranthus albus
AMARANTHACEAE

Prostrate Pigweed

Disturbed areas; up to 8200 ft.; non-native

This spring-blooming annual is a member of the amaranth family (Amaranthaceae), a group of plants that is characterized by its ability to tolerate harsh environments. Prostrate Pigweed is unremarkable in terms of its flowers, which are usually tiny. At the end of the growing season, the whole plant gets blown around like a tumbleweed, an efficient way to distribute seeds. Plant height to 3- ft.; leaves alternate, unlobed, margins toothed; tepals inconspicuous, 3, free; asymmetric; green

Eryngium castrense
APIACEAE

Great Valley Coyote Thistle

Vernal pools, riparian; up to 3000 ft.; native

Although it is not a true thistle (included in the sunflower family), this summer-blooming perennial herb resembles its namesake, with conspicuous spiny bracts below its flower clusters. Its roots have been used as a diuretic, a stimulant, and an expectorant. Plants are able to begin life submerged because of special "snorkel" cells that transport oxygen. **Plant height to 2 ft.; leaves alternate, pinnately compound, margins sharply toothed; flower clusters showy; petals small, 5, free; radial symmetry; green-gray**

Lomatium californicum
APIACEAE

California Rock Parsnip

Woodlands; 500–6000 ft.; native

This spring-blooming perennial herb has blue-green leaves that look and smell like celery. Like most species in the carrot family, individual flowers are tiny, but the cluster is showy. Reportedly, the Yuki people used root pieces as talismans for good luck when gambling. It is a larval host for Anise Swallowtails. **Plant height 1–4 ft.; leaves alternate, pinnately compound, margins toothed; flower clusters showy; petals small, 5, free; radial symmetry; green-yellow**

Tauschia hartwegii
APIACEAE

Hartweg's Umbrellawort

Chaparral, woodlands; up to 6000 ft.; native

This spring-blooming perennial herb grows only in California. Foliage is covered in short, rough hairs, and each leaf does not have a well-defined central axis. Its dime-sized or smaller fruits are rounded and ribbed. The genus is named after 19th century Bohemian botanist Ignaz Friedrich Tausch. **Plant height to 3 ft.; leaves alternate, pinnately compound, margins toothed; flower clusters showy; petals small, 5, free; radial symmetry; green-yellow**

Ambrosia chamissonis
ASTERACEAE

Silver Beachweed

Dunes; up to 100 ft.; native

The thick, hairy leaves of this summer-blooming shrub are an adaptation for water conservation and salt tolerance. Individual flowers are tiny. Flowerheads about the size of a nickel are grouped in conspicuous clusters along the stem. Fruits develop large prickles that can snag passersby. **Plant height to 4 ft.; leaves alternate, unlobed to dissected, margins smooth or toothed; flowerheads small, discoid; flowers tiny; radial symmetry; green**

Ambrosia dumosa
ASTERACEAE

Burrobush

Deserts; up to 5600 ft.; native

This rounded, spring- and fall-blooming shrub is a foundational species in the Mojave and Sonoran deserts, where it frequently occurs with Creosote Bush. Plants are wind-pollinated, with separate male and female flowers. They are long-lived, often surviving for more than 75 years. Burrobush roots exude chemicals that inhibit the growth of nearby shrubs. **Plant height to 3 ft.; leaves alternate, deeply lobed, margins smooth; flowerheads small, discoid; flowers tiny; radial symmetry; green**

Ambrosia salsola
ASTERACEAE

Cheesebush

Deserts; up to 6100 ft.; native

This short-lived, spring-blooming subshrub has yellow-green, threadlike leaves. It is commonly found in sandy flats and washes. The crushed foliage has an unpleasant odor reminiscent of rotten cheese—thus, the common name. White to pink, papery wings surround each developing fruit, creating an eye-catching display. **Plant height to 6 ft.; leaves alternate, unlobed, margins smooth; flowerheads small, discoid; flowers tiny; radial symmetry; green**

Artemisia californica
ASTERACEAE

Coastal Sagebrush

Chaparral, coastal sage scrub, woodlands; up to 2600 ft.; native

Large portions of Coastal California are dominated by this summer-blooming shrub. Its oily, narrow, hairy leaves are drought-deciduous. During the hot, dry summer, plants drop their leaves and their metabolisms slow. Very tiny flowers form raisin-sized flowerheads. The species provides important habitat for wildlife. **Plant height to 6 ft.; leaves alternate, dissected, margins smooth; flowerheads small; flowers tiny; radial symmetry; green**

Artemisia douglasiana
ASTERACEAE

California Mugwort

Many communities, wetlands; up to 7200 ft.; native

This perennial herb blooms from summer through fall and is common throughout the Western states, extending into Baja California, Mexico. Plants spread by underground rhizomes. Leaves are green on top and white-hairy beneath and emit a pungent aroma when handled. The crushed leaves have been used to soothe poison oak rash. **Plant height 2–8 ft.; leaves alternate, unlobed to lobed, margins smooth; flowerheads small, discoid; flowers tiny; radial symmetry; green**

Artemisia dracunculus
ASTERACEAE

Wild Tarragon

Coastal sage scrub, many communities; up to 11,200 ft.; native

Somewhat weedy in appearance, this perennial herb blooms in late summer through fall. It occurs from the coast to the alpine—often in dry, disturbed places. Its slender leaves can be scented but do not smell like the culinary herb. The tarragon used in French cuisine is a potent, but sterile, variety of *A. dracunculus*. **Plant height 2–5 ft.; leaves alternate, unlobed to lobed, margins smooth; flowerheads small, discoid; flowers tiny; radial symmetry; green**

Artemisia tridentata
ASTERACEAE

Big Sagebrush

Deserts, many communities; up to 10,500 ft., native

With a refreshing scent that is particularly pungent after a summer rain, this summer-blooming shrub is the dominant species of the Great Basin. Covering a vast area, Big Sagebrush is the backbone of the sage steppe ecosystem, which provides habitat for countless species of wildlife. Its specific name means "three-toothed," referring to its three-lobed leaves.

Plant height to 10 ft.; leaves alternate, lobed, margins smooth; flowerheads small, discoid; flowers tiny; radial symmetry; green

Xanthium strumarium
ASTERACEAE

Rough Cocklebur

Disturbed areas; up to 4600 ft.; native

This coarse annual occurs in wet, often alkaline areas worldwide. Conspicuous fruits develop from its tiny flowers in summer and fall. The spiny-hooked fruit easily attaches to passersby. The genus name, *Xanthium*, means "yellow" in Greek, referring to a dye that was made from the fruit. **Plant height to 32 in.; leaves alternate, unlobed to lobed, margins smooth or toothed; fruits showy; flowerheads discoid; flowers small; radial symmetry; green, white**

Streptanthella longirostris
BRASSICACEAE

Longbeak Streptanthella

Deserts, grasslands; 250–6500 ft.; native

This mustard family member is a common spring-blooming annual, primarily of desert habitats. Clusters of showy maroon flower buds appear at the tips of flower stalks. Once open, the short-petaled flowers are white to yellow and develop into delicate linear seed pods that hang down along the stems, with little seedless "beaks" at their tips. **Plant height 8–24 in.; leaves alternate, lobed or unlobed, margins smooth; petals showy, 4, free; radial symmetry; green, white, yellow, pink**

Cylindropuntia bigelovii
CACTACEAE

Teddybear Cholla

Deserts; 450–3500 ft.; native

This spring-blooming perennial has relatively demure flowers for a cactus but very impressive spines. Visitors to Joshua Tree National Park can enjoy these not-so-cuddly teddy bears at the park's Cholla Cactus Garden. A 2014 study showed that this species is sensitive to extreme drought; populations at low elevations are expected to struggle as global temperatures rise. **Plant height 1–7 ft.; leaves modified into spines; petals showy, many, free; radial symmetry; green-yellow**

Cylindropuntia echinocarpa
CACTACEAE

Silver Cholla

Deserts; -120–6500 ft.; native

This spring-blooming perennial occurs in
the Mojave Desert, which includes elevations
below sea-level. Like many cacti, this species has glochids, small, almost microscopic
prickles that detach from the plant and can
lodge in the skin, causing serious irritation.
The flowers are usually light green but can
be yellow-brown or red-tinged. **Plant height
6–10 ft.; leaves modified
into spines; petals showy,
many, free; radial sym-
metry; green-yellow**

Atriplex canescens
CHENOPODIACEAE

Four-wing Saltbush

Many communities; -230–8000 ft.; native

This summer-blooming shrub has distinctive,
densely packed fruit, each containing a single
seed with four leathery wings at right angles.
This species is important for several animal
species of conservation concern and is a primary food source for the Desert Tortoise (*Gopherus
agassizii*). Ecologists have planted Four-wing
Saltbush at Audubon Kern River Preserve in
Kern County to restore
Yellow-Billed Cuckoo
(*Coccyzus americanus*) habitat. **Plant height 1–10 ft.;
leaves alternate, unlobed,
margins smooth; fruits
showy, pink; flowers
green-yellow**

Atriplex hymenelytra
CHENOPODIACEAE

Desert Holly

Deserts; 280–8000 ft.; native

This spring-blooming shrub has a rounded growth form and distinctive silver-gray foliage. *Atriplex* species do not have showy flowers. Instead, fruits are used to differentiate among them. Desert Holly has dime-sized, kidney-shaped, single-seeded fruits. The toothed leaves and pink-tinged fruit are reminiscent of those of English Holly (*Ilex aquifolium*). **Plant height 1–3 ft.; leaves alternate, unlobed, toothed; fruits showy, pink; flowers green-yellow**

Atriplex semibaccata
CHENOPODIACEAE

Australian Saltbush

Many communities; up to 3300 ft.; non-native

Blooming from spring through winter, this perennial herb was introduced as livestock forage in the 1920s. Today it is a common invasive plant in coastal communities, where it tolerates harsh saline soils. Like all species of *Atriplex*, its flowers are not showy. Its bright red, fleshy fruits are attractive to birds. **Plant height 15–30 in.; leaves alternate, unlobed, margins smooth; fruits showy, red; flowers green**

Chenopodium album
CHENOPODIACEAE

White Goosefoot

Wetlands, gardens, disturbed areas; up to 5900 ft.; non-native

Most likely native to Europe, this annual weed (also known as Lambs Quarters) has naturalized to all parts of the world, except Antarctica. In California, White Goosefoot can be found flowering in summer and fall. High in protein and vitamins, it is sometimes eaten as a leafy vegetable. **Plant height to 5 ft.; leaves alternate, unlobed, toothed; sepals inconspicuous, 5, free; petals absent; radial symmetry; green**

Chenopodium californicum
CHENOPODIACEAE

California Goosefoot

Many communities; up to 7500 ft.; native

This spring-blooming perennial herb has spikes of pink-tinged green flower clusters, but like most members of the goosefoot family, individual flowers are tiny. All other *Chenopodium* species in California are annuals. California Goosefoot contains saponins, which foam up like soap in water. **Plant height 1–3 ft.; leaves alternate, unlobed, toothed; sepals inconspicuous, 5, free; petals absent; radial symmetry; green**

Grayia spinosa
CHENOPODIACEAE

Hopsage

Deserts; up to 9600 ft.; native

This late spring–blooming shrub is widely distributed throughout Western North America and has distinctive, thick, spoon-shaped leaves. Individual plants are dioecious, with either male (staminate) or female (pistillate) flowers, but not both. An estimated 6 percent of flowering plants in the world are dioecious. **Plant height 1–3 ft.; leaves alternate, unlobed, margins smooth; fruit bracts showy, pink; perianth inconspicuous, 5, free (male), perianth absent (female); radial symmetry; green**

Salsola tragus
CHENOPODIACEAE

Russian Thistle

Deserts, many communities; up to 9200 ft.; non-native

This annual species tumbles across lonely landscapes in Western movies. Ironically, it is native to Eurasia and was first documented in North Dakota in a contaminated shipment of flaxseed from Russia. It is considered a noxious weed in California, where a single plant can spread more than 200,000 seeds in windy conditions. **Plant height to 4 ft.; leaves alternate, unlobed, toothed; fruit wings pink; sepals inconspicuous; petals absent; radial symmetry; green-light brown**

Croton setiger
EUPHORBIACEAE

Doveweed

Disturbed areas; up to 3300 ft.; native

In this odd wildflower, male flowers have sepals and stamens, whereas the female flower
consists of a bare ovary. Although its flowers
are inconspicuous, it is an eye-catching species
with distinctive gray-green, mounded foliage.
It is very common along roadsides and trails
in California and beyond. This annual blooms
year-round, and doves love the seeds. **Plant
height to 8 in.; leaves
alternate, unlobed, mar-
gins smooth; flowers
inconspicuous; radial
symmetry; green-yellow**

Euphorbia crenulata
EUPHORBIACEAE

Chinese Caps

Many communities; up to 7600 ft.; native

This summer-blooming perennial occurs in
California and Oregon. Like in all spurges,
it has irritating white latex sap. Its flower
clusters are composed of reduced male and
female flowers. Each male flower is a single
stamen and the female flower is simply a
naked ovary on a stalk. Surrounding these
petalless flowers are crescent-shaped, horned
glands. **Plant height to 3
ft.; leaves alternate, unlobed, margins smooth;
bracts showy; sepals and
petals absent; radial symmetry; green**

Ricinus communis
EUPHORBIACEAE

Castor Bean

Disturbed areas; up to 1000 ft.; non-native

This shrubby noxious weed flowers year-round. Its seeds produce castor oil, which is used in food, medicine, and industrial applications. Seeds also contain ricin, which is highly toxic to humans. Nevertheless, it is sometimes planted in gardens for its huge, palmately lobed leaves. Unshowy male and female flowers appear in the same cluster. Each female flower has a red stigma. **Plant height 6–10 ft.; leaves alternate, lobed, toothed; fruits showy, spiny, red; sepals 3–5, petals absent; radial symmetry; green**

Fritillaria affinis
LILIACEAE

Mission Bells

Woodlands, grasslands, mixed forest; up to 5900 ft.; native

The nodding flowers of this delicate spring-blooming perennial herb have a mottled, green-maroon (sometimes yellow) pattern. Its petal margins are subtly undulate, whereas Brown Bells (*F. micrantha*) have flat margins, and its tepal tips are not reflexed. In some years, these beauties produce only leaves as they gather energy to bloom the following spring. **Plant height to 3 ft.; leaves whorled, un-lobed, margins smooth; tepals showy, 6, free; radial symmetry; yellow with green-maroon pattern**

Fritillaria atropurpurea
LILIACEAE

Spotted Fritillary

Dry meadows, rocky slopes, conifer forests; 3300–10,500 ft.; native

Widely distributed across Western North America, this perennial herb blooms in spring and summer. The half-nodding flowers are distinctively mottled with a maroon-green pattern. A similar species, Pinewoods Fritillary (*F. pinetorum*), has more erect flowers and leaves that get shorter toward the stem tip. **Plant height 4–24 in.**; leaves whorled, alternate above, unlobed, margins smooth; tepals showy, 6, free; radial symmetry; yellow with maroon-green pattern

Fritillaria micrantha
LILIACEAE

Brown Bells

Foothill woodlands, conifer forests; 1000–6000 ft.; native

The nodding flowers of this spring-blooming perennial herb are mottled in green and brown and are smaller than those of other *Fritillaria* species. Like many species in the lily family, the sepals and petals look the same and are called tepals. The genus name, *Fritillaria*, means "a dicebox," probably a reference to its geometric, winged fruit. Its whorled leaves become alternate higher on the stem. **Plant height 18–36 in.**; leaves whorled, unlobed, margins smooth; tepals showy, 6, free; radial symmetry; green-brown

Listera convallarioides
ORCHIDACEAE

Broad-lipped Twayblade

Conifer forests; 2500–9500 ft.; native

This summer-blooming perennial herb occurs throughout North America. Although its rounded leaves appear opposite, they are technically alternate, because they emerge from different nodes. The flower's lower petal extends forward and is notched at the tip, while the other two petals and three sepals sweep back, exposing an elegantly arched column reminiscent of a bird's neck. **Plant height to 10 in.; leaves alternate, unlobed, margins smooth; petals showy, 3, free; mirror symmetry; green, translucent**

Piperia unalascensis
ORCHIDACEAE

Alaska Rein Orchid

Woodlands, wetlands, many communities; 400–8500 ft.; native

Hundreds of tiny green flowers appear on each stem of this summer-blooming perennial. They have a musky, unpleasant odor that attracts moths in the evening, which pollinate the small flowers. Alaska Rein Orchid was named after Unalaska, an Aleutian Island, where it was first recognized by botanists. **Plant height to 30 in.; leaves alternate, unlobed, margins smooth; petals showy, 3, free; mirror symmetry; green, translucent**

Castilleja attenuata
OROBANCHACEAE

Valley Tassels

Woodlands, conifer forests, grasslands; up to 5200 ft.; native

This spring-blooming annual is hairy, but not sticky. The yellow flowers are visible among the white-tipped bracts. The specific name means "narrowed to a point," most likely referring to its pointy leaves and bracts. It is a hemiparasite: it can make its own food but also gets some of its glucose from other plants via root connections.

Plant height to 20 in.; leaves alternate, unlobed or lobed, margins smooth; petals inconspicuous, 5, fused; mirror symmetry; bracts green; flowers yellow, white

Castilleja pilosa
OROBANCHACEAE

Parrot-head Paintbrush

Conifer forests, shrublands; 3900–11,200 ft.; native

This low-growing summer-blooming perennial herb occurs in dry habitats throughout Western North America. Its narrow leaves may or may not be lobed and are soft-hairy but not glandular. Its pouched petals and prominent stigma are reminiscent of a parrot's head. Green bracts hide the cream-colored flowers. Plant height to 14 in.; leaves alternate, unlobed or lobed, margins smooth; petals inconspicuous, 5, fused; mirror symmetry; bracts green-yellow; flowers cream

Thalictrum fendleri
RANUNCULACEAE

Fendler's Meadow-rue

Conifer forests; 3600–10,800 ft.; native

This perennial herb has dainty, fernlike leaves. It blooms in spring through early summer. It is usually dioecious—each plant has either male or female flowers—though, rarely, male and female flowers appear on a single plant. Flowers are petalless. It is in its full glory when its dangly stamens are fully developed. Female flowers develop into beaked, dry fruits. **Plant** height 2–6 ft.; leaves alternate, compound, lobed leaflets, toothed; stamens almost showy, many, free; radial symmetry; green-yellow

Frangula californica
RHAMNACEAE

California Coffeeberry

Chaparral, shrubland, woodlands; up to 9000 ft.; native

Cherry-sized, red-black fruits are the most distinctive feature of this summer-blooming shrub. The fruits sustain many species of wildlife throughout the summer and fall. Its seeds are reminiscent of coffee beans. Currently, six subspecies are recognized based on variation in leaf characters. **Plant** height to 15 ft.; leaves alternate, unlobed, noticeably pinnately veined, margins smooth; petals inconspicuous, 5, free; radial symmetry; white-green, cream

Rhamnus ilicifolia
RHAMNACEAE

Hollyleaf Redberry

Woodlands; up to 4000 ft.; native

This spring-blooming subshrub is reminiscent of a miniature holly, with toothed leaves and vibrant, fleshy red berries in late summer. The flowers are tiny and numerous, producing copious nectar for pollinators. The succulent berries are forage for many animals, including foxes, coyotes, skunks, and bears. **Plant height to 15 ft.; leaves alternate, unlobed, toothed; sepals inconspicuous, 4, free; petals 0; radial symmetry; green-yellow**

Galium angustifolium
RUBIACEAE

Narrow-leaved Bedstraw

Many communities; up to 8000 ft.; native

This perennial herb blooms from spring through summer. Its sprawling stems are square in cross section, with leaves in whorls of four. The plants are dioecious, with each plant having clusters of either all male or all female flowers. Female flowers produce reddish nutlets with bristly hairs that seem to explode outward from the centers. **Plant height to 3 ft.; leaves whorled, unlobed, margins smooth; petals showy, 4, free; radial symmetry; green-yellow**

Galium californicum
RUBIACEAE

California Bedstraw

Coastal woodlands and forests; up to 6000 ft.; native

This perennial herb grows mainly in shady and moist coastal habitats. It blooms in spring and summer. In a female plant, one tiny flower emerges from the axil of the stem and leaf, whereas the male plant's small flowers form large clusters. Unlike the majority of bristly fruited *Galium* species in California, the fruit is a fleshy, smooth berry. **Plant height to 3 ft.; leaves whorled, unlobed, margins smooth; petals showy, 4, free; radial symmetry; green-yellow**

Galium triflorum
RUBIACEAE

Fragrant Bedstraw

Many communities; up to 8900 ft.; native

The common name of this summer-blooming annual refers to the vanilla-scented dried foliage. Historically, bedstraws were used to fill mattresses. The square, coarsely hairy stems feel rough to the touch. Tiny flowers usually appear in clusters of three and develop into bristly hair-covered fruits that are great at hitching a ride in animal fur (or socks!). **Plant height 7–30 in.; leaves whorled, unlobed, margins smooth; petals showy, 4, free; radial symmetry; green-yellow, white**

Acer glabrum
SAPINDACEAE

Mountain Maple

Montane to subalpine conifer forests; 5000–10,000 ft.; native

Flowers on this small tree are inconspicuous and have complex sexual identities. An individual plant can have only male flowers or only female flowers (dioecious), or both (monoecious). In late summer, maples produce conspicuous double-winged fruits (samaras) that helicopter down from the tree. Leaves of this deciduous species turn yellow or red-orange in the fall. **Plant height to 18 ft.; leaves opposite, lobed or compound, margins toothed; petals inconspicuous, 5, free; radial symmetry; green-yellow**

Pectiantia breweri
SAXIFRAGACEAE

Brewer's Mitrewort

Conifer forests; 5000–11,500 ft.; native

Look closely—the exquisitely delicate flower petals of this species are perfectly partitioned into whisker-like segments. Upwards of 50 flowers may be arranged on one side of the long-flower stalk. To find this perennial herb in bloom, visit moist, shaded mountainous habitats from late spring into summer. **Plant height 12–16 in.; leaves basal, shallowly lobed, margins wavy; flower clusters showy; petals 5, partially fused; radial symmetry; green-yellow**

Simmondsia chinensis
SIMMONDSIACEAE

Jojoba

Deserts, chaparral; up to 4400 ft.; native

Blooming from late winter through spring, this perennial shrub has attractive gray-green foliage and very smooth oval leaves. Unlike most plants, its male and female flowers appear on separate plants (dioecious). The female plants are economically important, because the seeds are used to produce jojoba oil, a highly desirable moisturizer. **Plant height 3–6 ft.; leaves opposite, unlobed, margins smooth; flowers small; sepals 5, free; radial symmetry; green-yellow**

Urtica dioica
URTICACEAE

Stinging Nettle

wetlands; up to 11,110 ft.; non-native

The hairs on the leaves of this summer- and fall-blooming perennial herb are like miniature hypodermic needles. When touched, they release histamine and formic acid, which cause a painful stinging sensation. Boiling the plants neutralizes the stinging hairs, making nettles edible and nutritious. This species is wind-pollinated and is a host plant for the Red Admiral butterfly. **Plant height 3–10 ft.; leaves opposite, unlobed, margins toothed; flowers inconspicuous; radial symmetry; green**

Vitis californica
VITACEAE

California Grape

Riparian; up to 4000 ft.; native

This vining perennial blooms in late spring through summer. It is easy to recognize when its stems are loaded with clusters of grapes. Growing vigorously in moist habitats, it is a choice food for wildlife, inspiring turf wars among squirrels and birds. Its distinctive palmately lobed leaves climb high into the forest canopy. **Plant height up to 3 ft.; leaves alternate, unlobed, margins toothed; flowers inconspicuous, petals 5, free; radial symmetry; green-yellow**

WHITE
FLOWERS

Chlorogalum angustifolium
AGAVACEAE

Narrowleaf Soap Plant

Grasslands, woodlands; up to 1600 ft.; native

This perennial herb blooms from late spring through early summer. Its common name is derived from the saponins in the bulbs that foam up like soap when crushed. This bulb extract was also used by indigenous tribes as a poison to stupefy fish. The bulbs were cooked for food and the coarse fibers coating the bulbs were used to make brushes. **Plant height to 2.5 ft.; leaves in basal rosette, unlobed, margins smooth; tepals showy, 6, free; radial symmetry; white**

Chlorogalum pomeridianum
AGAVACEAE

Wavyleaf Soap Plant

Many communities; up to 5000 ft.; native

This spring- and summer-blooming perennial often has long, wavy leaves that hug the ground. Each bud forms a slender, fragrant flower that lasts for a single afternoon and evening, withering the next day. The specific name means "past midday" in reference to its late-afternoon bloom time. Night-flying moths follow its sweet fragrance to find and pollinate its flowers. **Plant height to 7 ft.; leaves in basal rosette, unlobed, margins wavy; tepals showy, 6, free; radial symmetry; white**

Hesperocallis undulata
AGAVACEAE

Desert Lily

Deserts; up to 2000 ft.; native

This perennial herb blooms from late winter through spring. Definitely a favorite among desert-lovers, its large, trumpet-shaped, white flowers bloom after desert rains, attracting hawk moths. Leaves are blue-green and strap-like, usually with wavy margins. *Hesperocallis* is a monotypic genus, meaning that Desert Lily is the only species in the genus. **Plant height to 5 ft.; leaves in basal rosette, unlobed, margins wavy; tepals showy, 6, partially fused; radial symmetry; white**

Hesperoyucca whipplei
AGAVACEAE

Chaparral Yucca

Chaparral, deserts; up to 8200 ft; native

A spring-blooming perennial herb, this species has an impressive flowering stalk that can grow up to 6 inches in a single day. Its massive flower clusters can be up to 12 feet tall. At sunset, they look like candles lighting up the chaparral. Like Joshua Trees, Chaparral Yucca requires a particular species of yucca moth (genus *Tegeticula*) to pollinate its flowers. **Plant height to 12 ft.; leaves in basal rosette, unlobed, margins smooth; tepals showy, 6, free; radial symmetry; white**

Yucca brevifolia
AGAVACEAE

Joshua Tree

Deserts; 1300–6500 ft.; native

Joshua Tree is a treelike monocot with twisted branches and relatively short, spiky leaves, hence the specific name: *brevi* (short) *folia* (leaves). It blooms in spring in certain favorable conditions. As global temperatures rise, some studies indicate populations will shift northward. Sadly, there may come a day in the future when Joshua Tree National Park has no Joshua Trees. **Plant height 3–50 ft.; leaves alternate, unlobed, margins smooth; tepals showy, 6, free; radial symmetry; white, cream**

Yucca schidigera
AGAVACEAE

Mojave Yucca

Deserts; up to 8200 ft; native

This species has been used to treat various ailments, including arthritis. Today, you may notice it as an ingredient in your pet's food. Its stiff, succulent leaves emerge from a central rosette and have sharp terminal spines and long, tough fibers that may be visible at the leaf edges. This spring-blooming shrub is shorter than Joshua Tree, with longer leaves. **Plant height to 16 ft.; leaves alternate, unlobed; margins fibrous, shredding; tepals showy, 6, free; radial symmetry; white, cream**

Mesembryanthemum crystallinum
AIZOACEAE

Ice Plant
──────────

Dunes, disturbed areas; up to 350 ft.; non-native

This succulent perennial herb blooms from spring through fall. Originally from South Africa, it is considered an invasive plant in California. Clear, warty, fluid-filled vesicles on its leaf surfaces collect water and salt, and when the plant dies, the released salt increases soil salinity, making it difficult for less salt-tolerant plants to compete. **Plant height to 8 in., spreading to 3 ft.; leaves alternate or opposite, unlobed, margins smooth; petals and stamens showy, many, free; radial symmetry; white**

Alisma triviale
ALISMATACEAE

Northern Water-plantain
──────────

Wetlands; up to 5200 ft.; native

This perennial herb blooms from spring through fall and inhabits wet places in both natural and disturbed areas. Unlike some monocots with similar petals and sepals (tepals), its flowers have white petals with green, leaflike sepals. Its specific name, *triviale*, means "common," because it is common throughout North America. **Plant height to 3 ft.; leaves in basal rosette, unlobed, margins smooth; petals showy, 3, free; radial symmetry; white**

Damasonium californicum
ALISMATACEAE

Star Water-plantain

Wetlands, riparian; up to 5500 ft.; native

This perennial aquatic herb blooms in late summer in the shallows of ponds, rivers, and vernal pools. Like most flowering plants, it has both male and female parts in a single flower, but its pollen matures before the stigma is receptive, which decreases the likelihood of self-fertilization. Its ragged petals distinguish it from other plants in this family. **Plant height to 14 in.; leaves in basal rosette, unlobed, margins smooth; petals showy, 3, free; radial symmetry; white**

Sagittaria latifolia
ALISMATACEAE

Broadleaf Arrowhead

Wetlands; up to 5000 ft.; native

This summer-blooming perennial herb is found in aquatic habitats. In the 18th century, Carl Linnaeus, the creator of the scientific naming system that is still used today, named the genus *Sagittaria* in reference to the plant's arrow-shaped leaves. Plants produce edible tubers that are used as a food item by indigenous peoples of the Americas. **Plant height to 4 ft.; leaves in basal rosette, basally lobed, margins smooth; petals showy, 3, free; radial symmetry; white**

Allium amplectens
ALLIACEAE

Narrowleaf Onion

Grasslands, woodlands; up to 2000 ft.; native

Blooming from late spring through early summer, flowers of this perennial herb become papery in texture when they dry. This wild onion is found in heavy clay soils and can also tolerate serpentine-derived soils high in magnesium. "Graceful Beauty" is a selection that has been in cultivation since the 1850s. It is easy to grow and even deters rodents. **Plant height to 18 in.; leaves alternate, linear, unlobed, margins smooth; tepals showy, 6, free; radial symmetry; white, pink**

Malosma laurina
ANACARDIACEAE

Laurel Sumac

Chaparral; up to 3200 ft.; native

This summer-blooming shrub is a quintessential component of coastal sage scrub and chaparral communities in Southern California. Large, simple leaves are oriented to funnel moisture from fog down toward the roots. Its distinctive, bitter-apple aroma permeates Coastal California in the heat of summer; the genus name means "strong smell." **Plant height to 20 ft.; leaves alternate, unlobed, margins smooth; flower clusters showy; petals small, 4 or 5, free; radial symmetry; white**

Rhus aromatica
ANACARDIACEAE

Skunk Bush

Chaparral; up to 7200 ft.; native

This spring-blooming deciduous shrub resembles Poison-oak, but its shiny leaves with three leaflets will not cause severe dermatitis in most people; that said, those very sentitive to Poison-oak should not handle it. Its flower clusters are densely packed and fruits are bright red; Poison-oak has loose flower clusters and white fruit. **Plant height** 2–8 ft.; **leaves alternate, compound, margins wavy; flower clusters showy; petals small, 5, free; radial symmetry; white, cream**

Rhus integrifolia
ANACARDIACEAE

Lemonade Berry

Chaparral; up to 3000 ft.; native

This spring-blooming shrub is a common component of chaparral communities in Southern California. It has tough, evergreen, leathery leaves that hold water and enable the species to tolerate hot, dry summers. Its dense flower clusters mature into pleasantly sour-tasting pink-gray fruits, hence the common name. **Plant height to 25 ft.; leaves alternate, unlobed, margins smooth or toothed; buds and fruits pink; flower clusters showy; petals small, 5, free; radial symmetry; white, cream**

Rhus ovata
ANACARDIACEAE

Sugar Bush

Chaparral; up to 4200 ft.; native

Similar in appearance to Lemonade Berry, Sugar Bush is found in inland chaparral habitats. Its taco-shaped leaves fold up around the midvein and margins are smooth—as opposed to Lemonade Berry's flat leaf with margins that are usually toothed. The fruits of this spring-blooming shrub are important forage for small mammals and birds. **Plant height to 30 ft.; leaves alternate, unlobed, margins smooth; flower clusters showy; petals small, 5, free; radial symmetry; white, pink**

Toxicodendron diversilobum
ANACARDIACEAE

Poison Oak

Many communities; up to 5400 ft.; native

Poison Oak leaves have three leaflets that are often lobed and become leathery and reddish as they mature. Berries are white. This spring-blooming shrub produces an itchy rash in 85 percent of people who brush against or touch it. The reaction is caused by urushiol, a potent oil. Plant **height to 12 ft.; leaves alternate, compound, 3 leaflets, margins smooth or toothed; flower clusters showy; petals small, 5, free; radial symmetry; cream, white**

Angelica capitellata
APIACEAE

Ranger's Buttons

Meadows, riparian; up to 11,500 ft.; native

This tall, spring-blooming perennial herb grows in wet areas throughout Western North America. Individual flowers are tiny, but collectively, the flower clusters are showy. It is a nectar source for many pollinators and a larval host for Anise Swallowtails. An infusion made from its roots was used as a treatment for lice. **Plant height to 6 ft.; leaves alternate, pinnately compound, margins toothed; flower clusters showy; petals small, 5, free; radial symmetry; white, pink**

Angelica lineariloba
APIACEAE

Poison Angelica

Meadows, riparian; 5500–11,000 ft.; native

Like its sibling species Ranger's Buttons, this spring-blooming perennial herb is a host plant for Anise Swallowtails. Its large, feathery leaves have highly dissected leaflets. *Angelica* means "angel-like," an attribute bestowed upon the genus because a European species was used to treat plague. **Plant height to 6 ft.; leaves alternate, pinnately compound, margins smooth; flower clusters showy; petals small, 5, free; radial symmetry; white**

Anthriscus caucalis
APIACEAE

Bur Chervil
———
Disturbed areas, seasonally moist areas; up to 5000 ft.; non-native

Native to Eurasia, this annual blooms in spring and summer. Its specific name, *caucalis*, refers to the Caucasus, the region between the Black and Caspian seas. It is similar to Tall Sock-destroyer (*Torilis arvensis*), both of which have sock-grabbing, bristly fruits. Leaves are pinnately compound with highly dissected leaflets. **Plant height 1–3 ft.; leaves alternate, pinnately compound, leaflets dissected, margins minutely toothed; flower clusters showy; petals small, 5, free; radial symmetry; white**

Apiastrum angustifolium
APIACEAE

Mock Parsley
———
Chaparral, grasslands; up to 5000 ft.; native

This spring-blooming annual is a typical member of the carrot family, with finely dissected leaves and delicate white flowers in umbrella-like clusters. It can be found in many areas of Coastal California and Baja California. The specific name, *angustifolium*, describes its narrow leaves. **Plant height to 18 in.; leaves alternate, dissected, margins toothed; flower clusters showy; petals small, 5, free; radial symmetry; white, cream**

Conium maculatum
APIACEAE

Poison Hemlock

Disturbed wet areas; up to 5000 ft.; non-native

A funny thing about the carrot family is that many species are edible, while many others are deadly poisonous. Poison Hemlock is one of the latter. Ingesting even a small amount can cause respiratory failure. This robust annual blooms from late spring through summer and is common along trails and in ditches. Red-purple splotches on the hairless stems are its hallmark. **Plant height to 10 ft.; leaves alternate, pinnately compound, margins toothed; flower clusters showy; petals small, 5, free; radial symmetry; white**

Daucus carota
APIACEAE

Queen Anne's Lace

Many communities; up to 5400 ft.; non-native

Blooming in summer and fall, this annual is the wild form of the edible garden carrot. It was originally brought to North America by European settlers. The species looks similar to Poison Hemlock but has solid, unspotted stems that are usually hairy. The fruits are bristly. Sometimes a single tiny, dark purple flower in the center of the white flower cluster (umbel) attracts pollinators. **Plant height to 4 ft.; leaves alternate, dissected, margins toothed; flower clusters showy; petals small, 5, free; radial or bilateral symmetry; white**

Daucus pusillus
APIACEAE

Rattlesnake Weed

Many communities; up to 5400 ft.; native

This spring-blooming annual occurs through-out Western North America. Its scientific name literally means "very small." Indeed, this plant is much smaller than its sibling species, Queen Anne's Lace. After Rattlesnake Weed flowers, the stalks of its flower cluster curve upward, forming a little "cage" around the ripening seeds. **Plant height 2–24 in.; leaves alternate, dissected, margins toothed; flower clusters showy; petals small, 5, free; radial symmetry; white**

Heracleum maximum
APIACEAE

Common Cow Parsnip

Moist habitats in many communities; up to 8500 ft.; native

This summer-blooming perennial herb has thick, hairy stems; large leaves; and a large array of flat-topped flower clusters (umbels). Each leaf's wide, papery base wraps around the stem. All parts of this plant are quite large, earning it its genus name, *Heracleum*, after Heracles (Hercules). Its sap can blister the skin with sun exposure. **Plant height to 9 ft.; leaves alternate, compound, palmately lobed leaflets, margins toothed; flower clusters showy; petals small, 5, free; radial symmetry; white**

Ligusticum grayi
APIACEAE

Gray's Lovage

Meadows, conifer forests; 3200–11,000 ft.; native

This perennial herb has had many historical uses. Its leaves were cooked and eaten, and its roots have been used as a pain reliever, cold remedy, cough suppressant, and indigestion aid. It blooms in summer and fall and can be difficult to distinguish from Western Water Hemlock (*Cicuta douglasii*), which is deadly poisonous. **Plant height 8–30 in.; leaves alternate, pinnately compound; margins smooth; flower clusters showy; petals small, 5, free; radial symmetry; white**

Lomatium dasycarpum
APIACEAE

Wooly Fruited Lomatium

Grasslands, chaparral, woodlands; up to 5200 ft.; native

When not in flower, this perennial herb looks very similar to Mojave Lomatium (*L. mohavense*), but should have a longer stem. Often growing on rocky, open areas, especially on serpentine, this species blooms early in spring and then goes dormant during the hot, dry summer. Like California Rock Parsnip, it is a larval host for Anise Swallowtail. **Plant height 4–18 in.; leaves alternate, dissected, margins toothed; flower clusters showy; petals small, 5, free; radial symmetry; cream, white**

Lomatium macrocarpum
APIACEAE

Bigseed Biscuitroot

Chaparral, woodlands; 500–9800 ft.; native

Blooming in winter and early spring, this low-growing perennial herb has hairy, gray foliage. Clusters of tiny, cream-colored flowers form on dividing stalks that look like the spokes of an umbrella. The specific name, *macrocarpum*, means "with large seed pods." It is found throughout Western North America. **Plant height to 1 ft.; leaves basal, dissected, margins smooth; flower clusters showy; petals small, 5, free; radial symmetry; white, cream, purple**

Osmorhiza brachypoda
APIACEAE

California Sweet Cicely

Conifer forests, woodlands; up to 2200 ft.; native

This spring-blooming perennial herb grows in moist drainages and its roots smell like licorice. The plants have been used for various medicinal purposes by the Kawaiisu people of Southern California. It is an important larval host for *Greya suffusca*, a moth species found only in the Southern Sierra Nevada. **Plant height 12–18 in.; leaves alternate, pinnately compound; margins toothed; flower clusters showy; petals small, 5, free; radial symmetry; white, green**

Perideridia parishii
APIACEAE

Parish's Yampah

Meadows, conifer forests; 6500–11,000 ft.; native

This summer-blooming, tuberous perennial occurs throughout Southwestern North America. California has two subspecies: subsp. *latifolia* is widespread, whereas subsp. *parishii* is rare, restricted to the San Bernardino Mountains. The two are distinguished by subtle differences in their flower clusters and fruits. **Plant height to 3 ft.; leaves alternate, pinnately compound, margins smooth; flower clusters showy; petals small, 5, free; radial symmetry; white**

Torilis arvensis
APIACEAE

Tall Sock-destroyer

Disturbed areas; up to 5200 ft.; non-native

The mature fruit of this annual is covered in tiny hooks that cling tenaciously to clothing, hair, fur, and socks. Native to Europe, it has hitchhiked throughout North America. Its specific name, *arvensis*, means "in the fields," and it is considered an invasive plant in California. It blooms in spring and summer. **Plant height to 2 ft.; leaves alternate, pinnately compound, margins toothed; flower clusters showy; petals small, 5, free; radial symmetry; white**

Apocynum cannabinum
APOCYNACEAE

Hemp Dogbane

Grasslands, shrublands, riparian; 500–6500 ft.;
native

Flowers of this bushy perennial are borne in
summer and fall in clusters at the ends of long
stems, where they develop into conspicuous
long, narrow fruits. The common name refers
to its strong fibers, which, like hemp, are used
to make string, clothing, and even building
materials. All parts of the plant are poisonous. **Plant height to 6 ft.;**
leaves opposite, unlobed,
margins smooth; petals
showy, 5, partially fused;
radial symmetry; white,
light pink

Asclepias eriocarpa
APOCYNACEAE

Woolypod Milkweed

Woodlands, chaparral, grasslands; up to 6200
ft.; native

Similar to California Milkweed, but with
lighter flowers and hairier leaves, this perennial herb blooms from spring through fall. The
genus is named in honor of the ancient Greek
god of healing, Asclepius. Indeed, this plant
has many reported medicinal uses, including
as a cold remedy, an asthma treatment, and a
skin salve. Nevertheless,
all milkweeds have milky
sap that can irritate the
skin. **Plant height 1–3 ft.;**
leaves opposite, unlobed,
margins wavy; petals
showy, 5, free; radial sym-
metry; white, cream

Zantedeschia aethiopica
ARACEAE

Calla Lily

Moist disturbed areas; up to 1000 ft.; non-native

Originally from South Africa, this perennial herb has escaped cultivation in coastal areas. In spring and summer, the white, showy part of the plant is actually a large bract called a spathe. Within the spathe is a stalk of tiny yellow flowers clusters. Calla Lily is not in the lily family but is more closely related to philodendrons and other aroids. **Plant height 2–4 ft.; leaves alternate, basally lobed, margins smooth; bract showy, 1, fused, white; flowers yellow**

Aralia californica
ARALIACEAE

California Spikenard

Riparian; up to 8200 ft; native

One of the largest non-woody perennials in California, this species blooms in summer and fall with white flowers arranged in a round cluster. The flowers develop into purple fruit. Its roots have been used to treat various medical conditions, from colds to skin problems. Spikenard is in same family as English Ivy (*Hedera helix*). **Plant height to 10 ft.; leaves alternate, pinnately compound, margins toothed; petals showy, 5, free; radial symmetry; white, cream, green**

Achillea millefolium
ASTERACEAE

Yarrow

Woodlands, grasslands, many communities; up to 12,000 ft.; native

This spring- and summer-blooming perennial herb has a distinctive and pleasant smell, flat-topped flower clusters, and curly, cobwebby hairs on its leaves. It has been used medicinally to treat many conditions, including diarrhea, colds, arthritis, wounds, and liver disorders. Don't let your dog eat it, though; it's toxic to canines. **Plant height to 3 ft.; leaves in basal rosette, stem leaves alternate, dissected, margins smooth; flowerhead showy; radial symmetry; white, pink**

Layia glandulosa
ASTERACEAE

White-daisy Tidy Tips

Grasslands, many communities; up to 8900 ft.; native

This annual blooms in spring and summer in gravelly and sandy soils throughout Western North America. Stems and leaves have glandular hairs that may be sticky, and its flowers are aromatic, attracting butterflies, moths, and other insects. Flowers are generally white, but the petal-like rays may be pale or golden yellow. **Plant height to 2 ft.; leaves at base of stem opposite, alternate above, lobed or unlobed, margins toothed; flowerheads sunflower-like; radial symmetry; white, centers yellow**

Perityle emoryi
ASTERACEAE

Emory's Rock-daisy

Coastal shrublands, deserts; up to 4300 ft.; native

This little annual is an oddball. Rock-daisies in California are usually rare, but Emory's Rock-daisy occurs throughout Southwestern North America and has even naturalized in Hawaii. Despite its preference for dry, rocky areas, it is abundant where it is found, with a lush, well-watered appearance. It blooms in winter and spring. **Plant height to 2 ft.; leaves alternate, lobed, margins toothed; flowerheads sunflower-like; radial symmetry; white, centers yellow**

Hieracium albiflorum
ASTERACEAE

White Hawkweed

Conifer forests; up to 10,800 ft.; native

This perennial herb blooms in late spring and early summer, when flowering stems shoot up from fuzzy basal rosettes. Each plant has a branched flower cluster of 3–30 dime-sized, dandelion-like flowerheads that attract bumblebee pollinators. It occurs throughout Western North America. The specific name means "white-flowered." **Plant height to 4 ft.; leaves in basal rosette, stem leaves alternate, unlobed, margins smooth; flowerheads dandelion-like; radial symmetry; white**

Malacothrix saxatilis
ASTERACEAE

Cliff Aster

Coastal sage scrub, woodlands; up to 6600 ft.; native

Often growing on rocky banks and cliffs, this California endemic perennial herb or subshrub blooms in spring and summer. Though it has basal leaves, they generally dry up early. Hairiness and leaf shape are variable. Five varieties occur, including two that are rare. **Plant height to 3 ft.; basal leaves wither early, stem leaves alternate, unlobed to lobed, margins toothed; flowerheads dandelion-like; radial symmetry; white, underside pink**

Petasites frigidus
ASTERACEAE

Arctic Sweet Coltsfoot

Wetlands in conifer or mixed evergreen forests; up to 4600 ft.; native

The flowering stems on this creeping perennial herb often appear before the large basal leaves emerge. Fragrant flowerheads bloom in winter and early spring and are arranged in a nearly spherical cluster. Native to temperate regions of the Northern Hemisphere, it reaches the southernmost part of its range on the Central Coast of California. **Plant height to 32 in.; leaves basal, alternate, lobed, margins toothed; flowerheads discoid or with a few short ray flowers; radial symmetry; white, pale pink**

Rafinesquia californica
ASTERACEAE

California Chicory

Shrublands, woodlands; 330–5000 ft.; native

This charming annual blooms in spring and summer. Usually one main stem grows upright and may or may not be branched. As an opportunistic annual with wind-dispersed fruits that resemble those of dandelions, this wide-ranging species is often prolific after fires. The undersides of flowerheads are often pink-tinged. **Plant height to 5 ft.; leaves basal, alternate, lobed, stem leaves clasp the stem, margins smooth or toothed; flowerheads dandelion-like; radial symmetry; white, cream, pink**

Adenocaulon bicolor
ASTERACEAE

American Trailplant

Woodlands, conifer forests; up to 6600 ft.; native

This summer-blooming perennial herb generally grows in the shade, often along trails. The bright white undersides of the triangular leaves have long been used as a guide for hikers to help them mark their path or to see where others have walked before. The glandular, club-shaped fruits stick to passersby, dispersing seeds to new areas. **Plant height 12–40 in.; leaves in basal rosette, lobed, margins smooth; flowerheads inconspicuous, discoid; radial symmetry; white**

Anaphalis margaritacea
ASTERACEAE

Pearly Everlasting

Many communities; up to 10,500 ft.; native

This perennial herb blooms from summer to fall and spreads via underground stems (rhizomes). Leaves are green on top and white-hairy beneath. The pearly white bracts surrounding the flowers resemble tiny dried roses. Their color is reflected in both the common name and the specific name; *margaritacea* means "pearly." **Plant height to 3 ft.; leaves alternate, unlobed, margins smooth; flowerhead cluster showy, discoid; radial symmetry; bracts white**

Baccharis pilularis
ASTERACEAE

Coyote Brush

Chaparral, coastal scrub; up to 5000 ft.; native

This common component of coastal scrub habitats prefers full sun and has tough, drought-tolerant leaves. Mammals and birds hide from predators under this prostrate or erect shrub, and seedlings gain a foothold in its shade. The pea-sized flowerheads, blooming in fall and winter, often go unnoticed until the fruits develop fluffy hairs. **Plant height to 6 ft.; leaves alternate, unlobed, margins toothed; flowerhead clusters showy, discoid; radial symmetry; white, pale yellow**

Baccharis salicifolia
ASTERACEAE

Mule Fat

Shrublands, wetlands; up to 7900 ft.; native

Blooming year-round, this shrub favors wet areas. It has angled to upright stems and often sticky leaves. Like other *Baccharis* species, male and female flowers appear on separate plants (dioecious). The style branches of female flowers create a starburst effect, whereas pollen is visible on male flowerheads if you look closely. **Plant height to 13 ft.; leaves alternate, unlobed, margins toothed; flowerheads discoid; radial symmetry; white, pink**

Chaenactis douglasii
ASTERACEAE

Douglas' Pincushion

Many communities; up to 11,500 ft.; native

This wooly or hairy perennial herb blooms from spring through fall. Common in gravelly, rocky areas, the more widespread variety *douglasii* is taller, with a leafy stem adorned with many pincushiony flowerheads. Variety *alpina* occurs at high elevations, has a lower growth form, lacks a leafy stem, and usually has only one flowerhead per stalk. **Plant height to 20 in.; leaves in basal rosette, stem leaves alternate, dissected, margins smooth; flowerheads discoid; radial symmetry; white, pink**

Chaenactis fremontii
ASTERACEAE

Fremont Pincushion

Many communities; up to 5200 ft.; native

This annual is abundant in desert areas, where it favors sandy, gravelly openings. Occasionally, plants will grow up through shrubs, escaping hungry browsers such as Desert Tortoises, which are known to munch on them. Blooming in winter and spring, its flowerhead has larger blooms peripherally, growing smaller toward the center. **Plant height** 4–12 in.; leaves basal, alternate, dissected, margins smooth; flowerheads discoid; radial symmetry; white, pink

Chaenactis xantiana
ASTERACEAE

Mojave Pincushion

Many communities; 1000–8500 ft.; native

Flowering in spring and summer, this annual occurs in open, sandy areas and ranges into Oregon, Nevada, and Arizona. It can be distinguished from other *Chaenactis* species by its stout stems, fleshy leaves, and especially showy flowerheads. The peripheral flowers in the flowerheads are only slightly larger than those in the interior portion. **Plant height** 4–16 in.; leaves basal, alternate, dissected, margins smooth; flowerheads discoid; radial symmetry; white, beige

Logfia filaginoides
ASTERACEAE

California Cottonrose

Many communities; up to 6000 ft.; native

This common annual occurs in open or rocky habitats throughout Southwestern North America. It is more noticeable after a fire, when plants can be larger and huskier. The common name refers in part to the wooly, tangled hairs that appear on stems, leaves, and flowerheads. It is also known as Fluffweed. Plant height to 1 ft.; leaves alternate, unlobed, margins smooth; flowerheads inconspicuous, discoid; radial symmetry; white

Micropus californicus
ASTERACEAE

Q-Tips

Many communities; up to 5300 ft.; native

The common name perfectly fits this species, with its small, white, wooly flowerheads. (Note: we do not recommend using it to clean your ears!) Though not a showy plant, it often occurs in large numbers or with other colorful wildflowers in lovely springtime displays. Its distribution extends up to Western Oregon. Plant height to 20 in.; leaves alternate, unlobed, margins smooth; flowerheads inconspicuous, discoid; radial symmetry; white

Pseudognaphalium californicum
ASTERACEAE

California Everlasting

Chaparral, foothill woodland; up to 2600 ft.; native

Blooming from winter through summer, this annual or biennial grows from Western Oregon to Baja California, Mexico. Its small, pineapple-shaped flowerheads are wrapped in white, papery bracts that stay on the flowering stems for many months—thus everlasting. The leaves are quite aromatic, reminiscent of maple syrup. **Plant height to 4 ft.; leaves alternate, unlobed, margins smooth; flowerheads discoid; radial symmetry; white, pink**

Vancouveria hexandra
BERBERIDACEAE

White Inside-out Flower

Conifer forests; up to 6000 ft.; native

This striking perennial herb blooms in spring and summer on the forest floor in northwestern California, north to Washington. Its hairless pedicel (flower stalk) distinguishes it from the other two species in the genus. Its flowers' reflexed petals and pointy anthers resemble tiny umbrellas. The shapes of the leaflets on its compound leaves are reminiscent of duck feet. **Plant height 8–16 in.; leaves alternate, compound, margins wavy; petals and sepals showy, 6, free; radial symmetry; white**

Vancouveria planipetala
BERBERIDACEAE

Redwood Ivy

Conifer forests; up to 5100 ft.; native

This low-growing perennial herb occurs from the San Francisco Bay Area north to Southwest Oregon. It differs from other species of *Vancouveria* in that it has stalked glands on its flower stems (pedicels). The evergreen leaflets are triangular in shape, resembling the leaves of English Ivy. It blooms in spring and summer. **Plant height 6–12 in.; leaves alternate, compound, margins smooth; petals and sepals showy, 6, free; radial symmetry; white, lavender**

Corylus cornuta
BETULACEAE

Western Hazelnut

Conifer forests, many communities; up to 6800 ft.; native

Although not a wildflower in the classic sense, the showy, cream-colored, male flower clusters (catkins) of this shrub dangle in the wind, releasing pollen. Bright pink stigmas appear on petaless female flowers. The fruits are edible for both squirrels and humans. It grows in moist, shady areas, where it blooms in winter and early spring. **Plant height 5–25 ft.; leaves alternate, unlobed, margins toothed; petals absent; female stigmas pink; male catkins cream, brown**

Cryptantha flaccida
BORAGINACEAE

Weak-stem Cat's Eyes

Many communities; up to 6000 ft.; native

This annual grows in semibarren, gravelly, loose soils in rocky sites and washes. Small white flowers bloom in spring and summer. It is a fairly typical member of a large group of annuals covered with stiff hairs. The species name, *flaccida*, refers to its weak stem. Most *Cryptantha* species have four nutlets, but this species matures just a single nutlet. **Plant height 6–18 in.; leaves alternate, unlobed, margins smooth; petals showy, 5, partially fused; radial symmetry; white**

Cryptantha intermedia
BORAGINACEAE

Clearwater Cat's Eyes

Grasslands, chaparral, woodlands; up to 7500 ft.; native

This annual herb is covered in bristly hairs. It occurs throughout California and can form impressive wildflower displays. Blooming in spring and summer, flowers are white with bright yellow centers. Its specific name refers to the dense hairs that appear along the center of each sepal. **Plant height 6–18 in.; leaves alternate, unlobed, margins smooth; petals showy, 5, partially fused; radial symmetry; white**

Cryptantha pterocarya
BORAGINACEAE

Wing-nut Cat's Eyes

Deserts; 650–8500 ft.; native

There are dozens of *Cryptantha* species in California, and most are quite similar in their flowers and foliage. To tell species apart, botanists look at nutlets, which are ornamented fruits that usually have four seeds. As its specific name implies, this spring-blooming annual has winged nutlets: *ptero* means "wing" and *carya* means "nut." **Plant height to 15 in.; leaves alternate, unlobed, margins smooth; petals showy, 5, partially fused; radial symmetry; white**

Pectocarya penicillata
BORAGINACEAE

Sleeping Combseed

Disturbed areas; up to 7500 ft.; native

This spring-blooming annual has tiny flowers. Although not a showy wildflower in the classic sense, its most interesting characteristic is its 4-seeded fruits (nutlets), which collectively resemble a parrot's foot. The nutlets are quite small, so a magnifying lens can be helpful to see them. **Plant height 1–10 in.; leaves alternate, unlobed, margins smooth; petals tiny, 5, partially fused; radial symmetry; fruits yellow; flowers white**

Pectocarya setosa
BORAGINACEAE

Moth Combseed

Many communities; up to 7000 ft.; native

This tiny-flowered annual blooms from spring through summer and can be found growing in dry habitats throughout Western North America. As is true for many plants, the translation of its scientific name is its common name: *pectos* is Greek for "combed" and *carya* means "nut." Combseed fruits are lined with comblike bristles. **Plant height 1–10 in.; leaves alternate, unlobed, margins smooth; petals tiny, 5, partially fused; radial symmetry; fruits yellow; flowers white**

Plagiobothrys arizonicus
BORAGINACEAE

Arizona Popcorn Flower

Deserts, shrublands, woodlands; up to 7600 ft.; native

This annual blooms in winter and spring. Its flowers are similar to those of *Cryptantha* species, in that they have stiff hairs and small white flowers in coiled flower clusters. It has distinct red-staining sap and its calyx breaks off like a little cap as the fruit matures. Micro details of the fruits (nutlets) are used to differentiate among species. **Plant height to 16 in.; leaves in basal rosette, unlobed, margins smooth; petals showy, 5, partially fused; radial symmetry; white**

Plagiobothrys nothofulvus
BORAGINACEAE

Rusty Popcorn Flower

Woodlands, grasslands; up to 6500 ft.; native

Displays of this awesome spring-blooming annual look like fields of floating popcorn. Similar to Arizona Popcorn Flower, it has red-staining sap and caplike calyces. To tell the two plants apart, look for leaves among the flower clusters. Rusty Popcorn Flower does not have leaves among its flower clusters, whereas Arizona Popcorn Flower does. **Plant height to 2 ft.; leaves in basal rosette, unlobed, margins smooth; petals showy, 5, partially fused; radial symmetry; white**

Plagiobothrys tenellus
BORAGINACEAE

Slender Popcorn Flower

Grasslands, woodlands, conifer forests; up to 11,300 ft.; native

Blooming in spring and summer, this annual has a basal rosette and is covered with spreading, white hairs. Its specific name refers to its slender stems: *tenellus* means "quite delicate." To identify this species accurately, you need a magnifying lens to look closely at the fruit. It has unusual cross-shaped nutlets. **Plant height to 1 ft.; leaves in basal rosette, unlobed, margins smooth; petals showy, 5, partially fused; radial symmetry; white**

Athysanus pusillus
BRASSICACEAE

Sandweed

Many communities; up to 10,000 ft.; native

This annual is not showy by any means, but it has interesting delicate, round, hairy fruits. The plants are small but often occur in dense patches. It grows throughout the state, from grasslands to conifer forests, in wet soils or dry, rocky outcrops. Its tiny flowers bloom from winter through summer, depending on local conditions. *Pusillus* means "small." **Plant height to 12 in.; leaves basal rosette, unlobed, margins smooth; petals inconspicuous, 4, free; radial symmetry; white**

Capsella bursa-pastoris
BRASSICACEAE

Shepherd's Purse

Disturbed areas, grasslands, wetlands; up to 9100 ft.; non-native

Conspicuous heart-shaped fruits make this little annual weed easy to recognize. Originally from Europe, this species has made it around the world. It is cultivated as a commercial food crop in Asia and has many other documented uses, including as a treatment for inflammation and dysentery. The Latin *bursa-pastoris* means "shepherd's purse." **Plant height to 18 in.; basal leaves lobed, alternate stem leaves clasping, margins smooth; petals small, 4, free; radial symmetry; white**

Cardamine californica
BRASSICACEAE

Milk Maids

Conifer forests, woodlands; 300–9000 ft.; native

This perennial herb can bloom in all seasons. At one point, multiple varieties were recognized, but currently it is treated as single taxon with variable leaves. Basal leaves are usually unlobed with smooth margins. The stem leaves toward the flowers are usually lobed. It grows well in shady, moist woodlands. **Plant height to 1 ft.; leaves alternate, unlobed to deeply lobed, margins smooth to wavy, tip toothed; petals showy, 4, free; radial symmetry; white, pink**

Cardamine oligosperma
BRASSICACEAE

Little Western Bittercress

Grasslands, riparian; up to 9700 ft.; native

This annual mustard blooms in early spring. On a rosette of deeply lobed leaves, the terminal leaflet is larger than the others. Tiny white flowers produce long, skinny fruits that explode, scattering their seeds. Native to moist, mountainous habitats of Western North America, it has become a weedy pest in commercial nurseries and home gardens. **Plant height to 1 ft.; leaves basal rosette, deeply lobed, margins smooth; petals tiny, 4, free; radial symmetry; white**

Caulanthus lasiophyllus
BRASSICACEAE

California Mustard

Grasslands; 160–6000 ft.; native

This widespread annual can form massive spring wildflower displays of delicate white flowers in years with adequate rainfall. A similar species, Lemmon's Mustard (*C. anceps*), has lavender-tinged petals that open widely. Both species are harbingers of good wildflower years in Southern California. **Plant height to 3 ft.; basal rosette, leaves lobed, margins toothed; petals showy, 4, free; radial symmetry; white, lavender**

Caulanthus major
BRASSICACEAE

Slender Wild Cabbage

Woodlands; 2500–10,500 ft.; native

This charming summer-blooming perennial is widespread throughout Western North America. It has white flowers and deep green leaves with uneven lobes. Contrast these leaves with the leathery, symmetrical, gray-green leaves of Laguna Mountains Jewelflower. Both have white flowers and occur in the San Bernardino Mountains. **Plant height to 3 ft.; leaves alternate, lobed, margins smooth; petals showy, 4, free; radial or biradial symmetry; petals purple; sepals white**

Draba cuneifolia
BRASSICACEAE

Wedgeleaf Draba

Disturbed open shrublands; up to 8200 ft; native

Blooming in winter and spring, this annual grows in open areas in moist, sandy, disturbed soils. The specific name describes its distinctive wedge-shaped leaf; *cuneus* is the Latin root of *cuneiform*, which means "wedge," and *folia* means "leaf." Branched hairs on the foliage are best seen with a hand lens. **Plant height to 16 in.; leaves alternate, unlobed, margins toothed; petals showy, 4, free; radial symmetry; white**

Draba verna
BRASSICACEAE

Spring Draba

Disturbed open areas; up to 8200 ft; non-native

Because the flowers of this ephemeral annual are uniquely divided, they look as though they have eight petals rather than the standard four petals of the mustard family. Originally from Europe, settlers likely brought this attractive plant to North America. The specific name, *verna*, means "of spring," indicating its early blooming time from late winter into spring. **Plant height to 12 in.; leaves basal rosette, unlobed, margins smooth; petals showy, 4, free; radial symmetry; white**

Lepidium fremontii
BRASSICACEAE

Desert Pepperweed

Deserts; 130–9200 ft.; native

This hairless, small-flowered perennial blooms in spring. In general, fruits (silicles) are used to differentiate among pepperweed species. Desert Pepperweed has round, winged fruit with a notch. With a magnification lens, look for the persistent stigma visible in the notch. The edible seeds can be ground to make mustard smoothies (yum?). **Plant height to 3 ft.; leaves alternate, dissected, margins smooth; petals showy, 4, free; radial symmetry; white**

Lepidium nitidum
BRASSICACEAE

Shining Pepperweed

Grassland, shrublands, riparian; 250–9000 ft.; native

This spring-blooming annual is common throughout California. Its flat, round, hairless fruit is winged with a notch at the tip. The specific name refers to its shining fruit: the Latin word *nitidus* means "bright, glittering." A study from 1997 found that Shining Pepperweed increases in abundance around the nests of black seed–harvesting ants. **Plant height to 14 in.; leaves alternate, dissected, margins smooth; petals showy, 4, free; radial symmetry; white**

Lobularia maritima
BRASSICACEAE

Sweet Alyssum

Disturbed areas; up to 2000 ft.; non-native

Blooming from spring through fall, this perennial herb is often planted in gardens because of its attractive white flower clusters. Originally from the Macaronesian Islands off the coast of Africa, it has escaped cultivation and is considered an invasive plant in disturbed coastal dunes, scrub, bluffs, prairies, and riparian areas, where it can displace native species. **Plant height to 12 in.; leaves alternate, unlobed, margins smooth; petals showy, 4, free; radial symmetry; white**

Nasturtium officinale
BRASSICACEAE

Watercress

Wetlands, riparian; up to 10,600 ft.; native

This summer-blooming aquatic perennial grows in slow-moving streams, springs, and ditches. Confusingly, Nasturtium is also the common name of *Tropaeolum majus*, which demonstrates the importance of scientific names for dealing with redundancies. Watercress is the only truly aquatic mustard family species in California. **Plant height to 3 ft.; leaves alternate, deeply lobed, margins smooth; petals showy, 4, free; radial symmetry; white**

Streptanthus bernardinus
BRASSICACEAE

Laguna Mountains Jewelflower

Woodlands, conifer forests; 500–10,000 ft.; native

Locally abundant in the mountains of Southern California, this perennial herb is considered a rare species because of its limited distribution. The plant is hairless, often with a waxy texture. It grows in the understory of forests and woodlands. In summer, look for small, inflated, balloon-like white flowers that contrast with thick, gray-green leaves. **Plant height 2–3 ft.; leaves alternate, unlobed, margins smooth to toothed; sepals and petals showy, 4, free; biradial symmetry; white, green-yellow**

Thysanocarpus curvipes
BRASSICACEAE

Sand Fringepod

Chaparral, deserts, woodlands, grasslands; 700–9500 ft.; native

This spring-blooming annual's fruits are conspicuous en masse, especially when backlit by morning or evening sun. Each flattened, rounded fruit disk is perforated with a ring of holes at the margin. Stem leaf bases are arrow shaped and clasping. Reportedly, a tea made from the plant can be used to ease stomachaches. **Plant height 4–30 in.; leaves in basal rosette, unlobed, margins smooth; petals inconspicuous, 4, free; radial symmetry; white, pinkish**

Thysanocarpus laciniatus
BRASSICACEAE

Mountain Fringepod

Many communities; up to 7600 ft.; native

This spring-blooming annual is similar to
Sand Fringepod, but its leaf bases do not clasp
the stem. The plant has a waxy texture and
the fruit wings are fringed. The specific name
describes this lacy edge: *lacinia* means "torn."
It can be found growing in many habitats
throughout much of Western North America.
**Plant height to 2 ft.; leaves alternate, un-
lobed, margins smooth;
petals inconspicuous, 4,
free; radial symmetry;
white, purple**

Turritis glabra
BRASSICACEAE

Tower Mustard

Many communities; up to 9500 ft.; native

This spring-blooming, tall biennial to perennial herb has arrow-shaped stem leaves with
clasping leaf bases and narrow, erect seed pods
held close to the stem. This species is native
to North America, Europe, and Asia. Tower
Mustard was classified as a species of *Arabis*
until DNA evidence prompted its reclassification into the genus *Turritis*. **Plant height to
5 ft.; leaves in basal ro-
sette, unlobed, margins
smooth; petals showy,
4, free; radial symme-
try; sepals yellow-white;
petals white**

Campanula scouleri
CAMPANULACEAE

Scouler's Harebell

Conifer forests; up to 14,100 ft.; native

A summer-blooming perennial herb, Scouler's Harebell is found in mountain forests from California to Alaska, in shaded areas and along streams. The flower's style protrudes far beyond the petals, which are strongly reflexed. The stems tend to droop under the weight of the flower clusters. Calyx lobes are long and narrow. **Plant height to 2 ft.; leaves alternate, unlobed, margins toothed; petals showy, 5, partially fused; radial symmetry; white, pale blue, lavender**

Nemacladus montanus
CAMPANULACEAE

Mountain Threadplant

Woodlands, chaparral, serpentine soil; 250–2850 ft.; native

This summer-blooming annual has small yet spectacular flowers on plants so tiny you must lie on the ground to appreciate them. It is restricted to serpentine soils of the Inner Coast Ranges, including the Mount Hamilton Range, just east of San Jose. For those who can find them, they are a treat. **Plant height 3–7 in.; leaves in basal rosette, unlobed, margins smooth or somewhat toothed; petals showy, 5, partially fused; mirror symmetry; white with purple and yellow spots**

Nemacladus rubescens
CAMPANULACEAE

Desert Threadplant

Deserts; -225–4400 ft.; native

This little spring-blooming annual grows in dry, sandy, or gravelly soils. It has brownish purple stems and deep green–brown, hairy basal leaves. The genus name describes the delicate structure of the plant; in Greek, *nemos* means "thread" and *clados* means "branch." Upper petals of the tiny flowers have distinctive cilia, long marginal hairs. **Plant height 2–8 in.; leaves in basal rosette, unlobed, margins smooth; petals showy, 5, partially fused; mirror symmetry; white with brown patches**

Eremogone congesta
CARYOPHYLLACEAE

Ballhead Sandwort

Conifer forests, deserts, rock outcrops; 250–12,200 ft.; native

The leaves of this spring-blooming perennial herb are needle-like, up to 4 in. long, and only a fraction of an inch wide. Until recently, it was classified in the genus *Arenaria*. As the common name suggests, each stem is topped with a spherical flower cluster. It has been used for a variety of medicinal purposes by indigenous peoples.

Plant height to 18 in.; leaves opposite, unlobed, margins smooth; petals showy, 5, free; radial symmetry; white

Minuartia californica
CARYOPHYLLACEAE

California Sandwort

Many communities; up to 5000 ft.; native

This spring-blooming annual is a bonafide "dinkophyte" (a dinky plant). Its delicate flowers are supported on thread-thin stems. Although it is small, it is not picky and can be found growing in many sunny habitats, including gravelly slopes and vernally moist soils. Its distribution extends just into Southeastern Oregon. **Plant height to 5 in.; leaves opposite, unlobed, margins smooth; petals showy, 5, free; radial symmetry; white**

Minuartia douglasii
CARYOPHYLLACEAE

Douglas' Stitchwort

Many communities; up to 11,300 ft.; native

Sandy, rocky slopes provide habitat for this spring-blooming annual. It usually occurs in sparse patches but occasionally forms dense displays. Under magnification, you can see that the tiny seeds are winged. This is the only species of *Minuartia* in North America that has winged seeds. **Plant height to 12 in.; leaves opposite, unlobed, margins smooth; petals showy, tiny, 5, free; radial symmetry; white, pink**

Pseudostellaria jamesiana
CARYOPHYLLACEAE

Tuber Starwort

Conifer forests; up to 9000 ft.; native

This summer-blooming perennial herb has small, two-lobed flowers, each about the size of a pencil eraser. It does not usually form abundant displays but is widely distributed throughout Western North America. It forms an underground network of swollen stems (tubers) and often produces self-pollinating flowers that never open (cleistogamous). **Plant height 18–24 in.; leaves opposite, unlobed, margins smooth; petals showy, tiny, 5, free; radial symmetry; white**

Sagina decumbens
CARYOPHYLLACEAE

Western Pearlwort

Many communities; up to 8700 ft.; native

A spring-blooming annual, this weedy little plant grows in many types of habitat, from rocky outcrops to sidewalk cracks. Only *S. decumbens* subsp. *occidentalis* occurs in California, and its seeds are darker and smoother relative to subspecies that occur in Eastern North America. The genus name, *Sagina*, means "stuffing," which refers to its nutritional value for livestock. **Plant height 2–6 in.; leaves opposite, unlobed, margins smooth; petals showy, small, 5, free; radial symmetry; white**

Silene antirrhina
CARYOPHYLLACEAE

Sleepy Silene

Disturbed areas; up to 8100 ft.; native

Blooming in spring and summer, this annual is widespread but uncommon, except after fire, when it can become locally abundant. Flowers open at night and early morning. The species often has sticky hairs on the stem that trap insects, though there is no evidence that it absorbs nutrients from these creatures. **Plant height to 2.5 ft.; leaves opposite, unlobed, margins smooth; petals showy, 5, free; radial symmetry; buds red; flowers white, pink**

Stellaria media
CARYOPHYLLACEAE

Common Chickweed

Disturbed areas; up to 4900 ft.; non-native

This little annual can bloom throughout the winter in coastal areas but dries out in the summer heat. It grows almost anywhere, in sun or shade, rocky fields or shrubby hillsides. The subtle but diagnostic feature of the species is a single line of hairs on one side of the stem. Otherwise, the plant is hairless. Flower petals are deeply double-lobed. **Plant height to 16 in.; leaves opposite, unlobed, margins smooth; petals showy, tiny, 5, free; radial symmetry; white**

Krascheninnikovia lanata
CHENOPODIACEAE

Winter Fat

Deserts; 500–8800 ft.; native

Because of its high protein content, this spring-blooming shrub provides important forage for wildlife and livestock. Plants are covered in thick hair, hence the specific name, *lanata*, which means "wooly." Few plants have more reported uses. It has been used to treat ailments including Poison Ivy rashes, boils, sore muscles, headaches, and even datura poisoning. **Plant height 1–3 ft.; leaves alternate, unlobed, margins smooth; fruits showy, white, wooly; flowers insignificant; anthers pink**

Comandra umbellata
COMANDRACEAE

Bastard Toadflax

Dry rocky areas, sagebrush scrub, forests; up to 11,110 ft.; native

This unique spring-blooming perennial herb is a hemiparasite; it can produce its own carbohydrates through photosynthesis, but it also parasitizes a variety of other plants by attaching to their roots. It is an alternate host for Comandra Blister Rust, a fungal disease of ponderosa and lodgepole pines. The species is widespread in North America. **Plant height to 16 in.; leaves alternate, unlobed, margins smooth; petals showy, 5–6, partially fused; radial symmetry; white**

Calystegia macrostegia
CONVOLVULACEAE

Island Bindweed

Chaparral, grasslands; up to 3000 ft.; native

This herbaceous vining perennial responds well to disturbance, becoming abundant in areas opened by fire. Perennial moisture in the form of fog causes plants to be quite huge on the Channel Islands, with leaves almost 12 in. long. Populations growing in the dry interior parts of Southern California have tiny leaves. It blooms in spring and summer. **Plant stem** length to 4 ft.; leaves alternate, basally lobed, margins smooth, wavy; petals showy, 5, fused; radial symmetry; white, pinkish

Calystegia occidentalis
CONVOLVULACEAE

Chaparral Bindweed

Chaparral, woodlands, yellow pine forests; up to 4000 ft.; native

This vining perennial herb blooms in spring and summer, with showy white flowers, and tends to scramble over shrubs. Two subspecies have been described, one with basally lobed bracts and the other with unlobed bracts. This species commonly adorns roadsides and trails throughout California. *Occidentalis* means "western." **Plant stem** length to 6 ft.; leaves alternate, basally lobed, margins smooth; petals showy, 5, fused; radial symmetry; white, pinkish

Convolvulus arvensis
CONVOLVULACEAE

Field Bindweed

Disturbed areas, grasslands; up to 8500 ft.; non-native

This perennial herb is a problematic weed in agricultural fields and home gardens. Bindweeds often have robust underground rhizomes. In the case of Field Bindweed, plants can resprout from underground stems even after being poisoned, solarized, and tilled. Its seeds can live up to 50 years in the seed bank. It blooms in spring and summer. **Plant trailing to 10 ft.; leaves alternate, basally lobed, margins smooth, wavy; petals showy, 5, fused; radial symmetry; white to pink**

Cressa truxillensis
CONVOLVULACEAE

Alkaliweed

Saline and alkaline wetlands; up to 5000 ft.; native

Most morning glories are vining perennials, but Alkaliweed has an unusually upright habit. Its summer-blooming flowers are relatively small, each about the size of a penny. This species can be found growing along trails and beaches in coastal areas and can tolerate harsh, salty soils, such as those found in alkali sinks. It also tolerates disturbance. **Plant height to 1 ft.; leaves alternate, unlobed, margins smooth; petals showy, 5, partially fused; radial symmetry; white**

Cuscuta californica
CONVOLVULACEAE

Chaparral Dodder

Chaparral; up to 8000 ft.; native

This parasitic perennial vining plant obtains all of its carbohydrates from a host plant. Because it has completely lost its ability to perform photosynthesis; its leaves have been reduced to stem scales. If you see a shrub that looks as though it's covered with a large serving of orange spaghetti, you've probably found a dodder. Tiny flowers are visible from spring through fall. **Plant stem length to 5 ft.; leaves absent; petals inconspicuous, 5, partially fused; radial symmetry; white**

Cornus nuttallii
CORNACEAE

Pacific Dogwood

Conifer forests; up to 6000 ft.; native

This spring-blooming deciduous tree or shrub is beloved for its large white "flowers," which are actually tight clusters of tiny flowers surrounded by showy, petaloid bracts. The flowers develop into tightly packed red fruits. Leaves turn scarlet in the fall. If you are lucky, you may see a dogwood simultaneously flowering and fruiting while sporting autumn leaf color. **Plant height to 80 ft.; leaves opposite, unlobed, margins smooth; bracts showy, 4–7, free; radial symmetry; white**

Cornus sericea
CORNACEAE

Red Osier Dogwood

Riparian; up to 10,800 ft.; native

The young stems of this summer-blooming shrub are red when it grows in sunny areas. It prefers wet soils. Leaves have distinctive curving veins. Flower clusters mature into showy white berries that attract birds and are human-edible. In California, the subspecies are differentiated based on petal size and leaf hairs, which can cause dermatitis when handled. **Plant height 4–13 ft.; leaves opposite, unlobed, margins smooth; petals showy, 4, free; radial symmetry; white, pink**

Crossosoma bigelovii
CROSSOSOMATACEAE

Ragged Rockflower

Deserts; up to 5600 ft.; native

This spring-blooming shrub is native to the Mojave and Sonoran deserts, where it occurs sporadically. It has gray-green foliage. Reminiscent of roses, its fragrant flowers have crinkly petals and multiple rows of stamens. Ragged Rockflower is drought-deciduous, meaning it drops its leaves when water-stressed. Crossosomataceae is a small family that includes only six species. **Plant height 3–7 ft.; leaves alternate, unlobed, margins smooth; petals showy, 5, free; radial symmetry; white**

Marah fabacea
CUCURBITACEAE

California Manroot

Riparian and open areas; up to 5200 ft; native

This spring-blooming vining perennial has small, solitary, pale-green female flowers, with male flowers in elongated clusters arising from the leaf axils. Its distinctive spherical fruits are covered in prickles. The massive, fleshy underground stem (tuber) is reminiscent of a buried body, hence the common name. Roots of older plants can weigh more than 200 pounds. **Plant stem length to 15 ft.; leaves alternate, lobed, margins toothed; petals showy, 5, partially fused; radial symmetry; white, pale green**

Marah macrocarpa
CUCURBITACEAE

Wild Cucumber

Chaparral, woodlands; up to 3000 ft.; native

This vining perennial is one of the first plants to respond to winter rains with stems climbing up to 20 ft. Plants have separate male and female flowers. Blooming in winter and spring, multiple cup-shaped male flowers form a cluster at the ends of stems, while female flowers occur singly. The hanging fruits are tennis ball–sized, spike-covered spheres. **Plant stem length to 20 ft.; leaves alternate, lobed, margins toothed; petals showy, 5, partially fused; radial symmetry; white**

Allotropa virgata
ERICACEAE

Sugarstick

Conifer and hardwood forests; 300–10,300 ft.; native

This spring-blooming perennial is a myco-parasite that gets all of its carbohydrates from fungi in the soil, which in turn get their nutrients from tree roots. Genetic studies show that Sugarstick has completely lost the genes it would need to perform photosynthesis. It lacks green pigment, and its aboveground parts are reduced to a thick, flower-bearing stem. **Plant height to 20 in.; leaves reduced to bracts; petals showy, 5, free; radial symmetry; anthers red, turn black; flowers white**

Arctostaphylos glandulosa
ERICACEAE

Eastwood's Manzanita

Chaparral, conifer forests; up to 7900 ft.; native

This winter-blooming shrub's sticky, flattened, round fruits are about the size of a dime. Though manzanitas are not wildflowers in the strict sense, they have been described as "rock stars" of the California shrub scene, with their gorgeous evergreen foliage and abundant flower clusters that brighten winter landscapes. The fruits are an important food source for wildlife. **Plant height 3–12 ft.; leaves alternate, unlobed, margins smooth, pointed tip; petals showy, 5, fused; radial symmetry; white, pink**

Arctostaphylos glauca
ERICACEAE

Bigberry Manzanita

Chaparral, woodlands; up to 7200 ft.; native

This winter-blooming shrub has red, sticky, round fruits that are up to a half-inch wide. Its glaucous leaves are light green with a distinctive white, powdery coating. Plants tend to be taller along the coast and smaller in arid areas. Bigberry Manzanita is susceptible to leaf galls, which look like fruit but are actually the nests of egg-laying insects. **Plant height 3–20 ft.; leaves alternate, unlobed, margins smooth, pointed tip; petals showy, 5, fused; radial symmetry; white, pink**

Arctostaphylos manzanita
ERICACEAE

Common Manzanita

Conifer forests, woodlands, chaparral; up to 6100 ft.; native

This winter-blooming shrub has small, pea-sized flowers. The bright green leaves usually have a wedge-shaped base. Multiple subspecies can vary beyond the usual conditions, however. For example, *A. manzanita* subsp. *glaucescens* typically has glaucous leaves with a white, powdery coating. The common name means "little apple" and perfectly describes the fruits. **Plant height 6–25 ft.; leaves alternate, unlobed, margins smooth, pointed tip; petals showy, 5, fused; radial symmetry; white, pink**

Arctostaphylos viscida
ERICACEAE

Whiteleaf Manzanita

Conifer forests, woodlands, chaparral; up to 7200 ft.; native

The leaves of this winter-blooming shrub are green-gray on both sides, and its flower stems are covered in sticky glands. Like most manzanitas, it is slow-growing and can take up to 10 years to produce seeds. Low-intensity fires can completely kill the plant, which is often a dominant component of chaparral in Northern California. A flush of seedlings typically follows. **Plant height 8–16 ft.; leaves alternate, unlobed, margins smooth, toothed tip; petals showy, 5, fused; radial symmetry; white, pink**

Cassiope mertensiana
ERICACEAE

Western Moss Heather

Subalpine; 6000–11,500 ft.; native

This summer-blooming shrub grows on moist, rocky, high-elevation slopes from Alaska to California and Montana. Distinctive scale-like leaves cover the stems, giving the branches a reptilian quality. The habit can be spreading or upright. Records indicate that the plant was used by indigenous peoples as a treatment for tuberculosis. **Plant height to 1 ft.; leaves opposite, unlobed, margins smooth; petals showy, 5, fused; radial symmetry; sepals red; petals white**

Gaultheria shallon
ERICACEAE

Salal

Coastal conifer forests and scrub; up to 3500 ft.; native

This evergreen shrub grows densely along forest edges in Western North America. Stems create a distinctive zigzag pattern. Its leathery leaves are deep green on the upper surface and lighter below. Spring flowers are followed by attractive, edible black berries that provide food for wildlife and can be used to make a tasty jam. **Plant height 1–7 ft.; leaves alternate, unlobed, margins finely toothed; petals showy, 5, fused; radial symmetry; white, pink**

Orthilia secunda
ERICACEAE

Sidebells Wintergreen

Conifer forests; 3300–10,500 ft.; native

This summer-blooming perennial herb occurs in high latitudes across the Northern Hemisphere (circumboreal distribution). Its specific name means "side flowering," in reference to its one-sided flowering stalk. Although it occurs throughout the world, it has lost habitat and is no longer found in Maryland, Indiana, and Ohio. **Plant height to 8 in.; leaves alternate, unlobed, margins smooth; petals showy, 5, fused; radial symmetry; white**

Pterospora andromedea
ERICACEAE

Woodland Pinedrops

Conifer forests; up to 9500 ft.; native

This parasitic plant has taken an evolutionary path similar to that of Sugarstick and lost all of its leaves. All that is visible above ground is a robust, ghostly pink–flowering stalk. As soil fungi penetrate the roots of nearby trees and Woodland Pinedrops, the species is able to obtain nutrients from the trees via the fungi (mycoheterotrophy). **Plant height 1–3 ft.; leaves absent; petals showy, 5, fused; radial symmetry; cream, brown-yellow**

Pyrola picta
ERICACEAE

White-veined Wintergreen

Conifer forests; 1300–7900 ft.; native

This summer-blooming perennial herb is a little gem of the forest understory. It has leathery, white-veined leaves and is widely distributed throughout forests in Western North America to Alaska. Like many other species in the Ericaceae, it gets some of its carbohydrates from the trees around it via root associations with fungi. **Plant height to 8 in.; leaves in basal rosette, unlobed, margins smooth, rarely toothed; petals showy, 5, free; radial symmetry; white, pink**

Rhododendron occidentale

ERICACEAE

Western Azalea

Wetlands, riparian; up to 8900 ft.; native

This late-spring–blooming shrub has unex-pectedly wide ecological tolerances for an azalea, from cool coastal habitats to inland montane wetlands with hot summers. Its range extends to Western Oregon. It is the only deciduous *Rhododendron* species in Cal-ifornia, losing its leaves after they turn color in autumn. The floral fragrance is delicious. **Plant height 6–16 ft.; leaves alternate, un-lobed, margins smooth; petals showy, 5, partly fused; radial symmetry; white, yellow, pink tinge**

Euphorbia albomarginata

EUPHORBIACEAE

Rattlesnake Sandmat

Chaparral, deserts; up to 7500 ft.; native

This mat-forming perennial blooms from spring through fall. Technically, flowers of *Euphorbia* species lack petals, but Rattlesnake Sandmat has petal-like nectar appendages in its flower clusters. Each leaf has a thin white line around its margin. Its specific name means "white-edge." **Plant height to 1 in., mat forming; leaves opposite, unlobed, margins smooth; bracts showy, 4, free; radial to mirror symmetry; white, red**

Euphorbia misera
EUPHORBIACEAE

Cliff Spurge

Chaparral; up to 1600 ft.; native

Unlike most North American *Euphorbia* species, this plant is a woody subshrub. It blooms from winter through summer. It grows on steep slopes in a special vegetation type, called maritime succulent scrub. It is common in Baja California but has never been abundant in California, where coastal development has reduced its habitat further. **Plant height 1–3 ft.; leaves alternate, unlobed, margins smooth; bracts showy, 5, free; radial symmetry; white, red**

Acmispon americanus
FABACEAE

Spanish Lotus

Grasslands, woodlands, wetlands; up to 7900 ft.; native

This low-growing, hairy annual plant produces small, cream to pink, solitary flowers in spring. It is a larval food source for many butterflies, including Melissa Blue and Bald Duskywing. Its compound leaves comprise three leaflets. As an easily grown nitrogen fixer, it is often used in restoration seed mixes. Until recently, its scientific name was *Lotus purshianus*. **Plant height to 1 ft.; leaves alternate, pinnately compound, margins smooth; petals showy, 5, partially fused (keel); mirror symmetry; white, cream, pink**

Astragalus trichopodus
FABACEAE

Santa Barbara Milkvetch

Chaparral, grasslands, coastal bluffs; up to 10,000 ft.; native

This robust, bushy perennial has pale flower clusters that bloom in late winter and spring. Found in a wide range of open habitats, its inflated, papery fruits are food for Western Tailed Blue butterfly caterpillars. It is one of almost 100 species of milkvetch in California, some of which are toxic to livestock. **Plant height to 3 ft.; leaves alternate, pinnately compound, margins smooth; petals showy, 5, partially fused (keel); mirror symmetry; cream**

Glycyrrhiza lepidota
FABACEAE

Wild Licorice

Many communities; up to 6560 ft.; native

A tall, rangy, summer-blooming perennial, Wild Licorice has half-inch fruits covered with hooks, perfect for hitching rides on animal hair and human socks to disperse its seeds. It grows in damp, open, often disturbed habitats of Western North America. It is closely related to European Licorice (*G. glabra*), whose roots are used as a flavoring and as medicine. **Plant height to 4 ft.; leaves alternate, pinnately compound, margins smooth; petals showy, 5, partially fused (keel); mirror symmetry; white, tan**

Prosopis glandulosa
FABACEAE

Honey Mesquite

Deserts; up to 5600 ft.; native

This small desert tree is distinguished by wicked 2 in. thorns, twice-compound leaves, and spikes of tiny flowers. It blooms in summer. It is native to the U.S. Southwest and into Mexico. The species was introduced to Australia and South Africa, where it has become extremely invasive. Bees foraging on honey mesquite produce a flavorful and popular honey. **Plant height to 23 ft.; leaves alternate, pinnately compound, margins smooth; stamens showy, many, free; radial symmetry; cream**

Senegalia greggii
FABACEAE

Catclaw Acacia

Deserts; up to 7800 ft.; native

This shrub will stop you in your tracks if you are "grabbed" by its abundant clawlike prickles, which can rip your clothing and skin. Its numerous stamens are the most distinctive flower feature. *Acacia* species native to North America have been reassigned to genus *Senegalia*. This spring-blooming shrub was known as *Acacia greggii* until recently. **Plant height to 12 ft.; leaves alternate, pinnately compound, margins smooth; stamens showy, many, free; radial symmetry; cream, light yellow**

Trifolium monanthum
FABACEAE

Mountain Carpet Clover

Many communities; 5600–12,800 ft.; native

Blooming in spring and summer, the flowers of this perennial herb can occur singly, which is unusual for a clover, or in a cluster with up to six flowers per head. The specific name, *monanthum*, means "one-flowered" and describes this unusual arrangement. It often forms plush carpets in moist meadows or along streams. **Plant height to 3 in.; leaves alternate, palmately compound, 3 leaflets, margins toothed; petals showy, 5, partially fused (keel); mirror symmetry; white, lavender**

Garrya elliptica
GARRYACEAE

Coast Silktassel

Coastal scrub, chaparral, foothill woodlands; up to 2600 ft.; native

In winter, this coastal shrub has beautiful chains of flowers that dangle from the stems, resembling silky tassels. Male flower chains grow on separate plants from female flowers. Leathery, evergreen, opposite leaves are waxy on top, densely hairy below, and wavy-edged. Bare stamens and pistils peek out from the overlapping flower bracts. **Plant height to 15 ft.; leaves opposite, unlobed, margins wavy; petals of staminate flowers inconspicuous, 4; fused; radial symmetry; flower clusters (tassels) showy; white, gray-green**

Frasera albicaulis
GENTIANACEAE

Whitestem Frasera

Dry woodlands and forests, chaparral; 600–6100 ft.; native

This attractive perennial herb is native to Western North America and forms a tidy basal rosette of narrow, white-margined leaves. Blooming in spring to early summer, its flowers are borne in intermittent clusters along erect stems. The petals are flat and intricately spotted. The specific name, *albicaulis*, means "white stem." **Plant height to 2.5 ft.; leaves in basal rosette, unlobed; stem leaves opposite, margins smooth; petals showy, 4, fused at base; radial symmetry; white, light blue**

Frasera speciosa
GENTIANACEAE

Monument Plant

Montane meadows and openings in conifer forests; 5000–9800 ft.; native

This perennial herb blooms in summer in mountain meadows, producing hundreds of exquisite pale flowers per plant. Its large, oblong leaves inspired an alternative common name, Deer's Tongue. A single plant grows for decades as a basal rosette of leaves. Then, in one season, it produces a massive flower display, releases thousands of seeds, and dies. **Plant height to 6 ft.; leaves basal, stem leaves whorled, unlobed, margins smooth; petals showy, 4, fused at base; radial symmetry; white, green**

Gentiana newberryi

GENTIANACEAE

Alpine Gentian

Alpine, wetlands; 4000–13,100 ft.; native

Blooming in summer in wet montane meadows, this species is similar to Explorers' Gentian, but with even larger flowers. The flowers
of *G. newberryi* var. *tiogana* are usually white
but sometimes have a blue tinge; variety *newberryi* usually has bright gentian-blue flowers.
The flowering stems arise from underneath
the flat basal leaf rosette—an oddity. **Plant
height to 4 in.; leaves
in basal rosette, stem
leaves opposite, unlobed,
margins smooth; pet-
als showy, 5, partially
fused; radial symmetry;
white, blue**

Heliotropium curassavicum

HELIOTROPIACEAE

Salt Heliotrope

Many communities; up to 7400 ft.; native

Blooming in late spring, this fleshy, hairless,
sprawling perennial has a prominent coiled
flower cluster typical of the family. The flowers are five-lobed and white with yellow centers. As the flowers age the centers become
purple. The species favors disturbed saline
and alkaline soils and can become invasive in
these habitats outside its native range. **Plant
height 12–18 in.; leaves
alternate, unlobed,
margins smooth; pet-
als showy, 5, partially
fused; radial symmetry;
white with yellow centers
fading purple**

Philadelphus lewisii
HYDRANGEACEAE

Mock Orange

Conifer forests, woodlands; up to 8000 ft.; native

This spring-flowering montane shrub produces masses of 1 in. fragrant flowers. It was one of 200 species new to science when it was collected during the Lewis and Clark Expedition. Leaves are oppositely arranged and deciduous. If you carefully pull apart a leaf, the fibers in the veins stay connected as visible cottony threads. **Plant height 5–12 ft.; leaves opposite, unlobed, margins smooth or toothed; petals showy, 4, free; radial symmetry; white**

Whipplea modesta
HYDRANGEACEAE

Modesty

Coastal scrub, chaparral, forests, woodlands; up to 5000 ft.; native

Technically a spring-flowering woody sub-shrub, though it presents as a groundcover, Modesty occurs in coastal areas as far south as Monterey County and north to Washington State. It has opposite leaves and small flowers clustered at its stem tips. The genus honors Lieutenant A. W. Whipple, surveyor of the 35th Parallel in the 1850s. **Plant height to 8 in.; leaves opposite, unlobed, margins toothed; petals showy, 4–6, free; radial symmetry; white**

Eucrypta chrysanthemifolia
HYDROPHYLLACEAE

Spotted Hideseed

Coastal sage scrub, woodlands, deserts; up to 7500 ft.; native

A spring-flowering annual with dainty flowers and dissected leaves, Spotted Hideseed often pops up in response to fire or other disturbances. The genus name *Eucrypta* is Greek for "well-hidden," referring to the red seeds that are hidden in small green fruits. This species can be mistaken for White Fiesta Flower, which lacks the vinegary smell of Spotted Hideseed. Plant height 1–3 ft.; leaves alternate, lobed, margins toothed; petals showy, 5, partially fused; radial symmetry; white, veins purple

Nemophila heterophylla
HYDROPHYLLACEAE

Canyon Nemophila

Forests, woodlands, chaparral; up to 5600 ft.; native

This branching, spring-flowering annual inhabits dappled shade in various habitats of Northern California and Southwest Oregon. The specific name, which means "other leaf," reflects the plant's leaf variation. Its lower leaves are opposite and deeply lobed, whereas its upper leaves are alternate and shallowly lobed or unlobed. **Plant height to 18 in.; leaves alternate, opposite, lobed or unlobed, margins smooth; petals showy, 5, partially fused; radial symmetry; white**

Nemophila maculata
HYDROPHYLLACEAE

Fivespot

Woodlands, meadows; up to 8000 ft.; native

This spring-flowering annual is endemic to California. The common and scientific names of this species refer to the prominent purple spot on each petal of its large flowers; *maculata* means "spotted" in Latin. This species produces colorful displays in the Sierra Nevada and Coast Range foothills. It is also a common component of California wildflower seed mixes. **Plant height 6–12 in.; leaves opposite, lobed, margins smooth; petals showy, 5, partially fused; radial symmetry; white, purple**

Phacelia imbricata
HYDROPHYLLACEAE

Imbricate Phacelia

Chaparral, woodlands; up to 9100 ft.; native

A perennial herb with tightly coiled flower clusters, this species is recognizable by its thick coat of stiff hairs and deeply lobed leaves. The word imbricate means "overlapping"; although not super easy to see, the calyx lobes are imbricate in fruit. This widely distributed species is found on slopes, roadsides, flats, and canyons. **Plant height 1–3 ft.; leaves in basal rosette, lobed, margins smooth; petals showy, 5, partially fused; radial symmetry; white, fading to tan**

Phacelia ramosissima
HYDROPHYLLACEAE

Branching Phacelia

Coastal sage scrub, conifer forests; up to 10,500 ft.; native

This ecologically diverse species can grow in dune, salt marsh, coastal bluff, canyon, meadow, and woodland habitats. It could be confused with the white-flowered, spring-bloooming annual Distant Phacelia, but Branching Phacelia is a perennial that blooms from spring through fall. Its stamens extend beyond the petals and its leaves are highly divided. **Plant height to 4 ft.; leaves alternate, dissected, margins smooth; petals showy, 5, partially fused; radial symmetry; white, light pink, blue, lavender**

Pholistoma membranaceum
HYDROPHYLLACEAE

White Fiesta Flower

Dunes, woodlands, deserts; up to 8100 ft.; native

This rambling, tangled annual has stiff hairs that can attach to clothing and socks. Its small flowers are bee-pollinated. Blooming in winter and spring, each of the flower's five petals usually has a subtle purple streak down its center. The species is endemic to the southern half of the California Floristic Province to Baja California. **Plant height to 3 ft.; leaves alternate, lobed, margins smooth; petals showy, 5, partially fused; radial symmetry; nectary green; flowers white with purple spots**

Clinopodium douglasii
LAMIACEAE

Yerba Buena

Woodlands, chaparral; up to 3000 ft.; native

The square stems of this spring- and summer-blooming perennial herb run along the ground and are covered with thick, fragrant leaves. *Yerba buena* means "good herb" in Spanish. The Mexican settlement that eventually became San Francisco was once known as Yerba Buena for the plentiful *C. douglasii* plants in the area. It can be used to make a soothing tea. **Plant height to 4 in.; leaves opposite, unlobed, margins toothed; petals showy, 5, partially fused; mirror symmetry; white**

Marrubium vulgare
LAMIACEAE

White Horehound

Disturbed areas; up to 2000 ft.; non-native

The sepals of this summer-blooming perennial herb terminate in stiff prickles that can shred your socks. It has distinctive, deeply net-veined leaves. Native to Eurasia and North Africa, it has been used as a cough remedy for centuries. The U.S. Food and Drug Administration has approved its use as a food additive, but not as a medicine. **Plant height to 2 ft.; leaves opposite, unlobed, margins toothed; petals showy, 5, partially fused; mirror symmetry; white**

Salvia apiana
LAMIACEAE

White Sage

Coastal sage scrub, chaparral, pine forests; up to 4900 ft.; native

This gorgeous spring-blooming perennial herb or subshrub forms mounds of hairy, white-green foliage that sprout long, flower-covered stems up to three times the mound height. White Sage is an important component of Southern California coastal sage communities. Sadly, it has recently suffered serious decline as a result of unscrupulous overharvesting of wild plants. **Plant height to 5 ft.; leaves opposite, unlobed, margins minutely toothed; petals showy, 5, partially fused; mirror symmetry; white, lavender**

Scutellaria californica
LAMIACEAE

California Skullcap

Scrub, woodlands, forest openings; up to 7200 ft.; native

This sprawling perennial herb has oblong-triangular leaves that curl upward. Summer-blooming flowers are borne singly in leaf axils along the stem. Each has a tucked upper lip (petal) and a winged lower lip, giving the overall impression of disembodied nose and mustache. Unusual for a mint, it does not have a minty aroma. **Plant height to 18 in.; leaves opposite, unlobed, margins minutely toothed, smooth; petals showy, 5, partially fused; mirror symmetry; white, light yellow, pink- or blue-tinged**

Stachys albens
LAMIACEAE

Whitestem Hedge-nettle

Wetland habitats; up to 9800 ft.; native

This summer-blooming perennial herb has upright stems and leaves with distinctive round-toothed margins. The specific name means "covered in white," which describes the effect of the wooly hairs that cover the plant. Despite its common name, it is not a member of the nettle family. Its opposite leaves, square stems, and aroma give it away as a mint family member. **Plant height 2–8 ft.; leaves opposite, basally lobed or not, margins round-toothed; petals showy, 5, partially fused; mirror symmetry; white with pink spots**

Calochortus albus
LILIACEAE

White Globe Lily

Foothill woodlands, chaparral, pine forests; up to 6600 ft.; native

This beautiful spring-blooming perennial herb is endemic to California and adjacent Baja California. Its nodding flowers are folded into the shape of a globe. Petals are hairy on the inside and slightly bulged out at the base. The narrow sepals curve over the petals. Unlike many lily family members, its sepals and petals are different sizes and shapes. **Plant height to 2.5 ft.; leaves alternate, straplike, unlobed, margins smooth; petals showy, 3, free; radial symmetry; white, pink (red)**

Calochortus catalinae
LILIACEAE

Santa Catalina Mariposa Lily

Grasslands, shrublands; up to 2300 ft.; native

Like other mariposa lilies, this perennial herb
has upright, cup-shaped flowers. The petals
are white to pale lavender, each with a basal
deep purple patch with golden hairs. The
sepals are pale green, shorter and narrower
than the petals, and the stamens are lavender
to pink-red. It blooms in spring and early
summer. **Plant height to 2 ft.; leaves alternate, straplike, unlobed,
margins smooth; petals
showy, 3, free; radial symmetry; white, lavender**

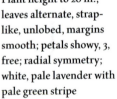

Calochortus invenustus
LILIACEAE

Plain Mariposa Lily

Conifer forests; 2300–10,000 ft.; native

Despite the scientific name—*invenustus* means
"plain"—the large, upright, cup-shaped flowers of this perennial herb are striking. The
outer side of each petal has a vertical pale
green stripe. The petals are usually unmarked
except for a darker base with golden hairs.
The sepals are upright and not curled back as
in Splendid Mariposa Lily, a similar species.
**Plant height to 20 in.;
leaves alternate, strap-
like, unlobed, margins
smooth; petals showy, 3,
free; radial symmetry;
white, pale lavender with
pale green stripe**

Calochortus leichtlinii
LILIACEAE

Smokey Mariposa Lily

Conifer forests, alpine; 4400–13,100 ft.; native

This summer-blooming perennial herb has upright, cup-shaped flowers, with white petals that are sometimes tinged pinkish. A bright yellow hairy patch adorns the base of each petal, with a small maroon patch just above. Stamens are white. Bruneau Mariposa Lily (*C. bruneaunis*) is similar, but with darker stamens. **Plant height 2 ft.; leaves alternate, straplike, unlobed, margins smooth; petals showy, 3, free; radial symmetry; white with yellow and purple patches**

Calochortus superbus
LILIACEAE

Superb Mariposa Lily

Grasslands, woodlands, pine forests; up to 5600 ft.; native

This perennial herb flowers in spring and summer. The white petals (sometimes yellow or lavender) have a dark blotch that is rimmed with a band of bright yellow above or around it. The petal base is dappled red and has an inverted V-shaped line of hairs that help distinguish it from other species. Sepal tips often roll backward. **Plant height to 2 ft.; leaves alternate, straplike, unlobed, margins smooth; petals showy, 3, free; radial symmetry; white, lavender, yellow, red**

Calochortus venustus
LILIACEAE

Butterfly Mariposa Lily

Grasslands, woodlands, pine forests; 700–8800 ft.; native

One of California's most beautiful spring lilies, this species has cup-shaped flowers with broad petals and narrow sepals. Background petal colors can be white, pink, lavender, or yellow. Each petal usually has two red blotches above a dappled red base. Its petal bases have a diagnostic square patch of hairs that help differentiate it from other mariposa lilies. **Plant height to 2 ft.; leaves alternate, unlobed, margins smooth; petals showy, 3, free; radial symmetry; white, pink, lavender, red, or yellow, with red blotches**

Clintonia uniflora
LILIACEAE

Bead Lily

Conifer forests; 3300–6200 ft.; native

This early spring–blooming perennial herb has a rosette of shiny green foliage. Each flowering stem usually produces a single flower (*uniflora* means "one flower"), which develops into a single, shiny, blue, erect berry. The plant has been used as a poultice to soothe sore eyes, and a blue dye can be made from the fruit. **Plant height 6–10 in.; leaves in basal rosette, unlobed, margins smooth; tepals showy, 6, free; radial symmetry; white**

Erythronium californicum
LILIACEAE

California Fawn Lily

Woodlands, chaparral, forests; up to 6200 ft.; native

This perennial herb blooms in spring, often forming large, low-growing colonies that become dormant when hot weather arrives. It grows wild only in Northern California. The attractive nodding flowers appear to float unsupported. The two glossy, straplike basal leaves usually have a mottled pattern, like the coat of a fawn, hence the common name. **Plant height to 12 in.; leaves basal, unlobed, margins wavy; tepals showy, 6, free; radial symmetry; white with yellow center**

Erythronium purpurascens
LILIACEAE

Purple Fawn Lily

Conifer forests, meadows; 3600–8900 ft.; native

This harbinger of spring is one of the first plants to bloom after the snow melts. Its wide and wavy, straplike, deep green leaves lack the mottled pattern characteristic of most fawn lilies. The elegant yellow-centered flowers of this perennial turn from white to purple after pollination. *Purpurascens* means "becoming purple," in reference to this process. **Plant height to 8 in.; leaves basal, unlobed, margins wavy, smooth; tepals showy, 6, free; radial symmetry; white, aging to purple**

Lilium washingtonianum
LILIACEAE

Washington Lily

Conifer forests, chaparral; 1000–6600 ft.; native

This summer-blooming perennial herb is restricted to the mountains of Northern California and Oregon, where it grows in dry, open areas, often among shrubs, where it gets some protection from foraging deer. It does not occur in Washington but was named in honor of the inaugural first lady of the United States, Martha Washington. **Plant height** 2–8 ft.; **leaves whorled, unlobed, margins smooth; tepals showy, 6, free; radial symmetry; white, pink**

Streptopus amplexifolius
LILIACEAE

Twisted Stalk

Conifer forests, streamsides; 800–5600 ft.; native

This early summer–blooming perennial herb grows in moist, shaded areas throughout much of North America and Eurasia. Distinctive characters are its zigzagging stems, delicate pendant flowers on sharply bent stalks, clasping leaves, and bright red berries. Like many lilies, the sepals and petals look the same and are called tepals. The sweet berries reportedly taste like watermelon. **Plant height** 1–4 **ft.; leaves alternate, unlobed, margins smooth, minutely toothed; tepals showy, 6, free; radial symmetry; white, green-yellow**

Limnanthes alba
LIMNANTHACEAE

White Meadowfoam

Winter-wet grasslands and woodlands, vernal pools; up to 6900 ft.; native

This spring-blooming annual grows in seasonal wet areas. The white flowers often have yellow-green centers and petals with darker veins. The common name describes the abundant floral displays that create what looks like a foam-covered field. The oil produced from its seeds is used to treat sun damage, stretch marks, and other skin issues. **Plant height to 1 ft.; leaves alternate, pinnately compound, margins smooth; petals showy, 5, free; radial symmetry; white**

Eucnide urens
LOASACEAE

Desert Stingbush

Deserts; up to 4600 ft.; native

This spring-blooming perennial herb is covered with toxin-filled, stinging hairs. When unsuspecting animals, or humans, brush by or touch the hairs, the resulting skin irritation is uncomfortable at best, and the hairs are difficult to remove. The specific name means "stinging" in Latin. Quite common in the Death Valley area, it occurs in desert areas outside of California as well. **Plant height to 2 ft.; leaves alternate, unlobed, margins toothed; petals showy, 5, partially fused at base; radial symmetry; cream, white**

Hibiscus lasiocarpos
MALVACEAE

Rose Mallow

Wetlands, riparian; up to 330 ft.; native

This deciduous perennial is narrowly distributed in the Central Valley. Blooming in summer and fall, it grows along perennial watercourses. Mediterranean plants often go dormant during summer droughts, but this wetland species always has water available and goes dormant in winter as temperatures drop. **Plant height 4–6 ft.; leaves alternate, unlobed to heart-shaped, margins toothed; petals showy, 5, fused at base; filaments fused; radial symmetry; white with red center**

Malva neglecta
MALVACEAE

Cheese Weed

Disturbed areas; up to 9800 ft.; non-native

This weedy species can be an annual or a perennial. The round fruits are shaped like a cheese wheel and break up into single-seeded wedges when ripe. Don't confuse it with Cheesebush, a species in the sunflower family that smells like rotten cheese. Cheese Weed blooms from spring through fall and its stem has star-shaped hairs, diagnostic of the mallow family. **Plant height to 2 ft.; leaves alternate, lobed, margins toothed; petals showy, 5, fused at base, filaments fused; radial symmetry; white, pink**

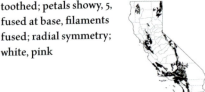

Toxicoscordion fremontii
MELANTHIACEAE

Fremont's Death Camas

Grasslands, woodlands; up to 3300 ft.; native

This spring-blooming perennial herb has a loose cluster of attractive, six-parted white flowers. Pollinators zero-in on the yellow-green nectaries at the base of each petal. Leaves are long and narrow. Meadow Death Camas (*T. venenosus*) is also common in California and has slightly smaller flowers. All parts of the plant are poisonous. **Plant height to 4 ft.; leaves basal, unlobed, margins smooth; tepals showy, 6, free; radial symmetry; white, yellow-green**

Trillium ovatum
MELANTHIACEAE

Western Trillium

Redwood forests, mixed evergreen forests, montane conifer forests; up to 6600 ft.; native

The stem of this spring-blooming perennial has a whorl of three elliptical leaves that are evenly deep green and not mottled. It is unique among *Trillium* species in California, because its flowers have pedicels and are held above the leaves on flower stalks. Western Trillium has two subspecies; the rare one has smaller flowers. White petals fade to pink. **Plant height to 1 ft.; leaves alternate, unlobed, margins smooth; petals showy, 3, free; radial symmetry; white, fading to pink**

Veratrum californicum
MELANTHIACEAE

California Corn Lily

Montane meadows, streambanks, forest margins; up to 11,500 ft.; native

This summer-blooming perennial has large, elliptical leaves up to 18 in. long on a heavily leaved stem that resembles a corn stalk. It produces hundreds of white flowers per cluster, creating impressive displays in wet meadows. All parts of the plant are toxic to mammals; as a result, it is avoided by livestock and can be an invasive plant in over-grazed meadows. **Plant height to 6 ft.; leaves alternate, unlobed, margins smooth; tepals showy, 6, free; radial symmetry; white**

Xerophyllum tenax
MELANTHIACEAE

Beargrass

Openings in montane forests; up to 7500 ft.; native

This summer-blooming perennial herb has narrow, wiry leaves. *Tenax* means "to hold" and refers to the tough, persistent leaves, which are harvested for basketry. Despite its common name, it is not a grass. Grasses have very reduced flowers that lack showy petals. This species has many small flowers with parts in sets of three that form large clusters. **Plant height to 5 ft.; leaves alternate, unlobed, margins smooth; tepals showy, 6, free; radial symmetry; white**

Menyanthes trifoliata
MENYANTHACEAE

Buckbean

Wetlands in montane conifer forests, often in ponds; 3000–10,500 ft.; native

This summer-blooming perennial herb is not super common, but its flowers are too interesting to pass up. Long, thick hairs grow from the inner surface of the flower's white petals. Further accenting the eccentric flowers are dark anthers. The trifoliate leaves resemble bean plant leaves, though bean plants and Buckbeans are not in the same plant family. **Plant height to 18 in.; leaves alternate, compound, 3 leaflets, margins smooth; petals showy, 5, partly fused; radial symmetry; white, pink-tinged**

Claytonia exigua
MONTIACEAE

Serpentine Spring-beauty

Many communities; up to 3300 ft.; native

This fleshy, hairless, spring-blooming annual grows throughout Western North America. It is often found on serpentine-derived soils, which are typically rich in heavy metals and poor in nutrients, making plant growth difficult. In California, two subspecies can be distinguished based on the shape of the leaves just below the flowers. **Plant height to 6 in.; leaves in basal rosette, unlobed; margins smooth; petals showy, 5, free; radial symmetry; white, pink**

Claytonia perfoliata
MONTIACEAE

Miner's Lettuce

Many communities; up to 6600 ft.; native

This annual blooms in late winter through spring. It grows in moist, shady places throughout Western North America. Its prominent leaves fuse around the stem, forming a disc below a cluster of small flowers. Basal leaves are long-stalked with triangular blades. The fleshy leaves are edible and contain vitamin C. **Plant height to 1 ft.; leaves in basal rosette, stem leaves opposite, fused, unlobed, margins smooth; petals showy, 5, free; radial symmetry; white, pink**

Claytonia sibirica
MONTIACEAE

Candy Flower

Woodlands, streambanks, marshes; up to 4300 ft.; native

Lance-shaped leaves and distinctly pendant flower buds characterize this short-lived, spring-blooming perennial herb. Often found in moist soils, its natural distribution extends beyond continental North America into the Commander Islands of Siberia. It is high in vitamin C and has been used as a treatment for dandruff. **Plant height to 2 ft.; leaves in basal rosette, unlobed, margins smooth; flowers small, petals showy, 5, free; radial symmetry; white, pink**

Lewisia nevadensis
MONTIACEAE

Nevada Lewisia

Open slopes and grassy flats in montane
forests, alpine fell-fields; 4300–9900 ft.; native

This summer-blooming perennial herb has
fleshy stems and leaves. Found throughout
Western North America, it usually has a single
flower per stem and many stems per plant.
The flower has some unusual qualities. The
petal number is not constant, varying from 5
to 10. The shape of the flower is oval—technically, it has mirror
symmetry. **Plant height
to 4 in.; leaves basal in rosette, unlobed, margins
smooth; sepals 2; petals
showy, 5–10, free; mirror;
white, yellow center**

Lewisia pygmaea
MONTIACEAE

Alpine Lewisia

Damp, rocky, gravelly, sandy slopes; meadows;
streambanks; 5600–13,200 ft.; native

This spring- and summer-blooming perennial
has fleshy, linear leaves with blunt tips. The
most striking aspect of this species is its size.
Alpine Lewisia is a "belly plant." To get a look
at it, you need to lie on your belly. This species
is an example of the tremendous diversity that
exists when you look closely at the natural
world. **Plant height to
2 in.; leaves in basal rosette, unlobed, margins
smooth; petals showy,
5–9, free; radial; white,
pink, magenta**

Lewisia rediviva
MONTIACEAE

Bitter-root

Conifer forests, woodlands; up to 10,300 ft.;
native

This spring-blooming perennial has thick,
linear, fleshy leaves. It occurs sporadically
throughout high-elevation areas on rocky substrate, and pink populations are common. It is
difficult not to be impressed by its numerous
flowers, each with many petals, as many as
nine sepals, and up to 50 stamens. The plant
is only a few inches tall
but can produce dozens
of large flowers. **Plant
height to 4 in.; leaves in
basal rosette, unlobed,
margins smooth; petals
showy, 10–19, free; radial;
white, pink, red**

Lewisia triphylla
MONTIACEAE

Three-leaf Lewisia

Open conifer forests, meadows, gravelly slopes;
4300–11,200 ft.; native

This spring- and summer-blooming perennial
is distinguished by a pair or whorl of three to
five leaves on its flowering stem. Basal leaves
dry up before flowering occurs. Unlike many
lewisias, this one lacks a basal leaf rosette.
Typical of lewisias, this species has shiny black
seeds. This is the only *Lewisia* species with a
globose (spherical) tuber-
ous root. **Plant height to
3 in.; basal leaves withering; stem leaves opposite
or whorled, unlobed;
margins smooth; petals
showy, 5–9, free; radial;
white, pink, yellow center**

Eriodictyon trichocalyx
NAMACEAE

Hairy Yerba Santa

Conifer forests, chaparral, deserts;
400–8500 ft.; native

This shrub has hairless, sticky upper leaves that appear shiny. The leaf underside has dense white hairs. Blooming in spring and summer are large, loosely coiled flower clusters. The species has dozens of documented medicinal uses, including treatment of colds, coughs, arthritis, fever, asthma, sore throat, and tuberculosis. **Plant height 3–7 ft.; leaves alternate, unlobed, margins toothed; flower clusters showy; petals 5, partially fused; radial symmetry; white**

Abronia turbinata
NYCTAGINACEAE

Transmontane Sand Verbena

Deserts; 3000–8200 ft.; native

This summer-blooming species is an annual or short-lived perennial. It is not super common in California, but you might happen upon it while exploring around the Mono Lake area of the Eastern Sierra. It has small, fleshy, round leaves. Flower clusters are umbrella-shaped, the showy flower parts are sepals, and the flowers have no petals. **Plant height to 18 in.; leaves opposite, unlobed, margins smooth; sepals showy, 5, partially fused; radial; white, pink**

Nymphaea odorata
NYMPHAEACEAE

Fragrant Water-lily

Aquatic; up to 8900 ft.; non-native

This aquatic perennial grows in shallow lakes and ponds. Blooming in spring and summer, the flower is emergent (out of the water) for a few days before being pulled underwater, where the fruit develops. Native to Northeastern North America, populations in California are garden escapees. It can quickly form dense populations that negatively affect lake ecology. **Plant height to 8 ft.; leaves alternate, basally lobed, margins smooth; petals showy, many, free; radial symmetry; white, pink**

Chylismia claviformis
ONAGRACEAE

Brown-eyes

Deserts; up to 9000 ft.; native

This spring-blooming species can be an annual or a perennial. White or yellow petals age to deep pink. The floral axis at the junction of male and female flower parts is bright red to maroon or brown. This variable species has been divided into 11 subspecies, 8 of which are in California. **Plant height to 2 ft.; leaves in basal rosette, unlobed to deeply lobed, margins toothed; petals showy, 4, free; radial symmetry; white or yellow**

Circaea alpina
ONAGRACEAE

Enchanter's Nightshade

Conifer forests, wetlands; up to 8900 ft.; native

This spring-blooming perennial herb has small flowers clustered at stem tips. Flowers have two reflexed sepals, two notched petals, and two stamens that extend beyond the petals. The inferior ovary and subsequent fruit are covered with hooked hairs. This widespread species is not a true nightshade, which is a common name for the Solanaceae family. **Plant height to 20 in.; leaves opposite, basally lobed, margins toothed; petals showy, 2, free; radial symmetry; white, pink**

Eremothera boothii
ONAGRACEAE

Booth's Suncup

Deserts; -230–7900 ft.; native

This spring-blooming annual has red-tinged, hairy stems and blotchy leaves. The nodding buds give way to short, erect clusters of many small flowers. Booth's Suncup is a preferred food of the Desert Tortoise (*Gopherus agassizii*). In a study of foraging behavior, tortoise would always feed on this species when it was encountered. **Plant height to 18 in.; leaves in basal rosette or not, unlobed, margins toothed; petals showy, 4, free; radial symmetry; white**

Gayophytum diffusum
ONAGRACEAE

Spreading Groundsmoke

Open montane forests, sagebrush scrub; 2600–12,100 ft.; native

This summer-blooming annual has thin red stems and very narrow leaves. The delicate plants en masse produce a smokelike haze over the ground, hence the common name. *Diffusum*, which means "spreading," describes the open growth form of the plant. The flower buds are pink, and then petals fade to white. It becomes more locally abundant after fire. **Plant height to 2 ft.; leaves alternate, opposite near base, unlobed, margins smooth; petals showy, 4, free; radial symmetry; white**

Oenothera californica
ONAGRACEAE

California Evening Primrose

Chaparral, woodlands; up to 10,000 ft.; native

This spring-blooming perennial herb has nodding buds that become erect as they open. It is native to Southwestern North America. Once common along roadsides in Southern California, its abundance has declined, presumably resulting from the use of herbicides. The fragrant flowers open at dusk and are pollinated by hawk moths. **Plant height to 30 in.; leaves in basal rosette, unlobed to lobed, margins toothed, smooth; petals showy, 4, free; radial symmetry; white fading to pink**

Oenothera deltoides
ONAGRACEAE

Birdcage Evening Primrose

Deserts; up to 5900 ft.; native

This annual blooms from spring through fall and has an unusual mode of seed dispersal. The plant begins as a basal rosette and then produces several foot-long flower stems. As the fruits mature, the stems dry, curving toward one another to form a cage of sorts. Strong winds eventually uproot the entire plant, which rolls like a tumbleweed, spreading its seeds. **Plant height to 1 ft.; leaves in basal rosette, lobed or unlobed, margins toothed; petals showy, 4, free; radial symmetry; white, fading to pink**

Cephalanthera austiniae
ORCHIDACEAE

Phantom Orchid

Conifer forests; up to 7200 ft.; native

This spring- and summer-blooming leafless perennial herb produces no chlorophyll and obtains its nutrients from other plants via soil fungi (mycoheterotrophy). Like most orchids, male and female parts are fused into a column. The name *Cephalanthera* combines the Greek words for "head" and "anther," which describes the position of the anther at the top of the flower column. **Plant height to 15 in.; leaves absent; petals showy, 3, free; mirror symmetry; white**

Cypripedium montanum
ORCHIDACEAE

Mountain Lady's Slipper

Forests, riparian; 600–7000 ft.; native

This perennial herb blooms from spring through summer. In *Cypripedium* species, the lip (lower petal) is modified into a pouch, which orients insects to climb across the stigma and one of the anthers. These plants are deceptive. Insects are attracted to the pouch because it smells like food, but it does not actually provide a nectar reward for the pollinators. **Plant height to 2 ft.; leaves alternate, unlobed, margins smooth; petals showy, 3, free; mirror symmetry; white and maroon**

Goodyera oblongifolia
ORCHIDACEAE

Rattlesnake Plantain

Conifer forests; up to 7000 ft.; native

This perennial herb blooms from spring through fall. The white netted pattern on its leaves, often resembling tire tracks, is its most distinctive characteristic. The tall, not very showy flower clusters tend to be one-sided. Plants can reproduce via seed or by sending out underground stems that give rise to new plantlets. **Plant height to 20 in.; leaves in basal rosette, unlobed, margins smooth; petals showy, 3, free; mirror symmetry; white**

Platanthera dilatata
ORCHIDACEAE

White Bog Orchid

Wet meadows, seeps, streambanks; up to 11,000 ft.; native

This summer-blooming perennial herb produces dozens of conspicuous, spicy-smelling flowers. This species has a modified petal (spur) that holds nectar—a sugary reward for its moth pollinators. Three varieties are recognized, but only the variety *leucostachys* occurs in California. Although not shown in the map, sparse collections of this species have been made along the south coast. **Plant height to 5 ft.; leaves alternate, unlobed, margins smooth; petals showy, 3, free; mirror symmetry; white**

Spiranthes romanzoffiana
ORCHIDACEAE

Hooded Lady's Tresses

Wet meadows, seeps, freshwater marshes; up to 10,700 ft.; native

This sweet-smelling perennial herb has small, white flowers arranged in a tight spiral. It is bee-pollinated and has a relatively straightforward pollination mechanism: the pollen sacs (pollinia) get stuck to the bee's face as it drinks nectar from the flower. The sepals and upper petals are fused, hence the hood referenced in the common name. **Plant height to 20 in.; leaves alternate, unlobed, margins smooth; petals showy, 3, partially fused; mirror symmetry; white**

Chloropyron maritimum
OROBANCHACEAE

Salt Marsh Bird's Beak

Coastal salt marshes, inland alkaline flats; up to 6200 ft.; native

This mat-forming annual blooms in summer and fall. The whole plant, other than its flowers, tends to be dark green, sometimes tinged purple-red. This species of saline environments is often encrusted with salt. It is a root parasite that gets some of its nutrients from other plants, but it can also perform photosynthesis. **Plant height to 16 in.; leaves alternate, unlobed, margins smooth; petals inconspicuous, 5, fused; mirror symmetry; white**

Cordylanthus rigidus
OROBANCHACEAE

Rigid Bird's Beak

Forests, woodlands, chaparral, dunes; up to 8900 ft.; native

This summer-blooming annual has branched, upright, yellow-green stems with stiff hairs. Its white flowers, also covered in hairs, are mostly hidden by leaves that often have dark tips. The corolla lips close around each other and resemble a bird's beak. Four subspecies have been described in California. The subspecies *littoralis* is restricted to dune habitats. **Plant height to 4 ft.; leaves alternate, lobed or unlobed, margins smooth; petals inconspicuous, 5, fused; mirror symmetry; bracts red; petals white**

Cordylanthus tenuis
OROBANCHACEAE

Slender Bird's Beak

Dunes, conifer forests, woodlands, chaparral, sagebrush scrub; up to 8500 ft.; native

This airy, summer-blooming annual has green-yellow foliage and narrow leaves on long, slender stems. Impressively, Slender Bird's Beak has been divided into six subspecies, including subspecies *capillaris*, an endangered species. Only a handful of populations remain and are threatened by illegal dumping, road maintenance, and development. Plant height to 4 ft.; leaves alternate, unlobed, margins smooth; petals inconspicuous, 5, fused; mirror symmetry; white, maroon

Argemone munita
PAPAVERACEAE

Prickly Poppy

Dry openings in forests, woodland, shrublands; up to 9800 ft.; native

This summer-blooming herb is either an annual or a short-lived perennial. The entire plant is covered with formidable prickles and spines. If you are brave enough to pull off a leaf, yellow sap will ooze from the injured part of the plant. Its flowers can be huge, up to 5 in., and are erect in bud. Populations often increase after wildfire. Plant height to 3 ft.; leaves alternate, lobed, margins toothed; petals showy, usually 6, free; radial symmetry; white

Canbya candida
PAPAVERACEAE

Pygmy Poppy

Deserts; 2000-4800 ft.; native

This charming spring-blooming annual is relatively rare and faces various threats including road maintenance, grazing, and mining. Nevertheless, it is not listed by state or federal agencies. The California Native Plant Society tracks rare, but unprotected, species such as the Pygmy Poppy and recommends that they be considered during project planning. **Plant height to 1 in.; leaves basal rosette, unlobed, margins smooth; petals showy, usually 6, free; radial symmetry; white**

Romneya coulteri
PAPAVERACEAE

Coulter's Matilija Poppy

Chaparral; up to 4000 ft.; native

This tall perennial herb blooms from early spring into summer. Its huge, white flowers have crinkly petals and numerous bright orange stamens. As is typical of poppies, the petals fall immediately after fertilization. This species is relatively rare in nature but is very commonly grown in gardens. It is named for Chief Matilija of the Chumash peoples. **Plant height 4–6 ft.; leaves alternate, whorled, lobed to dissected, margins toothed; petals showy, 6, free; radial symmetry; white**

Parnassia palustris
PARNASSIACEAE

Marsh Grass-of-Parnassus

Seeps, fens, wet meadows in montane conifer forests, woodlands; up to 11,800 ft.; native

The native distribution of this late summer–blooming perennial spans North America and Eurasia. Flowers have unusual gland-tipped, yellow sterile stamens (staminodes). These are shorter than the fertile stamens and are reminiscent of frog feet. As a traditional medicine, it has been used to treat liver problems, indigestion, and kidney stones. **Plant height to 16 in.; leaves in basal rosette, basally lobed or unlobed, margins smooth; petals showy, 5, free; radial symmetry; white**

Phytolacca americana
PHYTOLACCACEAE

American Pokeweed

Disturbed riparian areas, pastures, roadsides; up to 3300 ft.; non-native

This large perennial herb blooms in summer. Its flowers, with five sepals and no petals, develop into distinctive dark berries in drooping elongate clusters, contrasting in color with the bright pink fruiting stalks. The plant is poisonous, especially the roots and fruits. It is native to Eastern North America, the U.S. South, and the Midwest. **Plant height to 10 ft.; leaves alternate, unlobed, margins wavy, toothed; sepals showy, 5, partially fused; radial symmetry; white, pink**

Antirrhinum confertiflorum
PLANTAGINACEAE

Ghost Flower

Desert slopes and washes; up to 4100 ft.; native

Blooming in late winter to spring, this annual herb has opposite leaves low on the stem that transition to alternate. The gray-green foliage is covered with glandular hairs. White flowers have red splotches that guide pollinators to a nectar reward. Until recently, it was known as *Mohavea confertiflora* but was reclassified based on DNA evidence. **Plant height 4–16 in.; leaves opposite and alternate, unlobed, margins smooth; petals showy, 5, partially fused; mirror symmetry; white with red splotches**

Antirrhinum coulterianum
PLANTAGINACEAE

Coulter's Snapdragon

Chaparral; up to 8800 ft.; native

This large, spring-blooming annual becomes more common following a wildfire. The species has a basal rosette of leaves, which is unusual for a snapdragon. It is an upright species with long, hairy, wandlike flower clusters. The common name refers to the flowers' resemblance to the face of a dragon, which opens and closes its "mouth" when squeezed. **Plant height to 5 ft.; leaves alternate, basal, unlobed, margins wavy; petals showy, 5, partially fused; mirror symmetry; white, lavender**

Keckiella breviflora
PLANTAGINACEAE

Bush Beardtongue

Many communities; up to 9200 ft.; native

Blooming from late spring through summer, this scraggly shrub can get quite tall and uses its surrounds for support. The flower has four fertile stamens that snake under the lower lip of the corolla. It has one sterile stamen (staminode) that is hairless and barely peeks out of the tube opening. It also occurs in Nevada. **Plant height 3–6 ft.; leaves opposite, unlobed, margins toothed; petals showy, 5, partially fused; mirror symmetry; white, pink**

Plantago erecta
PLANTAGINACEAE

Dot-seed Plantain

Chaparral, grassland, woodlands; -160–4500 ft.; native

This spring-blooming annual has narrow, linear leaves covered in sparse, silky hairs. Each flower in its inconspicuous flower clusters has four tiny, paperlike petals that fold back, followed by dull-brown seeds. Dietary fiber supplements are made from the seed husks of various plantain species; most often, Desert Plantain (*P. ovata*) is used. **Plant height 5–8 in.; leaves in basal rosette, unlobed, margins smooth or toothed; petals inconspicuous, 4, partially fused; radial symmetry; white, tan**

Aliciella monoensis
POLEMONIACEAE

Mono Lake Aliciella

Deserts; 1600–8200 ft.; native

The genus *Aliciella* honors Alice Eastwood, a celebrated botanist at the California Academy of Sciences. In the immediate aftermath of the 1906 San Francisco Earthquake, she valiantly rescued 1500 of the most valuable herbarium specimens from the damaged building where they were housed. This skunky smelling annual blooms in spring and summer. **Plant height to 1 ft.; leaves in basal rosette, stem leaves alternate, lobed, margins smooth; petals showy, 5, partially fused; radial symmetry; white**

Gilia angelensis
POLEMONIACEAE

Chaparral Gilia

Sandy openings in coastal sage scrub, pine forests, chaparral; 700–6200 ft.; native

Ranging into Baja California, this annual was first discovered in Los Angeles—thus the specific name. Plants are upright and highly branched, with hairy leaves. Flowers occur singly or in clusters of 2–10, with the stamens and style protruding beyond the corolla lobes (petals). It blooms in winter and spring. **Plant height to 2 ft.; leaves basal, lobed, margins smooth or toothed; petals showy, 5, partially fused; radial symmetry; white, lavender**

Gilia stellata
POLEMONIACEAE

Star Gilia

Sandy desert flats and washes; up to 5800 ft.;
native

This spring-blooming annual occurs in sandy,
open habitats across Southwestern North
America and Baja California. Plants have
dense, white, sharply bent hairs near the base
of the stem, with black-tipped stalked glands
higher up. Funnel-shaped flowers have yellow
throats with purple spots and pink or white
corolla lobes (petals).

Plant height to 16 in.;
leaves in basal rosette,
stem leaves alternate,
unlobed to lobed, mar-
gins smooth or toothed;
petals showy, 5, partially
fused; radial symmetry;
white, pink

Ipomopsis congesta
POLEMONIACEAE

Ballhead Ipomopsis

Conifer forests, shrublands, alpine fell-fields;
3900–12,100 ft.; native

This perennial herb is usually quite hairy and
has spherical flowerheads densely packed with
small, white flowers. The specific name means
"crowded." Of the two subspecies, *I. congesta*
subsp. *montana* usually occurs at higher elevations, with the small, tufted plants growing
up into the alpine zone. It is native to much
of Western North Amer-
ica. **Plant height to 1 ft.;**
leaves in basal rosette,
stem leaves alternate,
lobed, margins smooth;
petals showy, 5, partial-
ly fused; radial sym-
metry; white

Leptosiphon liniflorus
POLEMONIACEAE

Narrowflower Flaxflower

Openings in many communities; up to 5600 ft.; native

Seeming to hover in midair, the funnel-shaped flowers on this delicate, spring-blooming annual are supported by the narrowest of stalks. Plants branch above the base in this species, and the calyx membranes (the thin material between the calyx lobes) are wider than the lobes themselves. Flowers are generally purple-veined. **Plant height to 20 in.; leaves opposite, lobed, margins smooth; petals showy, 5, partially fused; radial symmetry; white, pale blue, with purple veins**

Leptosiphon parviflorus
POLEMONIACEAE

Variable Linanthus

Chaparral, oak woodlands; up to 7200 ft.; native

This delightful spring-blooming annual occurs in large numbers and is worth admiring up close. The tiny flowers—with their impossibly narrow, threadlike tubes—are pollinated by butterflies and moths. The petals often have red markings near the base. The three-parted stigma lobes, characteristic of the family, are huge relative to the flower size. **Plant height to 16 in.; leaves opposite, lobed, margins smooth; petals showy, 5, partially fused; radial symmetry; white, lavender, yellow**

Linanthus dichotomus
POLEMONIACEAE

Evening Snow

Chaparral, deserts, woodland openings; up to 5900 ft.; native

This spring-blooming annual ranges into Nevada, Arizona, and Baja California. Relatively large, funnel-shaped flowers grace the tips of wiry, forking (dichotomous) stems—opening only in the evening or during the day, depending on the subspecies. Some find the potent scent of these flowers pleasing, while others do not. **Plant height to 8 in.; leaves opposite, lobed, margins smooth; petals showy, 5, partially fused; radial symmetry; white, lavender**

Linanthus pungens
POLEMONIACEAE

Granite Prickly Phlox

Open rocky areas in scrub, woodlands, conifer forests; 4900–13,100 ft.; native

Large, scented, funnel-shaped flowers open in the evening on this prickly perennial herb or subshrub. Occurring up into the alpine zone, it is a common sight in rocky, montane areas. Of the two subspecies, subsp. *pulchriflorus* is more common, occurring throughout the state into Utah. It blooms in spring and summer. **Plant height to 1 ft.; leaves alternate, unlobed to lobed, margins smooth; petals showy, 5, partially fused; radial symmetry; white, pink**

Navarretia intertexta
POLEMONIACEAE

Needle-leaf Navarretia

Seasonally wet grasslands, vernal pools; up to 6900 ft.; native

This annual has needle-like leaf and bract lobes and an upright growth form. With ample rainfall, this little gem can grow as wide as it is tall. A single plant can have many separate "heads" of tiny flower clusters. Note that the anthers visibly protrude from the flowers on this species. It is native to Western North America and blooms in spring and early summer. **Plant height to 10 in.; leaves alternate, lobed, margins smooth; petals showy, 5, partially fused; radial symmetry; white, light blue**

Navarretia leucocephala
POLEMONIACEAE

Whitehead Navarretia

Vernal pools; up to 7200 ft.; native

This annual has five subspecies—three are rare and two are wide-ranging, extending into Washington, Oregon, and Utah. *Leucocephala* means "white head," referring to the pincushion-like white flowerheads typical of the species. Two of the rare subspecies sometimes have blue flowers. It blooms in spring and summer. **Plant height to 6 in.; leaves alternate, lobed, margins smooth; petals showy, 5, partially fused; radial symmetry; white, blue**

Phlox diffusa
POLEMONIACEAE

Spreading Phlox

Open, rocky slopes in conifer forests, alpine; 3600–11,800 ft.; native

This matted subshrub blooms from late spring through summer and is a food source for bumble bees and butterflies. It has short, stiff, linear leaves and pinwheel-shaped flowers that produce a delicate perfume. The plant can be completely covered in flowers. *Diffusa* means "spreading," which describes its growth pattern. **Plant height 1–8 in.; leaves opposite, unlobed, margins smooth, pointed tip; petals showy, 5, partially fused; radial symmetry; white, pink, lavender**

Centrostegia thurberi
POLYGONACEAE

Red Triangles

Deserts, shrublands; 1000–7900 ft.; native

This annual is the only species in the genus. It grows in sandy and gravelly habitats across Southwestern North America, into Mexico. The whole plant often has a reddish hue. The involucre, the structure that contains the two tiny, hairy flowers, is a bizarre-looking contraption, with sharp angles and teeth. It blooms in spring and summer. **Plant height to 8 in.; leaves in basal rosette, unlobed, margins smooth; tepals inconspicuous, 6, free; radial symmetry; white, pink**

Eriogonum angulosum
POLYGONACEAE

Angle-stem Buckwheat

Woodlands, grasslands, deserts; up to 2700 ft.; native

This annual grows in clay or loam and blooms all year. Its flowers are covered with glandular hairs, and the stem leaves are narrow. The wild buckwheats (*Eriogonum* spp.) mostly occur in Western North America; the genus is one of the most species-rich in California. Cultivated buckwheat, used to make pancakes, is in the genus *Fagopyrum*. **Plant height to 20 in.; leaves in basal rosette, unlobed, margins smooth; flower clusters small, tepals inconspicuous, 6, free; radial symmetry; white, pink**

Eriogonum baileyi
POLYGONACEAE

Bailey's Buckwheat

Deserts, openings in scrub, woodlands, pine forests; 1600–9500 ft.; native

Common in sandy and gravelly areas, this annual occurs throughout Western North America. The involucres (structures that contain the small flowers) are appressed (lie flat) to the stems. It blooms from spring through fall. Two subspecies are recognized: one has hairy flower clusters, and the other's clusters are hairless. **Plant height to 16 in.; leaves in basal rosette, unlobed, margins smooth, wavy; flower clusters small; tepals inconspicuous, 6, free; radial symmetry; white, pink**

Eriogonum davidsonii
POLYGONACEAE

Davidson's Buckwheat

Chaparral, woodlands, pine forests; 3000–8500 ft.; native

This dainty annual prefers sandy or gravelly soils. Its range extends into Arizona, Utah, and Northern Baja California. Leaves are long-stalked, round, and hairy underneath. Blooming in spring and summer, one upright stem emerges from the leaves and is branched above, with small clusters of flowers arranged along the branches. **Plant height to 20 in.; leaves basal, unlobed, margins smooth, wavy; flower clusters small; tepals inconspicuous, 6, free; radial symmetry; white, pink**

Eriogonum elongatum
POLYGONACEAE

Longstem Buckwheat

Chaparral, woodlands; 200–6200 ft.; native

This common perennial herb can be variable in form, but it generally appears gray from a distance because of its hairy foliage. The short-petioled leaves are elliptical to oval, and spherical flower clusters are arrayed along the elongated, often many-forked stems. It occurs in sand and clay and blooms in the summer and fall. **Plant height 2–5 ft.; leaves basal, alternate, unlobed, margins smooth, wavy; tepals inconspicuous, 6, free; radial symmetry; white, pink**

Eriogonum fasciculatum
POLYGONACEAE

California Buckwheat

Scrub, grasslands, woodlands; up to 8200 ft; native

This shrub is the most common buckwheat found in the southern half of California. *Fasciculatum* means "bundled," referring to the leaves, which grow in clusters. It blooms all year, attracting a wide variety of insects including European Honeybees, which make delicious honey. It is used extensively for roadside revegetation projects. **Plant height to 5 ft.; leaves alternate, un-lobed, margins smooth; flower clusters showy; tepals inconspicuous, 6, free; radial symmetry; white, pink**

Eriogonum nudum
POLYGONACEAE

Naked Buckwheat

Woodlands, forests, chaparral, grasslands; up to 12,500 ft.; native

This wide-ranging perennial herb blooms in spring, summer, and fall. Of the fourteen varieties described, based mostly on variation in flower color and hairiness, six are rare. Common along dry roadsides, it has long, often leafless stems with widely forking branches. The spherical flower clusters atop the branches bob in the breeze. **Plant height to 3 ft.; leaves in basal rosette, unlobed, margins smooth, wavy; flower clusters showy; tepals inconspicuous, 6, free; radial symmetry; white, yellow, pink**

Eriogonum ovalifolium
POLYGONACEAE

Cushion Buckwheat

Deserts, conifer forests, alpine fell-fields; 2000–13,800 ft.; native

This gorgeous, mat-forming perennial herb has eight varieties in California, three of which are rare. It grows in sandy-gravelly or rocky areas up into the alpine, often on granite. Though *ovalifolium* means "oval-leaved," the leaves can also be narrow or round. Dense, often spherical flower clusters bloom in spring and summer. **Plant height to 16 in.; leaves basal, unlobed, margins smooth; flower clusters showy; tepals inconspicuous, 6, free; radial symmetry; white, yellow, pink, burgundy**

Eriogonum parvifolium
POLYGONACEAE

Seacliff Buckwheat

Dunes, grasslands, scrub; up to 1300 ft.; native

This subshrub can be found in bloom all season of the year. *Parvifolium* means "small-leaved," which is typical of the species. Leaf shape varies from narrow to round in shape. Flower clusters are borne on simple or branched stalks and attract many pollinators. It is the larval host plant for the El Segundo Blue butterfly, an endangered species. **Plant height 12–40 in.; leaves alternate, unlobed, margins smooth; tepals inconspicuous, 6, free; radial symmetry; white, pink, yellow**

Eriogonum saxatile
POLYGONACEAE

Hoary Buckwheat

Conifer forests, deserts; 2600–11,200 ft.; native

The specific name, *saxatile*, means "rock-dwelling." True to its name, this matted perennial is common in sandy, gravelly, and rocky areas. The beautiful, rounded, white-hairy (hoary) basal leaves are immediately recognizable. Blooming in spring through fall, flowers are clustered in heads subtended by glandular bracts (involucres). **Plant height 8–16 in.; leaves basal, alternate, unlobed, margins smooth; flower clusters showy; tepals inconspicuous, 6, free; radial symmetry; white, pink, yellow**

Eriogonum spergulinum
POLYGONACEAE

Spurry Buckwheat

Openings in conifer forests; 3900–11,500 ft.; native

With its narrow leaves, threadlike stems, and flowers that appear singly rather than in clusters, this species is clearly atypical for annual buckwheats. Multitudes of this small, delicate, summer-blooming species can fill large areas in sandy or gravelly openings. Of the three varieties, *E. spergulinum* var. *reddingianum* is the most commonly encountered. **Plant height to 16 in.; leaves in basal rosette, unlobed, margins smooth; flowers small; tepals inconspicuous, 6, free; radial symmetry; white, pink**

Eriogonum wrightii
POLYGONACEAE

Bastard Sage

Deserts, woodlands, conifer forests; 100–11,800 ft.; native

This wide-ranging subshrub blooms for most of the year and can be found growing in sandy, gravelly, and rocky areas. With six varieties in California (one is rare), it can have a low-matting form or can grow upright. Plants are often gray-hairy, with narrow leaves and many-flowered, upright stems. **Plant height 6–40 in.; leaves alternate, unlobed, margins smooth; flower clusters showy; tepals inconspicuous, 6, free; radial symmetry; white, pink**

Polygonum aviculare
POLYGONACEAE

Prostrate Knotweed

Disturbed areas, grasslands; up to 6600 ft.; non-native

This mat-forming to upright annual is a most resilient plant. It can withstand being walked on or driven on and is able to grow in poor quality, compacted soil. It will even thrive with its roots in a sidewalk crack. Blooming from spring through fall, Prostrate Knotweed has tiny flowers borne along wiry stems with narrow leaves. **Stem length to 6 ft. though usually shorter; leaves alternate, unlobed, margins smooth; tepals inconspicuous, 6, free; radial symmetry; white**

Actaea rubra
RANUNCULACEAE

Red Baneberry

Conifer forests, woodlands; up to 9200 ft.; native

Blooming in early summer, the delicate flowers of this species have inconspicuous, threadlike petals and many showy stamens. The flowers develop into red (rarely white), shiny berries that cause severe stomach discomfort if ingested by humans, though birds love them. The species is widespread in moist woods across the North-ern Hemisphere. **Plant height 1–3 ft.; leaves basal, compound, margins toothed; petals 4–10; stamens showy, many, free; radial symmetry; white**

Anemone occidentalis
RANUNCULACEAE

Western Anemone

Open rocky slopes, montane to subalpine; 3900–10,500 ft.; native

This spring- and summer-blooming perennial herb is native to Western North America and grows in gravelly soils and moist meadows. The flower lacks petals but has attractive sepals and more than 150 showy stamens. As the flower develops, the styles elongate, becoming feath-ery; the fruiting head is reminiscent of a tiny Truffula Tree from Dr. Seuss' *The Lorax*. **Plant height 4–24 in.; leaves basal, compound, dis-sected leaflets, margins toothed; sepals showy, 5–7, free; radial symme-try; white, lavender**

Aquilegia pubescens
RANUNCULACEAE

Sierra Columbine

Alpine; 8500–12,000 ft.; native

This summer-blooming perennial herb's flowers have sepals that flare at a right angle to the tubular petals, ending in nectar spurs. The petal blades are white, and the sepals and petal tubes are pink. At the end of the spur is a brownish nectary. It is primarily pollinated by hawk moths, whose long tongues can reach the nectary. **Plant height 8–20 in.; leaves basal, compound, lobed, margins toothed; sepals showy, 5, free; radial symmetry; sepals pink; petals white**

Caltha leptosepala
RANUNCULACEAE

White Marsh Marigold

Wetlands in montane conifer forests; 3000–10,800 ft.; native

This perennial herb blooms in late spring, as the snow melts. The large, shiny, rounded leaves have a distinctly fleshy feel. The flowers do not have petals: the showy white structures are actually sepals. White Marsh Marigold occurs throughout Western North America. The plants in California were once classified as their own species, *C. bifora*. **Plant height 6–12 in.; leaves basal, unlobed or lobed, margins entire, toothed; sepals showy, many, free; radial symmetry; white**

Clematis ligusticifolia
RANUNCULACEAE

Western White Clematis

Wetlands, riparian; up to 7900 ft.; native

This vining or scrambling species blooms in summer when other *Clematis* species are in fruit. Each flower is either male or female, but not both. The flowers lack petals. Instead, the sepals and sexual parts are showy, and the fluffy seedheads are as showy as the flowers. Chaparral Clematis (*C. lasiantha*), another native, is more common in drier habitats. **Plant height 10–20 ft.; leaves opposite, pinnately compound, margins toothed; sepals showy, 4, free; radial symmetry; white**

Delphinium hansenii
RANUNCULACEAE

Eldorado Larkspur

Grasslands, oak woodlands, chaparral; 200–11,000 ft.; native

This perennial herb blooms in spring through early summer. By the time the plant is in flower, the basal leaves have usually withered away or are dry. The undersides of its leaves are distinctly hairy and the fruits are narrow and erect. Flower color is variable, from blue-violet to pink-white. Three varieties are recognized in California. **Plant height to 3 ft.; leaves alternate, lobed, margins toothed; sepals showy, 5, free; mirror symmetry; white, lavender, purple**

Enemion occidentale
RANUNCULACEAE

Western Rue-anemone

Chaparral, woodlands, conifer forests; 700–4900 ft.; native

This dainty perennial blooms in early spring in woodland habitats. The foliage is fernlike and flowers are solitary or loosely grouped. This genus differs from true anemones in that each of its pistils becomes a dry, multiseeded fruit (follicle) that splits along one side. True anemones have dry, single-seeded fruits (achenes) that do not split open at maturity. **Plant height 4–16 in.; leaves alternate, compound, lobed leaflets, margins toothed; sepals showy, 5, free; radial symmetry; white**

Myosurus minimus
RANUNCULACEAE

Mousetail

Vernal pools; up to 9800 ft.; native

This diminutive spring-blooming annual grows in wet areas throughout much of the Northern Hemisphere. Each flower is borne singly on a long, flowering stem. A flower has five sepals and five petals closely associated with each other, making them difficult to tell apart. The female part of the flower forms an elongated cone as fruits develop. **Plant height to 5 in.; leaves basal rosette, unlobed, margins smooth; flowers small, petals showy, 5, free; radial symmetry; white**

Ranunculus aquatilis
RANUNCULACEAE

White Water Buttercup

Wetlands, riparian; up to 10,500 ft.; native

Blooming in late spring and summer, this perennial herb can be fully aquatic and has an almost worldwide native range that includes Western North America. The submerged leaves are dissected, whereas the floating leaves are simple with three lobes. The fresh plant is toxic and its juice can cause skin blisters. **Plant height 1–2 ft.; leaves basal, compound, simple, margins smooth; petals showy, usually 5, free; radial symmetry; white, yellow center**

Ceanothus cuneatus
RHAMNACEAE

Buckbrush

Chaparral; up to 6200 ft.; native

This is the most common *Ceanothus* species in California. Its thick, leathery leaves have tapered bases. This shrub has a distinctive architecture created by stems that branch at right angles. In the spring, it produces thousands of aromatic flowers, organized into round clusters. Swarms of bees create an audible buzz when it blooms. **Plant height to 7 ft.; leaves opposite, unlobed, margins smooth; flower clusters showy; petals 5, free; radial symmetry; white, lavender**

Ceanothus integerrimus
RHAMNACEAE

Deerbrush

Many communities; up to 8500 ft.; native

This deciduous shrub blooms in late spring and summer. Deerbrush has fragrant flower sprays up to 8 in. long that attract many pollinators including crawling insects, bees, and butterflies. Its soft leaves are dark above and pale below, with three distinctive veins. The long-lived seeds sprout vigorously after fire and can contribute to slope stabilization. **Plant height to 13 ft.; leaves alternate, unlobed, margins smooth; flower clusters showy; petals 5, free; radial symmetry; white, blue, lavender, pink**

Adenostoma fasciculatum
ROSACEAE

Chamise

Chaparral; up to 5900 ft.; native

Chamise often dominates chaparral communities throughout California. The plant is covered with tiny, fragrant, white blooms when summer heat is at its highest. Narrow, clustered, stiff leaves and deep roots are adaptations that enable it to flower and fruit during the hottest, driest part of the season. It responds to fire by resprouting and germinating from seed. **Plant height to 8 ft.; leaves alternate, unlobed, margins smooth; flower clusters showy; petals 5, free; radial symmetry; white**

Adenostoma sparsifolium
ROSACEAE

Redshanks

Chaparral; 660–6600 ft.; native

The shredded ribbons of red bark and sparse foliage are the most distinctive features of this shrub. Its leaves are tiny and filamentous. A fall-blooming species, it has exceptionally small flowers. Redshanks, along with Chamise, sprout and produce new seedlings vigorously after fires, providing forage for wildlife. **Plant height to 13 ft.; leaves alternate, unlobed, margins smooth; flower clusters showy; petals 5, partially fused; radial symmetry; white**

Amelanchier alnifolia
ROSACEAE

Saskatoon Serviceberry

Conifer forests; 4600–8530 ft.; native

This beautiful flowering shrub is common in Northern California. It is known for its sweet and nutty, edible purple fruits, which are enjoyed by many species of birds and mammals. Blooming in summer, it attracts a large suite of pollinators and is a larval host to several species of butterflies. It grows in open, moist habitats. **Plant height 3–35 ft.; leaves alternate, unlobed, margins toothed; petals showy, 5, partially fused with sepals at base; radial symmetry; white**

Amelanchier utahensis
ROSACEAE

Utah Serviceberry

Conifer forests; 700–11,150 ft.; native

This shrub grows on rocky slopes, along creek banks, and in canyons. When in flower, this spring-bloomer attracts many species of pollinators. Its small, dark berries are important forage for wildlife. Its leaves have finely hairy undersides and its fruits are small, whereas its sibling species, Saskatoon Serviceberry, has hairless leaves and larger fruits. **Plant height to 15 ft.; leaves alternate, unlobed, margins toothed; petals showy, 5, partially fused with sepals at base; radial symmetry; white**

Cercocarpus betuloides
ROSACEAE

Birch-leaf Mountain Mahogany

Chaparral; up to 8,200 ft; native

The genus name, *Cercocarpus*, means "fruit with a tail" in Greek. The flower of this spring-blooming shrub has a persistent style that matures to form a long, fluffy tail. The wood is incredibly dense and strong, and its leaves are wide and toothed. **Plant height 8–20 ft.; leaves alternate, clustered, unlobed, margins toothed; petals inconspicuous, 5, partially fused with sepals at base; feathery fruits showy; radial symmetry; white, cream**

Cercocarpus ledifolius
ROSACEAE

Curl-leaf Mountain Mahogany

Deserts, chaparral, woodlands; 4000–9800 ft.;
native

Known for its longevity, this iconic high-desert shrub can live more than 1000 years. Its narrow, leathery leaves are curled under along the margins. Blooming in early spring, the persistent styles of the inconspicuous flowers give rise to fruits with hairy appendages that glisten when backlit in the summer sun. **Plant height to 30 ft.; leaves alternate, clustered, un- lobed, margins smooth; petals inconspicuous, 5, partially fused with se- pals at base; fruit mass- es showy; radial sym- metry; white**

Chamaebatia foliolosa
ROSACEAE

Mountain Misery

Conifer forests; 2000–7700 ft.; native

This summer-blooming shrub is responsible for the aroma of the low-elevation conifer forests of the Sierra. Its fernlike leaves form a groundcover, and it vigorously resprouts after a fire. Called Mountain Misery because of its sticky leaf resin, which smells similar to sagebrush, other common names include Kit-kit-dizzy (Miwok), Tarweed, and Bear Clover. **Plant height 6–24 in.; leaves alternate, dis- sected, margins toothed; petals showy, 5, partially fused with sepals at base; radial symmetry; white**

Chamaebatiaria millefolium

ROSACEAE

Fern Bush

Deserts, sagebrush scrub; 3000–11,100 ft.; native

This hairy, resinous shrub has fernlike foliage and is sweetly aromatic. The profusion of flowers in summer attracts a wide variety of pollinators. Interestingly, this plant occurs in a discontinuous range, in the sagebrush scrub of the Eastern Cascades as well as in the high-desert areas of the Southern Sierra and White Mountains. **Plant height 2–7 ft.; leaves alternate, dissected, margins toothed; petals showy, 5, partially fused with sepals at base; radial symmetry; white**

Cotoneaster pannosus

ROSACEAE

Silverleaf Cotoneaster

Disturbed areas; up to 3300 ft.; non-native

Native to China, this shrub grows in moderate climates and disturbed areas in Coastal California. It produces a cascade of white flowers in summer that turn into large clusters of fleshy, red berries, with two stonelike seeds per fruit. Its berries look similar to those of Toyon, but its smaller leaves have smoother margins. **Plant height to 6 ft.; leaves alternate, unlobed, margins smooth; petals showy, 5, partially fused with sepals at base; radial symmetry; white**

Drymocallis glandulosa
ROSACEAE

Sticky Cinquefoil

Conifer forests, wetlands; 1,300–6,500 ft.; native

Found throughout California except in the interior valleys, this plant resembles a strawberry plant at first glance. The leaves and stems are covered with glandular hairs that create a somewhat sticky surface. This perennial herb blooms in spring and summer and becomes more common after a fire. Several rodent species favor this plant as a food source. **Plant height 8–24 in.; leaves alternate, pinnately compound, margins toothed; petals showy, 5, free; radial symmetry; white, pale yellow, cream**

Fallugia paradoxa
ROSACEAE

Apache Plume

Pinyon–juniper woodlands; 3300-7200 ft.; native

In late spring, the snow-white flowers of Apache Plume give rise to fluffy, pink, hairy styles, each attached to a single-seeded fruit (achene). The style plumes aid wind-dispersal of the seeds. This shrub occurs throughout Southwestern North America and is exceedingly drought-tolerant. It does well in a xeric landscape in full sun. **Plant height to 6 ft.; leaves alternate, pinnately compound, margins smooth; petals showy, 5, partially fused with sepals at base; radial symmetry; white**

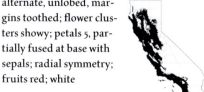

Fragaria vesca
ROSACEAE

Woodland Strawberry

Conifer forests; up to 6,500 ft.; native

Blooming in spring, the flowers of this perennial herb develop into luscious red fruits that
are high in vitamin C. To verify the species, examine the teeth on the terminal leaflet, which
are roughly equal in size. In similar *Fragaria*
species, the teeth at the tip of the leaflet are
shorter than adjacent teeth. **Plant height to 6
in.; leaves basal, ternately compound, leaflets, 3, margins toothed;
petals showy, 5, partially
fused with sepals at base;
radial symmetry; white**

Heteromeles arbutifolia
ROSACEAE

Toyon

Chaparral, woodlands; up to 4300 ft.; native

This shrub is a common chaparral and
foothill-woodland species with distinctive
glossy, leathery, toothed, evergreen leaves. The
dense, summer-blooming white flower clusters turn into thousands of red berries in late
fall. The fruits persist on the plant until birds
pick them off, often lasting well into winter.
Plants resprout vigorously after wildfire. **Plant
height to 20 ft.; leaves
alternate, unlobed, mar-
gins toothed; flower clusters showy; petals 5, partially fused at base with
sepals; radial symmetry;
fruits red; white**

Holodiscus discolor
ROSACEAE

Oceanspray

Conifer forests; up to 13,000 ft.; native

This summer-blooming shrub grows along
moist woodland edges and on rocky slopes.
Its habit can be open, tall, or wispy, or it is low
and compact, depending on the variety. The
leaves are delicately scalloped. It is a common
understory shrub in the Pacific Northwest. Its
small flowers have a faintly sweet scent. **Plant
height 4–19 ft.; leaves alternate, lobed or unlobed, margins toothed;
flower clusters showy;
petals 5, partially fused
at base with sepals; radial
symmetry; white**

Horkelia tridentata
ROSACEAE

Three-tooth Horkelia

Conifer forests; up to 8,200 ft; native

This perennial herb blooms in late spring
and summer. Flowers have a near perfect
ring of pink anthers that attract insects
to their blooms. Each hairy leaflet has a
trident-shaped tip, hence its very appropriate
common and scientific names. Its distribution
extends into the mountains of Southern Oregon and Nevada. **Plant height to 17 in.; leaves
basal, pinnately com-
pound, margins toothed;
petals showy, 5, partially
fused at base with sepals;
radial symmetry; white**

Ivesia santolinoides
ROSACEAE

Mousetail Ivesia

Conifer forests; 5000–12,000 ft.; native

Each leaf of this perennial herb comprises 120–180 tiny, hairy leaflets that overlap tightly to form a wooly, tail-like, cylindrical leaf. In summer, upwards of 200 white flowers with reddish purple anthers bloom on each plant. Endemic to the Sierra Nevada and Transverse ranges of California, it grows in sandy, bare places and granitic ledges. **Plant height 6–16 in.; leaves basal, pinnately compound, margins smooth; petals showy, 5, partially fused at base with sepals; radial symmetry; white**

Oemleria cerasiformis
ROSACEAE

Oso Berry

Chaparral, woodlands, conifer forests; up to 6000 ft.; native

This early spring–blooming shrub produces pendant flower clusters. Each plant in this dioecious species has either male or female flowers, but not both. The female plant produces large, purple-black, plumlike fruits. *Cerasiformis* means "cherry-shaped" and refers to the fruit cluster. It is a favorite snack for bears and other wildlife—*oso* is Spanish for "bear." **Plant height to 20 ft.; leaves alternate, unlobed, margins smooth; petals showy, 5, partially fused at base with sepals; radial symmetry; white**

Physocarpus capitatus
ROSACEAE

Pacific Ninebark

Streamsides, moist slopes in conifer forests; up to 4600 ft.; native

This shrub has distinctive palmately lobed, maple-like leaves. Its thinly layered bark shreds and peels away in strips. Blooming in late spring and summer, flowershead are dense and rounded, resembling a bridal bouquet. Look closely to see the red-tipped stamens. Its distribution extends into much of Western North America. Plant height 3–8 ft.; leaves alternate, lobed, margins toothed; flower clusters showy; petals 5, partially fused with sepals at base; radial symmetry; white

Prunus emarginata
ROSACEAE

Bitter Cherry

Conifer forests; up to 9800 ft.; native

Common throughout California mountain forests, this summer-blooming tree has distinctive silver-white bark and brilliant red berries. In the fall, its dense foliage turns yellow. As the common name implies, the fruits are incredibly bitter. This does not, however, deter wildlife, including bears, from devouring them. It is a larval host for various butterfly species. Plant height to 45 ft.; leaves alternate, unlobed, margins toothed; flower clusters showy; petals 5, partially fused with sepals at base; radial symmetry; white

Prunus fasciculata
ROSACEAE

Desert Almond

Deserts; up to 7200 ft.; native

This winter-blooming shrub occurs in drier habitats, where it forms thorny thickets. The narrow leaves are clustered into bundles (fascicles), and the bark is smooth and gray. Plants are either male or female (dioecious); only the female plant produces fruit. Native Americans considered the fruit a delicacy, probably after leaching out the cyanogenic compounds. **Plant height to 6 ft.; leaves alternate, unlobed, margins smooth; flowers showy en masse; petals 5, partially fused with sepals at base; radial symmetry; white**

Prunus virginiana
ROSACEAE

Western Chokecherry

Woodlands; up to 9800 ft.; native

The long, pendulous flower clusters of this spring-blooming shrub develop into striking red-black fruit clusters. The branches are thin and pliable and have been used by Native Americans for basket weaving, as well as utensils. The fruits can be made into jams and jellies but must be sweetened to overcome the sourness. **Plant height to 20 ft.; leaves alternate, unlobed, margins toothed; flower clusters showy; petals 5, partially fused with sepals at base; radial symmetry; white**

Purshia tridentata
ROSACEAE

Antelope Bitterbrush

Deserts, sagebrush scrub; 3000–11,500 ft.; native

This low, spreading shrub is an iconic component of sagebrush scrub. The specific name describes its small, drought-adapted, trident-shaped leaves. Its roots harbor bacteria that fix nitrogen, enabling it to survive in poor soil. A purplish dye can be made from the outer seed coat. It blooms in late spring and summer. **Plant height to 8 ft.; leaves alternate, lobed, margins smooth; flowers showy en masse; petals 5, partially fused with sepals at base; radial symmetry; white, pale yellow**

Rubus armeniacus
ROSACEAE

Himalayan Blackberry

Riparian, woodlands; up to 5200 ft; non-native

This spring- and summer-blooming shrub is considered a noxious weed in California. The robust, five-angled stems have abundant backward-pointing, stout prickles. This beast crowds out native plants, covering many riparian areas with dense, impenetrable thickets. Contrary to its common name, it is not from the Himalayas but is native to the Middle East. **Plant height to 6 ft.; leaves alternate, palmately compound, margins toothed; petals showy, 5, partially fused to sepals at base; radial symmetry; white, light pink**

Rubus parviflorus
ROSACEAE

Western Thimbleberry

Conifer forests; up to 8000 ft.; native

This spring-blooming shrub grows in damp, shaded forest edges and along streams. Thimbleberry has large, maple-like leaves that are very soft to the touch. No prickles whatsoever on this plant! Why its specific name is *parviflorus*, which means "small flowered," is a mystery, because its flowers are larger than most *Rubus* species. **Plant height to 6 ft.; leaves alternate, lobed, margins toothed; petals showy, 5, partially fused to sepals at base; radial symmetry; white**

Rubus ursinus
ROSACEAE

California Blackberry

Wetlands, woodlands, shrublands; up to 5000 ft.; native

Leaves and branches of this low, trailing shrub are covered in prickles. Leaves can be lobed or compound with three leaflets. Blooming in winter and early spring, its white flower petals are separated by green, leafy sepals. Unusual for this genus, male and female flowers grow on separate plants. **Plant height (length) to 6 ft.; leaves alternate, lobed or compound, margins toothed; petals showy, 5, partially fused to sepals at base; radial symmetry; white**

Sorbus californica

ROSACEAE

California Mountain Ash

Moist conifer forests; 4000–14,000 ft.; native

This summer-blooming shrub puts on a dramatic color display in the fall. It produces brilliant red berries and golden leaves that contrast with the surrounding conifer forest. The bitter berries are eaten by a host of wildlife. Its leaves resemble those of true ashes (*Fraxinus* spp.), but they are not closely related. **Plant height to 16 ft.; leaves alternate, pinnately compound, margins toothed; flower clusters showy; petals 5, partially fused to sepals at base; radial symmetry; white**

Cephalanthus occidentalis

RUBIACEAE

Button-willow

Wetlands, riparian; up to 3000 ft.; native

In midsummer, when most other species are dormant, this species' dense, round flower-heads erupt like little exploding fireworks (or giant coronaviruses). The flowers are a rich source of nectar to bees and butterflies. When not flowering, it can be recognized by its distinctive shoots with three leaves per node. **Plant height to 15 ft.; leaves whorled, unlobed, margins smooth; flower clusters showy; petals 4, partially fused; radial symmetry; white, cream**

Galium aparine
RUBIACEAE

Stickywilly

Grasslands, woodlands, shrublands; up to 4900 ft.; native

This spring-blooming annual is native to North America and Eurasia. It has whorled leaves and square stems. The plant's surface is covered in hooked prickles that stick to passersby. When they latch on, the brittle stems break off and a whole section of the plant hitches a ride. **Plant height to 3 ft.; leaves whorled, unlobed, margins smooth but with marginal hooked prickles; petals inconspicuous, 4, fused at base; radial symmetry; white**

Maianthemum stellatum
RUSCACEAE

Starry False Lily of the Valley

Woodlands; up to 7900 ft.; native

This perennial herb is native to North America and grows on moist slopes and in meadows. Its shiny, deep green leaves create a beautiful background for the small constellation of tiny, starlike flowers. It blooms in late spring and summer and is similar to False Solomon's Seal (*Maianthemum racemosum*). **Plant height to 2 ft.; leaves alternate, unlobed, margins smooth; petals showy, 6, free; radial symmetry; white**

Nolina parryi
RUSCACEAE

Parry's Beargrass

Deserts, chaparral; 3000–6900 ft.; native

This perennial herb has a dense rosette of long, stiff leaves with fine sawtoothed margins. The rosette itself can be up to 5 ft. tall. Blooming in spring, it produces a massive stalk that can double the plant's height. The epic flower cluster attracts moth pollinators, and the fruits are eaten by birds. **Plant height to 10 ft.; leaves basal rosette, unlobed, margins toothed; flower clusters showy; petals 6, fused at base; radial symmetry; white**

Aesculus californica
SAPINDACEAE

California Buckeye

Foothill woodlands, dry slopes; up to 5500 ft.; native

This tree is covered in sweet-smelling blooms from late spring into summer. Numerous flower clusters up to 8 in. long protrude from the dome-shaped tree. As summer temperatures rise, it drops its leaves. Then large, dangling, fuzzy fruits develop, splitting open in autumn to reveal polished, mahogany-colored seeds. All parts of the plant are poisonous. **Plant height to 30 ft.; leaves opposite, palmately compound, margins smooth; petals showy, 5, free; radial symmetry; white, pink**

Anemopsis californica
SAURURACEAE

Yerba Mansa

Wetlands, saline and alkaline soils; up to 6500 ft.; native

This spring-blooming perennial prefers to have its feet wet. In early spring, white petal-like bracts surround the base of a cone-like cluster of tiny flowers. Like many of the plants in this lineage, the species is aromatic. Records indicate that it was used to treat colds, open sores, and stomach ulcers. In Spanish, *yerba* means "herb" and *mansa* means "calm or tranquil." **Plant height 3–31 in.; leaves basal, unlobed, margins smooth; bracts showy, many, free; radial symmetry; white**

Boykinia occidentalis
SAXIFRAGACEAE

Brook Foam

Wet, shaded banks in chaparral, coastal scrub, woodlands, and forests; up to 5000 ft.; native

This delicate-looking perennial herb grows in seeps and springs. Its roots deeply penetrate rock crevices, where they receive constant moisture. This species is primarily a coastal dweller, though is also abundant in inland ranges. Blooming in spring, the flowering stems produce open flower clusters. The dried leaves are fragrant. **Plant height 6–36 in.; leaves basal, lobed, margins toothed; flower clusters showy; petals 5, free; radial symmetry; white**

Boykinia rotundifolia
SAXIFRAGACEAE

Roundleaf Brook Foam

Riparian, chaparral; up to 6500 ft.; native

This summer-blooming perennial herb is primarily a resident of shaded streambanks in the coastal mountains of Southern California. It has rounded, scalloped leaves with small stipules (leaf bases). The tiny flowers are crowded and overlapping on the flower stem, which can be more than 2 ft. tall. Petals barely emerge from the calyx. **Plant height 18–30 in.; leaves alternate, shallowly lobed, margins toothed; flower clusters mostly greenish from prominent calyx, petals inconspicuous, 5, free; radial symmetry; white**

Heuchera micrantha
SAXIFRAGACEAE

Crevice Alumroot

Conifer forests; up to 8200 ft; native

This perennial herb grows in vernally moist, rocky crevices, but it is also commonly planted in gardens. Blooming from late spring into summer, the tiny flowers resemble smoke or mist floating over the understory. The family name comes from the Latin word *saxifrage*, which means "stone-breaker." This is exactly what the roots do as they grow into weaknesses in the rocks. **Plant height 12–40 in.; leaves basal, lobed, margins toothed; flower clusters showy; petals 5, free; radial symmetry; white**

Jepsonia heterandra
SAXIFRAGACEAE

Foothill Jepsonia

Woodlands; up to 2300 ft.; native

This perennial herb blooms from late summer through early winter, producing a delicate spray of white flowers on tall stems. It is often found growing out of rock crevices on slopes in the Sierra Nevada foothills. Its name honors Willis Linn Jepson, the original author of *The Jepson Manual*, the most comprehensive species identification resource for California plants. **Plant height 3–11 in.; leaves basal, shallowly lobed, margins toothed; flower clusters showy; petals 5, free; radial symmetry; white**

Lithophragma affine
SAXIFRAGACEAE

Common Woodland Star

Grasslands, shrublands, woodlands; up to 6500 ft.; native

Blooming in spring, this perennial has a unique mutualistic relationship with Greya moths. An adult moth pollinates the plant's delicate flowers and then lays eggs in the ovaries. Larvae feed on the developing seeds but don't eat all of them. Counter to intuition, fruits infected with moth larvae produce more seeds than self-pollinated flowers, because the moths are very effective pollinators. **Plant height 4–24 in.; leaves basal, lobed, margins toothed; petals showy, 5, free; radial symmetry; white**

Micranthes californica
SAXIFRAGACEAE

California Saxifrage

Woodlands; up to 4000 ft.; native

This delicate foothill perennial is ephemeral, growing aboveground parts that are visible for only a few weeks in spring. When spring rains fade, its leaves and flowers fade as well. The plant spends most of the year underground, waiting for favorable conditions to return. Look closely for the 10 orange-tipped stamens in each flower. **Plant height 6–14 in.; leaves basal, unlobed, margins toothed; petals showy, 5, free; radial symmetry; white**

Micranthes tolmiei
SAXIFRAGACEAE

Tolmie's Saxifrage

Subalpine conifer forests, alpine tundra, and fell-fields; up to 6500 ft.; native

Unlike most saxifrages that have basal leaves, this perennial herb has a long, trailing stem crowded with overlapping fleshy leaves, reminiscent of a stonecrop. Blooming in late summer, the flowers are densely clustered on the top of the flowering stalk. The stamens are almost petal-like and end in orange-red anthers. **Plant height to 6 in.; leaves alternate, unlobed, margins smooth; petals showy, 5, free; radial symmetry; white**

Myoporum laetum
SCROPHULARIACEAE

Ngaio Tree

Chaparral, riparian; up to 1500 ft.; non-native

This evergreen shrub blooms from spring
through summer. It has attractive dark green
foliage and penny-sized white flowers with
pink spots that develop into purple fruits.
Its native distribution is restricted to New
Zealand, but in Southern California it has escaped cultivation into wildlands, often forming dense stands that crowd out native vegetation. **Plant height 5–20
ft.; leaves alternate, unlobed, margins smooth
to finely toothed; petals
showy, 5, partially fused;
radial symmetry; white,
pink spots**

Datura wrightii
SOLANACEAE

Sacred Datura

Many communities, roadsides; up to 7200 ft.;
native

This perennial herb, which is in the same family as potatoes, tomatoes, and tobacco, can
be found in bloom in California nearly any
month of the year. Opening at night, its flowers are fragrant and pollinated by hawk moths.
The plant contains psychoactive alkaloids that
are both potentially dangerous and integral
to certain spiritual and
religious practices. **Plant
height 1–5 ft.; leaves alternate, unlobed, mar-
gins wavy; petals showy,
5, fused; radial symme-
try; white, pink-tinged**

Lycium andersonii
SOLANACEAE

Water Jacket

Deserts; up to 6200 ft.; native

This spring-blooming shrub has hairless, thorny branches. Its flowers develop into small red fruits. Its leaves are fleshy with a high water content. *Lycium* species are differentiated based on the shape of the leaf's cross section. If you used a razor blade to cut through a Water Jacket's leaf, its cross section would be oval shaped. **Plant height 1–10 ft.; leaves alternate, clustered, unlobed, margins smooth; flowers small, petals showy, 5, partially fused; radial symmetry; violet, white**

Lycium cooperi
SOLANACEAE

Peach Thorn

Deserts; up to 6500 ft.; native

This spring-blooming shrub grows in sandy, rocky flats and washes throughout Southwestern North America. Its calyx lobes reflex distinctively as the flower matures. Peach Thorn has small, fleshy, peach-colored fruits. A recent chemical analysis found that the plant produces antioxidants that may help treat macular degeneration. **Plant height 3–5 ft.; leaves alternate, unlobed, margins smooth; petals showy, 5, partially fused; radial symmetry; white-green, lavender**

Nicotiana attenuata
SOLANACEAE

Coyote Tobacco

Disturbed openings in grasslands, woodlands, shrub, and forests; 700–9000 ft.; native

Blooming in summer and fall, this robust annual has long, tubular flowers that are pollinated at night by moths. The plant synthesizes nicotine in its roots, which is transported up to the leaves, where it acts as a natural insect repellent. It has been used for a variety of medicinal purposes and smoked ceremonially by many indigenous peoples. **Plant height 1–5 ft.; leaves alternate, unlobed, margins smooth; petals showy, 5, fused; radial symmetry; white**

Nicotiana quadrivalvis
SOLANACEAE

Sacred Tobacco

Grasslands, shrublands, woodlands; up to 5000 ft.; native

This annual has sweet-smelling, long, tubular flowers that open at night, drawing in a suite of pollinating moths, including hawk moths. Its elliptical leaves are short-stalked or sessile, connected directly to the main stem, whereas the leaves of Coyote Tobacco have petioles. It has a long history of cultivation by the indigenous peoples of Western North America. **Plant height 1–6 ft.; leaves alternate, unlobed, margins smooth; petals showy, 5, fused; radial symmetry; white**

Solanum americanum
SOLANACEAE

American Black Nightshade

Many communities; up to 3300 ft.; native

The flowers of this highly toxic, spring-blooming annual or perennial are classically characteristic of the nightshades. Tightly clustered, yellow stamens surround the central pistil, and petals are reflexed backward when mature. Glossy, black fruits are perhaps its most distinctive feature. It is distributed worldwide. **Plant height 1–3 ft.; leaves alternate, unlobed, margins wavy; petals showy, 5, partially fused; radial symmetry; white**

Styrax redivivus
STRYRACACEAE

Snowdrop Bush

Woodlands, mixed evergreen forests; up to 5000 ft.; native

Blooming in spring, the lightly scented, large, bell-shaped flowers with fat yellow stamens superficially resemble orange blossoms. The common name describes the shrub's propensity to drop its petals after blooming, carpeting the ground in white. It is not super abundant in wildlands, but it is a favorite in native plant gardens. **Plant height to 12 ft.; leaves alternate, unlobed, margins smooth; petals showy, usually 5 but up to 10; fused below; radial symmetry; white, cream**

Odontostomum hartwegii
TECOPHILAEACEAE

Hartweg's Doll's-lily

Grasslands, woodlands; up to 2000 ft.; native

This spring-blooming perennial herb is endemic to Northern California and is the only member of the genus *Odontostomum*. Also known as Inside Out Lily, its sepals and petals are fused into a tube at the base and the lobes are swept backward, exposing the purplish anthers. It grows in clay and serpentine soils. **Plant height 6–18 in.; leaves basal, unlobed, margins smooth; tepals showy, 6, partially fused; radial symmetry; white, cream, yellow**

Muilla maritima
THEMIDACEAE

Sea Muilla

Grasslands; up to 7500 ft.; native

The flowers of this spring-blooming perennial herb are similar in appearance to the flowers of *Allium* (onion) species. In fact, muilla is allium spelled backward. You can tell it is not an onion, though, because it does not have an oniony smell. The anthers are green, blue, or purple, and a brown-green stripe appears under each petal. **Plant height 6–24 in.; leaves basal, unlobed, margins smooth; tepals showy, 6, free; radial symmetry; white**

Triteleia hyacinthina
THEMIDACEAE

Wild Hyacinth

Grasslands, woodlands, montane meadows; up to 6500 ft.; native

This perennial herb is a graceful member of many sunny, vernally moist habitats. It blooms in late spring through summer, with flower clusters that resemble those of *Allium* (onions) species, but they do not smell like onions. The anthers are yellow and the midribs of the petals are green. It is a good choice for pollinator gardens. **Plant height 1–3 ft.; leaves basal, unlobed, margins smooth; petals showy, 6, partially fused; radial symmetry; white**

Triantha occidentalis
TOFIELDIACEAE

Western False Asphodel

Wetlands; up to 10,000 ft.; native

This summer-blooming perennial herb has tight clusters of small flowers grouped on mostly leafless flower stalks. Its ovaries and stamens turn reddish in color as the flowers go to seed. Its stems are covered in sticky hairs that trap insects. Researchers recently realized that the species is carnivorous and is able to absorb nutrients from the trapped insects. **Plant height 1–3 ft.; leaves basal, unlobed, margins smooth; tepals showy, 6, free; radial symmetry; white, yellow**

Valeriana californica
VALERIANACEAE

California Valerian

Conifer forests; 5000–12,100 ft.; native

In summer, tall stalks of this perennial herb are topped with tight clusters of tiny flowers, with stamens that protrude above the petals. Growing in moist, forested habitats, its distribution includes Oregon and Nevada. It is part of a large genus that includes medicinal Valerian (*V. officinalis*), which has been used as a sedative for centuries in Eurasia. **Plant height 8–24 in.; leaves opposite, lobed, margins smooth; flower clusters showy, petals 5, partially fused; mirror symmetry; white, pink-tinged**

Phyla nodiflora
VERBENACEAE

Turkey Tangle Fogfruit

Wetlands, grasslands, woodlands; up to 1300 ft.; native

This mat-forming perennial herb blooms from spring through fall. Its native range is quite large, spanning the lower latitudes of the Americas. At one time, any low-growing species that colonized fields after hay was cut were called fogfruits; this has been misinterpreted as frogfruits by many. It is a larval food source for various butterfly species. **Plant height 1–6 in.; leaves opposite, unlobed, margins toothed; petals showy, 5, partially fused; mirror symmetry; white with purple center**

Sambucus mexicana
VIBURNACEAE

Black Elderberry

Many communities; up to 9000 ft.; native

This spring-blooming shrub is widely distributed in North America. Large, flattened flower clusters develop dark berries that are attractive to wildlife. Although the flowers and ripe berries may be edible, all other plant parts and unripe berries, including the seeds, are toxic. Cooking the berries makes them safer and more palatable. **Plant height to 25 ft.;** leaves opposite, pinnately compound, margins toothed; flower clusters showy; petals small, 5, free; radial symmetry; white, cream

Sambucus racemosa
VIBURNACEAE

Red Elderberry

Riparian, conifer forests; 6000–12,000 ft.; native

This robust shrub blooms in spring and summer. It usually produces shiny, red fruits at the end of summer, which can also be dark purple, similar to those of Black Elderberry. Red Elderberry fruit is also toxic if it is not cooked properly. Clusters of fragrant flowers are elongated, not flattened, and visited by hummingbirds and pollinators. **Plant height to 20 ft.;** leaves opposite, pinnately compound, margins toothed; flower clusters showy; petals small, 5, free; radial symmetry; white

Viola macloskeyi
VIOLACEAE

Macloskey's Violet

Meadows, riparian, conifer forests; 2000–11,100 ft.; native

This perennial herb blooms in spring through summer across its large elevational range. The little plants hide out in wet meadows. Its striking flower is quite small, less than a half-inch across, with an elongated lower petal that forms a pouchlike spur behind the sepals. Purple guides on the lower petals lead pollinators into its nectaries. **Plant height to 6 in.; leaves basal, unlobed, margins smooth; petals showy, 5, free; mirror symmetry; white with purple nectar guides**

PURPLE TO BLUE FLOWERS

Camassia leichtlinii
AGAVACEAE

Great Camas

Wetlands; 3000–8500 ft.; native

This attractive spring- and summer-blooming perennial herb is used as a garden ornamental and sold by bulb suppliers. The variety native to California is not as floriferous as European horticultural selections, but our local plants still produce masses of intense blue flowers that mature from the base of the flower stalk toward the growing tip. **Plant height to 3 ft.; leaves basal, unlobed, margins smooth; tepals showy, 6, free; radial symmetry; blue**

Allium fimbriatum
ALLIACEAE

Fringed Onion

Dry slopes and flats in grasslands, chaparral, woodlands, forests; 1000–8800 ft.; native

Blooming in spring, this perennial herb grows from a reddish brown bulb that is about the size of a quarter. The specific name means "having a fringe." Some onions have a ring of tissue that rests atop the ovary; in this species, the ring is deeply cut into fringes, and it has a single, narrow leaf that is longer than the flower stem. **Plant height to 1 ft.; leaf 1, unlobed, margins smooth; tepals showy, 6, free; radial symmetry; purple-red, pink**

Allium howellii
ALLIACEAE

Howell's Onion

Open slopes in grasslands, woodlands; 600–6000 ft.; native

Wild onion identification relies heavily on bulb characteristics. The bulb of this spring-blooming perennial has a reddish brown outer coat. It is quite tall for an onion and has a single cylindrical leaf. It is native to the West Coast of North America, from British Columbia to Baja California, and it grows in granite and serpentine soils. **Plant height to 2 ft.; leaf 1, unlobed, margins smooth; tepals showy, 6, free; radial symmetry; lavender, pink, white**

Sanicula bipinnatifida
APIACEAE

Purple Sanicle

Grasslands, woodlands; up to 6000 ft.; native

The highly divided basal leaves of this perennial herb are up to 5 in. long. Blooming in spring, the flowerheads are small and spherical, about 1 in. across. They can be purple or yellow and comprise a few dozen tiny flowers with protruding stamens. It prefers open habitats and often grows in serpentine-derived soils. **Plant height to 2 ft.; leaves basal, pinnately compound, margins toothed; flower clusters showy; petals small, 5, free; radial symmetry; purple, yellow**

Vinca major
APOCYNACEAE

Big-leaf Periwinkle

Garden escapee; up to 4500 ft.; non-native

Blooming in spring and summer, this perennial herb is widely used as a garden ornamental. Unfortunately, it often escapes into natural areas, where it outcompetes and smothers other species, especially in ideal moisture conditions. For this reason, it should never be planted intentionally. Solarizing under clear, UV-resistant plastic is an effective way to kill it. **Plant height to 10 in.; leaves opposite, unlobed, margins smooth; petals showy, 5, partially fused; radial symmetry; blue**

Corethrogyne filaginifolia
ASTERACEAE

Common Sandaster

Coastal scrub, grasslands, woodlands; up to 8500 ft.; native

Blooming summer and fall, this perennial herb has sunflower-like flowerheads and white-hairy foliage. It occurs in dry habitats from Southern Oregon to Baja California. Variation within the species is astonishing, and it was divided into more than 30 taxa across 7 species, but today only a single, undivided species is recognized. **Plant height 4–40 in.; leaves alternate, unlobed; margins smooth or toothed; flowers small; flowerheads sunflower-like; radial symmetry; purple, pink, white**

Dieteria canescens
ASTERACEAE

Hoary Tansy-aster

Deserts, montane slopes; 2500–11,200 ft.; native

Blooming from spring through fall, this annual or perennial herb occurs throughout much of North America. "Hoary" describes the short, dense white-grey hairs that cover its leaves and stems. Its distinguishing features include spaced ray flowers and pointy, backward-curling involucre bracts below the flowerhead. There are five varieties in California. **Plant height to 2** ft.; leaves alternate, unlobed, margins smooth or minutely toothed; flowers small; flowerheads showy, daisy-like; radial symmetry; purple, pink, white

Erigeron breweri
ASTERACEAE

Brewer's Fleabane

Conifer forests, deserts; 990–10,200 ft.; native

Generally found in dry, rocky areas, this perennial herb occurs in five varieties in California. Its stems have dense, short, reflexed hairs. Blooming in spring and summer, it is one of many specific named to honor William H. Brewer, a botanical explorer on the groundbreaking Geological Survey of California between 1860 and 1864. **Plant height 9–24 in.;** leaves alternate, unlobed, margins smooth; flowers small; flowerheads showy, daisy-like; radial symmetry; lavender with yellow center

Erigeron foliosus
ASTERACEAE

Leafy Fleabane

Chaparral, conifer forests, woodlands; up to 9500 ft.; native

The flowers of this perennial herb are similar to those of Brewer's Fleabane, but its stems are less hairy, or hairless. The specific name, *foliosus*, means "leafy," referring to the stems with their regularly spaced, often threadlike leaves. It is native to Western North America, from Oregon to Baja California. It blooms from spring through fall. **Plant height to 3 ft.; leaves alternate, unlobed, margins smooth; flowers small; flowerheads showy, daisy-like; radial symmetry; lavender with yellow center**

Erigeron glaucus
ASTERACEAE

Seaside Fleabane

Dunes; up to 100 ft.; native

Blooming in spring and summer, this perennial herb is a common sight on beaches, dunes, and coastal bluffs from California to Oregon. It has a tidy growth form and gorgeous flowerheads with numerous ray petals. It is a popular choice for coastal native gardens. Bees and butterflies are attracted to the pollen reward. **Plant height to 1 ft.; leaves alternate, unlobed, margins smooth or toothed; flowers small; flowerheads showy, sunflower-like; radial symmetry; lavender, white, pink, with yellow center**

Oreostemma alpigenum
ASTERACEAE

Tundra Aster

Wetlands in montane forests; 4000–11,000 ft.; native

In late spring and summer, the flowerheads on this erect, perennial herb are easily spotted in mountain meadows throughout Western North America. Unlike many asters, it has a single, large flowerhead on each stem. Three varieties occur in North America; California has variety *andersonii*. In Northwest California, it often grows with California Pitcherplant. **Plant height to 16 in.; leaves basal, alternate, unlobed, margins smooth; flowers small; flowerheads showy, daisy-like; radial symmetry; light purple**

Symphyotrichum chilense
ASTERACEAE

Pacific Aster

Grasslands, wetlands, disturbed areas; up to 1650 ft.; native

This creeping perennial herb spreads by underground stems (rhizomes), creating widespread colonies. Blooming summer and fall, its multiple daisy-like flowerheads are an important food source for pollinators. This species intergrades with Douglas' Aster (*S. subspicatum*). The two can be difficult to distinguish. **Plant height 16–40 in.; leaves basal, alternate, unlobed, margins smooth or toothed; flowers small; flowerhead clusters showy, flowerheads daisy-like; radial symmetry; blue, violet, pink**

Xylorhiza tortifolia
ASTERACEAE

Mojave Woody Aster

Deserts; 800–6600 ft.; native

Blooming in spring and fall, the eye-catching flowerheads of this species look like they belong on a garden ornamental. In summer, the whole plant turns brown. The genus name, *Xylorhiza*, means "woody root." This perennial herb has tough roots that help it grow in dry, rocky areas. Its distribution extends to Southwestern Utah and Western Arizona. **Plant height 8–24 in.; leaves alternate, unlobed, margins toothed; flowers small; flowerheads showy, daisy-like; radial symmetry; lavender, light blue, white**

Cichorium intybus
ASTERACEAE

Chicory

Disturbed areas; up to 5000 ft.; non-native

Blooming from spring through fall, this perennial herb is common in disturbed areas. Related to lettuce, its bitter foliage has been used as a salad green, and roots can be baked or roasted and used as a coffee substitute. A good forage for livestock, it may reduce intestinal parasites. **Plant height 16–80 in.; leaves in basal rosette, stem leaves alternate, unlobed to lobed, margins smooth or toothed; flowers small; flowerheads showy, dandelion-like; radial symmetry; blue, pink, white**

Cynara cardunculus
ASTERACEAE

Cardoon

Disturbed areas; up to 1600 ft.; non-native

This perennial herb blooms in spring and summer. Its leaf stalks and midribs are reported to be edible, and some sources indicate that the unopened bud is as well. This species regularly escapes cultivation (as a garden ornamental) along the coast and is considered invasive. Plants can be massive, forming dense stands that displace native vegetation. **Plant height 2–8 ft.; leaves in basal rosette, deeply lobed, margins toothed; flowerheads showy, discoid; flowers small; radial symmetry; purple, blue**

Adelinia grandis
BORAGINACEAE

Pacific Hound's Tongue

Woodlands, chaparral; up to 7000 ft.; native

The large leaves of this perennial herb are wide at the base and narrow at the tip. From late winter to spring, its blue flowers have white nectar pouches at their centers. The roots are reportedly used to treat burns and stomachaches. It was previously known as *Cynoglossum grande*. **Plant height to 2 ft.; leaves in basal rosette, lobed or unlobed at base, margins smooth, wavy; flower clusters showy; flowers small, petals 5, partially fused; radial symmetry; blue, purple**

Echium candicans
BORAGINACEAE

Pride of Madeira

Disturbed shrublands near the coast; up to 1500 ft.; non-native

Blooming from spring through fall, this sub-shrub has striking flower clusters of up to a foot tall. Its appearance and low care needs makes it a popular choice in coastal gardens. Unfortunately, it can escape cultivation and invade natural communities. It requires summer moisture and is not freeze tolerant, so it does not become weedy inland. **Plant height 4–8 ft.; leaves alternate, unlobed, margins smooth; flower clusters showy; petals 5, partially fused; radial symmetry; violet**

Hackelia micrantha
BORAGINACEAE

Meadow Stickseed

Wetlands, woodlands; 2000–12,200 ft.; native

This perennial herb graces a wide range of montane habitats. It is the most common *Hackelia* species in California, where it forms large populations. It has smaller flowers than most other stickseeds; *micrantha* means "small flowered." Fruits are covered with hooked barbs that attach to animal fur. It blooms in late spring and summer. **Plant height to 3 ft.; leaves alternate, unlobed, margins smooth; flower clusters showy; petals 5, partially fused; radial symmetry; blue, lavender**

Mertensia ciliata
BORAGINACEAE

Streamside Bluebells

Wetlands, riparian; 2500–11,000 ft.; native

This perennial herb grows in wet habitats. Blooming in late spring and summer, its delicate, drooping clusters of bell-shaped flowers are pollinated by bumble bees. The insects create a high frequency vibration with their wings that causes the flower's anthers to release pollen (buzz pollination). Variety *stomatechoides* is the only California variety. **Plant height to 5 ft.; leaves alternate, unlobed, margins smooth; flower clusters showy; petals 5, partially fused; radial symmetry; blue**

Myosotis laxa
BORAGINACEAE

Bay Forget-me-not

Wetlands, riparian; up to 8000 ft.; native

This uncommon but locally abundant perennial herb has delicate flowers that bloom in spring and summer. It is the only native *Myosotis* species in California; other non-native species may be invasive garden escapees. About this species, Henry David Thoreau wrote in his journal, "it is the more beautiful for being small and unpretending." **Plant height to 15 in.; leaves alternate, unlobed, margins smooth; flower clusters showy; petals 5, partially fused; radial or biradial symmetry; blue with yellow center**

Boechera breweri
BRASSICACEAE

Brewer's Rockcress

Woodlands; 1000–7500 ft.; native

Blooming in late winter and spring, this perennial herb grows in rocky crevices. It has attractive, arching, purple seed pods (siliques). The more common form of this species, *B. breweri* subsp. *breweri*, is smaller and hairier than the less common form, subspecies *shastaensis*. Mustards can have either long, thin siliques or more round fruits (silicles). **Plant height to 8 in.; basal leaves unlobed, stem leaves alternate, clasping, margins smooth; flower clusters showy; petals 4, free; radial symmetry; lavender, pink**

Boechera pulchra
BRASSICACEAE

Beautiful Rockcress

Chaparral, desert scrub, woodlands; 1200–9300 ft.; native

Blooming in spring and summer, this gorgeous little perennial herb may be spotted as you hike along desert slopes in Southern California. Its specific name, *pulchra*, means "pretty." Distributed throughout Southwestern North America, five varieties have been described based on hairiness and fruit form. Fruits are straight, narrow silicles and strongly reflexed. **Plant height 12–30 in.; basal rosette, stem leaves alternate, unlobed, margins smooth; flowers small, petals showy, 4, free; radial symmetry; lavender, pink**

Boechera sparsiflora
BRASSICACEAE

Sicklepod Rockcress

Dry, rocky openings in sagebrush steppe, conifer woodlands, forests; up to 12,800 ft.; native

Blooming spring and summer, this perennial herb occurs from Northern California to Utah and north to British Columbia. Coarse hairs and leaves vary from linear to arrowhead shaped. Narrow, arched fruits (siliques) up to 6 inches long. An important host for Western Orange Tip caterpillars. **Plant height to 3 ft.; stem leaves alternate, unlobed to basally lobed, margins smooth or toothed; flower clusters showy; flowers small, petals 4, free; radial symmetry; lavender, pink**

Caulanthus amplexicaulis
BRASSICACEAE

Clasping-leaf Wild Cabbage

Chaparral; 850–10,045 ft.; native

This annual grows on rocky slopes or openings in more dense habitats. It blooms in spring and summer with delicate, balloon-shaped flowers. The plant's basal leaves are often the same color as the rocks surrounding the plant, which is thought to provide camouflage to prevent them from being eaten. **Plant height to 3.5 ft.; stem leaves alternate, lobed or clasping at base, margins smooth or toothed; petals and sepals showy, 4, free; radial or biradial symmetry; purple, yellow, white**

Phoenicaulis cheiranthoides
BRASSICACEAE

Dagger Pod

Desert scrub, barrens, rocky slopes; 500–11,800 ft.; native

Blooming in spring, this hardy perennial herb grows in rocky, barren areas. Its common name refers to its conspicuously dagger-shaped fruits. The genus name is likely derived from *phaneros*, meaning "visible," and *kaulos*, which means "stem." Reports indicate that it was used in a tonic administered after childbirth. **Plant height to 1 ft.; leaves in basal rosette, unlobed, margins smooth; flower clusters showy; petals 4, free; radial symmetry; purple**

Streptanthus cordatus
BRASSICACEAE

Heartleaf Twistflower

Sagebrush scrub, pinyon–juniper woodlands, chaparral; 2500–11,500 ft.; native

Whereas most jewelflowers have narrow distributions, this perennial herb occurs throughout Western North America, often on limestone outcrops. It has a distinct basal rosette of gray, toothed leaves. Its stem leaves are heart-shaped and clasping. Blooming in spring and summer, the green to purple sepals mostly hide the purple petals. **Plant height to 3 ft.; leaves in basal rosette, toothed; stem leaves alternate, clasping, smooth; sepals and petals showy, 4, free; radial or biradial symmetry; maroon, purple**

Streptanthus farnsworthianus
BRASSICACEAE

Farnsworth's Jewelflower

Woodlands; 500–6000 ft.; native

This spring-blooming, rare annual grows in the foothills of the Southern Sierra Nevada. In contrast to many other wildflowers, its most showy part is a large, purple bract located around each flower. A good place to observe this species is in the Greenhorn Mountains in Kern and Tulare counties. **Plant height to 3 ft.; leaves in basal rosette, pinnately lobed, margins smooth or toothed; flowers small, sepals and petals 4, free; radial or biradial symmetry; sepals purple, petals white**

Streptanthus glandulosus
BRASSICACEAE

Bristly Jewelflower

Woodlands, chaparral; 250–2500 ft.; native

This spring- and summer-blooming annual has colorful, inflated petals and hairy leaves and stems. Eight named varieties are recognized. Many of them are rare and geographically restricted. These plants grow in a variety of habitats, but the rare species are often associated with serpentine outcrops, which are inhospitable to most plants. **Plant height 5–35 in.; basal leaves lobed, stem leaves unlobed, margins toothed or smooth; sepals and petals showy, 4, free; radial or biradial symmetry; purple**

Streptanthus polygaloides
BRASSICACEAE

Milkwort Jewelflower

Barrens, woodlands, chaparral; 350–7000 ft.; native

Blooming in spring and summer, the flowers of this annual are asymmetrical and range from green to purple. It can accumulate large quantities of elemental nickel in its tissues, which is present in the soil (serpentine) where it grows, and which may make the plants unpalatable to herbivores. **Plant height 8–30 in.;** leaves in basal rosette, deeply lobed; stem leaves lobed at base; margins smooth; sepals and petals showy, 4, free; radial or biradial symmetry; purple, yellow

Streptanthus tortuosus
BRASSICACEAE

Shieldplant

Conifer forests, woodlands; up to 14,000 ft.; native

Blooming in spring, this widely distributed species occurs in foothills and mountainous areas where vegetation is sparse and the substrate is rocky. It has conspicuous shieldlike bracts that wrap around the flowering stems. It is hairless, has small flowers, and can be a biennial or short-lived perennial. **Plant height to 4 ft.; leaves alter-**nate, unlobed, margins toothed; sepals and petals showy, 4, free; radial or biradial symmetry; petals purple, yellow, or white; sepals purple to white

Asyneuma prenanthoides
CAMPANULACEAE

California Harebell

Conifer or mixed evergreen forests; up to 6500 ft.; native

The long style in the flower of this summer-blooming perennial herb extends beyond its delicately recurved petals. It grows in Northern California and into Oregon, often on roadsides or trail margins. With more than 33 *Asyneuma* species from Eurasia, this is the only one found in North America. **Plant height to 4 ft.; leaves alternate, unlobed, margins toothed; petals showy, 5, partially fused; radial symmetry; blue, lavender, rarely white**

Downingia cuspidata
CAMPANULACEAE

Toothed Calico Flower

Vernal pools, lake margins, meadows; up to 5600 ft.; native

This spring-blooming annual is a widely distributed species in a genus known for having narrow distributions. Flower markings help with identification in this group. In Toothed Calico Flower, the yellow region on the lower petals is completely surrounded by white, and the very center of the flower is not purple. **Plant height to 16 in.; leaves alternate, unlobed, margins smooth; petals showy, 5, partially fused; mirror symmetry; blue, yellow, white**

Downingia pulchella
CAMPANULACEAE

Valley Calico Flower

Vernal pools, roadside ditches; up to 5100 ft.;
native

The flowers of this spring-blooming annual
are similar to Toothed Calico Flower, but with
purple spots. A suite of native bees nest in
the uplands adjacent to the vernal pools that
support calico flowers. The bees and flowers
respond to moisture synchronously, so the
bees emerge and reproduce when the vernal
pool annuals are in flow-
er. Plant height to 16
in.; leaves alternate, unlobed, margins smooth;
petals showy, 5, partially
fused; mirror symmetry;
blue, yellow, white, with
purple center

Githopsis specularioides
CAMPANULACEAE

Common Bluecup

Oak woodlands, chaparral; up to 5000 ft.;
native

This spring-blooming annual has dime-sized,
upright flowers framed by long, linear sepals.
This little gem is most common after fire and
occurs sporadically on slopes in open, rocky
habitats. In California, it has hundreds of occurrences, but in Washington, Oregon, and
Montana, it is less abundant and is considered a vulnerable species.

Plant height 2–16 in.;
leaves alternate, unlobed,
margins toothed; flow-
ers small, petals showy,
5, partially fused; radial
symmetry; purple with
white throat

Heterocodon rariflorum
CAMPANULACEAE

Western Pearl-flower

Vernally wet places in many communities; up to 8100 ft.; native

This spring- and summer-blooming annual grows in moist soils throughout Western North America. *Heterocodon* means "other bell," in reference to its flower types. It has typical showy, but very small, bell-shaped flowers that attract pollinators. It also has even smaller flowers that never open but can produce seeds (cleistogamous). **Plant height to 1 ft.; leaves alternate, clasping bases, margins toothed; petals showy, 5, partially fused; radial symmetry; purple**

Porterella carnosula
CAMPANULACEAE

Fleshy Porterella

Open wetlands in conifer forests; 4300–11,500 ft.; native

This spring-blooming annual occurs east of the Sierra Nevada in areas with wet soil. Fleshy Porterella is similar to species in the genus *Downingia*, but with a distinct difference: *Porterella* species have slender flower stems (pedicels) that attach the flower to the main plant body, whereas most *Downingia* species have flowers attached directly to the plant. **Plant height 1–12 in.; leaves alternate, unlobed, margins smooth; petals showy, 5, partially fused; mirror symmetry; blue, yellow, with white center**

Amorpha californica
FABACEAE

California False Indigo

Conifer forests, woodlands, chaparral; up to 7600 ft.; native

Blooming in spring and summer, this shrub's flower clusters comprise hundreds of tiny flowers, each with a single petal (the banner). This plant is not super abundant but can be found in shady understory habitats. This species and *A. fruticosa* are the only larval hosts for California's state insect, California Dogface Butterfy (*Zerene eurydice*). **Plant height to 6 ft.; leaves alternate, pinnately compound, margins smooth; flower clusters showy; petal 1, free; mirror symmetry; purple, white**

Astragalus didymocarpus
FABACEAE

Dwarf White Milkvetch

Coastal sage scrub, woodlands, deserts; -150–5000 ft.; native

This spring-blooming annual has distinctive black-and-white hairs on the flower buds. The specific name is not only fun to say, but it describes another distinguishing feature of the plant. *Didymocarpus* means "fruits in pairs." The seeds are paired, one on each side of the fruit. Four subspecies are recognized based on flower color and size. **Plant height to 12 in.; leaves alternate, pinnately compound, margins smooth; petals showy, 5, partially fused (keel); mirror symmetry; light purple**

Astragalus lentiginosus
FABACEAE

Freckled Milkvetch

Deserts, conifer forests, woodlands; up to 12,000 ft.; native

This perennial herb has inflated, freckled fruits. The number of varieties described within this species is also impressive, with more than 15 in California alone. Keel size and fruit characters are used to differentiate varieties. It occurs throughout Western North America, often on talus slopes. **Plant height to 18 in.**; leaves alternate, pinnately compound, margins smooth; petals showy, 5, partially fused (keel); mirror symmetry; fruits red and tan; petals violet, pink, cream

Astragalus purshii
FABACEAE

Woolypod Milkvetch

Conifer forests; 600–12,300 ft.; native

This perennial herb has ridiculously hairy fruits that could be mistaken for a pile of cotton balls. Common in arid areas throughout Western North America, it blooms in spring and summer. Milkvetches are also known as locoweeds, because they contain a toxin that can cause neurological damage, emaciation, and death in livestock. **Plant height to 7 in.**; leaves alternate, pinnately compound, margins smooth; petals showy, 5, partially fused (keel); mirror symmetry; purple, pink, white

Hoita macrostachya
FABACEAE

California Hemp

Riparian areas, wetlands; up to 8200 ft; native

This summer-blooming perennial herb resembles a giant clover. It grows in shaded to sunny, moist areas. Until recently, it was included in the genus *Psoralea*, which now includes only South African species. *Hoita* is an indigenous name from the people who lived in the Feather River area. It is pronounced "ho-I-tay," with emphasis on the middle syllable. **Plant height to 6 ft.; leaves alternate, compound, margins smooth; petals showy, 5, partially fused (keel); mirror symmetry; purple, lavender**

Lathyrus vestitus
FABACEAE

Pacific Pea

Conifer forests, chaparral; up to 8600 ft.; native

This vining perennial scrambles over other plants, with large purple flowers that smell subtly of grapes. It makes a great garden plant, especially along the coast, where it grows in full sun. If grown inland, it requires light shade. Its flower clusters attract various pollinators, and it is a larval host to several butterflies. **Plant stem length to 10 ft.; leaves alternate, pinnately compound, margins smooth; petals showy, 5, partially fused (keel); mirror symmetry; lavender, white, pink**

Lupinus albifrons
FABACEAE

Silver Lupine

Chaparral, conifer forests, woodlands; up to 8,200 ft; native

This shrubby lupine blooms in spring and early summer. Different varieties occur in a range of habitats, but all have purple and white flowers. The specific name, *albifrons*, means "white fronded," in reference to its leaves, which are often silvery. It is a host plant for Mission Blue larvae, a federally endangered butterfly species.

Plant height to 10 ft.; leaves alternate, palmately compound, margins smooth; petals showy, 5, partially fused (keel); mirror symmetry; violet, pink, white

Lupinus benthamii
FABACEAE

Spider Lupine

Woodlands, grasslands; up to 5000 ft.; native

This spring-blooming annual has distinctive long, narrow leaflets that resemble spider legs. It is common in lower elevation areas, where it forms massive wildflower displays. The flowers of this species are similar to a few other lupines, but the doppelgängers have wider leaflets and tend to bloom after Spider Lupine. **Plant height to 2 ft.; leaves alternate, palmately compound, margins smooth; petals showy, 5, partially fused (keel); mirror symmetry; blue**

Lupinus bicolor
FABACEAE

Miniature Lupine

Many communities; up to 5200 ft; native

Abundant from British Columbia to Baja California, this spring-blooming species covers seasonally moist, open fields in a sea of blue. The flower has two colors—blue and white—hence the specific name. Many subspecies have been described within this variable species, but none are currently recognized. It is an annual that may live for two years. **Plant height to 15 in.; leaves alternate, palmately compound, margins smooth; petals showy, 5, partially fused (keel); mirror symmetry; blue, violet, white**

Lupinus concinnus
FABACEAE

Bajada Lupine

Open or disturbed areas, deserts; up to 5600 ft.; native

This annual is covered with long, shaggy hairs. Like Miniature Lupine, it has two-colored flowers. The upper-most petal (banner) is white, whereas the rest of the flower is pink or lavender. It is found in dry, sandy, disturbed soils. In Latin *concinnus* means "well-made, elegant" referring to the tidy growth form of this little plant. **Plant height to 1 ft.; leaves alternate, palmately compound, margins smooth; petals showy, 5, partially fused (keel); mirror symmetry; lavender, white, pink**

Lupinus excubitus
FABACEAE

Grape Soda Lupine

Desert slopes and washes; up to 10,400 ft.;
native

This spring- and summer-blooming perennial
herb gets its common name from its young
flowers, which smell like grape soda. It is
highly variable and can be large and woody or
small and herbaceous. In all pea flowers, the
lower two petals wrap around the reproductive structure, forming a keel. In Grape Soda
Lupine, the keel curves
upward sharply. **Plant
height** 2–6 ft.; leaves alternate, palmately com-
pound, margins smooth;
petals showy, 5, partially
fused (keel); mirror sym-
metry; purple

Lupinus nanus
FABACEAE

Sky Lupine

Woodlands, coastal scrub, grasslands; up to
4300 ft.; native

Few species create a more beautiful wildflower display than the Sky Lupine. Blooming in
spring, this robust annual can completely cover
large areas in blue-and-white flowers. Its fragrance attracts a host of pollinators, including
moths and butterflies. Like all lupines, it has
compound leaves that resemble little hands. It
is native to Western North
America. **Plant height**
to 2 ft.; leaves alternate,
palmately compound,
margins smooth; petals
showy, 5, partially fused
(keel); mirror symmetry;
blue, purple, white

Lupinus succulentus
FABACEAE

Arroyo Lupine

Open disturbed areas, roadsides, many communities; up to 4300 ft.; native

This spring-blooming annual has fingerlike leaflets that are wider near their tips and feel rubbery. The plant is succulent, meaning it feels fleshy, as though it is holding water. *Succus* means "juice," and *ulentus* means "an abundance of." The banner has a large white patch until the flower is pollinated, when the patch turns reddish purple. **Plant height to 3 ft.; leaves alternate, palmately compound, margins smooth; petals showy, 5, partially fused (keel); mirror symmetry; violet, blue, white**

Medicago sativa
FABACEAE

Alfalfa

Disturbed areas; up to 8000 ft.; non-native

Blooming from spring through autumn, this perennial herb has an upright growth form and is usually hairless. Its unique coiled fruits are smooth. Grown as livestock feed, it is often found growing near agricultural fields or roadsides. Its history of use starts in ancient Iran more than 2000 years ago. *Sativa* means "cultivated." **Plant height to 30 in.; leaves alternate, palmately compound, 3 leaflets, margins toothed at tip; flower clusters showy; petals 5, partially fused (keel); mirror symmetry; purple**

Psorothamnus arborescens
FABACEAE

Mojave Indigobush

Deserts; 400–6200 ft.; native

This thorny shrub grows on lower desert mountain slopes, flats, and washes. Blooming in spring, flowers often have red sepals and indigo petals, creating an almost unearthly color combination. The seed pods are distinctive, with large, warty glands. It is similar to Fremont's Indigobush (*P. fremontii*) but has larger fruit glands. **Plant height to 3 ft.; leaves alternate, pinnately lobed to compound, margins smooth; flower clusters showy; petals 5, partially fused (keel); mirror symmetry; blue**

Trifolium gracilentum
FABACEAE

Pinpoint Clover

Woodlands, chaparral, grasslands; up to 5900 ft.; native

Though this spring-blooming annual can vary in size, growth habit, and flower number and color, its flowers always droop with age, forming points at their tips. This feature gives the species its common name. To distinguish it from Rancheria Clover, check the calyx lobes—they are smooth, rather than bristly. **Plant height to 10 in.; leaves alternate, compound, 3 leaflets, margins toothed; flower clusters showy; petals small, 5, partially fused (keel); mirror symmetry; purple, magenta, with pink tips**

Trifolium variegatum
FABACEAE

Whitetip Clover

Coastal scrub, conifer forests, wetlands; up to 8200 ft; native

This annual clover flowers in spring and summer. It has white flower tips and a wheel-shaped structure (involucre) below the flowerhead. It is currently divided into three varieties: *major*, the showiest variety, has 10-plus flowers per head; *geminiflorum*, the smallest, has 1–5 flowers; and *variegatum* has 5–10 flowers. **Plant height to 20 in.; leaves alternate, compound, 3 leaflets, margins toothed; flower clusters showy; petals small, 5, partially fused (keel); mirror symmetry; purple, magenta, with white tips**

Trifolium willdenovii
FABACEAE

Tomcat Clover

Conifer forests, woodlands, chaparral; up to 8200 ft; native

A common clover, this variable, spring-blooming annual can be spotted along trails and is tolerant of harsh, serpentine environments. Generally, it can be distinguished by its narrow leaflets, though shapes may vary. The plant often turns reddish in color. Honey-scented flowerheads attract beneficial insects. **Plant height to 16 in.; leaves alternate, compound, 3 leaflets, margins toothed; flower clusters showy; petals small, 5, partially fused (keel); mirror symmetry; purple, pink**

Vicia americana
FABACEAE

American Vetch

Conifer forests; up to 7800 ft.; native

This vining, spring-blooming perennial has relatively large flowers. The vetches (*Vicia* spp.) are similar to sweet peas (*Lathyrus* spp.). However, *Lathyrus* species have usually flat styles that are hairy near the middle, whereas *Vicia* species have round styles that are hairy at the tip near the stigma, like a toothbrush. Plant height to 3 ft.; leaves alternate, pinnately compound, margins smooth or toothed at tip; petals showy, 5, partially fused (keel); mirror symmetry; purple fading to blue, white

Vicia sativa
FABACEAE

Common Vetch

Disturbed areas; up to 5200 ft.; non-native

This vining annual blooms in spring, with one to three flowers per cluster, attached directly to the stem (sessile). Each leaflet is tipped with a distinct tooth. The final leaflet is modified into a tendril that helps the plant climb. Common Vetch is considered a weed and grows in disturbed areas and roadsides. Plant stem length to 6 ft.; leaves alternate, pinnately compound, margins smooth; petals showy, 5, partially fused (keel); mirror symmetry; purple, red

Vicia villosa
FABACEAE

Winter Vetch

Disturbed areas; up to 6900 ft.; non-native

This vining annual forms showy clusters of
10 or more small flowers, arranged on one
side of a prominent stalk. The scientific name
references the hairiness of the upper stems
and leaves: *villosa* means "soft-hairy." Though
it blooms in spring and summer, it is called
Winter Vetch because it is more cold-hardy
than Common Vetch. **Plant stem length to
3 ft.; leaves alternate,
pinnately compound,
margins smooth; petals
showy, 5, partially fused
(keel); mirror symme-
try; purple**

Gentiana calycosa
GENTIANACEAE

Explorers' Gentian

Wet mountain meadows, streamsides; 4300–
12,800 ft.; native

Blooming in summer and early autumn,
this perennial herb has large flowers, up to 2
in. long, borne on short stems. Unlike most
gentians, it does not have a basal rosette,
and its leaves are ovate-rounded rather than
long-linear. This species likes to have its feet
wet, occurring in seeps and meadows. The
scientific name *calycosa*,
means "full-calyx." **Plant
height to 8 in.; leaves opposite, unlobed, margins
smooth; petals showy,
5, partially fused; radial
symmetry; blue, purple**

Gentianopsis simplex
GENTIANACEAE

Hiker's Fringed Gentian

Wet montane meadows; 3900–11,500 ft.; native

This perennial herb is a typical representative of the family, growing in moist, open areas at high elevations. Blooming in summer and early autumn, its flowers are borne singly on long stems. The flowers have distinctly fringed petal margins. It is similar to Sierra Gentian (*G. holopetala*) but has evenly green sepals as opposed to sepals with dark midribs. **Plant height to 16 in.; leaves opposite, unlobed, margins smooth; petals showy, 4, partially fused; radial symmetry; purple, blue**

Nemophila menziesii
HYDROPHYLLACEAE

Baby Blue Eyes

Grasslands, woodlands, meadows; up to 6200 ft.; native

Dense, showy displays of this annual are common in coastal areas and the foothills of the Sierra Nevada. Blooming in spring, its most typical form has blue flowers with white centers, but it can be quite variable. Variety *atomaria* has white flowers with black dots. Plants are usually hairy and have distinctly lobed leaves. **Plant height to 12 in.; leaves opposite, lobed, margins smooth; flowers showy, petals 5, partially fused; radial symmetry; blue with white center**

Phacelia campanularia
HYDROPHYLLACEAE

Desert Bluebell

Deserts; up to 7800 ft.; native

Blooming in late winter and spring, this unforgettable desert annual has large flowers up to 2 in long. Sprays of flowers among granite boulders delight photographers and botanists alike. The glandular trichomes can cause skin irritation. It is similar to California Bluebell (*P. minor*), but it has a less constricted flower tube opening. **Plant height to 2 ft.; leaves alternate, unlobed, margins toothed; flower clusters showy; petals 5, partially fused; radial symmetry; blue**

Phacelia ciliata
HYDROPHYLLACEAE

Great Valley Phacelia

Grasslands, shrublands; up to 600 ft.; native

This annual produces one of the most spectacular wildflower displays in California. When conditions are favorable, the clay soils of the Carrizo Plain are covered in blossoms. As the specific name implies, the leaves are ciliate with hairs around the edges. It blooms in early spring through summer, providing a much needed pollen source for bees. **Plant height to 22 in.; leaves alternate, compound with lobed leaflets, margins toothed; flower clusters showy; petals 5, partially fused; radial symmetry; blue**

Phacelia distans
HYDROPHYLLACEAE

Distant Phacelia

Openings in conifer forests, woodlands, chaparral; up to 8800 ft.; native

This spring-blooming annual has highly divided, fernlike leaves and showy flowers in a long, coiled cluster. The male parts, anthers and filaments, extend outside of the corolla tube. The foliage can be boiled and eaten as a green. Lacy phacelia (*P. tanacetifolia*) is similar but with a more compact inflorescence and longer filaments. **Plant height to 2.5 ft.; leaves alternate, dissected, margins toothed; flower clusters showy; petals 5, partially fused; radial symmetry; blue, lavender, white**

Pholistoma auritum
HYDROPHYLLACEAE

Blue Fiesta-flower

Dunes, shrublands, woodlands; 3800–7600 ft.; native

The foliage of this spring-blooming annual is coated in hairs and bristles, which enables it to attach to clothing. It has a distinctive winged leaf stalk (petiole). There are two subspecies: the smaller flowered form is rare in California, occurring only in the Sonoran Desert, and the widespread subspecies has larger flowers. **Plant height to 4 ft. (sprawling); leaves alternate, lobed, margins smooth; flower clusters showy; petals 5, partially fused; radial symmetry; blue**

Tricardia watsonii
HYDROPHYLLACEAE

Three Hearts

Deserts; 450–7500 ft.; native

This perennial herb usually grows under other shrubby species. Three of its five sepals are large and heart shaped, hence the name. Blooming in spring, flowers are white with purple around the flower opening. It does not produce grand wildflower displays, but it is a real desert gem if you can find it. **Plant height to 16 in.; leaves in basal rosette, unlobed, margins smooth; flower clusters showy; petals 5, partially fused; radial symmetry; white, purple**

Iris douglasiana
IRIDACEAE

Douglas Iris

Grasslands, especially near the coast; up to 700 ft.; native

This perennial herb has narrow, straplike basal leaves with parallel veins. Blooming in spring, multicolored flowers provide a floriferous feast for their preferred pollinators. Bees in particular hone in on blue, violet, and white. The genus name pays homage to the Greek goddess of rainbows. **Plant height to 2 ft.; leaves basal, unlobed, margins smooth; sepals and petals showy, 3 each, partially fused; radial symmetry; purple, pink, blue, white**

Iris hartwegii
IRIDACEAE

Rainbow Iris

Dry slopes and flats in woodlands, pine forests; 1300–7500 ft.; native

This perennial herb has a short floral tube and spreading leaves. The flower color is variable, from lavender to yellow, with dark veins. This iris goes dormant in the cold winter months, with leaves reemerging from underground parts in the spring. Impressively, four subspecies have been described within this California endemic. **Plant height to 16 in.; leaves basal, unlobed, margins smooth; sepals and petals showy, 3 each, partially fused; radial symmetry; lavender, yellow, maroon**

Iris macrosiphon
IRIDACEAE

Bowl-tube Iris

Dry slopes in oak or pine woodlands; up to 3300 ft.; native

Blooming in spring, this perennial herb has a long flower tube that reaches almost to the base of the leaves. Like all irises, it has an inferior ovary. Nestled among straplike leaves, its flower can be almost any color, from deep indigo-blue to lavender, or yellow to white. **Plant height to 1 ft.; leaves basal, unlobed, margins smooth; sepals and petals showy, 3 each, partially fused; radial symmetry; purple, white, yellow**

Iris missouriensis
IRIDACEAE

Western Blue Flag

Vernally wet, open areas; 3000–11,200 ft.; native

This spring-blooming perennial herb is one of the few native irises found in wet places. It has large, usually blue flowers with contrasting nectar guides that provide a visual cue to pollinators. This species is common throughout mountainous regions of Western North America, and it can also be found in low-elevation coastal areas. **Plant height to 18 in.; leaves alternate, unlobed, margins smooth; petals showy, 5, partially fused; radial symmetry; blue, rarely white**

Sisyrinchium bellum
IRIDACEAE

Western Blue-eyed Grass

Grasslands, woodlands; up to 7900 ft.; native

Blooming in spring, this perennial herb looks like a grass with a handsome blue flower on top. A yellow center guides bees toward a nectar reward. Tepals are tipped with a slender point. Flowers close at night and reopen with the sun. It is quite common in vernally moist areas throughout California and beyond. **Plant height to 2 ft.; leaves basal, unlobed, margins smooth; tepals showy, 6, free; radial symmetry; purple, violet**

Condea emoryi
LAMIACEAE

Desert Lavender

Deserts; up to 3300 ft.; native

This shrub blooms in the winter and spring. Distributed across the Southwest in desert washes, it is restricted to the southern deserts in California. The plant is covered in fine, white hairs. Until recently, Desert Lavender was in the genus *Hyptis*. Based on DNA evidence, plant scientists moved it into the genus *Condea*. **Plant height to 14 ft.; leaves opposite, unlobed, margins toothed; flower clusters showy; petals small, 5, partially fused; mirror symmetry; lavender**

Lepechinia calycina
LAMIACEAE

Woodbalm

Chaparral, woodlands; 500–3000 ft.; native

This shrub has a strong minty odor; some find it pleasant, others say overpowering. Its triangular evergreen leaves are hairy with a rough texture. Blooming in late spring and early summer, its tubular flowers are reminiscent of water spouts. It flourishes after fire for a period, before being crowded out by more robust species. **Plant height to 6 ft.; leaves opposite, unlobed, margins smooth or toothed; petals showy, 5, partially fused; mirror symmetry; white, lavender**

Mentha spicata
LAMIACEAE

Spearmint

Wetlands, riparian; up to 7700 ft.; non-native

Blooming in summer and fall, this perennial herb is native to Eurasia and is naturalized in much of the rest of the world. The leaves are mostly hairless, wrinkly, and have pointed tips; flowers grow in spikelike clusters. Its most distinguishing characteristic is its fragrance. It is widely used as a medicinal and culinary herb. **Plant height to 2 ft.; leaves opposite, unlobed, margins toothed; flower clusters showy; petals small, 5, partially fused; mirror symmetry; lavender, white**

Monardella breweri
LAMIACEAE

Brewer's Monardella

Woodlands, chaparral; up to 11,000 ft.; native

This spring- to autumn-blooming annual is fragrant and colorful, with purple stems and soft, linear leaves. Its inflorescence bracts are green with purple tips. The species is endemic to California. Recent research indicates that it is one of the species preferred by bumble bees after fire in upland communities. **Plant height to 2 ft.; leaves opposite, unlobed, margins smooth; flower clusters showy; petals small, 5, partially fused; mirror symmetry; calyx pink; flower purple**

Monardella odoratissima
LAMIACEAE

Mountain Coyote Mint

Rocky openings in sagebrush scrub, conifer forests; up to 13,500 ft.; native

This summer-blooming subshrub is native to mountainous regions of Western North America. It is low-growing and can form impressive floriferous mats. Its most distinctive characteristic is its intense minty fragrance. The oil glands responsible for the fragrance are often visible on its triangular leaves. **Plant height to 1.5 ft.; leaves opposite, unlobed, margins smooth; flower clusters showy; petals small, 5, partially fused; mirror symmetry; lavender, white**

Monardella villosa
LAMIACEAE

Coyote Mint

Coastal scrub, chaparral, woodlands, openings in montane forests; up to 4900 ft.; native

This summer-blooming, mat-forming subshrub has a woody base in older plants. It has narrowly triangular leaves that are covered with soft, white hairs, making the plant look gray. The specific name, *villosa*, means "soft hairs." Coyote Mint prefers rocky substrate and well-drained soils. Like most *Monardella* species, pollinators love it. **Plant height to 2 ft.; leaves opposite, unlobed, margins minutely toothed; flower clusters showy; petals small, 5, partially fused; mirror symmetry; lavender, pink, white**

Pogogyne douglasii
LAMIACEAE

Douglas' Mesamint

Vernal pools, swales; up to 3000 ft.; native

This spring- and summer-blooming annual has an erect growth form and hairless foliage that contrasts with its densely hairy flower clusters. Mesamints grow in vernal pools that fill with water during wet winter and spring seasons; they dry up via evaporation when the rains stop. This species occurs only in California. **Plant height to 18 in.; leaves opposite, unlobed; margins minutely toothed; flower clusters showy; petals 5, partially fused; mirror symmetry; purple**

Prunella vulgaris
LAMIACEAE

Self-heal

Moist, often disturbed areas in woodlands and forests; up to 8200 ft; native

This summer-blooming perennial herb has a less minty fragrance, but it does have the opposite leaves and square stems diagnostic of species in the mint family. Dense flower clusters have intensely maroon bracts and sepals, studded with violet flowers. Recent studies of diabetic mice have shown that extracts from Self-heal can reduce blood-sugar levels. **Plant height to 20 in.; leaves opposite, unlobed, margins smooth; flower clusters showy; petals 5, partially fused; mirror symmetry; violet, lavender**

Salvia carduacea
LAMIACEAE

Thistle Sage

Deserts, chaparral, grasslands; up to 4600 ft.; native

Blooming in spring, the flower clusters on this annual sage resemble cotton balls, adorned with spiny bracts and large, lavender flowers with fringed petal margins. The anthers protrude well beyond the corolla and have bright orange anther sacs. The entire effect resembles a dragon's head. **Plant height 10–24 in.; leaves opposite, lobed, margins toothed; flower clusters showy; petals 5, partially fused; radial symmetry; lavender, blue, white**

Salvia clevelandii
LAMIACEAE

Cleveland Sage

Chaparral; up to 4400 ft.; native

This summer-blooming shrub has a mounded growth form and elliptical, gray-green, wrinkled leaves. Leaf bases narrow gradually to the petiole. Its sweet fragrance makes it one of the most attractive of all the mints in California. The flowers do not self-pollinate, because the stigma becomes receptive well after the pollen has been removed by pollinators. **Plant height to 5 ft.; leaves opposite, unlobed, margins minutely toothed; flower clusters showy; petals 5, partially fused; mirror symmetry; blue, violet**

Salvia columbariae
LAMIACEAE

Chia

Chaparral, woodlands; up to 8200 ft; native

Blooming in spring, this annual grows in dry, sunny spots throughout much of California and beyond. Each stem usually has a few flower clusters subtended by prickly maroon bracts. Chia is similar to Thistle Sage, but it is not wooly. Its documented uses are extensive. The nutritious seeds can be eaten directly or made into a drink. **Plant height to 20 in.;** leaves opposite, lobed, margins smooth; flower clusters showy; petals 5, partially fused; mirror symmetry; blue

Salvia dorrii
LAMIACEAE

Desert Sage

Deserts; 1500–10,500 ft.; native

This spring-blooming shrub forms low mounds of silver-gray foliage with spoon-shaped leaves. The flower clusters are surrounded by bright pink bracts. In California, three varieties have been described based on bract hairiness and petiole shape. Variety *pilosa*, which has hairy magenta bracts, is the most common. It grows in alluvial fans and washes. **Plant height to 2 ft.;** leaves opposite, un-lobed, margins smooth; flower clusters showy; petals 5, partially fused; mirror symmetry; blue, purple, pink

Salvia leucophylla
LAMIACEAE

Purple Sage

Chaparral, coastal sage; up to 4100 ft.; native

This upright, sprawling shrub has leaves that are wrinkled and white on both sides. Blooming in early summer, its flower has a long, narrow corolla tube and equal-length upper and lower corolla lips. Purple Sage and Cleveland Sage (*Salvia clevelandii*) are similar, though the latter has bluer flowers and a short lower corolla lip. **Plant height to 5 ft.; leaves opposite, unlobed, margins minutely toothed; flower clusters showy; petals 5, partially fused; mirror symmetry; lavender, pink**

Salvia mellifera
LAMIACEAE

Black Sage

Chaparral, coastal sage scrub; up to 4400 ft.; native

This spring- and summer-blooming shrub has dark green, wrinkled leaves with a hairy lower surface. The middle lobe of the flower's lower lip (petal) looks like a whale tail. As an adaptation to California's regular summer heat and drought, its leaves curl up, making the whole plant look dark, hence the name Black Sage. **Plant height to 6 ft.; leaves opposite, unlobed, margins minutely toothed; petals showy, 5, partially fused; mirror symmetry; pale blue, lavender, white**

Salvia pachyphylla
LAMIACEAE

Blue Sage

Pinyon–juniper woodlands and pine forests; 3900–10,000 ft.; native

This shrub blooms from spring through fall and is found on dry, rocky slopes and well-drained flats at high elevations through the Desert Southwest. The contrast of its silver-gray foliage with the violet flower clusters is almost unearthly. *Pachyphylla* means "thick-leaf," which describes its leathery leaves. It is similar to Desert Sage but has larger flowers. **Plant height to 3 ft.; leaves opposite, unlobed, margins smooth; flower clusters showy; petals 5, partially fused; mirror symmetry; lavender, pink**

Salvia sonomensis
LAMIACEAE

Creeping Sage

Chaparral, woodlands, mixed evergreen forests; up to 6600 ft.; native

Creeping Sage forms massive, gray-green mats in the understory of chaparral and near rocky forest edges and road cuts. This subshrub is endemic to California and can be very abundant where it occurs. Blooming in spring and summer, the flower clusters hold small, blue-fringed flowers surrounded by sepals with maroon margins. **Plant height to 1 ft., spread 15 ft.; leaves opposite, unlobed, margins minutely toothed; flower clusters showy; petals 5, partially fused; mirror symmetry; lavender, white**

Scutellaria mexicana
LAMIACEAE

Paperbag Bush

Deserts; up to 6200 ft.; native

The young stems of this shrub are gray-green, turning brown with age. Blooming in spring, the flower's calyx lobe becomes inflated as the fruits mature, resembling paper bags. It has a distinct architecture: its lateral shoots are opposite each other at right angles to the main stem. This desert species loses its leaves during summer drought. **Plant height to 4 ft.;** leaves opposite, unlobed, margins smooth; flower clusters showy; petals 5, partially fused; mirror symmetry; purple, white

Scutellaria tuberosa
LAMIACEAE

Common Skullcap

Conifer forests, woodlands, chaparral; up to 4800 ft.; native

This weak-stemmed perennial herb has oval leaves, and the entire plant is hairy, even the flowers. It becomes abundant after fires in open vegetation. In early spring, stems sprout from underground tubers. In the heat of summer, its aboveground parts dry up, leaving no trace of the plant until the next spring. **Plant height to 10 in.;** leaves opposite, unlobed, margins toothed infrequently; flower clusters showy; petals 5, partially fused; mirror symmetry; blue with white nectar guides

Trichostema lanatum
LAMIACEAE

Wooly Bluecurls

Chaparral; up to 4100 ft.; native

This spring-blooming shrub has a pungent odor and striking flower clusters. Its linear, deep green leaves are hairless above and hairy below. The hairy sepals range from magenta to white. The long, shiny style and stamens extend well beyond the blue corolla, forming a strong arch. Its sticky foliage can be irritating to the skin. **Plant height to 5 ft.; leaves opposite, unlobed; margins smooth; flower clusters showy; petals 5, partially fused; mirror symmetry; blue, rarely white**

Trichostema lanceolatum
LAMIACEAE

Vinegar Weed

Woodlands, chaparral; up to 7200 ft.; native

This summer- and fall-blooming annual, true to its common name, smells strongly of vinegar when touched. It is commonly found in dry, disturbed areas. The odiferous oils it produces reduce germination and growth of other seedlings, thereby reducing competition. The specific name refers to its narrow, lance-shaped leaves. **Plant height to 3 ft.; leaves opposite, unlobed, margins smooth; flower clusters showy; petals small, 5, partially fused; mirror symmetry; blue**

Pholisma arenarium
LENNOACEAE

Desert Christmas Tree

Dunes, chaparral, deserts; up to 6400 ft.; native

Although this perennial herb is not the most common of species, it is too interesting to pass up. Because it is fully parasitic and cannot perform photosynthesis, it gets all of its nutrients from other plants, usually *Eriodictyon* species or various shrubby asters. In spring and summer, its short flowering stem emerges from the sand. **Plant height to 1 ft.; leaves alternate or absent, margins smooth; flower clusters showy; petals small, 5, fused; radial symmetry; deep purple**

Calochortus coeruleus
LILIACEAE

Beavertail Grass

Gravelly openings in conifer woodlands and forests; 2000–8200 ft.; native

This spring-blooming perennial herb is not really a grass. It is similar to Tolmie Star-tulip, but it often has more hairs along the petal margins and the stems are less likely to be branched. Both species are variable and sometimes only a specialist can distinguish between them. Beavertail Grass grows at higher elevations, seldom below 2000 ft. **Plant height to 6 in.; leaves alternate, unlobed, margins smooth; petals showy, 3, free; radial symmetry; lavender, white**

Calochortus splendens
LILIACEAE

Splendid Mariposa Lily

Grasslands, conifer forests; up to 9200 ft.; native

Blooming in late spring and summer, this tall perennial herb has large, bowl-shaped flowers. Long hairs appear on the lower half of the flower, with a purple or dark area often at the petal base. Stamens are purple. It is similar to Plain Mariposa Lily, except its sepals curl outward and it has no green petal stripe. **Plant height 2–3 ft.; leaves alternate, unlobed, margins smooth; petals showy, 3, free; radial symmetry; lavender, pink, white**

Calochortus tolmiei
LILIACEAE

Tolmie Star-tulip

Grasslands, woodlands, conifer forests; up to 6600 ft.; native

Dense, long, furlike hairs on purplish petals are striking on this spring-flowering perennial herb. The hairs are absent from the base, where a dark purple patch appears. Stamens are purple. The nodding seed pods are sharply triangular in cross section. These plants often nestle among grasses. **Plant height to 16 in.; leaves basal, unlobed, margins smooth; petals showy, 3, free; radial symmetry; lavender, white**

Linum bienne
LINACEAE

Pale Flax

Coastal grasslands, disturbed areas; up to 3300 ft.; non-native

This garden escapee is a biennial to short-lived perennial with long, narrow leaves, slender stems, and dark veins on the petals. Flowers are receptive for one day, and then the petals fall off. The species is monecious, meaning that each flower has male or female parts, not both, but both kinds of flowers occur on each individual plant. **Plant height to 2 ft.; leaves alternate, unlobed, margins smooth; petals showy, 5, free; radial symmetry; white, light blue**

Linum lewisii
LINACEAE

Prairie Flax

Dry sunny openings in conifer forests, woodlands; up to 12,000 ft.; native

This spring- and summer-blooming perennial herb has large flowers on wispy stems. Its petals are delicate and fall off a short time after the flower opens. The seeds of Prairie Flax are an important food source for birds and small mammals. A pollination study indicates that bumble bees are its most effective pollinators, but smaller insects are also important. **Plant height to 3 ft.; leaves alternate, unlobed, margins smooth; petals showy, 5, free; radial symmetry; blue, white**

Eriodictyon californicum
NAMACEAE

California Yerba Santa

Chaparral, woodlands; up to 6000 ft.; native

This spring- and early summer–blooming shrub is a common species in chaparral communities. The plant has narrow, dark blue–green, leathery leaves that conserve water. Its coiled clusters of pale lavender flowers attracts butterflies and bees. Few plants have more documented medicinal uses, from pain treatment to asthma relief. **Plant height to 6 ft.; leaves alternate, un-lobed, margins toothed; flower clusters showy; petals 5, partially fused; radial symmetry; lavender, white**

Eriodictyon parryi
NAMACEAE

Poodle-dog Bush

Chaparral; 400–8000 ft.; native

Blooming in late spring through early summer, this shrub is relatively uncommon until after a fire. It then blankets hillsides with its shaggy foliage. During summer drought, its leaves curl in a way that is reminiscent of a poodle's coat, hence the common name. It has attractive flowers, but beware! Touching this plant causes a severe rash. **Plant height to 10 ft.; leaves alternate, unlobed, margins toothed; flower clusters showy; petals 5, partially fused; radial symmetry; blue, pink**

Aphyllon californicum
OROBANCHACEAE

California Aphyllon

Coastal strand, conifer forests, deserts; up to
8200 ft; native

This summer-blooming, parasitic perennial does not have true leaves and looks like a
mound of bright flowers popping out of the
ground. It is completely parasitic and lacks
chlorophyll, so it cannot make its own food
via photosynthesis. Instead, it has specialized structures called haustoria that tap into
the roots of neighboring
plants. **Plant height to 14
in.; leaves absent; flower
clusters showy; petals 5,
partially fused; mirror
symmetry; purple, white,
pink, rarely yellow**

Castilleja densiflora
OROBANCHACEAE

Dense-flower Paintbrush

Grasslands; up to 5200 ft.; native

This spring-blooming, erect annual is similar
to Valley Tassels, but its bract tips are usually pink instead of white. Like all species of
Castilleja, it is hemiparasitic and gets carbohydrates through root connections with other
plants. Three subspecies are recognized based
on calyx size and flower color variation. **Plant
height to 16 in.; leaves alternate, unlobed or
lobed, margins smooth;
bracts showy; petals 5,
fused; mirror symmetry;
pink, lavender, white**

Castilleja exserta
OROBANCHACEAE

Purple Owl's Clover

Shrublands, woodlands, grasslands; up to 5200 ft.; native

This common annual species forms large displays in grassland habits. Blooming in spring, it has short, sticky hairs and narrow leaves. Although it is called Purple Owl's Clover, the showy bracts can be white, yellow, pink, or purple. If you look closely, you can see the upper flower petal is long and the style is straight. **Plant height to 18 in.; leaves alternate, dissected, margins smooth; bracts showy; petals 5, fused; mirror symmetry; purple, pink, white**

Castilleja lemmonii
OROBANCHACEAE

Lemmon's Paintbrush

Moist meadows; 4900–12,1000 ft.; native

This summer-blooming perennial herb grows in moist places in California and into Nevada. It has unbranched stems, glandular hairs, and linear leaves. The erect flower clusters have showy pink bracts and inconspicuous green or cream-colored flowers. The genus is named after Domingo Castillejo Muñoz, an 18th-century Spanish botanist and surgeon. **Plant height to 8 in.; leaves alternate, unlobed or lobed, margins smooth; bracts showy; petals 5, fused; mirror symmetry; bracts pink; flowers pale yellow-green**

Kopsiopsis strobilacea
OROBANCHACEAE

California Ground-cone

Mixed evergreen forests, woodlands, chaparral; up to 9800 ft.; native

This parasitic perennial herb blooms in late spring. California Ground Cone resembles a pinecone sticking out of the ground. It does not have true leaves, and the aboveground parts of the plant include a thick, red-brown stem that produces purple flowers. It is a parasite that gets its nutrients from other plants, usually manzanita or madrone. **Plant height to 7 in.; leaves absent; flower clusters showy; petals 5, partially fused; mirror symmetry; purple, red, pink**

Oxalis oregana
OXALIDACEAE

Redwood Sorrel

Conifer forests; up to 3300 ft.; native

Growing in the dark, moist understory along the coast of Western North America, this perennial herb blooms in spring. Its distinctive leaves have three heart-shaped leaflets. Superficially, it resembles a clover, but its flowers are different from clovers. If stressed by drought or too much light, the leaflets will fold to protect themselves. **Plant height to 6 in.; leaves in basal rosette, compound, 3 leaflets, margins smooth; flowers small, petals showy, 5, free; radial symmetry; lavender, pink, white**

Antirrhinum kelloggii
PLANTAGINACEAE

Kellogg's Snapdragon

Chaparral; up to 4300 ft.; native

This spring-blooming annual occurs along the coast from Central California into Baja California. It is mostly hairless and has tendril-like flower stalks that enable the plant to climb among other species. The lower, bulbous flower petal is mottled white with purple veins. As is true for many snapdragons, the species becomes more common after fire. **Plant height to 3 ft.; leaves alternate, unlobed, margins smooth; flowers small, petals showy, 5, partially fused; mirror symmetry; blue, purple**

Antirrhinum nuttallianum
PLANTAGINACEAE

Nuttall's Snapdragon

Chaparral; up to 4300 ft.; native

This species is an annual or, rarely, a biennial. The leaves are opposite at the base of the stem and transition to alternate higher up. The upper petals resemble rabbit ears, similar to those of Coulter's Snapdragon, and the three-lobed lower lip has white splotches. Blooming in spring and summer, the flowers are usually lavender but can be magenta. **Plant height 1–3 ft.; leaves alternate, unlobed, margins smooth; petals showy, 5, partially fused; mirror symmetry; lavender, magenta**

Antirrhinum vexillocalyculatum
PLANTAGINACEAE

Wiry Snapdragon

Gravelly slopes in chaparral, grasslands; up to 6600 ft.; native

This summer-blooming annual has a weak upright stem and usually uses other vegetation for support. Its flower clusters have sticky hairs, and the calyx lobes are unequal in length. Flower petals are partially fused, with an upper lip and a prominent lower lip. **Plant height to 5 ft.; leaves alternate, opposite, unlobed, margins smooth; petals showy, 5, partially fused; mirror symmetry; purple, lavender, white**

Collinsia heterophylla
PLANTAGINACEAE

Innocence

Woodlands, chaparral; 1000–5600 ft.; native

This spring- and summer-blooming annual has narrow to triangular leaves and is common throughout California and Northern Baja California. Flowers are arranged in a tower of dense whorls, similar in shape to a pagoda. The upper lip (petals) is usually white or light colored with purple markings, and the lower lip is solid purple. **Plant height 1–2 ft.; leaves opposite, unlobed, margins smooth or toothed; flower clusters showy; petals 5, partially fused; mirror symmetry; purple, white, red**

Collinsia parryi
PLANTAGINACEAE

Parry's Blue-eyed Mary

Chaparral; 1600–5200 ft.; native

This spring-blooming annual has a lanky stem covered in long hairs. It is endemic to the mountains of Southern California. Unusual for a *Collinsia* species, the flowers are not densely clustered. The flower stem (pedicel) is usually longer than the calyx, and the petal edges have minute hairs. **Plant height to 16 in.; leaves opposite, unlobed, margins minutely toothed or smooth; petals showy, 5, partially fused; mirror symmetry; purple**

Collinsia sparsiflora
PLANTAGINACEAE

Few-flowered Collinsia

Grasslands, woodlands, chaparral; up to 3900 ft.; native

This spring-blooming annual has light pink flowers with two white petals. The specific name, *sparsiflora*, describes its low-density flower clusters. The flower stalks are usually longer than the calyx. It has long, sparse hairs on its filaments and lower petal lobes. Like all *Collinsia* species, the middle lower flower petal is folded into a keel shape. **Plant height to 1 ft.; leaves opposite, unlobed, margins smooth; petals showy, 5, partially fused; mirror symmetry; lavender, pink, white**

Nuttallanthus texanus
PLANTAGINACEAE

Blue Toadflax

Grasslands, woodlands, chaparral, pine forests; up to 5900 ft.; native

This erect, slender, spring-blooming annual (rarely a biennial) is native from Florida to California. The plant is mostly hairless, but some glandular hairs are associated with the flower clusters. Each small flower has a slender, recurved spur that extends from the rear of the corolla. Spurs hold nectar as a reward for pollinators. **Plant height to 2 ft.; leaves opposite, unlobed, margins smooth; flowers small, petals showy, 5, partially fused; mirror symmetry; purple**

Penstemon davidsonii
PLANTAGINACEAE

Davidson's Beardtongue

Montane to alpine outcrops and talus; 6600–12,300 ft.; native

This low-growing shrub blooms in summer throughout the high country. Its sterile stamen is densely covered with short, yellow hairs and its anthers are white-wooly. In Western North America, three varieties are recognized based on flower size and leaf margin characters. Only variety *davidsonii*, which has rounded leaf tips, occurs in California. **Plant height to 4 in.; leaves opposite, unlobed, margins smooth or toothed; petals showy, 5, partially fused; mirror symmetry; blue, purple, pink**

Penstemon heterophyllus
PLANTAGINACEAE

Foothill Penstemon

Conifer forests, woodlands, chaparral; 160–6200 ft.; native

This spring- and summer-blooming perennial is endemic to California. The color of a single flower is difficult to characterize, with electric blue, purple, and pink hues intermingling. A single, hairless, infertile stamen is visible just at the bottom of the corolla opening. It is easy to grow and attracts bees, making it a popular choice in native gardens. **Plant height to 3 ft.; leaves opposite, unlobed, margins smooth; petals showy, 5, partially fused; mirror symmetry; blue, pink, purple**

Penstemon rydbergii
PLANTAGINACEAE

Meadow Beardtongue

Montane meadows and streambanks; 3300–11,800 ft.; native

The flowers of this summer-blooming perennial are grouped in clusters along the stem. Each flower has a hairy, sterile stamen and lower corolla lip. Three varieties have been described across its distribution in Western North America. Only variety *oreocharis* occurs in California. **Plant height to 2 ft.; leaves opposite, unlobed, margins smooth; petals showy, 5, partially fused; mirror symmetry; blue, pink, purple**

Penstemon speciosus
PLANTAGINACEAE

Royal Beardtongue

Deserts, dry openings in conifer forests; 2800–12,400 ft.; native

This spring- and summer-blooming perennial herb has narrow, leathery leaves. Flowers are blue with purple tubes. This beardtongue can be hairless, but it usually has short yellow hairs just at the tip of its sterile stamen. The flower color can be variable, usually with a light area around the corolla tube opening and striped with pollinator guides. **Plant height 2–24 in.; leaves opposite, unlobed, margins smooth; petals showy, 5, partially fused; mirror symmetry; blue, pink, purple**

Penstemon spectabilis
PLANTAGINACEAE

Showy Penstemon

Chaparral; 330–5900 ft.; native

The distribution of this spring-blooming perennial herb extends into Baja California. The plant has distinctive leaves that fuse around the stem, and its staminode is hairless. It is one of the remarkable species that causes "penstemania," an affliction found among gardeners who become enamored with this special group of plants. **Plant height 2–4 ft.; leaves opposite, unlobed, margins toothed; petals showy, 5, partially fused; mirror symmetry; blue, pink, purple**

Veronica americana
PLANTAGINACEAE

American Speedwell

Wetlands; up to 10,800 ft.; native

This summer-blooming perennial herb has a wide native range that includes Asia and North America. It grows in streams and in moist soils. The plant resembles a mint, but its stems are rounded instead of square. Although some sources say it is edible, one of its documented medical uses is to induce vomiting. **Plant height 2–20 in.; leaves opposite, unlobed, margins toothed; petals inconspicuous, 4, partially fused; mirror symmetry (subtle); blue, lavender**

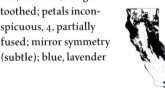

Limonium californicum
PLUMBAGINACEAE

Marsh Rosemary

Coastal wetlands; up to 150 ft.; native

This summer-blooming perennial occurs from Oregon through Baja California. The hairy sepals are white-tipped and the petals are purple or lavender. A handful of non-native *Limonium* species have naturalized in California: Statice (*L. sinuatum*) is commonly used in flower arrangements and has bright blue sepals, white petals, and winged stems. **Plant height to 18 in.; leaves in basal rosette, unlobed, margins smooth; flower clusters showy; petals 5, partially fused; radial symmetry; purple, lavender**

Allophyllum gilioides
POLEMONIACEAE

Dense False Gillyflower

Conifer forests, woodlands; 700–9500 ft.; native

This variable annual blooms in spring and summer. It has narrow leaves and dark flowers, and its short stalks are minutely glandular. Two subspecies are recognized in California based on the density of flowers. The flowers of subspecies *violaceum* are loosely clustered, whereas those of subspecies *gilioides* are dense. It prefers open, sandy habitats. **Plant height to 16 in.; leaves basal, alternate, dissected, margins smooth; flowers small, petals showy, 5, partially fused; radial symmetry; blue, purple**

Eriastrum densifolium
POLEMONIACEAE

Giant Woolystar

Many communities; up to 9500 ft.; native

Blooming in late spring and summer, this perennial herb has beautiful, funnel-shaped flowers and dense leaves. *Densifolium* means "dense leaves." Five subspecies have been described within this variable and wide-ranging species. The Santa Ana River Woolystar (subsp. *sanctorum*) is listed as endangered and is limited to Riverside and San Bardion Counties. **Plant height 10–20 in.; leaves alternate, unlobed to lobed, margins smooth; flower clusters showy; petals 5, partially fused; radial symmetry; blue, lavender**

Eriastrum pluriflorum
POLEMONIACEAE

Tehachapi Woolystar

Conifer forests, chaparral, deserts; up to 6600 ft.; native

This annual has a mass of trumpet-shaped flowers surrounded by spiny bracts covered in dense, cobwebby hairs. Blooming in spring and summer, the flower throat is often yellow to red and the stamens are visible past the corolla. Subspecies *pluriflorum* is most common and has showy flowers of almost an inch long. **Plant height to 13 in.; leaves alternate, un-lobed to lobed, margins smooth; flower clusters showy; petals 5, partially fused; radial symmetry; blue, white**

Eriastrum sapphirinum
POLEMONIACEAE

Sapphire Woolystar

Woodlands, chaparral; 2300–8900 ft.; native

The specific name means "sapphire blue." Blooming in spring and summer, the flowers of this annual come in several shades of blue, though, rarely, they may be white. Unlike other *Eriastrum* species, Sapphire Woolystar flowers can have mirror symmetry. The flower throat is yellow or white, sometimes with purple, zigzaged pollinator guides. **Plant height to 16 in.; leaves alternate, unlobed to lobed, margins smooth; flower clusters showy; petals 5, partially fused; radial or mirror symmetry; blue, white, yellow**

Eriastrum wilcoxii
POLEMONIACEAE

Wilcox's Woolystar

Deserts; up to 9500 ft.; native

This upright annual can be densely hairy to almost hairless. Leaves can be unlobed or may have up to seven lobes near the base of the plant. Flowers bloom in late spring through summer, with visible stamens emerging from the funnel-shaped blossoms. It is widely distributed, extending into Idaho and Wyoming. **Plant height to 1 ft.; leaves alternate, unlobed to lobed, margins smooth; flowers small; petals showy, 5, partially fused; radial symmetry; blue, white**

Gilia capitata
POLEMONIACEAE

Bluehead Gilia

Woodlands, conifer forests, shrublands; up to 7900 ft.; native

The specific name, *capitatus*, means "head-like," referring to the spherical flower clusters, which can include dozens of flowers. Eight subspecies are recognized by various characters, including whether the area just below the head is hairless, glandular, or white-hairy. This annual blooms prolifically from spring through summer. **Plant height to 3 ft.; leaves basal, alternate, dissected, margins toothed; flower clusters showy; petals 5, partially fused; radial symmetry; blue-violet, white**

Gilia tricolor
POLEMONIACEAE

Bird's-eye Gilia

Woodlands, grasslands; 300–5000 ft.; native

This lovely annual can cover entire hillsides with masses of purple-tinted flowers. Blooming in spring and summer, flowers are arranged in open to dense clusters, with yellow to orange centers and large purple spots. The stigma, style, and stamens—tipped with blue pollen—protrude from the flower. It is popular in wildflower mixes. **Plant height to 15 in.; leaves basal, alternate, lobed, margins smooth; flower clusters showy; flowers small, petals 5, partially fused; radial symmetry; blue, violet**

Linanthus parryae
POLEMONIACEAE

Parry's Linanthus

Deserts; up to 6600 ft.; native

In spring, these small, tufted annuals are covered with large, white or blue-purple, funnel-shaped flowers. Some populations tend toward one color or the other, though most populations have a mixture of the two. White flowers produce more fruit in wet years, and blue flowers produce more fruit in dry years. **Plant height to 4 in.; leaves opposite, lobed, margins smooth; petals showy, 5, partially fused; radial symmetry; blue, white**

Navarretia pubescens
POLEMONIACEAE

Downy Pincushion Plant

Woodlands, chaparral; up to 6100 ft.; native

This prickly, glandular annual generally has a single, upright stem. Jewel-like blooms appear on the plant in spring and summer—the protruding, white-tipped anthers almost sparkling against the darker throats of the blue-purple flowers. The specific name and common name both refer to the short, soft hairs on the leaves and stems. **Plant height 6–13 in.; leaves alternate, lobed, margins smooth or toothed; flower clusters showy; petals 5, partially fused; mirror symmetry; blue-purple**

Polemonium eximium
POLEMONIACEAE

Sky Pilot

Alpine; 9800–13,800 ft.; native

This lofty perennial herb is a high-elevation specialist. It has small, sticky, deeply lobed leaflets covered in glandular, aromatic hairs. Sky Pilot is endemic to the Sierra Nevada. Blooming in summer, the short-lived, blue-purple flowers reportedly have a urine-like odor that attracts fly pollinators. **Plant height 4–15 in.; leaves basal, compound, lobed leaflets, margins smooth; petals showy, 5, partially fused; radial symmetry; blue, purple**

Polemonium occidentale
POLEMONIACEAE

Western Polemonium

Conifer forests, riparian; 3000–10,800 ft.; native

The stem of this perennial herb is hairless below and glandular above. Blooming in summer, the flowers form an open cluster and have conspicuous sexual parts that extend beyond the flower. It can tolerate dry areas but is most commonly found in habitats with moist soils. *Occidentale* means "western," which describes its North American distribution. **Plant height 6–36 in.; leaves alternate, pinnately compound, margins smooth; petals showy, 5, partially fused; radial symmetry; blue, white**

Polemonium pulcherrimum
POLEMONIACEAE

Jacob's Ladder

Alpine talus; 7900–12,100 ft.; native

The flowers of this summer-blooming, mat-forming perennial herb have a skunky odor. The leaflets are quite regular and resemble the rungs of a ladder. *Polemonium pulcherrimum* var. *pulcherrimum* is widely distributed up to Alaska and has blue-purple flowers, whereas variety *shastense* is restricted to Northern California and has pink-tinged flowers. **Plant height to 12 ft.; leaves basal, pinnately compound; margins smooth; petals showy, 5, partially fused; radial symmetry; blue, white, pink**

Aconitum columbianum
RANUNCULACEAE

Monkshood

Conifer forests; 1000–11,500 ft.; native

The erect stem of this perennial herb produces impressive flower clusters up to 2 ft. long in summer. Within the showy, blue-purple sepal are small petals. This plant is super toxic! If ingested, it can be fatal to humans and livestock. Subspecies *viviparum* has small bulblets in upper axils, which fall off and become new plants. **Plant height to 5 ft.; leaves alternate, lobed, margins toothed; sepals showy, 5, free; mirror symmetry; blue-purple, rarely white**

Delphinium glaucum
RANUNCULACEAE

Sierra Larkspur

Wet thickets and streambanks; up to 12,000 ft.; native

This perennial herb prefers moist soils. In summer, when in bloom, the plant can be up to 6 ft. tall. The bright blue spurred sepals are showy and the petals are relatively inconspicuous. It is native to Western North America. In Canada, seed sales are banned because the plant is a leading cause of cattle poisoning. **Plant height to 8 ft.; leaves alternate, lobed, margins toothed; sepals showy, 5, free; mirror symmetry; deep purple, blue**

Delphinium parryi
RANUNCULACEAE

San Bernardino Larkspur

Chaparral, desert scrub, juniper woodlands; up to 5600 ft.; native

This spring-blooming perennial herb has two distinct leaf forms. Lower on the stem, leaf lobes are broad; they become more narrowly divided toward the stem tip. Five subspecies are recognized based on leaf, flower, and habitat differences. The genus name is derived from the Greek word for dolphin, in reference to the arched flower buds. **Plant height to 2 ft.; leaves alternate, lobed, margins toothed; sepals showy, 5, free; mirror symmetry; sepals and petals deep purple, upper petals white**

Delphinium patens
RANUNCULACEAE

Zigzag Larkspur

Conifer forests, woodlands, chaparral; 980–9200 ft.; native

This spring-blooming perennial herb can have zigzagging stems, hence the common name. Not all stems are zigzagged, however, and leaf characters are necessary for identification. The leaves have up to five lobes. Like all larkspurs, the sepals form the showy part of the flower. The small inner petals are white with blue streaks. **Plant height 4–20 in.; leaves alternate, lobed, margins toothed; sepals showy, 5, free; mirror symmetry; deep purple, blue**

Ceanothus lemmonii
RHAMNACEAE

Lemmon's Ceanothus

Woodlands; 1200–2500 ft.; native

This shrub with whitish branches and small green leaves may be easily overlooked throughout the year, but when it blooms in spring, the rich flowers make it a standout woodland beauty. Look closely and you will see the five yellow anthers, like tiny antennae, extending above each flower. This plant is named for 19th-century botanist J. G. Lemmon. **Plant height to 6 ft.; leaves alternate, unlobed, margins toothed; flower clusters showy; petals 5, free; radial symmetry; blue, purple**

Ceanothus leucodermis
RHAMNACEAE

Chaparral Whitethorn

Chaparral, woodlands; 900–7000 ft.; native

This spring-blooming shrub forms impenetrable thickets in woodlands and chaparral areas. Prominent thorns occur at the end of each skeletal white branchlet. A stunning display of floral color and fragrance attracts pollinators, including bees, birds, and butterflies. Hard to imagine, but many ungulates, such as deer, forage on the thorny branches. **Plant height to 12 ft.; leaves alternate, unlobed, margins smooth; flower clusters showy; petals 5, free; radial symmetry; pale blue, white**

Thamnosma montana
RUTACEAE

Turpentine Broom

Deserts; up to 6800 ft.; native

This perennial herb looks like a mass of bare stems most of the year, because it loses its tiny leaves in response to drought stress. Small purple flowers bloom in spring and develop into two-lobed fruits that resemble a pair of tiny limes. In fact, Turpentine Broom is one of three species in the citrus family native to California. **Plant height 1–2 ft.; leaves alternate, unlobed, margins smooth; flowers small, petals showy, 5, free; radial symmetry; deep purple**

Solanum elaeagnifolium
SOLANACEAE

Silverleaf Nightshade

Disturbed areas; up to 4000 ft.; non-native

The dense, star-shaped hairs on the leaves and stems of this perennial herb give the plant a silvery appearance. Flowers bloom in summer and fall, with yellow stamens and pistils that are tightly clustered in the centers. It produces toxic red-orange berries. The California Department of Food and Agriculture considers it a noxious weed. **Plant height to 1 ft.; leaves alternate, unlobed, margins wavy; petals showy, 5, partially fused; radial symmetry; purple, blue**

Solanum xanti
SOLANACEAE

Chaparral Nightshade

Conifer forests, woodlands, chaparral; up to 8900 ft.; native

The stamens of this perennial herb form a tight circle around the carpel. Flowers bloom in spring and summer. Each of the corolla lobes has two white-margined green spots at its base. This plant, especially its fruits, contains solanine, a toxic chemical that is common in the nightshade family and causes gastrointestinal and neurological problems when consumed. **Plant height 1–3 ft.; leaves alternate, unlobed, margins smooth; petals showy, 5, fused; radial symmetry; blue, lavender**

Brodiaea coronaria
THEMIDACEAE

Crown Brodiaea

Grasslands, vernal pools, oak woodlands; 2500 ft.; native

The starchy underground bulbs of this low-growing perennial herb can be eaten raw. Blooming in spring, the flowers have three sterile stamens (staminodes) alternating with three fertile stamens. The flower cluster is an umbel with long pedicels. The flat or rolled-in staminodes lean in toward the stamens but are not pressed against them. **Plant height 4–12 in.; leaves basal, unlobed, margins smooth; tepals showy, 6, partially fused; radial symmetry; purple, lavender**

Brodiaea elegans
THEMIDACEAE

Harvest Brodiaea

Grasslands, woodlands, chaparral; up to 8000 ft.; native

This perennial herb blooms in late spring when similar species are already in fruit. Look closely into the center of the flower, and you will see white, sterile stamens (staminodes) that are held away from the true stamens. Two other species, Crown Brodiaea and Dwarf Brodiaea, are similar, but they have subtle flower size and shape differences. **Plant height 6–18 in.; leaves basal, unlobed, margins smooth; tepals showy, 6, partially fused; radial symmetry; blue, purple**

Brodiaea terrestris
THEMIDACEAE

Dwarf Brodiaea

Grassland, woodlands; up to 1500 ft.; native

Blooming in late spring and summer, this perennial herb is similar to Harvest Brodiaea, but it has shorter flowering stems. The specific name means "on land" and refers to flowers that seem to grow straight out of the ground. Subspecies *kernensis* has violet sterile stamens and long-flowering stems relative to subspecies *terrestris*. **Plant height 4–10 in.; leaves basal, unlobed, margins smooth; petals showy, 6, partially fused; radial symmetry; purple, white**

Dipterostemon capitatus
THEMIDACEAE

Blue Dicks

Grasslands, woodlands, deserts, scrub; up to 7500 ft.; native

This early spring–blooming perennial herb is easily identified by the deep purple bracts under the compact head of flowers with short pedicels. If you look closely inside each flower, you will see three white, forked appendages enclosing the six fertile stamens. The flowers are a favorite nectar source for Pipevine Swallowtail butterflies. **Plant height to 2 ft.; leaves basal, unlobed, margins smooth; tepals showy, 6, partially fused; radial symmetry; blue, lavender**

Triteleia laxa
THEMIDACEAE

Wally Basket

Grasslands, woodlands, open conifer forests; up to 5000 ft.; native

This perennial herb typically starts to bloom just when the Blue Dicks have started to fade in late spring. Each flower is on a long pedicel, giving the appearance of an open basket. Six stamens are attached at two different levels. Species in this group resemble onions (*Allium* spp.) but do not have an oniony aroma. **Plant height 1–4 ft.; leaves basal, unlobed, margins smooth; tepals showy, 6, partially fused; radial symmetry; pale blue, purple**

Verbena gooddingii
VERBENACEAE

Gooding Verbena

Deserts; 3900–6600 ft.; native

This short-lived perennial herb has a water-dependent flowering period from early spring through fall. It has soft, hairy foliage and large headlike spikes of flowers. In a study of Sonoran Desert plants that aimed to find anticancer drugs, chemicals extracted from this plant were able to kill cancer cells. **Plant height 8–18 in.; leaves opposite, lobed, margins toothed; flower clusters showy; petals 5, partially fused; mirror symmetry; purple, pink, white**

Verbena lasiostachys
VERBENACEAE

Western Verbena

Conifer forests, woodlands, chaparral; up to 8000 ft.; native

This perennial herb blooms from spring through early fall. It is widely distributed in moist soils throughout California into Oregon. The charming dime-sized flowers attract butterflies. Verbenas have square stems and nutlets, which might lead you to think they are in the mint family. Indeed, the verbena and mint families are closely related. **Plant height 1–3 ft.; leaves opposite, lobed, margins toothed; flower clusters showy; petals 5, partially fused; mirror symmetry; lavender, pink**

Viola beckwithii
VIOLACEAE

Beckwith's Violet

Deserts; 3000–8900 ft.; native

This spring-blooming perennial herb grows in seasonally moist, open habitat from northeastern California into Oregon, Idaho, and Utah. The flower has two deep purple upper petals, while the lower petal is lavender with a deep yellow center. The lower petals are white in some populations. The fleshy dissected leaves are usually hairy. **Plant height to 7 in.; leaves basal, compound, dissected leaflets, margins smooth; petals showy, 5, free; mirror symmetry; purple, lavender, with yellow throat**

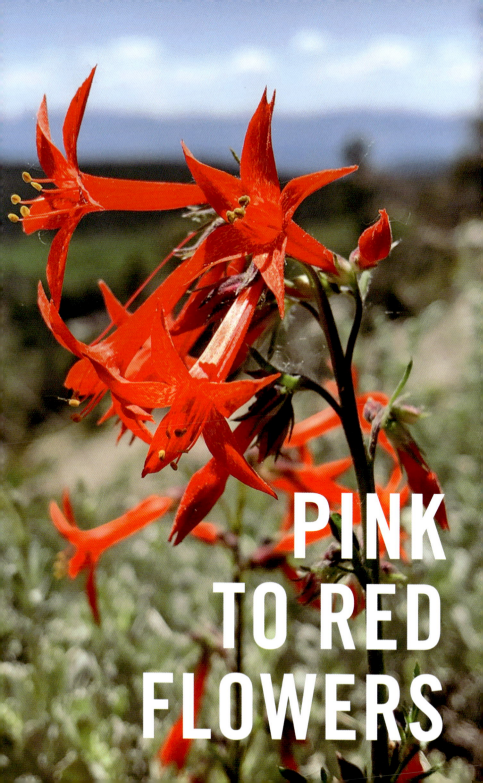

PINK
TO RED
FLOWERS

Justicia californica
ACANTHACEAE

Chuparosa

Deserts; up to 3000 ft.; native

This spring-blooming shrub has spectacular nectar-filled flowers that are irresistible to hummingbirds—*chuparosa* means "hummingbird" in Spanish. It naturally occurs in rocky desert washes and can tolerate very intense light and dry conditions in garden settings. It is one of only two native California species in the acanthus family. **Plant height to 6 ft.; leaves opposite, unlobed, margins smooth; petals showy, 5, partially fused; mirror symmetry; red, rarely yellow**

Carpobrotus edulis
AIZOACEAE

Freeway Iceplant

Dunes, disturbed areas; up to 350 ft.; non-native

Originally planted as a dune stabilizer, this fleshy perennial herb is now considered a noxious weed, completely invading coastal habitats, displacing natives. Originally from South Africa, where it has yellow or light pink flowers, it has hybridized with *C. chilensis* in California, and both yellow and hot-pink flowers can occur on the same plant. **Plant height to 5 ft., scrambling; leaves opposite, unlobed, margins smooth; petals and sterile stamens showy, many, free; radial symmetry; hot-pink, yellow**

Allium campanulatum
ALLIACEAE

Sierra Onion

Grasslands, woodlands; 2000–8500 ft.; native

The pointed petals of this summer-blooming perennial herb spread widely. Common throughout the Sierra, Klamath, and Coast Ranges, this plant grows in dry, thin soils and around rock outcrops. A similar species, Twincrest Onion (*A. bisceptrum*), occurs in the Eastern Sierra, with leaves that stay green while the plant is in flower. **Plant height to 1 ft.; leaves alternate, unlobed, margins smooth; tepals showy, 6, free; radial symmetry; pink, white**

Allium falcifolium
ALLIACEAE

Scytheleaf Onion

Grasslands, woodlands; 300–7000 ft.; native

This perennial herb blooms in late spring and early summer. Like most *Allium* species, it has a typical oniony smell. The common name refers to its leaves, which are curved like the blade of a scythe. The plant has a distinctive flat stem. It grows in rocky soils from Western California into Southern Oregon and can tolerate serpentine soils. **Plant height to 6 in.; leaves basal, unlobed, margins smooth; tepals showy, 6, free; radial symmetry; pink**

Allium haematochiton
ALLIACEAE

Red-skinned Onion

Grasslands, chaparral; up to 2500 ft.; native

This spring-blooming perennial herb has bulbs (fleshy leaves) clustered along stout rhizomes (underground stems). The outer bulb coat is reddish brown and the inner bulb layers are deep red to white. The species is common on dry slopes and ridges in Northern Baja California and Southern California to Kern County. **Plant height to 1 ft.; leaves alternate, unlobed, margins smooth; tepals showy, 6, free; radial symmetry; pink, white**

Allium peninsulare
ALLIACEAE

Peninsula Onion

Grasslands; up to 1000 ft.; native

This perennial herb blooms in spring. Two varieties are recognized within the species: one has straight leaves and the other has curly leaves. To identify wild onions, you must dig up the bulbs to look at the bulb coat pattern, which is recommended only when essential. **Plant height to 1 ft.; leaves alternate, unlobed, margins smooth; tepals showy, 6, free; radial symmetry; red-purple**

Allium validum
ALLIACEAE

Pacific Onion

Wetlands; up to 3500–11,000 ft.; native

The bulbs of this summer-blooming perennial herb are quite large, similar to those of
Red-skinned Onion. However, this species has
very different habitat preferences. It is found
in wetlands, whereas Red-skinned Onion
prefers drier habitats. The genus *Allium* was
considered part of the lily family (Liliaceae)
but is now classified in its own family, the
Alliaceae. **Plant height
to 3 ft.; leaves alter-
nate, unlobed, margins
smooth; tepals showy, 6,
free; radial symmetry;
pink, white**

Asclepias californica
APOCYNACEAE

California Milkweed

Grasslands, shrublands; 600–6800 ft.; native

This distinctive perennial herb is covered in
soft, white hairs that make the foliage look
gray-green in color. Blooming in spring and
summer, dark maroon flower clusters droop
downward at the ends of branches. This
drought-tolerant species is a host for larvae of the Monarch butterfly and Clio Tiger
moth. **Plant height to 3 ft.; leaves opposite,
unlobed, margins wavy;
petals showy, 5, partially
fused; radial symmetry;
maroon, pink**

Asclepias cordifolia
APOCYNACEAE

Heart-leaf Milkweed

Conifer forests, woodlands, chaparral; up to 6500 ft.; native

This perennial herb has hairless, leathery leaves. The species and common names refer to its heart-shaped leaves, which clasp the stem. Blooming in late spring and summer, flowers are purple and white, contrasting with blue-green foliage. Like all milkweeds, the plant contains a toxic cardiac glycoside that caterpillars ingest and sequester to deter predators. **Plant height 1–3 ft.; leaves opposite, basally lobed, margins smooth; sepals showy, 5, fused at base; radial symmetry; purple, white**

Asclepias fascicularis
APOCYNACEAE

Narrow-leaf Milkweed

Riparian, disturbed areas; up to 7000 ft.; native

This summer-blooming perennial herb is an important food source for Monarch caterpillars. Studies have shown that Monarchs prefer it over other species of *Asclepias*. When caterpillars feed on these plants, they sequester toxins that make them unpalatable to predators. Narrowleaf Milkweed has the precise amount of toxin required to make it tolerable to caterpillars but toxic to predators. **Plant height to 3 ft.; leaves opposite, narrow, unlobed, margins smooth; petals showy, 5, free; radial symmetry; pink, white**

Funastrum cynanchoides
APOCYNACEAE

Climbing Milkweed

Deserts; up to 5200 ft.; native

Blooming in spring and summer, this vining perennial produces large, showy flower clusters. Its foliage has a pungent odor that is reminiscent of hot rubber. It usually grows in dry washes. Like other milkweeds, it attracts butterflies. Although Climbing Milkweed is toxic at some level, its milky sap has been heated and used as chewing gum. **Plant stem length to 3 ft.; leaves opposite, unlobed, margins smooth; petals showy, 5, free; radial symmetry; pink, white**

Aristolochia californica
ARISTOLOCHIACEAE

California Pipevine

Riparian, woodlands; up to 2300 ft.; native

This vining perennial is one of the most interesting species in California. The large purple flowers are shaped like tobacco pipes, hence the common name. Blooming in winter and spring, the flowers smell like rotting meat, a strategy used to attract fly pollinators. It is the only known larval host for the Pipevine Swallowtail. **Plant stem length to 20 ft.; leaves alternate, basally lobed, margins smooth; petals showy, 5, fused; mirror symmetry; maroon**

Asarum caudatum
ARISTOLOCHIACEAE

Creeping Wild Ginger

Conifer forests, woodlands; up to 7200 ft.; native

This perennial herb is not a true ginger, but the leaves and rhizomes do have a ginger-like aroma. Blooming in spring and summer, the distinctive cup-shaped flowers have long-tailed sepals. The species has dozens of reported medicinal and traditional uses. A study published in the *Journal of Ethnopharmacology* indicated that it was able to kill fungi. **Plant height to 1 ft.; leaves alternate, basally lobed, margins smooth; sepals showy, 3, partially fused; radial symmetry; maroon**

Hulsea heterochroma
ASTERACEAE

Redray Alpinegold

Conifer forests, chaparral; 1000–8900 ft.; native

This species can be an annual or a perennial and becomes abundant following fire. The foliage is sticky and aromatic. Blooming in spring and summer, its large, striking flowers develop into spherical seedheads. Seeds can live in the soil for 75 years or more, waiting until the next disturbance stimulates germination. **Plant height to 5 in.; leaves basal, alternate, unlobed, margins toothed; flowers small; flowerheads sunflower-like; radial symmetry; red, orange**

Acourtia microcephala
ASTERACEAE

Sacapellote

Chaparral, woodlands; up to 5100 ft.; native

This summer-blooming perennial herb is commonly observed after fires. Sticky leaves densely cover the stems. Each pink to white flower has two ligulate petals, which is unique among the asters. The flowerheads develop into fluffy seedheads for wind dispersal. Then the entire plant dies back, reemerging the following year. **Plant height 2–5 ft.; leaves alternate, unlobed, margins toothed; flower clusters showy; flowers small; radial symmetry; pink, white**

Pleiacanthus spinosus
ASTERACEAE

Thorn Skeletonweed

Deserts; 1400–10,000 ft.; native

Pleiacanthus is a monotypic genus, meaning it contains only one species. The genus name means "unusually thorny," which sums up the initial impression of this subshrub. In summer, dainty pink flowerheads adorn the branches, providing a striking contrast to the rigid, thorny, blue-gray architecture of the plant. **Plant height to 20 in.; leaves alternate, unlobed, margins smooth; flowers small; radial symmetry; pink, lavender, white**

Stephanomeria exigua
ASTERACEAE

Small Wire Lettuce

Conifer forests, woodlands, chaparral; up to 9200 ft.; native

Blooming from spring through fall, this variable species can be either an annual or a perennial. The common name refers to the slender, wiry branches that spread out above a single stem. Because the basal leaves quickly wither, the stems, branches, and flowerheads are all that is visible when the plant is in flower. **Plant height to 6 ft.; leaves in basal rosette, stem leaves alternate, unlobed to lobed, margins smooth or toothed; flowers small; radial symmetry; pink, white**

Carduus pycnocephalus
ASTERACEAE

Italian Thistle

Disturbed areas, grasslands; up to 4000 ft.; non-native

Native to the Mediterranean region and North Africa, this annual blooms in spring and summer. The entire plant is covered in prickles. Its stems are winged, and the slightly wooly flowerheads are clustered. It is considered a noxious weed, because it creates impenetrable stands that exclude native plants and grazing animals. **Plant height 1–7 ft.; leaves in basal rosette, stem leaves alternate, lobed, margins toothed; flowerheads discoid; flowers small; radial symmetry; pink, purple**

Cirsium occidentale
ASTERACEAE

Cobweb Thistle

Chaparral, conifer forests, woodlands; up to 11,800 ft.; native

This biennial blooms in winter, spring, and summer. It is the most common native thistle in California. Unlike the non-native thistles that form dense impenetrable stands, these plants occur sporadically. The species varies in terms of stature, hairiness, and flowerhead color and has been divided into eight named varieties. **Plant height 20–80 in.; leaves in basal rosette, stem leaves alternate, lobed, margins toothed; flowerheads showy, discoid; flowers small; radial symmetry; red, pink, purple, white**

Cirsium vulgare
ASTERACEAE

Bull Thistle

Disturbed areas; up to 7800 ft.; non-native

This perennial herb pops up following disturbances such as fire and is invasive in coastal grasslands, moist areas in forests, and marshes. It blooms from spring through fall and has slender spines and distinctive thickened ridges on the bracts surrounding the flowerheads. The spiny plants are unpalatable to grazing animals. **Plant height 12–80 in.; leaves in basal rosette, stem leaves alternate, lobed, margins toothed; flowerheads showy, discoid; flowers small; radial symmetry; pink, lavender**

Palafoxia arida
ASTERACEAE

Desert Palafox

Deserts; up to 3300 ft.; native

This upright, branched annual blooms from winter through summer. Plants have rough-hairy, narrow leaves. The attractive flowerheads are accented by branched pink-purple stigmas that emerge from dark anther tubes. The petal lobes are white and tiny. *Palafoxia arida* var. *gigantea* is rare and is taller than variety *arida*, with longer flowerheads. **Plant height to 6 ft.; lower leaves opposite, upper alternate, unlobed, margins smooth; flowerheads showy, discoid; flowers small; radial symmetry; stigma pink, petals white**

Pluchea sericea
ASTERACEAE

Arrowweed

Shrublands, riparian; up to 3100 ft.; native

Blooming in spring and early summer, this shrub occurs throughout Southwestern North America into Mexico. The upright stems have been used to make arrow shafts, thus the common name. The leaves are silky-hairy; *sericea* means "silky." Saltmarsh Fleabane (*P. odorata*) is a similar species with larger, well-spaced, toothed leaves. **Plant height 3–16 ft.; leaves alternate, unlobed, margins smooth; flowerheads showy, discoid; flowers small; radial symmetry; pink, lavender**

Silybum marianum
ASTERACEAE

Milk Thistle

Disturbed areas; up to 3000 ft.; non-native

Blooming in winter and spring, this species can be either an annual or a perennial herb. It has distinctive mottled white markings on its leaves. Its basal rosette is similar to that of Italian Thistle, but the large flowerheads are usually one per stem and the stems lack spiny wings. **Plant height to 10 ft.; leaves in basal rosette; stem leaves alternate, lobed; margins toothed, wavy, spiny-margined; flowerheads showy, discoid; flowers small; radial symmetry; pink, lavender**

Chilopsis linearis
BIGNONIACEAE

Desert Willow

Deserts; up to 6800 ft.; native

Blooming in spring, summer, and fall, this desert tree is covered in large, delicate flowers. Although it resembles a willow because of its narrow leaves, it has tubular flowers, not catkins, and it is not part of the willow family (Salicaceae). It is common in dry, sandy washes where its large pink flowers attract hummingbirds. **Plant height 12–40 ft.; leaves alternate, unlobed, margins smooth; petals showy, 5, partially fused; mirror symmetry; pink**

Andersonglossum occidentale
BORAGINACEAE

Western Hound's Tongue

Open, dry conifer forests; up to 8500 ft.; native

This perennial herb was known as *Cynoglossum occidentale* until DNA analysis and other evidence prompted scientists to rearrange the borage family. Blooming in spring and summer, its flowers are urn-shaped with prominent green sepals that largely hide the petals. It looks similar to Pacific Hound's Tongue (*Adelinia grande*), which has blue flowers. **Plant height 6–18 in.; leaves alternate, unlobed, margins smooth, wavy; flowers small, petals showy, 5, partially fused; radial symmetry; deep pink, burgundy, cream**

Cakile maritima
BRASSICACEAE

Horned Sea Rocket

Dunes; up to 300 ft.; non-native

This herbaceous perennial is common on California beaches, where it blooms year-round. Originally from Europe, its seeds can germinate after being in seawater for extended periods, which has enabled it to travel around the world in the ballast holds of ships. It is considered a minor pest plant in California. **Plant height to 18 in.; leaves alternate, lobed, margins smooth; flowers small, petals showy, 4, free; radial symmetry; pink**

Caulanthus californicus
BRASSICACEAE

California Jewelflower

Grasslands; up to 6000 ft.; native

In a good wildflower year, look for this rare species in the Carrizo Plain, growing among grasses. Clusters of dark maroon flower buds open to creamy or white flowers. Once common in the San Joaquin Valley, urban development and agriculture have reduced it to a fraction of its former range. **Plant height 4–20 in.; leaves in basal rosette to alternate, lobed to clasping base, margins toothed; sepals and petals showy, 4, free; biradial symmetry; buds maroon, petals white**

Caulanthus coulteri
BRASSICACEAE

Coulter's Wild Cabbage

Grasslands; up to 7100 ft.; native

This spring-blooming annual can be abundant in the San Joaquin Valley and adjacent foothill areas. Though similar to California Jewelflower, which has flattened fruits, its fruits are distinctly round in cross section. The clusters of dark maroon flowers at the tips of stalks are often a first clue that you have found this little gem. **Plant height to 5 ft.; leaves in basal rosette then alternate, unlobed to clasping, margins toothed; petals showy, 4, free; biradial symmetry; buds maroon, petals white**

Caulanthus inflatus
BRASSICACEAE

Desert Candle

Deserts, grasslands; up to 5500 ft.; native

One of California's most memorable wild-flowers blooms in spring, when inflated flower stalks emerge, often en masse. In the sunlight, fields covered in these plants appear as though they are filled with glowing candles. Look for impressive displays of this annual in years when Southern California receives ample rainfall. **Plant height to 3 ft.; leaves in basal rosette, unlobed to clasping, margins variable; petals showy, 4, free; radial symmetry; buds maroon, petals white**

Raphanus sativus
BRASSICACEAE

Wild Radish

Disturbed areas; up to 5000 ft.; non-native

This spring- and summer-blooming annual is the wild relative of the cultivated radish. Most likely native to Southeast Asia, it is found throughout the world. In California, it frequently invades grasslands, open areas, disturbed areas, and roadsides. It successfully outcompetes native plant species and can be toxic to livestock. **Plant height to 20 in.; leaves in basal rosette to alternate, lobed to deeply lobed, margins toothed; petals showy, 4, free; radial symmetry; pink, yellow, white**

Cylindropuntia prolifera
CACTACEAE

Coastal Cholla

Ocean bluffs; coastal scrub; up to 7000 ft.; native

Cacti usually make people think of deserts, but this spring-blooming, succulent perennial is strictly coastal in California and Baja California, growing on ocean bluffs. Like all chollas, its stems form long, cylindrical segments. Plants often reproduce asexually. Stem segments fall off and root, creating clonal colonies. Plants bloom in spring and summer. **Plant height to 6 ft.; leaves modified into spines; petals showy, many, free; radial symmetry; red**

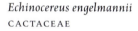

Echinocereus engelmannii
CACTACEAE

Engelmann's Hedgehog Cactus

Deserts; up to 7800 ft.; native

This spring-blooming succulent has a compact growth habit. It can have a single stem or multiple tightly clustered stems. It is common and abundant throughout Southwestern North America. Impressively, more than nine varieties have been described based on variation in spine color, growth form, and flower color. **Plant height to 2 ft.; leaves modified into spines; petals showy, many, free; radial symmetry; red, magenta**

Echinocereus mojavensis
CACTACEAE

Mojave Kingcup Cactus

Deserts; 1075–9300 ft.; native

This spring-blooming succulent is common throughout the deserts of Southwestern North America and Northern Mexico. Its stems are rounded to cylindrical and can occur in mounds of up to 100 stems. It has super-showy, hummingbird-pollinated flowers that can be 4 in. across. It has also been treated as a variety of *E. triglochidiatus*. **Plant height to 18 in.; leaves modified into spines; petals showy, many, free; radial symmetry; red with yellow center**

Mammillaria tetrancistra
CACTACEAE

Common Fishhook Cactus

Deserts; up to 5000 ft.; native

This spring-blooming perennial has spines shaped like fishhooks, hence its common name. Its genus name, *Mammillaria*, means "nipple" in Latin, referring to the small mound around each spine cluster. The species is small, with cylindrical stems that occur singly or in small clusters. The distinctive fruits are spineless and shiny. **Plant height to 10 in.; leaves modified into spines; fruit bright red; petals showy, many, free; radial symmetry; pink, lavender**

Opuntia basilaris
CACTACEAE

Beavertail Prickly-pear

Chaparral, woodlands, deserts; up to 7000 ft.; native

The pads, or modified stems, of this spring-blooming perennial are shaped like beaver tails. The plant generally lacks a main stem and the pads branch from the base. The specific name, *basilaris*, which means "from the base," describes the growth form. Pads lack long spines but are covered in tiny barbed bristles (glochids) that can penetrate and irritate the skin. **Plant height to 2 ft.; leaves modified into spines; petals showy, many, free; radial symmetry; pink, magenta**

Calycanthus occidentalis
CALYCANTHACEAE

Spice Bush

Woodlands, riparian; up to 4900 ft.; native

The pungent aroma of this shrub has been described as sweet, spicy, camphor-like, and reminscent of old wine barrels. It grows along streams and in moist canyons. Blooming in late spring and summer, the flowers have numerous strap-shaped sepals and petals. The only other species in the genus is Carolina All-spice (*C. floridus*), which grows in Southeastern North America. **Plant height 3–13 ft.; leaves opposite, unlobed, margins smooth; petals showy, many, free; radial symmetry; red, maroon**

Lonicera ciliosa
CAPRIFOLIACEAE

Orange Honeysuckle

Forests; up to 8800 ft.; native

This perennial vine can scramble up to 20 ft. It grows sporadically in Northern California and is quite common in the Pacific Northwest. Below each flower cluster are two opposite leaves that are fused around the stem. Blooming in spring, the sweetly scented, red-orange flowers produce nectar for hummingbirds, and its bright berries attract birds. **Plant height 10–20 ft.; leaves opposite, unlobed, margins smooth; petals showy, 5, partially fused; mirror symmetry; red, orange**

Lonicera hispidula
CAPRIFOLIACEAE

Pink Honeysuckle

Woodlands, riparian; 3600 ft.; native

Blooming in spring and summer, this species' pink, tubular flowers offer a nectar reward that attracts hummingbirds. Petal tips roll back, exposing the flower's reproductive parts. At the base of each flower cluster are two fused leaves that surround the stem. This hairy perennial grows on slopes and streambanks from Coastal Southern California to Oregon. **Plant height to 20 ft.; leaves opposite, unlobed, margins smooth; petals showy, 5 (2-lipped), partially fused; mirror symmetry; pink**

Lonicera involucrata
CAPRIFOLIACEAE

Twinberry Honeysuckle

Coastal strand, conifer forests, wetlands; up to 11,500 ft.; native

This summer-blooming shrub ranges from California to Wisconsin, and from Alaska to Mexico. Like all honeysuckles, the flowers are an important source of nectar for humming-birds, butterflies, and moths. Its red bracts are more conspicuous than its yellow-orange flowers. The black fruits are eaten by birds and bears but are likely toxic to humans. **Plant height 2–16 ft.; leaves opposite, unlobed, margins smooth, wavy; petals showy, 5, partially fused; radial symmetry; bracts red; petals red, yellow**

Symphoricarpos albus
CAPRIFOLIACEAE

Common Snowberry

Woodlands, conifer forests; up to 9700 ft.; native

This summer-blooming shrub is quite erect for a snowberry, whose branches usually tend to creep or trail. Snowberry fruits provide forage for bighorn sheep, white-tailed deer, and grizzly bears and cover for birds and small animals. Humans, however, should avoid the fruits. Similar to honeysuckle fruits, consuming the berries can cause vomiting. **Plant height 3–6 ft.; leaves opposite, unlobed to lobed, margins smooth; fruit white; petals showy, 5, partially fused; radial symmetry; pink**

Symphoricarpos mollis
CAPRIFOLIACEAE

Creeping Snowberry

Conifer forests, woodlands, chaparral; up to 11,110 ft.; native

Blooming in spring and summer, this shrub is similar to Common Snowberry but is more sprawling with smaller flower clusters. The specific name, *mollis*, means "soft, smooth" in Latin. The name refers to the velvety hairs on the leaves or the hairs inside the flower. Some individual plants have hairless leaves. **Plant height 6–30 in.; leaves opposite, unlobed, margins smooth; fruit white; petals showy, 5, partially fused; radial symmetry; pink**

Symphoricarpos rotundifolius
CAPRIFOLIACEAE

Round-leaved Snowberry

Conifer forests, deserts; up to 12,200 ft.; native

Blooming in spring and summer, this shrub has only one or two flowers per cluster; other snowberries have many flowers per cluster. New stems have fuzzy hairs, and the bark of older stems shreds in strips. The specific name, *rotundifolia*, means "round leaf." Plants often produce flowers and fruits at the same time. **Plant height to 4 ft.; leaves opposite, unlobed, margins smooth; petals showy, 5, partially fused; radial symmetry; pink, white**

Petrorhagia dubia
CARYOPHYLLACEAE

Hairy Pink

Grasslands, disturbed areas; up to 6000 ft.; non-native

This spring-blooming annual was introduced from Europe into the Sierra Nevada foothills in the 1920s. It has spread and become common in disturbed areas of Northern California. The dry and membranous (scarious) involucre can be mistaken for a calyx, as only one flower peeks out at a time. **Plant height 4–24 in.;** leaves opposite, unlobed, margins smooth; petals showy, 5, free; radial symmetry; pink, magenta, with dark veins

Silene gallica
CARYOPHYLLACEAE

Windmill Pink

Disturbed areas; up to 3300 ft.; non-native

Blooming in winter and spring, this annual is native to Eurasia. The plant is covered in rough hairs and its petals are much longer than the calyx. The genus is named after Silenus, the foam-covered, perennially intoxicated father of Bacchus (god of winemaking). The species is not foamy, but it does have sticky glands. **Plant height 4–16 in.;** leaves opposite, unlobed, margins smooth; petals showy, 5, free; radial symmetry; pink, white

Silene laciniata
CARYOPHYLLACEAE

Cardinal Catchfly

Chaparral, woodlands, conifer forests; up to 7200 ft.; native

Blooming in spring and summer, this perennial herb's red, tubular flowers are hummingbird magnets. The sepals are fused into a tube, while the petals are free to the base. It is covered with sticky hairs that sometimes trap small flies. It reaches its northern limit in California very near the Oregon border. **Plant height to 2.5 ft.; leaves opposite, unlobed, margins smooth; petals showy, 5, free; radial symmetry; red**

Silene verecunda
CARYOPHYLLACEAE

Dolores Campion

Chaparral, woodlands; up to 12,500 ft.; native

This spring- and summer-blooming perennial herb is quite variable. It is distributed widely in California, Nevada, and Utah but is named for the site of its first collection, near Mission Dolores Park in San Francisco. The specific name, *verecunda*, means "shy or modest," presumably referring to its delicate flowers. **Plant height to 18 in.; leaves opposite, unlobed, margins smooth; petals showy, 5, free; radial symmetry; pink, white**

Spergularia macrotheca
CARYOPHYLLACEAE

Sticky Sandspurry

Chaparral, wetlands; up to 2600 ft.; native

Blooming in spring, this scruffy perennial herb occurs in wet, often alkaline or saline soils. The flower clusters are covered in sticky hairs. In California, three forms are differentiated based on flower size and color. The name comes from the Latin term *spergere*, which means "to scatter," probably in reference to the winged, sandlike seeds. **Plant height to 16 in.; leaves opposite, unlobed; margins smooth; flowers small, petals showy, 5, free; radial symmetry; pink, white**

Spergularia rubra
CARYOPHYLLACEAE

Red Sandspurry

Disturbed areas, wetlands; up to 7900 ft.; non-native

This annual blooms from spring through fall. It is a Eurasian weed that prefers sandy soils and often grows in sidewalk cracks and agricultural areas. Although it is non-native, it is relatively small and innocuous. The sepals are free with a thin, papery margin. *Rubra* means "red," presumably referring to the flowers, though they are actually pink. **Plant height to 10 in.; leaves opposite, unlobed, margins smooth; flowers small, petals showy, 5, free; radial symmetry; pink, rarely white**

Calystegia purpurata
CONVOLVULACEAE

Pacific Bindweed

Chaparral, woodlands; up to 1000 ft.; native

Blooming in late spring, this robust perennial can climb to 20 ft., forming a thick, flower-covered curtain in coastal habitats. Morphologically, it is similar to Chaparral Bindweed, but it has a very sharp angle (sinus) between its basal leaf lobes and leaf blade. It is easy to grow but requires water a few times per month in the dry season. **Plant height to 20 ft.; leaves alternate, basally lobed, margins smooth; petals showy, 5, fused; radial symmetry; pink, white**

Dudleya lanceolata
CRASSULACEAE

Lanceleaf Dudleya

Chaparral; up to 7600 ft.; native

This summer-blooming, succulent perennial herb is relatively widespread. More typically, *Dudleya* species are rare and geographically restricted. Lanceleaf Dudleya grows on rocky slopes, and its rosette produces a flowering stem up to 3 ft. tall. The specific name, *lanceolata*, means "lancelike," which describes its leaf shape. **Plant height to 3 ft.; leaves in basal rosette, unlobed, margins smooth; petals showy, 5, partially fused; radial symmetry; pink, yellow, orange**

Dudleya pulverulenta
CRASSULACEAE

Chalk Dudleya

Rocky cliffs and canyons; up to 3300 ft.; native

This summer-blooming perennial has unusually large rosettes, up to 24 in. wide, covered
with a chalky white, waxy coating. In the spring,
stout flower stalks produce tubular flowers
that attract hummingbirds and bumble bees.
The species can be quite common on cliffs and
canyons in coastal areas of Southern California and Baja California. **Plant height to 3 ft.;**
leaves basal rosette, un-
lobed, margins smooth;
petals showy, 5, partially
fused; radial symme-
try; pink, red

Rhodiola integrifolia
CRASSULACEAE

Western Roseroot

Montane to alpine; 5900–13,000 ft.; native

This succulent perennial has a wide distribution that includes Western North America
and Eastern Russia. Blooming in summer,
dense clusters of deep red flowers contrast
with its blue-green foliage. For centuries, root
extracts of this species have been used medicinally to treat a wide range of ailments, from
depression to infection. **Plant height to 12 in.;**
leaves in basal rosette,
unlobed; stem leaves al-
ternate, margins smooth
or toothed; petals showy,
5, partially fused; radial
symmetry; red, magenta

Drosera rotundifolia
DROSERACEAE

Round-leaved Sundew

Wetlands, conifer forests; up to 8900 ft.; native

In summer, this small perennial herb produces delicate white flowers on a slender stem. Its prominent, unearthly-looking red leaves have large, sticky glands that trap and digest insects. This carnivorous plant derives some of its nutrients from trapped insects, rather than from the nitrogen-poor wetlands in which it grows. Plant height 2–10 in.; leaves in basal rosette, unlobed, margins smooth; flowers small, petals showy, 5, free; radial symmetry; flower white, leaves red

Tiquilia plicata
EHRETIACEAE

Fanleaf Crinklemat

Deserts; up to 4100 ft.; native

Blooming in spring and summer, this prostrate perennial or subshrub has small, ovate leaves with distinct crinkly ridges. It has very long hairs on the inside of the calyx. It is the main host plant of Sandfood (*Pholisma sonorae*), a rare parasitic species that gets its nutrients from other plants. Plant height to 1 in.; leaves alternate, unlobed, margins smooth; flowers small, petals showy, 5, partially fused; radial symmetry; pink, white

Chimaphila umbellata
ERICACEAE

Pipsissewa

Conifer forests; up to 9500 ft.; native

This summer-blooming perennial herb prefers dry, shady forests. Its evergreen leaves are arranged in irregular whorls and are technically alternate. The genus name, *Chimaphila*, is from Greek, meaning "winter loving," referring to its evergreen leaves. Its roots are traditionally used to make root beer. **Plant height to 18 in.; leaves alternate, unlobed, margins toothed; petals showy, 5, free; radial symmetry; pink, white**

Kalmia polifolia
ERICACEAE

Bog Laurel

Meadows, conifer forests; 3300–11,500 ft.; native

Blooming in late spring, this shrub can sometimes be found growing in cold, acidic fens (a type of peaty wetland) throughout the northern parts of North America. It has distinctly rolled leaf margins and flowers borne on long flower stalks. Its anthers are held in petal pits until they pop out when disturbed by insects, scattering pollen. **Plant height to 18 in.; leaves opposite, unlobed, margins smooth; petals showy, 5, partially fused; radial symmetry; pink**

Phyllodoce breweri
ERICACEAE

Brewer's Mountain Heather

Conifer forests, alpine; 4000–11,500 ft.; native

This summer-blooming subshrub occurs in the mountains of California and Nevada. Honey created from the the nectar of this plant contains grayanotoxin, a chemical that, when consumed, can cause dangerously low blood pressure and even death. The chemical is also found in species of other genera in the Ericaceae, including *Rhododendron*, *Pieris*, *Agarista*, and *Kalmia*. **Plant height to 1 ft.; leaves needle-like, alternate, unlobed, margins smooth; petals showy, 5, partially fused; radial symmetry; pink, rose-purple**

Rhododendron macrophyllum
ERICACEAE

Pacific Rhododendron

Conifer forests; up to 5000 ft.; native

This showy, spring-blooming shrub is relatively common along the coast from Central California through British Columbia. The leaves are evergreen, with a soft and leathery texture, and they curl under when overstressed. The upper lobe of each petal is spotted. It is the state flower of Washington and the star of Port Townsend's annual Rhododendron Festival. **Plant height 10–15 ft.; leaves alternate, unlobed, margins smooth; petals showy, 5, partially fused; radial symmetry; pink, white, purple**

Sarcodes sanguinea
ERICACEAE

Snow Plant

Conifer or mixed forests; up to 10,000 ft.; native

This fleshy perennial herb blooms from late spring through summer. Not only are its flowers red, but the entire aboveground part of the plant is red as well. It resembles a bright red cone, rising up through snow or pine needles. It completely lacks chlorophyll and must gather nutrients from underground fungi that collect carbon from nearby conifers. **Plant height to 1 ft.; leaves absent; whole plant showy; petals 5, fused; radial symmetry; red**

Vaccinium ovatum
ERICACEAE

Evergreen Huckleberry

Conifer forests; 2600 ft.; native

The purple-black berries of this evergreen, spring-blooming shrub are edible and can be used to make jam and syrup. Its thick, shiny leaves are reddish when they emerge in spring. The small, urn-shaped flowers usually have a red tinge but can also be white. Its distribution is mostly coastal, from California to Canada. **Plant height to 9 ft.; leaves alternate, unlobed, margins toothed; flower clusters showy; petals 5, fused; radial symmetry; pink, white**

Xylococcus bicolor
ERICACEAE

Mission Manzanita

Chaparral; up to 2100 ft.; native

This winter-blooming shrub is the SoCal cousin of the true manzanitas. The upper leaf surface is deep green, while the underside is densely covered in white hairs. The specific name, *bicolor*, refers to the two-toned leaves. Like many manzanita, it can resprout from its base (burl) after a moderate fire. **Plant height to 8 ft.; leaves alternate, unlobed, margins smooth, rolled under; flower clusters showy; petals 5, fused; radial symmetry; pink, white**

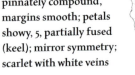

Astragalus coccineus
FABACEAE

Scarlet Milkvetch

Deserts; 2100–8000 ft.; native

This spring-blooming perennial herb is not widespread, but it can be locally abundant and is definitely eye-catching. It has spectacularly loud flowers set off by attractive, fuzzy-gray foliage. It is easy to identify because it is the only milkvetch with red flowers in North America. It is a favorite among hummingbirds and humans alike. **Plant height to 12 in.; leaves alternate, pinnately compound, margins smooth; petals showy, 5, partially fused (keel); mirror symmetry; scarlet with white veins**

Calliandra eriophylla
FABACEAE

Pink Fairy Duster

Deserts; 300–4900 ft.; native

Blooming in late winter and early spring, the flowers of this shrub have tiny petals and many long, showy pink stamens. It is not super common in California but is easily found in Anza-Borrego Desert State Park in Southern California. Baja Fairy Duster (*C. californica*), endemic to Baja California, is a closely related species with bright red stamens. **Plant height 1–2 ft.; leaves alternate, twice pinnately compound, margins smooth; stamens showy, many, free; radial symmetry; pink, red-purple**

Cercis occidentalis
FABACEAE

Western Redbud

Woodlands, chaparral; up to 4900 ft.; native

This robust shrub often grows as a small tree. It is incredibly showy and common in foothill areas throughout California. In spring it flushes with bright flowers against bare stems, so the entire plant looks like a giant flower cluster. The mass of flowers attracts pollinators of all sorts. **Plant height 10–20 ft.; leaves alternate, basally lobed, margins smooth; petals showy, 5, partially fused (keel); mirror symmetry; seed pods pink to purple; flowers pink**

Lathyrus latifolius
FABACEAE

Perennial Sweet Pea

Wetlands, riparian; up to 6600 ft.; non-native

This garden escapee can be recognized by its distinctive winged stems and large pink flowers. Native to Central Europe, this deeply rooted, summer-blooming perennial thrives in disturbed areas, where it chokes out native plants. Its pealike fruits are edible but can cause muscle cramping if eaten in large quantities. **Plant height to 6 ft. (sprawling); leaves alternate, pinnately compound, margins smooth; petals showy, 5, partially fused (keel); mirror symmetry; pink**

Lupinus microcarpus
FABACEAE

Chick Lupine

Disturbed areas; up to 5200 ft; native

This small, spring-flowering annual lupine has dense whorls of flowers. Its specific name means "tiny fruits." As the fruits develop, the stems sprawl, and the flower whorls reorient themselves upward. Palmately compound leaves have long petioles. Individual plants are inconspicuous, but in years with adequate rain, thousands of plants can color the landscape. **Plant height to 2.5 ft.; leaves alternate, palmately compound, margins smooth; petals showy, 5, partially fused (keel); mirror symmetry; pink, white, yellow, purple**

Trifolium albopurpureum
FABACEAE

Rancheria Clover

Woodlands, grasslands; up to 6900 ft.; native

Although the tiny flowers of this spring-blooming annual are white and purple, the overall hue of the plant is pink. Like many clovers, this species' flowers are clustered in a head, but unlike most, the tiny flowers are surrounded by hairy calyces. **Plant height to 10 in., spreading; leaves alternate, compound, 3 leaflets, margins toothed; flower clusters showy; petals small, 5, partially fused (keel); mirror symmetry; pink, purple, with white tips**

Trifolium ciliolatum
FABACEAE

Foothill Clover

Grasslands, chaparral, disturbed areas; up to 5600 ft.; native

The flowers on this upright, spring-blooming annual droop downward with age, often turning reddish. Though other clovers also have reflexing flowers, this species is easily distinguished by its bristly calyx lobes with narrow, pointed tips. The pale green, elongated leaflets mostly lack hairs and often sport whitish markings. **Plant height 8–20 in.; leaves alternate, compound, 3 leaflets, margins toothed; flower clusters showy; petals small, 5, partially fused (keel); mirror symmetry; pink, magenta**

Trifolium depauperatum
FABACEAE

Sack Clover

Woodlands, grasslands; up to 3000 ft.; native

The tiny, white-tipped flowers on this diminutive, spring-blooming annual inflate in fruit, creating the appearance of sacks, balloons, or, in the imagination of some, cow udders. The three varieties are differentiated based on characteristics of the fused bracts (involucres), located immediately below the flowers. **Plant height to 5 in.; leaves alternate, compound, 3 leaflets, margins toothed; flower clusters showy; petals small, 5, partially fused (keel); mirror symmetry; fruits pink; flowers magenta with white tips**

Trifolium hirtum
FABACEAE

Rose Clover

Disturbed areas, grasslands; up to 6800 ft.; non-native

Often growing in dry, disturbed areas, this spring-blooming annual was introduced for forage and erosion control. Now it's invasive in wildlands, displacing native clovers and other species. It is unusual in that its spherical flowerheads sit directly above one or two reduced leaves, whereas most clovers have many leaves below the flowerhead. **Plant height to 1 ft.; leaves alternate, palmately compound, margins toothed; flower clusters showy; petals small, 5, partially fused (keel); mirror symmetry; pink**

Trifolium longipes
FABACEAE

Longstalk Clover

Many communities; up to 9900 ft.; native

This spring-flowering montane perennial occurs in meadows and streamsides in all Northern California mountain ranges. Flowers range from white to purple, and leaflets can be very narrow to relatively broad. It always has a long stalk beneath the flowerhead, hence the specific name *longipes*, which means "long foot." **Plant height 2–16 in.; leaves alternate, compound, 3 leaflets, margins toothed; flower clusters showy; petals small, 5, partially fused (keel); mirror symmetry; pink, white, purple**

Trifolium microcephalum
FABACEAE

Small-headed Clover

Conifer forests, woodlands, chaparral; up to 8900 ft.; native

Blooming in spring and summer, this annual is common throughout Western North America. It is covered in fine-textured, white-wavy hairs, and its small, gray-green leaflets are notched. Fused bracts make a cup-shaped structure (involucre) that encloses the base of the flowerhead. In fruit, the seedhead becomes prickly to the touch. **Plant height to 6 in.; leaves alternate, palmately compound, margins toothed; flower clusters showy; petals small, 5, partially fused (keel); mirror symmetry; pink**

Trifolium wormskioldii
FABACEAE

Springbank Clover

Conifer forests, woodlands, wetlands, riparian; up to 10,500 ft.; native

From beaches to montane meadows, this perennial herb keeps its feet wet in moist or marshy areas. Plants vary from matted to long-stemmed and spread by horizontal, underground stems (rhizomes). Blooming from spring through fall, this clover's large flowerheads are a favorite food of hungry cattle. **Plant height to 3 ft.; leaves alternate, compound, 3 leaflets, margins toothed; flower clusters showy; petals small, 5, partially fused (keel); mirror symmetry; magenta, pink**

Fouquieria splendens
FOUQUIERIACEAE

Ocotillo

Deserts; up to 2300 ft.; native

Joshua Tree National Park is known for its iconic namesake, though a second impressive plant adorns the landscape in the southeastern part of the park. Ocotillo is a striking desert shrub that resembles a giant, upside-down octopus. Like cacti, it is covered in spines, but it is actually closely related to the phlox family (Polemoniaceae). **Plant height 10–30 ft.; leaves alternate, unlobed, margins smooth; petals showy, 5, fused; radial symmetry; red-orange**

Frankenia salina
FRANKENIACEAE

Alkali Seaheath

Salt marshes, alkali flats; up to 2400 ft.; native

This subshrub blooms from spring to late summer. Leaf margins roll under and flowers are long and tubular. Its sepals are fused into a calyx tube, but the petals are free. It is common and is one of the showiest plants in salt marshes. The specific name means "salty." **Plant height to 1 ft.; leaves opposite, unlobed, margins smooth; flowers small, petals showy, 5, free (sepals fused); radial symmetry; pink**

Zeltnera venusta
GENTIANACEAE

Charming Centaury

Grasslands, chaparral, woodlands; up to 5900 ft.; native

This annual is common during a year with adequate rain, but it can be found in drier conditions as well. It is also found in Oregon and Baja California. Blooming from early spring through midsummer, it has bright pink flowers with white centers. The bright yellow anthers corkscrew after they shed their pollen. *Venusta* means "charming or elegant." **Plant height to 18 in.; leaves opposite, unlobed, margins smooth; petals showy, 5, partially fused; radial symmetry; pink, white**

Erodium botrys
GERANIACEAE

Long-beak Stork's Bill

Disturbed areas, grasslands; up to 3200 ft.; non-native

Like all stork's bills, this weedy annual has long, thin fruits. In spring, after flower fertilization, the style elongates and thickens, and the carpel that develops resembles the head and beak of a stork. Fruit beaks can be up to 5 in. long. The specific name means "bunch of grapes," presumably referring to the flower cluster. **Plant height to 3 ft.; leaves in basal rosette, lobed to dissected, margins toothed; petals showy, 5, free; radial symmetry; pink, purple**

Erodium cicutarium
GERANIACEAE

Redstem Stork's Bill

Disturbed areas, grasslands; up to 6600 ft.; non-native

This weedy annual blooms from late winter into summer. The compound leaves have dissected leaflets. At maturity, its stems and midveins are reddish. Petals and sepals are about the same length and the fruit beak is relatively short, up to 2 in. Pollen evidence indicates it hitchhiked with early Europeans in the mid-1700s. **Plant height to 20 in.; leaves in basal rosette, pinnately compound, margins toothed; flowers small, petals showy, 5, free; radial symmetry; pink, purple**

Erodium texanum
GERANIACEAE

Texas Stork's Bill

Deserts; up to 4000 ft.; native

This annual blooms from late winter through early summer. Petal length is variable; the longest petal can be twice the length of the shortest. Its seeds are self-burying: pointed seedheads are pushed into the ground by a fruit tail of up to 3 in. long that coils and uncoils in response to moisture levels. **Plant height to 20 in.; leaves in basal rosette, lobed, margins toothed, wavy; flowers small, petals showy, 5, free; mirror symmetry; magenta**

Geranium dissectum
GERANIACEAE

Cutleaf Geranium

Many communities, disturbed areas; up to 4300 ft.; non-native

This annual herb blooms from spring through fall. Its lower leaves are deeply divided, creating narrow, pointed segments. The specific name, *dissectum*, means "to cut up" in Latin. The delicate petals are heart-shaped. This is another weedy member of the geranium family from Eurasia, which now grows in many places throughout the world. **Plant height to 30 in.; leaves opposite, dissected, margins toothed; flowers small, petals showy, 5, free; radial symmetry; bright pink**

Ribes cereum
GROSSULARIACEAE

Wax Currant

Dry montane forests, openings, among rocks, scrub; up to 12,600 ft.; native

This summer-blooming shrub occurs through-out Western North America. Its scent has been described as both spicy and unpleasant. Its leaves have visible resin glands. The showy part of the flower is its white-pink tubular calyx, which conceals small petals. Because it does not have nodal spines, it is considered a currant rather than a gooseberry. **Plant height 1–3 ft.; leaves alternate, shallow lobed, margins toothed; sepals showy, 5, partially fused; radial symmetry; pale pink, green, white**

Ribes malvaceum
GROSSULARIACEAE

Chaparral Currant

Chaparral, woodlands; up to 5,000 ft.; native

This upright, spineless shrub has thick, crinkled, sticky leaves that are bright green above and light green below (bright green in variety *viridifolium*). With age, the bark tends to shred. Blooming in winter and spring, the flowers' showy pink sepal lobes are twice as long as the actual petals. Its fruits are purple and waxy, with white glandular hairs. **Plant height 5–7 ft.; leaves alternate, lobed, margins toothed; sepals showy, 5, partially fused; radial symmetry; pink, white**

Ribes nevadense
GROSSULARIACEAE

Sierra Currant

Conifer forests, riparian; up to 10,000 ft.; native

Blooming in spring, the flowers of this shrub have pink bracts, red sepals, and white petals, which create the overall impression of pink flowers. This striking species has 6 in. flower clusters and deep blue fruits. The upper leaf surface is hairless and the lower surface can be glandular. It is relatively common in mountainous interior regions. **Plant height to 6 ft.; leaves alternate, lobed, margins toothed; sepals showy, 5, partially fused; radial symmetry; pink**

Ribes roezlii
GROSSULARIACEAE

Sierra Gooseberry

Conifer forests, woodlands, chaparral; up to 9300 ft.; native

Sierra gooseberry is a midsized, open shrub, topping out at 5 ft. tall. Widespread in the California foothills and mountains, it has stiff spines at leaf nodes, large and densely prickly red berries, and small, lobed leaves. In late spring, one to three flowers dangle from upper leaf nodes, with purple reflexed sepals and white petals. **Plant height to 5 ft.; leaves alternate, lobed, margins toothed; sepals showy, 5, partially fused; radial symmetry; purple, white**

Ribes sanguineum
GROSSULARIACEAE

Red Flowering Currant

Conifer forests, woodlands, chaparral; up to 7600 ft.; native

One of the earliest blooming spring shrubs of northwestern California, this currant's hot-pink flowers stand out against fresh green leaves. Introduced to cultivation in Britain in 1826 by Scottish botanist David Douglas, it was an immediate hit; it's also a favorite of native-plant gardeners in California. Abundant nectar attracts hummingbirds and butterflies. **Plant height to 10 ft.; leaves alternate, lobed, margins toothed; sepals showy, 5, partially fused; radial symmetry; bright pink to white**

Ribes speciosum
GROSSULARIACEAE

Fuchsia-flowered Gooseberry

Coastal sage scrub, chaparral; up to 7000 ft.; native

This shrub has attractive flowers that bloom in late winter and spring. Appropriately, the specific name is *speciosum*, which means "showy, brilliant." All of its flower parts are bright red, even the long-protruding stamens. The plant is aggressively armed with both nodal spines and prickles along the stem. It is a favorite nectar source for Anna's Hummingbird. **Plant height to 7 ft.; leaves alternate, lobed, margins toothed; sepals showy, 5, partially fused; radial symmetry; red**

Phacelia bicolor
HYDROPHYLLACEAE

Two-color Phacelia

Deserts, shrublands; up to 11,000 ft.; native

Blooming in late spring, this annual has a distinctive two-colored flower. The flower tube is yellow, and the rest of the flower is lavender. This delightful, low-growing species produces a showy display in sandy, alkaline soils. It can be confused with Fremont's Phacelia (*P. fremontii*), which also has yellow and lavender flowers. **Plant height to 16 in.; leaves alternate, dissected, margins toothed; flower clusters showy; petals 5, partially fused; radial symmetry; lavender with yellow tube**

Krameria bicolor
KRAMERIACEAE

White Rhatany

Deserts; up to 4600 ft.; native

This spring-blooming shrub has small, linear leaves and stems that look gray-green as they mature. The branch tips are thorny. The flower has both typical petals and petals with small oil-filled sacs. Its globose, purple fruit is spiny, with tiny, recurved barbs at the tips of the spines. This hemiparasite obtains nutrients via root connections with other species. **Plant height 2–5 ft.; leaves opposite, unlobed, margins smooth; sepals showy, 5, free; mirror symmetry; maroon, pink**

Agastache urticifolia
LAMIACEAE

Nettle-leaf Giant Hyssop

Conifer forests, woodlands, chaparral; 1300–9800 ft.; native

This spring-blooming perennial is common throughout Western North America. A typical mint, its stems are square and its foliage is aromatic. The small flowers have long stamens that protrude past the corolla lobes. The species cannot self-pollinate. The flowers attract a variety of pollinators, and it is a preferred nectar source for Monarch butterflies. **Plant height to 5 ft.; leaves opposite, unlobed, margins toothed; flower clusters showy; petals 5, partially fused; mirror symmetry; pink, lavender, white**

Lamium amplexicaule
LAMIACEAE

Giraffe Head

Disturbed areas; up to 2600 ft.; non-native

This weedy annual blooms from late winter through fall. It is one of two species of *Lamium* in California; both are non-native. This species in the mint family has a long flower tube protruding from the calyx, and the lower lip of the flower is often purple-spotted. **Plant height to 16 in.; leaves opposite, unlobed, margins toothed; flower clusters showy; petals 5, partially fused; mirror symmetry; pink, lavender**

Monardella macrantha
LAMIACEAE

Red Monardella

Chaparral, woodlands; 2000–6600 ft.; native

Blooming in summer and fall, this low-growing perennial herb has shiny, green leaves and produces showy clusters of bright red, tubular flowers. Subspecies *hallii* is rare in the wild but has attracted horticulturists. A long-flowered cultivar, "Marian Sampson," is available from native plant nurseries. **Plant height to 1 ft.; leaves opposite, unlobed, margins smooth or finely toothed; flower clusters showy; petals small, 5, partially fused; mirror symmetry; scarlet, yellow**

Salvia spathacea
LAMIACEAE

Hummingbird Sage

Chaparral, oak woodlands, coastal sage scrub; up to 2600 ft.; native

This spring-blooming perennial herb tends to have a sprawling habit, spreading by rhizomes. Its fruity-minty smell comes from oil stored in wavy glandular hairs that cover the plant. The large, green, sticky leaves are arrowhead- or spatula-shaped. It is the only *Salvia* species in California with truly red flowers. **Plant height to 3 ft.; leaves opposite, basally lobed, margins minutely toothed; flower clusters showy; petals 5, partially fused; mirror symmetry; red**

Stachys bullata
LAMIACEAE

California Hedge-nettle

Damp places in coastal sage scrub, chaparral, forests; up to 1600 ft.; native

The leaves of this perennial herb have deep veins that give the leaf surface a wrinkled apearance. Most hedge-nettles in California have a pouch at the base of their corollas, but California Hedge-nettle is the exception: it has a straight corolla tube. Common in cultivation, the species thrives in wet, boggy areas. **Plant height to 2.5 ft.; leaves opposite, unlobed, margins toothed; flower clusters showy; petals 5, partially fused; mirror symmetry; pink, white**

Stachys rigida
LAMIACEAE

Rough Hedge-nettle

Many communities; up to 8200 ft; native

This perennial herb has stiff, rough hairs that are sometimes sticky. Blooming in spring and summer, the flower's corolla is pink or purple with white splotches and a pouched base. Variety *rigida* can be common in small streams and seeps. Variety *quercetorum* has heart-shaped leaf bases and grows in wet clay soil. **Plant height to 3 ft.; leaves opposite, unlobed or lobed at base, margins toothed; flower clusters showy; petals 5, partially fused; mirror symmetry; pink, purple, white**

Calochortus plummerae
LILIACEAE

Plummer's Mariposa Lily

Chaparral, pine forests; up to 5600 ft.; native

This perennial herb flowers from spring into summer and occurs in dry habitats. It has upright, cup-shaped flowers that are pale pink to lavender. The petals are yellow at the base, with long yellow hairs in the midpetal. The narrower sepals can be longer than the petals. The linear leaves usually wither by flowering time. **Plant height 2–3 ft.; leaves alternate, unlobed, margins smooth; petals showy, 3, free; radial symmetry; pink, lavender**

Clintonia andrewsiana
LILIACEAE

Andrew's Clintonia

Conifer forests, redwood forests; up to 1300 ft.; native

This perennial herb blooms in early summer. It is an unusually showy inhabitant of the shady redwood forest floor. Beautiful bright pink or red bell-shaped flowers form an eye-catching umbel at the end of the long stem. The sepals and petals are indistinguishable, collectively called tepals. Its shiny, blue fruits attract wildlife. **Plant height 1–3 ft.; leaves in basal rosette, unlobed, margins smooth; fruits blue; tepals showy, 6, free; radial symmetry; red, pink**

Fritillaria recurva
LILIACEAE

Scarlet Fritillary

Conifer forests, woodlands, chaparral; up to 7200 ft.; native

This spring-blooming perennial bulb is a real eye-catcher. Its bell-shaped, red flowers are checkered with yellow and purple. The overlapping tepals are free to the base and strongly recurved at the tips. Flowering plants have narrow leaves. Look for nearby plants with a single broadly ovate leaf—these leaves are storing food for next season's blooms. **Plant height 1–3 ft.; leaves whorled, alternate above, unlobed, margins smooth; tepals showy, 6, free; radial symmetry; red, orange**

Scoliopus bigelovii
LILIACEAE

Fetid Adder's Tongue

Redwood forests; up to 3600 ft.; native

This perennial blooms in late winter and early spring. The sepals of the musky, fly-pollinated flowers have distinctive maroon striations. The genus name means "curved foot" and describes the way the flower stem curves over to deposit seeds on the forest floor. The seed has a fatty appendage (elaiosome) that attracts ant dispersers. **Plant height to 4 ft.; leaves basal, spotted, unlobed, margins smooth; sepals wide, spreading, narrow, 3, erect, free; radial symmetry; maroon stripes**

Linnaea borealis
LINNAEACEAE

Twinflower

Conifer forests, wetlands; 650–8500 ft.; native

On a warm day, the flowers of this summer-blooming species may smell of vanilla or licorice. It has two delicate, nodding flowers per flower stem. This perennial herb is relatively infrequent in California but is quite common in the Pacific Northwest. It is named after Carl Linnaeus, the Swedish naturalist who formalized the way species are named. **Plant height to 8 in.; leaves opposite, unlobed, margins toothed; petals showy, 5, partially fused; radial symmetry; pink, white**

Lythrum californicum
LYTHRACEAE

California Loosestrife

Marshes, ponds, stream margins; up to 7200 ft.; native

Blooming from spring to late summer, this upright, hairless perennial is native to Southwestern North America. Flowers have wrinkled petals and two whorls of stamens—one within the flower, the other poking out. Its ribbed fruits hug the stem as they mature. The leaves transition from opposite to alternate along the stem. **Plant height to 2 ft.; leaves opposite at base, alternate above, unlobed, margins smooth; flower clusters showy; petals 6, free; radial symmetry; pink, purple**

Eremalche parryi
MALVACEAE

Parry's Mallow

Grasslands, scrub, alkali flats, woodlands; up to 3300 ft.; native

This spring-blooming annual is endemic to California. It can create tremendous wildflower displays given well-timed rainfall. Subspecies *kernensis* (Kern Mallow), a rare plant that is federally listed as an endangered species, is known only from western Kern County, and adjacent counties, and has shorter and thinner sepals. **Plant height to 20 in.; leaves alternate, lobed, margins toothed; petals showy, 5, free, filaments fused; radial symmetry; pink, lavender, white**

Eremalche rotundifolia
MALVACEAE

Desert Five-spot

Deserts; -160–4000 ft.; native

This spring-blooming annual may have the most appropriate common name ever coined: it has a prominent red spot on each of its five pink petals, and its distribution is restricted to the deserts of Southwestern North America. It also has red stems and hairy calyces. The specific name, *rotundifolia*, refers to its round leaves. **Plant height to 2 ft.; leaves alternate, unlobed, margins toothed; petals showy, 5, free, filaments fused; radial symmetry; pink with red spots**

Hibiscus denudatus
MALVACEAE

Pale Face

Deserts; up to 2600 ft.; native

This spring-blooming subshrub has small, densely hairy leaves that are often folded, presumably to reduce water loss. Hibiscus flowers invoke images of Hawaiian shirts and tropical landscapes. Pale Face, however, is a desert species of Western North America. Its pink flowers are red-blushed, and petals are almost translucent. **Plant height to 3 ft.; leaves alternate, unlobed, margins toothed; petals showy, 5, free, filaments fused; radial symmetry; pink, white**

Malacothamnus fasciculatus
MALVACEAE

Chaparral Bush Mallow

Coastal scrub, chaparral; 200–2000 ft.; native

Blooming in spring, the flowers of this shrub form dense clusters along the stems, so that the whole plant resembles a bouquet. The specific name means "bundle" and refers to the flower clusters. It is common in the foothills of Southern California. Fremont's Bush Mallow (M. *fremontii*) is a similar but hairier species that grows in Northern California. **Plant height to 6 ft.; leaves alternate, lobed, margins toothed; petals showy, 5, free, filaments fused; radial symmetry; pink**

Malva assurgentiflora
MALVACEAE

Royal Mallow

Chaparral; up to 1100 ft.; native

This perennial herb or shrub blooms in spring and summer, producing large flowers with dark venation that provide nectar and pollen for wildlife. It has attractive green-gray foliage. The Channel Islands are the only place where the species occurs naturally. On the mainland, it escaped cultivation and can be found in coastal wildlands. **Plant height 4–13 ft.; leaves alternate, lobed, margins toothed; petals showy, 5, free, filaments fused; radial symmetry; red, pink**

Sidalcea diploscypha
MALVACEAE

Fringed Checkerbloom

Woodlands, grasslands; up to 2800 ft.; native

This spring-blooming annual is covered with bristly hairs. Leaves are deeply divided with forked lobes. The delicate petals have red patches and pale veins. In a study that used fire to control the noxious weed Yellow Star-thistle (*Centaurea solstitialis*), Fringed Checkerbloom was one of the annual herbs that rebounded in place of that weed. **Plant height to 2 ft.; leaves alternate, deeply lobed, margins smooth; petals showy, 5, free, filaments fused; radial symmetry; pink**

Sidalcea hartwegii
MALVACEAE

Valley Checkerbloom

Woodlands, grasslands; up to 2000 ft.; native

This spring- and early-summer-blooming annual has mostly hairless stems and densely hairy sepals. The leaves are highly divided and look almost palmately compound. Its male parts are unique for an annual mallow. The filaments of most annual mallows are completely fused, but this species has partly free filaments toward the anthers. **Plant height to 1 ft.; leaves alternate, deeply lobed, margins toothed; petals showy, 5, free, filaments partly fused; radial symmetry; pink**

Sidalcea malviflora
MALVACEAE

Checker Bloom

Coastal bluffs, conifer forests, woodlands, grasslands; up to 7500 ft.; native

Blooming in summer, this perennial herb can produce a notable display when conditions are favorable. The circular leaves are highly lobed and can be fleshy. As is typical of Mediterranean-climate species, it prefers cool, wet winters and dry summers. It supports a host of butterflies, including the West Coast Lady. **Plant height 2–4 ft.; leaves alternate, lobed, margins toothed; petals showy, 5, free, filaments fused; radial symmetry; pink**

Sidalcea oregana
MALVACEAE

Oregon Checkerbloom

Marshes, meadows, streamsides; up to 9800 ft.; native

This perennial herb prefers moist soils. Blooming in spring and summer, the flower cluster is dense and the petals look as though they have been cut at their tips, giving the flowers a distinct raggedy appearance. Of five subspecies, the subspecies *oregana* and subspecies *spicata* are quite common; the others are considered rare. **Plant height 2–4 ft.; leaves alternate, dissected, margins toothed; petals showy, 5, free, filaments fused; radial symmetry; pink**

Trillium chloropetalum
MELANTHIACEAE

Giant Wakerobin

Conifer forests, woodlands; up to 6600 ft.; native

This early spring–blooming perennial has large, sessile, ovate leaves with mottled brown-green patches. Like all *Trillium* species, leaves and flower parts are in groups of three. Its maroon or white flowers have a subtle sweet-spicy aroma. The fruit is a fleshy, six-sided star shape. The plant and its roots can be mildly toxic. **Plant height to 2 ft.; leaves whorled, unlobed, margins smooth; petals showy, 3, free; radial symmetry; maroon, red, white**

Calandrinia menziesii
MONTIACEAE

Redmaids

Grasslands, woodlands, cultivated fields; up to 7200 ft.; native

Given the right conditions, this spring-blooming annual can paint entire hillsides in bright pink flowers. The seeds are high in nutrients and have been an important food source for birds, insects, and small mammals. Brewers's Calandrinia (*C. breweri*) is a less-common coastal species that has longer fruits than Redmaids. **Plant height to 1 ft.; leaves alternate, unlobed, margins smooth; flowers small, petals showy, 5, free; radial symmetry; magenta**

Calyptridium monospermum
MONTIACEAE

One-seeded Pussypaws

Conifer forests; 1000–13,000 ft.; native

This summer-blooming perennial herb has a short stem and a flat basal rosette. Leaves are hairless and tongue-shaped. Its pink, papery sepals are round and usually larger than the flowers. A similar species with a similar name, *C. monandrum* (Common Pussypaws), grows in Southern California but is an annual and has less congested flower clusters. **Plant height to 18 in.; leaves basal, unlobed, margins smooth; sepals showy; flowers small, petals 4, free; radial symmetry; red, white**

Calyptridium umbellatum
MONTIACEAE

Mount Hood Pussypaws

Conifer forests; 800–14,100 ft.; native

This summer-blooming annual or perennial is similar to One-seeded Pussypaws, but with lighter petals and a single flower cluster per basal rosette. Plants often have many basal rosettes close together. In both species, the flowering stems rise during the heat of the day and lie flat when it cools off. **Plant height to 2 ft.; leaves basal rosette, unlobed, margins smooth; sepals showy; flowers small, petals 4, free; radial symmetry; sepals pink; flowers red, white**

Lysimachia latifolia
MYRSINACEAE

Starflower

Conifer forests, woodlands; up to 4600 ft.; native

This spring-blooming perennial has alternate leaves that transition to a whorl along the stem. Its star-shaped flowers have variable petal numbers and are borne singly on threadlike stalks. Native to Western North America, it grows in shaded, seasonally moist areas. It was recently moved from the genus *Trientalis* based on morphological and DNA evidence. **Plant height to 6 in.; leaves whorled, sometimes opposite, unlobed, margins smooth; flowers small, petals showy, 5–9, free; radial symmetry; pink, white**

Nama demissa
NAMACEAE

Purplemat

Deserts; 300–6500 ft.; native

Blooming in spring, this annual herb forms a carpet of pink over sandy flats throughout the deserts of Southwestern North America. Restricted to the Eastern Mojave, variety *covillei* has gray-green foliage and leaves with long, thin bases (petioles). The common form, variety *demissum*, has green foliage and sessile leaves. **Plant height 1–8 in.; leaves alternate, unlobed, margins smooth; flower clusters showy; petals 5, partially fused; radial symmetry; pink**

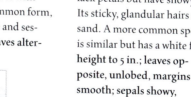

Abronia maritima
NYCTAGINACEAE

Red Sand Verbena

Dunes; up to 330 ft.; native

This rare perennial herb can bloom year-round. Typical of the sand verbenas, it has red stems, fleshy ovate leaves, and umbrella-shaped flower clusters. The flowers lack petals but have showy petal-like sepals. Its sticky, glandular hairs can be covered in sand. A more common species, *A. umbellata*, is similar but has a white flower center. **Plant height to 5 in.; leaves opposite, unlobed, margins smooth; sepals showy, 5, partially fused; radial symmetry; red, magenta**

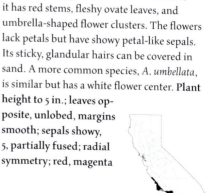

Abronia villosa
NYCTAGINACEAE

Desert Sand Verbena

Deserts; up to 5200 ft.; native

Like its coastal relatives, this annual has round leaves covered in sticky hairs. It resembles Pink Sand Verbena (*A. umbellata*) but has a less fleshy appearance. It is native to the deserts of Southwestern North America. Winter rain can cause it to germinate in abundance, carpeting the desert in pink, umbrella-shaped flower clusters from winter through summer. **Plant height to 6 in.; leaves opposite, unlobed, margins smooth; sepals showy, 5, partially fused; radial symmetry; pink, red**

Mirabilis laevis
NYCTAGINACEAE

Desert Wishbone Bush

Chaparral, woodlands, deserts, grasslands up to 8200 ft; native

This spring-blooming subshrub has a distinct architecture because of its evenly forked, branching pattern. The repeating V-shapes of its light-colored branches are reminiscent of wishbones, hence its common name. Three varieties have been described in California based on variation in hairiness, flower color, and fruit shape. **Plant height to 30 in.; leaves opposite, basally lobed or not, margins smooth; sepals showy, 5, partially fused; radial symmetry; pink, magenta, white**

Mirabilis multiflora
NYCTAGINACEAE

Giant Four O'clock

Deserts; up to 8200 ft; native

This perennial herb's round leaves become less hairy with age. Blooming in spring and summer, it produces an impressive floral display, with clusters that can include up to six large flowers. Two varieties have been described: one has warty fruits and the other's fruits are smooth. It has many documented uses, including as a tobacco substitute. **Plant height to 2 ft.; leaves opposite, unlobed, margins smooth; sepals showy, 5, partially fused; radial symmetry; magenta**

Chamerion angustifolium
ONAGRACEAE

Fireweed

Conifer forests, wetlands; up to 10,800 ft.; native

This perennial herb blooms in late summer and early fall. It has a circumboreal distribution, meaning it is found in boreal (northern) zones throughout the world. The leaves resemble those of willows and are often opposite, transitioning to alternate along the stem. It grows in open places and becomes abundant after fire. **Plant height 1–6 ft.; leaves opposite to alternate, unlobed, margins smooth to minutely toothed; petals showy, 4, free; radial symmetry; pink, magenta**

Clarkia amoena
ONAGRACEAE

Farewell-to-spring

Coastal scrub, conifer forests, woodlands; up to 2300 ft.; native

This showy annual can be found blooming in late spring along the western seaboard, from San Francisco Bay to Canada. The common name captures a main life-history characteristic of this annual. It is one of the last spring wildflowers to bloom, signaling the transition to summer. Records indicate that its seeds can be dried, ground, and used for food. **Plant height to 3 ft.; leaves opposite, unlobed, margins smooth; petals showy, 4, free; radial symmetry; pink, lavender**

Clarkia concinna
ONAGRACEAE

Red Ribbons

Conifer forests, woodlands; up to 4200 ft.; native

Blooming in spring, this annual has erect stems topped with impressive flowers. Each petal has three lobes, like a trident. The sepals curl back like a ribbon tied into a bow, hence the common name. Wild Red Ribbons are found only in the Northern Coast Ranges and Northern Sierra Foothills of California. It is often included in wildflower seed mixes. **Plant height to 16 in.; leaves opposite, unlobed, margins smooth; petals showy, 4, free; mostly radial symmetry; pink, lavender, red**

Clarkia gracilis
ONAGRACEAE

Slender Clarkia

Conifer forests, woodlands; up to 4900 ft.; native

This spring-blooming annual has erect stems and nodding buds. It includes four subspecies based on variation in flower color patterns. Flowers of subspecies *gracilis* are pink with light petal bases; flowers of subspecies *sonomensis* have a red spot in the center of each petal. **Plant height to 3 ft.; leaves opposite, unlobed, margins smooth; petals showy, 4, free; radial symmetry; pink, magenta**

Clarkia purpurea
ONAGRACEAE

Winecup Clarkia

Grasslands, shrublands, woodlands; up to 4900 ft.; native

The flower color of this spring-blooming annual varies from pink to deep wine-red. The defining characteristic of the species is its ribbed ovary. Multiple subspecies have been described based on flower color patterns and stigma length. It has been used to make pinole, a seed mixture that is ground and eaten as a mash. **Plant height to 2 ft.; leaves opposite, unlobed, margins smooth; petals showy, 4, free; radial symmetry; pink, lavender, magenta**

Clarkia rubicunda
ONAGRACEAE

Ruby Chalice Clarkia

Shrublands, woodlands; up to 2700 ft.; native

Clarkias are often called Farewell-to-spring because they are usually the last wildflowers to bloom in spring. Blooming in summer, this erect annual could be called "Hello Summer." It has a very narrow distribution surrounding the San Francisco Bay Area. It is similar to Farewell-to-spring (*C. amoena*), but the flower has a dark center. **Plant height to 4 ft.; leaves opposite, unlobed, margins smooth; petals showy, 4, free; radial symmetry; pink, red**

Clarkia speciosa
ONAGRACEAE

Redspot Clarkia

Woodlands, chaparral; up to 2300 ft.; native

The specific name of this late spring– and summer-blooming annual means "showy." Its common name refers to the dark spots in the centers of the petals, which appear sometimes, but not always. Pismo Clarkia (*C. speciosa* subsp. *immaculata*) is a rare and endangered coastal plant with unspotted petals. **Plant height to 20 in.; leaves opposite, unlobed, margins smooth; petals showy, 4, free; radial symmetry; pink, lavender, white**

Clarkia unguiculata
ONAGRACEAE

Elegant Clarkia

Woodlands; up to 4900 ft.; native

The flowers of this summer-blooming annual resemble fireworks. The specific name, *unguiculata*, is Latin for "with a small claw." The petals are clawed, or paddle-shaped, with long, narrow bases. The flower's red anthers and white-tipped pistil make it a real show-stopper. It is a common component of wildflower seed mixes. **Plant height to 3 ft.; leaves alternate, unlobed, margins smooth; petals showy, 4, free; radial symmetry; magenta**

Clarkia xantiana
ONAGRACEAE

Gunsight Clarkia

Woodlands, chaparral; 800–9000 ft.; native

Each petal of this spring-blooming annual has two lobes at the tip with a small tooth in between. There are two subspecies: one has larger flowers (subsp. *xantiana*) that are usually pollinated by insects, and another has smaller flowers (subsp. *parviflora*) and is usually self-fertile. Research indicates that fewer pollinators are available in areas where subspecies *parviflora* grows. **Plant height to 30 in.; leaves opposite, unlobed, margins smooth; petals showy, 4, free; mostly radial symmetry; pink, lavender**

Epilobium canum
ONAGRACEAE

California Fuchsia

Coastal sage scrub, conifer forests, chaparral; up to 11,200 ft.; native

This herb produces a massive display of flowers. Unlike most showy perennials, it continues flowering well into late-summer and fall, brightening gardens during the heat of summer. It is an important nectar source for hummingbirds during their fall migration. It was formerly placed in the genus *Zauschneria*. **Plant height to 30 in.; leaves opposite, sometimes alternate, unlobed, margins rarely toothed; sepals and petals showy, 4, partially fused; mirror symmetry; red, orange**

Epilobium densiflorum
ONAGRACEAE

Denseflower Willowherb

Many communities; up to 8500 ft.; native

This spring-blooming annual occurs in Western North America, generally in habitats with moist soils. It has hairy, lance-shaped, green leaves. The specific name, *densiflorum*, describes its flowers, which occur in a dense, leafy inflorescence. The petals are deeply two-lobed. Its small seeds are important forage for small birds. **Plant height to 1 ft.; leaves opposite below, alternate above, unlobed, margins minutely toothed; flower clusters showy; petals 4, free; radial symmetry; pink**

Epilobium obcordatum
ONAGRACEAE

Rockfringe Willowherb

Conifer forests, alpine; 5600–13,100 ft.; native

This attractive, summer-blooming perennial herb grows from a woody underground stem. It is native to Western North America, where it grows along rocky ridges, hence the common name. It has a compact growth form, typical of high-elevation species. Its leaves are round and borne on short stems. Deep lobes make the petals appear heart-shaped. **Plant height to 6 in.; leaves opposite, unlobed, margins toothed; petals showy, 4, free; radial symmetry; pink**

Epilobium siskiyouense
ONAGRACEAE

Siskiyou Fireweed

Conifer forests, alpine; 5600–8200 ft.; native

The large pink flowers of this rare summer-blooming perennial herb can be found creeping among red or blue serpentine rocks. Often found on slopes, it is a welcome sight during steep, uphill hikes. Like all *Epilobium* species, it has four petals and four sepals; its distinctive features are its large and heart-shaped petals, cross-shaped stigma, pointed leaves, and low stature. **Plant height to 10 in.; leaves opposite, unlobed, margins smooth; petals showy, 4, free; radial symmetry; pink**

Calypso bulbosa
ORCHIDACEAE

Fairy Slipper

Conifer forests; up to 5900 ft.; native

Growing in moist, rich needle duff, this perennial herb produces a single leaf in spring from a thick underground stem (corm). Its flowering stem bares a single flower with a pouchlike lower lip, reminiscent of a fairy's slipper. Though a single flower alone is a treat, this species can grow en masse, producing incredible flower displays. **Plant height to 7 in.; leaf basal, unlobed, margins smooth; petals and sepals showy, 3 each, free; mirror symmetry; pink, white**

Corallorhiza maculata
ORCHIDACEAE

Spotted Coral Root

Conifer forests; up to 11,000 ft.; native

This perennial herb blooms from early spring through summer. The genus name refers to its knotted and branched underground stems, or rhizomes, that resemble coral. It is a mycoheterotroph that gets its nutrition from soil fungi that are connected to tree roots. The specific name means "spotted." Each stem has multiple small flowers. **Plant height to 2 ft.; leaves absent; flower clusters showy; petals and sepals 3 each, free; mirror symmetry; red, brown, white, with pink spots**

Corallorhiza striata
ORCHIDACEAE

Striped Coral Root

Conifer forests; up to 8600 ft.; native

Blooming in summer, this perennial herb occurs throughout Western North America. Similar to Summer Coral Root, it is leafless and obtains its nutrients from fungi via mycoheterotrophy. Petals and sepals have prominent dark veins, hence the name *striata*, which means "striped." It produces dozens of flowers that attract insect pollinators. **Plant height to 20 in.; leaves absent; flower clusters showy; sepals and petals 3 each, free; mirror symmetry; pink with red stripes**

Epipactis gigantea
ORCHIDACEAE

Stream Orchid

Seeps, wet meadows, riparian; 2800-8500 ft.; native

This widespread, North American perennial orchid blooms from spring through fall. Its flowers produce a scent that mimics the smell of honeydew, the liquid waste produced by aphids, which are a favorite food of syrphid fly larvae. Adult flies are attracted to the scent, lay their eggs, and, in the process, inadvertently pollinate the flowers. **Plant height to 3 ft.; leaves alternate, unlobed, margins smooth; sepals and petals showy, 3 each, free; mirror symmetry; pink, yellow-green**

Castilleja applegatei
OROBANCHACEAE

Wavy-leaf Paintbrush

Chaparral, sagebrush scrub, conifer forests, alpine; 1000–11,800 ft.; native

Blooming in late spring, this perennial herb has sticky foliage and wavy leaf margins. It is a common paintbrush in California and is highly variable. The brightly colored parts of the plant are bracts, which are usually red but may be orange or yellow. The flower is slender, tubular, and mostly hidden by the bracts. **Plant height to 14 in.; leaves alternate, unlobed, margins wavy; bracts showy; petals 5, fused; mirror symmetry; bright red, yellow**

Castilleja foliolosa
OROBANCHACEAE

Wooly Paintbrush

Chaparral; up to 5900 ft.; native

This spring-blooming perennial herb is covered in white-gray hairs. Rarely, the showy bracts can be yellow instead of red. Like all *Castilleja* species, it is hemiparasitic, meaning it obtains some of its carbohydrates from other species—usually small shrubs in this case. The specific name of this leafy plant, *foliolosa*, means "full of leaves." **Plant height to 2 ft.; leaves alternate, unlobed or lobed, margins smooth; bracts showy; petals 5, fused; mirror symmetry; red, yellow, green**

Castilleja miniata
OROBANCHACEAE

Scarlet Paintbrush

Wet montane meadows, streamsides, Darlingtonia wetlands; up to 11,500 ft.; native

The leaves of this summer-blooming perennial herb are coated in hairs and are distinctively veined. Paintbrushes are hemiparasites that obtain some of their food through root connections. Although this species is tall and showy, you won't find it growing in gardens, because both the hemiparasite and its host plants are difficult to cultivate together. **Plant height to 30 in.; leaves alternate, unlobed, margins smooth; bracts showy; petals 5, fused; mirror symmetry; bracts red, purple; petals yellow-green**

Pedicularis attollens
OROBANCHACEAE

Little Elephant's Head

Wet meadows, streamsides; 3900–13,100 ft.; native

The flowers of this summer-blooming perennial herb resemble tiny elephant heads. The flower's upper petal is curved, like an elephant's trunk, and the lobed lower petals resemble elephant ears. It grows in mountainous areas along streams in wet or moist soils and is pollinated by bees. **Plant height to 2 ft.; leaves in basal rosette, stem leaves alternate, dissected, margins toothed; flower clusters showy; petals 5, partially fused; mirror symmetry; pink, purple**

Pedicularis densiflora
OROBANCHACEAE

Warrior's Plume

Chaparral, conifer and mixed forests; up to 6,900 ft.; native

This perennial herb blooms in winter and early spring. Clusters of bright red flowers with long, tubular corollas attract pollinators. Its brown, fernlike leaves age to green. Although its roots invade nearby shrubs to obtain nutrients and it is technically a hemiparasite, it can survive without parasitizing other plants. **Plant height to 2 ft.; leaves in basal rosette, dissected, margins toothed; flower clusters showy; petals 5, partially fused; mirror symmetry; red, lavender, yellow-orange**

Pedicularis groenlandica
OROBANCHACEAE

Elephant's Head

Conifer forests, wetlands; 3300–11,800 ft.; native

This perennial herb is larger and less hairy than Little Elephant's Head, and it blooms in the spring. It is native to mountainous regions in the Western United States and Northeastern Canada. Its specific name means "of Greenland," where it was first identified, though it is not abundant. **Plant height to 30 in.; leaves in basal rosette, stem leaves alternate, dissected, margins toothed; flower clusters showy; petals 5, partially fused; mirror symmetry; pink, purple**

Triphysaria pusilla
OROBANCHACEAE

Dwarf Owl's Clover

Grasslands; up to 3900 ft.; native

This spring-blooming annual has hairy foliage and ranges in color from light green to deep maroon. It grows in moist areas along the West Coast of North America. It is hemiparasitic and obtains some of its nutrients from other plants via root connections. A chemical mechanism prevents it from parasitizing the roots of other *Triphysaria* species. **Plant height to 8 in.; leaves alternate, lobed, margins toothed; petals inconspicuous, 5, partially fused; mirror symmetry; red, pink, purple**

Paeonia californica
PAEONIACEAE

California Peony

Coastal scrub, chaparral; up to 4900 ft.; native

This herbaceous perennial produces fresh shoots each spring from fleshy roots. The thick leaves have deeply lobed leaflets, and its large, solitary flowers nod toward the ground. One other *Paeonia* species is present in California: Brown's peony (*P. brownii*) is similar but has more rounded leaf tips and occurs in the Sierra Nevada. **Plant height to 2.5 ft.; leaves basal, stem leaves alternate, compound, lobed leaflets, margins smooth; petals showy, 5–6, free; radial symmetry; maroon**

Dicentra formosa
PAPAVERACEAE

Pacific Bleeding Heart

Conifer forests, woodlands; up to 7900 ft.; native

This spring- and summer-blooming perennial herb has large clusters of distinctive, heart-shaped flowers and fernlike leaves. A recent study determined that Bleeding Heart contains alkaloids that may have pain-relieving effects, and there is interest in its potential anticancer properties. **Plant height to 18 in.; leaves alternate, compound, leaflets dissected, margins toothed; petals showy, 4, outer 2 free, inner 2 partially fused; mirror symmetry; pink, purple, pale yellow**

Dicentra uniflora
PAPAVERACEAE

Steer's Head

Gravelly forest openings, alpine; 3300–10,800 ft.; native

Growing in rocky places throughout Western North America, this perennial herb has a short bloom period that follows snowmelt. Leaves are delicate and fernlike. The genus name is Greek for "double spurred," which describes the flower's two recurved petals. The unique flower resembles a horned steer's head. **Plant height to 4 in.; leaves basal, compound, lobed leaflets, margins smooth; petals showy, 4, partially fused; mirror symmetry; pink, lavender, white**

Diplacus bigelovii
PHRYMACEAE

Bigelow's Monkeyflower

Deserts, shrublands; up to 11,000 ft.; native

This annual blooms from late winter to early summer. All monkeyflowers were once included in the genus *Mimulus*. DNA evidence was used to reclassify species into several groups. *Diplacus* and *Erythranthe* have different pedicel-to-calyx length ratios: in general, *Erythranthe* species have long pedicles, whereas *Diplacus* species' pedicels are short. **Plant height 1–10 in.; leaves opposite, unlobed; margins smooth; petals showy, 5, partially fused; mirror symmetry; magenta with yellow spots**

Diplacus douglasii
PHRYMACEAE

Purple Mouse Ears

Riparian, grasslands; up to 3900 ft.; native

This spring-blooming annual grows in gravelly, open habitats in California and Southwest Oregon. The tiny flowers are distinctive. The two upper petals are large, and the three lower petals are reduced, giving the overall impression of magenta mouse ears. They produce large, open flowers in wet years and self-pollinate in dry ones. **Plant height to 2 in.; leaves basal, unlobed, margins smooth; petals showy, 5, partially fused; mirror symmetry; pink, magenta, purple**

Diplacus fremontii
PHRYMACEAE

Fremont's Monkeyflower

Conifer forests, woodlands; up to 6900 ft.; native

Blooming in spring, the magenta flowers of this species are not clustered. The inside of the corolla tube is yellow and usually hairless or has a few fine hairs. The calyx is inflated and very hairy. Each calyx lobe is about the same length, which helps distinguish it from similar species. Rarely, flower color is yellow. **Plant height 1–8 in.; leaves opposite, unlobed, margins smooth; petals showy, 5, partially fused; mirror symmetry; magenta, yellow**

Diplacus kelloggii
PHRYMACEAE

Kellogg's Monkeyflower

Conifer forests, woodlands; up to 5000 ft.; native

Growing on rock slides or in disturbed areas, this annual blooms from late winter to early summer. Its calyx is hairy with unequal lobes, and its oval leaves are deep green with distinct venation. The conspicuously long corolla tube is dark with yellow patches on the inside, which help guide bee pollinators to the nectar reward. **Plant height 1–12 in.; leaves opposite, unlobed, margins smooth; petals showy, 5, partially fused; mirror symmetry; magenta, yellow**

Diplacus layneae
PHRYMACEAE

Layne's Monkeyflower

Woodlands, chaparral; 700–2000 ft.; native

This summer-blooming annual occurs only in California. It is relatively abundant and grows in open, rocky, disturbed places. The ribbed calyx has pointed lobes that are equal in length. The corolla tube opening (throat) has a mottled pattern. The most common corolla color is pink with white splotches. **Plant height 1–10 in.; leaves opposite, unlobed, margins smooth; petals showy, 5, partially fused; mirror symmetry; pink, white**

Diplacus mephiticus
PHRYMACEAE

Skunky Monkeyflower

Sagebrush scrub, open slopes; up to 13,500 ft.; native

Growing in open, often disturbed granitic areas of the Eastern Sierra and into Nevada, this annual herb blooms in late spring and summer. It is covered with glandular hairs that have an unpleasant odor, hence its common name and scientific name: *mephitic* means "foul-smelling" in Latin. Calyx lobes are more or less equal. **Plant height 1–6 in.; leaves opposite, unlobed, margins smooth; petals showy, 5, partially fused; mirror symmetry; pink, yellow**

Erythranthe cardinalis
PHRYMACEAE

Scarlet Monkeyflower

Many communities, streams, seeps; up to 7900 ft.; native

This perennial herb blooms in riparian areas throughout spring and summer. Its two-lobed stigma closes quickly when touched. The genus name comes from two Greek words: *erythr* means "red" and *anthos* means "flower." The genus *Erythranthe* includes many species, many of which do not have red flowers.

Plant height to 2.5 ft.; leaves opposite, unlobed, margins toothed; petals showy, 5, partially fused; mirror symmetry; red

Erythranthe lewisii
PHRYMACEAE

Lewis' Monkeyflower

Montane to alpine streams and seeps; 2100–10,200 ft.; native

Found throughout Western North America, this summer-blooming perennial herb is covered in fine hairs, and its leaves have prominent veins. This species is part of a model system used to study pollinator-mediated speciation and flower-color evolution. Because monkeyflowers were recently reclassified, these studies refer to *Mimulus lewisii*.

Plant height 10–30 in.; leaves opposite, unlobed, margins toothed; petals showy, 5, partially fused; mirror symmetry; pink, magenta

Collinsia tinctoria
PLANTAGINACEAE

Tincture Plant

Conifer forests, woodlands, chaparral; up to 8200 ft; native

Blooming in spring and summer, this annual produces flowers that are arranged into a tower of dense whorls. The flower stalk (pedicel) is short or absent. The leaf underside is densely hairy, whereas the upper surface is less hairy and blotchy. *Tinctoria* means "to dye" and refers to the species' brown sap , which temporaily can stain one's skin when plants are touched. **Plant height to 2 ft.; leaves opposite, unlobed, margins smooth or toothed; flower clusters showy; petals 5, partially fused; mirror symmetry; pink, lavender, white**

Digitalis purpurea
PLANTAGINACEAE

Foxglove

Disturbed areas; up to 5600 ft.; non-native

This garden escapee has displaced native vegetation, especially near the coast. This hairy, spring-blooming biennial has tall, eye-catching flower clusters. Dark spots appear inside its large, pink-purple corollas. All parts of the plant are toxic. Historically, it was a commercial source of digitalin, a powerful cardiac stimulant. **Plant height 2–5 ft.; leaves in basal rosette, stem leaves alternate, unlobed, margins minutely toothed; flower clusters showy; petals 5, partially fused; mirror symmetry; pink, purple, white**

Keckiella cordifolia
PLANTAGINACEAE

Heart-leaved Keckiella

Chaparral, forest; up to 5200 ft.; native

This shrub blooms from late spring through summer. Flowers that have evolved with hummingbird pollinators are often red with long flower tubes. The stamens sit just below the upper petals and touch the head of the hummingbird as it drinks nectar. It has distinctive heart-shaped leaves. **Plant height 6–8 ft.; leaves opposite, basally lobed; margins toothed; flower clusters showy; petals 5, partially fused; mirror symmetry; red**

Penstemon centranthifolius
PLANTAGINACEAE

Scarlet Bugler

Chaparral, oak woodlands; up to 5900 ft.; native

Blooming in spring and summer, this perennial herb is hairless and covered with a chalky powder, making the plant look gray-green. Flowers are borne along impressive wandlike stems. Like all *Penstemon* species, its sterile stamen (staminode) sits on the corolla floor. Its leaves are heart-shaped with clasping leaf bases. **Plant height 2–4 ft.; leaves opposite, basally lobed, margins smooth; petals showy, 5, partially fused; mirror symmetry; scarlet**

Penstemon eatonii
PLANTAGINACEAE

Firecracker Penstemon

Sagebrush scrub, pinyon–juniper woodlands, yellow pine forests; up to 5900 ft.; native

The red, tubular flowers of this perennial herb bloom in spring and summer throughout the desert mountains of Southwestern North America. Its sterile stamen is hairless or sparsely hairy at the tip. When its anthers release pollen, they split near the tip—a characteristic that distinguishes it from similar species. **Plant height 2–3 ft.; leaves opposite, unlobed, margins smooth; petals showy, 5, partially fused; mirror symmetry; scarlet**

Penstemon grinnellii
PLANTAGINACEAE

Grinnell's Beardtongue

Conifer forests, woodlands; 1000–9400 ft.; native

This early summer–blooming perennial herb has a low-mounded growth form and hairless, leathery leaves. The flower has short, sticky hairs and a short, wide-open corolla tube, reminiscent of a gaping mouth. All *Penstemon* species have sterile stamens (staminodes). Those with hairy staminodes are known as beardtongues. **Plant height to 3 ft.; leaves opposite, unlobed, margins toothed to nearly smooth; petals showy, 5, partially fused; mirror symmetry; pink, purple, white**

Penstemon newberryi
PLANTAGINACEAE

Mountain Pride

Rocky outcrops and talus slopes in the
mountains; 1600–12,100 ft.; native

This photogenic spring- and
summer-blooming, mat-forming subshrub
has leathery, egg-shaped leaves. Its distribution extends into Oregon and Nevada. Wooly
white hairs ornament its corolla floor and stamens. It is named after a physician from the
1800s. Historically, physicians had to be good
botanists, because their
remedies were often herb-
al. Plant height 4–12 in.;
leaves opposite, unlobed,
margins toothed; petals
showy, 5, partially fused;
mirror symmetry; pink

Penstemon rostriflorus
PLANTAGINACEAE

Beaked Penstemon

Sagebrush, Joshua Tree woodland, pinyon–
juniper woodlands, montane forests; 1600–
11,500 ft.; native

The flower of this summer-blooming perennial herb has a strongly reflexed lower lobe
and a hairless staminode. It evolved to be pollinated by hummingbirds, which have good
color vision and are attracted to red flowers.
They use their slender beaks and bottle-brush
tongues to drink nectar
from the long, tubular
flowers. Plant height 2–3
ft.; leaves opposite, un-
lobed, margins smooth;
petals showy, 5, partially
fused; mirror symmetry;
red, orange

Armeria maritima
PLUMBAGINACEAE

Sea Thrift

Ocean bluffs, coastal strand, grasslands; up to 800 ft.; native

This perennial herb blooms in coastal areas from late winter through summer. It is native to coastal and mountainous regions throughout the Northern Hemisphere. Dense flower clusters on stalks adorn this mounding plant. This species was featured on the British 3-pence coin from 1937 to 1952, reportedly to encourage citizens to "be thrifty." **Plant height to 1 ft.; leaves basal, unlobed, margins smooth; flower clusters showy; petals 5, free; radial symmetry; pink, lavender, white**

Allophyllum divaricatum
POLEMONIACEAE

Purple False Gilia

Woodlands, chaparral; 1000–5900 ft.; native

Often occurring after fire or disturbance, this variable annual has a skunky odor and is generally covered with long-stalked glands. *Allophyllum* means "with diverse leaves," referring to the leaf-lobe number that ranges from three to thirteen. In spring, the plant is covered in clusters of flowers with very long flower tubes. **Plant height to 2 ft.; leaves alternate, deeply lobed, margins smooth; flowers small, petals showy, 5, partially fused; radial symmetry; magenta, pink, lavender**

Collomia heterophylla
POLEMONIACEAE

Variable-leaf Collomia

Openings in forests, woodlands, chaparral; up to 6600 ft.; native

This spring-blooming, glandular-hairy annual can be especially prolific in disturbed or burned areas. Its range extends to British Columbia and Idaho. *Heterophylla* means "variable-leaved," referring to the various leaf shapes present on a single plant. *Collomia* means "glue," referring to its seeds, which are gelatinous and sticky when wet. **Plant height to 8 in.; leaves alternate, unlobed to lobed, margins smooth; flower clusters showy; petals 5, partially fused; radial symmetry; pink, white**

Collomia tinctoria
POLEMONIACEAE

Staining Collomia

Openings in chaparral, woodlands, forests; 2000–9900 ft.; native

Blooming in late spring and summer, this annual is common in gravelly, rocky openings. Its range extends to Washington, Idaho, and Nevada. Plants have long, glandular hairs and stems that branch at wide angles off of the main stem. The dainty flowers have blue pollen that will stain your hands yellow when crushed. **Plant height to 3 in.; leaves alternate, unlobed, margins smooth; flowers small, petals showy, 5, partially fused; radial symmetry; pink**

Ipomopsis aggregata
POLEMONIACEAE

Scarlet Gilia

Openings in conifer forests, woodlands; 3600–10,800 ft.; native

It is always a treat to see this stunning perennial herb in bloom. In late spring and summer, the lateral clusters of red, trumpet-shaped, tubular flowers are hummingbird magnets. Two subspecies occur in California, while six other subspecies grow in the Rocky Mountains. The genus name, *Ipomopsis*, means "striking appearance" in Greek. **Plant height 2–3 ft.; leaves in basal rosette, stem leaves alternate, lobed, margins smooth; petals showy, 5, partially fused; radial symmetry; red**

Leptosiphon ciliatus
POLEMONIACEAE

Whiskerbrush

Conifer forests, woodlands, chaparral; up to 9900 ft.; native

This dainty annual is common in dry openings, where it creates swaths of color. Blooming in spring and summer, the small, yet exquisite, long-tubed flowers often have dark pink or red spots near the yellow centers. The flowers emerge from a dense, headlike structure composed of bracts that are fringed with short, white hairs. **Plant height to 1 ft.; leaves opposite, deeply palmately lobed, margins smooth; petals showy, 5, partially fused; radial symmetry; pink, white**

Linanthus californicus
POLEMONIACEAE

California Prickly Phlox

Chaparral, coastal sage scrub, forests, dunes; up to 4900 ft.; native

The lush flowers on this subshrub contrast strikingly with its scrubby, gray-green, sharp-pointed leaves. It blooms from winter through summer. Of the three subspecies, subspecies *tomentosus* is the hairiest and has the narrowest range—occurring in coastal dunes. Subspecies *californicus* has the widest distribution. **Plant height 12–40 in.; leaves alternate, deeply palmately lobed, margins smooth; petals showy, 5, partially fused; radial symmetry; pink, lavender**

Loeseliastrum matthewsii
POLEMONIACEAE

Desert Calico

Deserts; up to 5900 ft.; native

Common in sandy areas in the southern half of California, east into Nevada, the exquisite floral markings on this bristly annual are unique. The calico pattern on the flowers is responsible for its common name. Long stamens exceed the length of the upper lip (petal) of the strongly bilateral (mirror symmetry) flower. It blooms in spring and summer. **Plant height to 6 in.; leaves alternate, unlobed, margins toothed; petals showy, 5, partially fused; mirror symmetry; pink, white, yellow**

Microsteris gracilis
POLEMONIACEAE

Slender Phlox

Conifer forests, woodlands, chaparral; up to 11,000 ft.; native

Microsteris means "small star," alluding to the effect created by these charming, generally pink flowers with lobed tips. Ranging throughout much of Western North America, this variable species also occurs in South America. Flowering in spring and summer, the annual is single-stemmed to many-branched and is glandular-hairy above. Plant height to 8 in.; leaves opposite, unlobed, margins smooth; flowers small, petals showy, 5, partially fused; radial symmetry; pink, white

Phlox speciosa
POLEMONIACEAE

Showy Phlox

Openings in sagebrush scrub, woodlands, forests; 1600–7900 ft.; native

This spring-blooming perennial herb has large, pinwheel-shaped flowers up to 2 in. across, with heart-shaped petals. *Speciosa* means "showy" in Latin, which this species certainly is! Wide-ranging and morphologically variable, molecular analysis was used to help determine whether subspecies should be recognized, but little genetic variation was found. Plant height to 16 in.; leaves opposite, unlobed, margins smooth; petals showy, 5, partially fused; radial symmetry; pink, white

Phlox stansburyi
POLEMONIACEAE

Cold Desert Phlox

Sagebrush scrub, pinyon–juniper woodlands, roadsides; 5600–9800 ft.; native

Growing in the deserts of Western North America, this spring-blooming perennial herb can have white or pink flowers. The leaves are universally hairy but can be quite variable, from linear to more oval. It includes three subspecies, differentiated by woodiness and flower size. *Phlox* means "flame" in Greek and refers to the group's bright flowers. **Plant height to 10 in.; leaves opposite, unlobed, margins smooth; petals showy, 5, partially fused; radial symmetry; pink, white**

Saltugilia splendens
POLEMONIACEAE

Splendid Woodland Gilia

Openings in woodlands, chaparral; 1000–7900 ft.; native

Blooming in spring and summer, this annual has delicate flowers borne on slender, gland-dotted, wiry stems. It is endemic to Southern California, where it occurs on rocky soils. Historically, the genus was classified as part of the larger genus *Gilia*, but DNA and other evidence support including it in the genus *Saltugilia*. **Plant height 4–40 in.; leaves basal, lobed, margins smooth; petals showy, 5, partially fused; radial symmetry; pink**

Polygala californica
POLYGALACEAE

California Milkwort

Chaparral, conifer forests; up to 4600 ft.; native

Blooming in spring and summer, this perennial herb has prominent winged sepals that are the same color as the flower. Its flowers resemble pea flowers, reflecting the close evolutionary relationship between the milkworts (Polygalaceae) and the legumes (Fabaceae). It grows in coastal areas from the Channel Islands to Southwest Oregon. **Plant height 2–14 in.; leaves alternate, unlobed, margins smooth; flower clusters showy; petals 3 or 5, fused; mirror symmetry; pink, purple, white**

Polygala cornuta
POLYGALACEAE

Sierra Milkwort

In spring and summer, the pink-tinged, pealike flowers of Sierra Milkwort bloom. In Greek, *gala* means "milk," which refers to European species that were thought to increase milk yields when fed to cattle. There is an odd gap in the distribution of this species; it skips over the Southern Sierra Nevada. **Plant height to 6 ft.; leaves opposite, unlobed, margins smooth; flower clusters showy; petals 5, free; mirror symmetry; pink, lavender, white**

Chorizanthe membranacea
POLYGONACEAE

Pink Spineflower

Woodlands, chaparral, grasslands; 100–5000 ft.; native

Found in sandy-rocky areas, this annual has an unusual appearance for a spineflower. Unlike many others, it grows upright and has leafy stems. Atop the hairy stems are spherical structures composed of many papery floral bracts (involucres) with hooked awns. Each involucre contains a single, tiny flower. It blooms in spring and summer. **Plant height to 2 ft.; leaves basal, alternate, unlobed, margins smooth; flower clusters showy; tepals 6, free; radial symmetry; pink, white

Chorizanthe polygonoides
POLYGONACEAE

Knotweed Spineflower

Conifer forests, woodlands, chaparral; 100–5000 ft.; native

Like many spineflowers, this small, reddish, spring-blooming annual hugs the ground, growing in sand or gravel. The single flowers are surrounded by floral bracts (involucres) that have three teeth tipped with hooked awns. Variety *longispina*, from Southern California and Northern Baja, has longer awns and is rare. **Plant height to 2 in.; leaves basal, alternate, unlobed, margins smooth; tepals inconspicuous, 6, free; radial symmetry; red, pink, white

Chorizanthe staticoides
POLYGONACEAE

Turkish Rugging

Chaparral; 1000–5600 ft.; native

Growing in sandy, gravelly, or rocky areas, this hairy, often reddish annual grows upright and branches above with flattish flower clusters composed of many small flowers. As the specific name alludes, the species resembles Statice (*Limonium sinuatum*), a Mediterranean ornamental used in flower arrangements. It blooms in spring and summer. **Plant height to 2 ft.; leaves basal, un-lobed, margins smooth; flower clusters showy; tepals inconspicuous, 6, free; radial symmetry; pink, white**

Eriogonum latifolium
POLYGONACEAE

Coast Buckwheat

Dunes, grasslands; up to 260 ft.; native

This perennial is common in sandy areas along the coast. It has matted, gray-green, hairy foliage and eye-catching, pompom clusters of many small flowers. Like other coastal species, these plants bloom throughout the year. It is a host and food plant of Smith's Blue butterfly, an endangered species. **Plant height 8–28 in.; leaves alternate, unlobed, margins smooth, wavy; flower clusters showy; tepals 6, free; radial symmetry; pink, white**

Eriogonum lobbii
POLYGONACEAE

Lobb's Buckwheat

Conifer forests; 5200–12,500 ft.; native

One of the more striking buckwheats, this common montane species often grows on or near rocks. This perennial herb has large, oval, gray-hairy leaves and often stems that grow horizontally. It blooms in late spring and summer. Each flowering stem is capped with a large cluster of flowers that turn orange-red with age. **Plant height to 1 ft.; leaves basal, un-lobed, margins smooth; flower clusters showy; tepals 6, free; radial symmetry; pink, white, aging to orange or cherry-red**

Eriogonum maculatum
POLYGONACEAE

Spotted Buckwheat

Deserts; 300–8200 ft.; native

Maculatum means "spotted," and this common annual can be distinguished from other small buckwheats by the pink-purple spots on its outer tepals. Found in sandy-gravelly areas, this densely branched species has glandular-hairy flowers that appear somewhat inflated. Its little flower clusters bloom from spring through fall. **Plant height 4–8 in.; leaves in basal rosette, unlobed, margins smooth; flower clusters small; tepals inconspicuous, 6, free; radial symmetry; white, yellow, pink**

Eriogonum roseum
POLYGONACEAE

Wand Buckwheat

Openings in conifer forests, chaparral, woodlands; up to 7200 ft.; native

Common in sandy or gravelly areas, this annual blooms in spring, summer, and fall. Its distribution extends north to Southern Oregon and south to Northern Baja California. Its common name refers to its long branches, which are adorned with small, evenly spaced flower clusters. Plants are variably hairy. **Plant height to 32 in.; leaves in basal rosette, stem leaves alternate, unlobed, margins smooth; flower clusters small; tepals 6, free; radial symmetry; pink, white, yellow**

Oxyria digyna
POLYGONACEAE

Alpine Mountain Sorrel

Alpine; 5900–13,100 ft.; native

Occurring throughout northern latitudes, in California this perennial herb favors rock crevices and talus slopes in mountainous areas. Emerging from the green to reddish, fleshy, kidney-shaped leaves are elongated flowering stems with many small flowers in summer, turning reddish in fruit. *Oxyria* means "sour," referring to the taste of the leaves. **Plant height to 20 in.; leaves in basal rosette, basally lobed, margins smooth; tepals inconspicuous, 6, free; radial symmetry; flowers green, winged fruit red**

Oxytheca perfoliata
POLYGONACEAE

Roundleaf Oxytheca

Deserts; 1900–6200 ft.; native

This dainty, green to reddish annual deserves a close inspection. Tiny flowers appear in spring and summer. More notable are the large, disc- or funnel-shaped structures that surround the stem at each node, which are composed of three fused bracts with a sharply pointed awn at each corner. **Plant height to 8 in.; leaves basal, unlobed, margins smooth; tepals inconspicuous, 6, free; radial symmetry; flowers white, bracts red**

Persicaria lapathifolia
POLYGONACEAE

Pale Smartweed

Moist, disturbed areas; up to 4900 ft.; native

Blooming in summer and fall, this annual has upright stems and prefers disturbed areas. Thin, papery sheathing leaf bases (ocreae) surround the stems. The lance-shaped leaves are narrow to wide, sometimes with darker markings. It is considered native to California but has a worldwide distribution. **Plant height to 3 ft.; leaves alternate, unlobed, margins smooth, wavy; flower clusters showy; pink, green-white**

Pterostegia drymarioides
POLYGONACEAE

Fairy Mist

Conifer forests, woodlands, chaparral; up to 5300 ft.; native

This common annual with a sprawling habit grows in sandy or gravelly areas near rocks—or under other plants. In the shade, plants are green, but they often turn red in the sun. The tiny flowers are unisexual, meaning that each flower has either male or female parts, but not both. It blooms in spring and summer. **Plant height to 4 ft.; leaves opposite, 2-lobed or un-lobed, margins smooth; tepals inconspicuous, 6, free; radial symmetry; fruits pink, yellow**

Rumex acetosella
POLYGONACEAE

Sheep Sorrel

Wetlands-riparian, disturbed areas; up to 9800 ft.; non-native

This reddish perennial herb flowers in spring and summer. It has fleshy, arrow-shaped leaves with two downward- to outward-pointing basal lobes. Leaves are sour to the taste. This species is dioecious, meaning that male and female flowers are on separate individual plants. Plants often spread, creating colonies. **Plant height to 16 in.; leaves basal, alternate, basal lobes, margins smooth; tepals incon-spicuous; radial sym-metry; flowers green, fruits pink**

Rumex crispus
POLYGONACEAE

Curly Dock

Disturbed areas; up to 8900 ft.; non-native

Native to Eurasia, this stout perennial herb is found in moist areas. The specific name, *crispus*, means "curly," referring to the leaves. Blooming year-round, the upright flowering stems support a dense array of small flowers. These turn rust-colored in fruit and persist on the plant for some time. **Plant height 16–40 in.; leaves basal, alternate, unlobed, margins smooth, wavy; tepals inconspicuous; radial symmetry; flowers green, fruits pink**

Rumex hymenosepalus
POLYGONACEAE

Wild Rhubarb

Chaparral, grasslands, deserts; up to 6600 ft.; native

This perennial herb occurs in dry areas of Southwestern North America. Its tuberous roots are rich in tannins and have been used as a dye. Its leaves can be eaten as a green after being boiled to remove toxins. Its winged, pink fruits are far showier than its flowers, which bloom in winter and spring. **Plant height 10–35 in.; leaves basal, alternate, unlobed, margins smooth, wavy; tepals inconspicuous; radial symmetry; flowers green, fruits pink**

Rumex salicifolius
POLYGONACEAE

Willow Dock

Conifer forests, woodlands, chaparral; up to 11,500 ft.; native

Blooming in spring and summer, this perennial herb has a wide elevational range, occurring in wet or dry areas into Nevada, Arizona, and Northern Mexico. The specific name, *salicifolius*, means "willow-leafed." Indeed, its long narrow leaves resemble those of willows. In Europe, it is considered a roadside weed. **Plant height 1–2 ft.; leaves basal, alternate, unlobed, margins wavy; tepals inconspicuous; radial symmetry; flowers green, fruits red-brow**

Primula clevelandii
PRIMULACEAE

Padre's Shooting Star

Chaparral, woodlands, grasslands; up to 2000 ft.; native

This spring-blooming perennial herb produces new growth from underground parts each spring. Basal rosettes produce a single flowering stem, which is tipped with flowers that have distinctive reflexed petals. Buds initially point up; then, as the flower opens, the stem (pedicel) points downward. As the fruit develops, the pedicel straightens again. **Plant height 7–16 in.; leaves in basal rosette, unlobed, margins minutely toothed; petals showy, 5, fused near base; radial symmetry; pink, lavender, white**

Primula hendersonii
PRIMULACEAE

Mosquito Bill

Forests, woodlands, chaparral, grasslands; up to 6200 ft.; native

This perennial herb blooms from winter through early spring. The petals of its downward-pointing flowers fold sharply backward, reminiscent of a shooting star. A yellow ring appears at the base of the petals, and stamens are purple. The top of the fruit pops off like a cap, releasing ripe seeds. **Plant height 5–20 in.; leaves in basal rosette, unlobed, margins smooth or minutely toothed; petals showy, 5, sometimes 4, fused near base; radial symmetry; pink, lavender, white**

Primula jeffreyi
PRIMULACEAE

Sierra Shooting Star

Meadows and streambanks; 2000–9800 ft.; native

Found throughout Western North America, this summer-blooming perennial herb has hairless leaves and glandular-hairy stems. Like all shooting stars, the flowers are buzz-pollinated by bumble bees. A bee holds on to the flower with its legs while engaging its flight muscles to make vibrations, which cause pollen to shoot out of the anthers. **Plant height 4–24 in.; leaves basal rosette, unlobed, margins smooth, minutely toothed; petals showy, 5, sometimes 4, fused near base; radial symmetry; pink, lavender, white**

Primula suffrutescens
PRIMULACEAE

Sierra Primrose

Montane to alpine rock outcrops and cliffs; 6600–13,800 ft.; native

This summer-blooming subshrub grows in low, dense patches. Basal rosettes of hairless, spoon-shaped leaves give rise to bright pink flower clusters atop leafless stems. When conditions are favorable, this beauty forms impressive displays. It grows in rock crevices kept moist by snowmelt. **Plant height 4–6 in.; leaves in basal rosette, unlobed, margins toothed; petals showy, 5, partially fused; radial symmetry; pink**

Aquilegia formosa
RANUNCULACEAE

Western Columbine

Streambanks, seeps, wet ditches; up to 10,800 ft.; native

Structurally interesting flowers appear every spring on this perennial, with sepals at right angles to the tubular petals. Bumble bees and hummingbirds can reach the nectar in the petal spurs with their long tongues; honey bees often chew holes through the petals to access the reward. **Plant height 1–4 ft.; leaves basal, compound or simple, lobed leaflets; margins toothed; petals showy, 5, free; radial symmetry; petals red, yellow; sepals red**

Delphinium cardinale
RANUNCULACEAE

Scarlet Larkspur

Chaparral, woodlands; 150–4900 ft.; native

This large perennial herb blooms from spring through summer, with showy red sepals and small yellow petals. Hummingbirds are attracted to the bright flowers and nectar. The genus name is derived from the Greek word that means "dolphin." Look for the dolphin-shaped buds near the tip of the flower cluster. **Plant height** 2–5 ft.; leaves alternate, lobed, margins toothed; sepals showy, 5, free, upper sepal spurred; petals 4, free; mirror symmetry; scarlet, yellow

Delphinium nudicaule
RANUNCULACEAE

Red Larkspur

Moist talus and seasonally damp rocky areas in forests, woodlands, chaparral; up to 8500 ft.; native

This early spring–blooming perennial herb has impressive flower clusters up to 20 in. long. It is similar to Scarlet Larkspur, but it has curved fruits and is more common in Northern California. Like most species in the buttercup family, this plant is toxic. **Plant height** 8–20 in.; leaves alternate, lobed; margins toothed; sepals showy; 5, free, upper sepal spurred; petals 4, free; mirror symmetry; red

Prunus andersonii
ROSACEAE

Desert Peach

Pinyon–juniper woodlands; 3000–8500 ft.; native

Typically found in dry, Eastern Sierran habitats, this shrub blooms in spring. Although the fruit may look tempting, the plant arms itself with spine-tipped twigs. Wildlife eat the fruits and cache any leftovers for leaner times. The Paiute people have used the plant for tea and herbal remedies. **Plant height to 9 ft.; leaves alternate, un-lobed, margins toothed; flower clusters showy; petals 5, free; radial symmetry; pink, white**

Rosa californica
ROSACEAE

California Wild Rose

Moist areas, streambanks; up to 6000 ft.; native

Growing in moist areas, this summer-blooming deciduous shrub has distinctive downward-curving prickles and shaggy-hairy leaves. The fragrant flowers are visited by a myriad of pollinators, including native bees. The orange-red rose fruits (hips) are high in vitamins and are relished by wildlife in winter. **Plant height 2–8 ft.; leaves alternate, pinnately compound, margins toothed; petals showy, 5, free; radial symmetry; pink**

Rosa woodsii
ROSACEAE

Woods' Rose

Moist places, desert springs; 3600–11,000 ft.; native

Blooming in late spring and summer, this shrub forms thickets in moist habitats. Distinguishing features include straight prickles on reddish stems and a terminal leaflet that is wider above the middle. The delicate flower is visited by pollinating insects. The rose fruit (hip), which ripens in fall, has been used medicinally and to make tea. **Plant height 2–10 ft.; leaves alternate, pinnately compound, margins toothed; petals showy, 5, free; radial symmetry; pink**

Rubus spectabilis
ROSACEAE

Salmonberry

Coastal forests, wetlands; up to 1600 ft.; native

The hot-pink flowers of Salmonberry bloom on prickly branches with newly emerging leaves in late winter. It is the only native *Rubus* species in California with flowers that are not white. Fruits resemble blackberries in shape but are salmon-colored to red—and tasty. Salmonberry grows in dense, upright thickets. Leaves are compound, with three leaflets. **Plant height to 13 ft.; leaves alternate, compound, margins toothed; petals showy, 5, free; radial symmetry; bright pink**

Spiraea douglasii
ROSACEAE

Rose Spiraea

Moist places, conifer forests; up to 6800 ft.; native

This summer-blooming shrub is associated with forests in Northern California. Its flower clusters resemble spire-shaped tufts of pink cotton candy. Native to Alaska, Canada, and the Pacific Northwest, it was introduced to Europe circa 1803, and is now considered a noxious weed in Denmark and Latvia. **Plant height to 6 ft.; leaves alternate, unlobed, margins toothed; flower clusters showy; petals 5, free; radial symmetry; pink, red**

Spiraea splendens
ROSACEAE

Rose Meadowsweet

Meadows, streamsides, conifer forests; 1800–11,000 ft.; native

Native to Western North America and typically found in higher elevation forests and damp rocky meadows, this shrub blooms in summer. It has a flat-topped cluster of fragrant flowers. The deciduous leaves turn yellow in the fall, blanketing the ground like a carpet. It was formerly known as *S. densiflora*. **Plant height to 3 ft.; leaves alternate, unlobed, margins toothed; flower clusters showy; petals 5, free; radial symmetry; pink, red**

Kelloggia galioides
RUBIACEAE

Milk Kelloggia

Conifer forests; 2300–10,200 ft.; native

Growing in the forest understories throughout Western North America, this delicate perennial herb blooms in summer, with tiny flowers on slender, erect stems. The flower parts attach to the top of the ovary (inferior ovary), which develops into a tiny, hairy fruit. The genus is named for Albert Kellogg, a pioneering California botanist of the 19th century. **Plant height 6–16 in.; leaves opposite, unlobed, margins smooth; flowers small, petals showy, 4–5, free; radial symmetry; pink, white**

Darlingtonia californica
SARRACENIACEAE

California Pitcherplant

Wetlands; 200–7200 ft.; native

The tubular leaves of the California Pitcherplant resemble a cobra about to strike. This perennial herb is a carnivore that attracts insects into a leaf trap by producing a sweet, sticky, nectarlike residue. Trapped insects are digested by enzymes, and the nutrients are absorbed into the plant. Like most carnivorous plants, it grows in wet, sunny locales in low-nutrient soils. **Plant height 2–3 ft.; leaves basal, unlobed, margins smooth; petals showy, 5, free; radial symmetry; maroon**

Darmera peltata
SAXIFRAGACEAE

Umbrella Plant

Riparian; up to 6500 ft.; native

Growing along streams in mountainous areas, this perennial herb blooms in late spring and summer. The umbrella-like, peltate leaves can be very large—upwards of 4 ft. in diameter. The flowers emerge on long stalks before the leaves are released from bud. Its leaves turn yellow, red, and purple in autumn before dying back for winter. **Plant height 1–5 ft.; leaves basal, lobed, margins toothed; flower clusters showy; petals 5, free; radial symmetry; white, pink**

Heuchera rubescens
SAXIFRAGACEAE

Pink Alumroot

Conifer forests, pinyon–juniper woodlands, alpine fell fields; 3300–13,000 ft.; native

This perennial herb grows in seasonally moist, rocky banks and cliffs. Blooming in late spring and summer, feather-like flowers emerge from the basal leaves in delicate sprays. The pink-flowering stems sometimes overshadow the delicate white flowers. The calyx (sepals) age to pink. Native Americans have used its astringent roots medicinally. **Plant height 3–21 in.; leaves basal, shallowly lobed, margins toothed; flower clusters showy; petals 5, free; radial symmetry; white, pink**

Tellima grandiflora
SAXIFRAGACEAE

Fringe Cups

Conifer forests; up to 6500 ft.; native

The tiny flower petals of this perennial herb look raggedly fringed along their edges. They grow under canopies in moist evergreen forests on the coast as well as in the Klamath Ranges and Sierra Nevada. *Tellima* is an anagram of *Mitella*, a closely related genus. It blooms in late spring and summer. **Plant height 1–3 ft.; leaves basal, lobed, margins toothed; flower clusters showy; petals 5, free; radial symmetry; red, white**

Scrophularia californica
SCROPHULARIACEAE

California Bee Plant

Chaparral, conifer forests, wetlands; up to 8,200 ft; native

Found throughout Western North America, this tall, spring-blooming perennial herb has large arrowhead-shaped leaves. Flowers have a club-shaped sterile stamens (staminodes). The flowers produce nectar that attracts bees, hummingbirds, and small wasps. It is also a host plant for Common Buckeye caterpillars. **Plant height to 4 ft.; leaves opposite, unlobed, margins toothed; flower clusters showy; petals 5, partially fused; mirror symmetry; red**

Tamarix ramosissima
TAMARICACEAE

Saltcedar

Riparian; up to 6500 ft.; non-native

This shrub or small tree blooms from early spring through fall. It has scale-like leaves and produces a profusion of tiny pink flowers. Native to Eurasia, it has been widely planted as a windbreak. In California, and other warm climates, it forms thickets that displace natives, drain the water table, and increase fire frequency. **Plant height to 25 ft.; leaves alternate, unlobed, margins smooth; flower clusters showy; petals 5, free; radial symmetry; pink**

Dichelostemma volubile
THEMIDACEAE

Snake Lily

Woodlands; 350–5300 ft.; native

As its common name implies, this perennial herb has a very long, twining stalk that wraps around other vegetation. Blooming in spring and summer, the dense flowerhead comprises urn-shaped flowers with white staminodes (sterile stamens). Historically, the underground stems (corms) were harvested as a starchy staple. **Plant height 2–6 ft.; leaves basal, unlobed, margins smooth; tepals showy, 6, partially fused; radial symmetry; pink, lavender, white**

Plectritis ciliosa
VALERIANACEAE

Longspur Seablush

Conifer forests, woodlands, chaparral; up to 7000 ft.; native

Growing in many habitats throughout Western North America, this annual blooms in spring. Each tiny flower has a nectar spur at its base. Its stems are square in cross section. The specific name describes the fine hairs around the margin of the fruits. Its nectar is a favorite of checkerspot butterflies. **Plant height 2–30 in.; leaves opposite, unlobed, margins smooth; flower clusters showy; petals 5, partially fused; mirror symmetry; pink, white**

ORANGE
FLOWERS

Amsinckia eastwoodiae
BORAGINACEAE

Eastwood's Fiddleneck

Woodlands, grasslands; up to 5000 ft.; native

This spring-blooming annual, with large flowers for a fiddleneck, is covered in bristles that grow sharper as the plant ages. It was named for famed botanist Alice Eastwood, who saved much of the California Academy of Science's botany collections from fire following the 1906 earthquake. *Amsinckia* species identification often requires the examination of its nutlets. **Plant height to 4 ft.; leaves alternate, unlobed, margins smooth; flower clusters showy; flowers small, petals 5, partially fused; radial symmetry; orange, yellow**

Amsinckia menziesii
BORAGINACEAE

Menzies' Fiddleneck

Grasslands, woodlands; up to 5500 ft.; native

This annual blooms in spring and summer. It prefers open areas but is also shade-tolerant and can be found growing at the forest edge. Common Fiddleneck (*Amsinckia intermedia*) is a similar species that has larger flowers, exceeding seven millimeters in diameter, whereas Menzies' Fiddleneck has smaller flowers. Fiddleneck seeds are the favorite food of Lawrence's Goldfinch during its nesting season in spring and early summer. **Plant height to 4 ft.; leaves alternate, unlobed, margins smooth; flower clusters showy; flowers small, petals 5, partially fused; radial symmetry; orange, yellow**

Amsinckia tessellata
BORAGINACEAE

Devil's Lettuce

Deserts, woodlands, grasslands; up to 7200 ft.; native

Blooming in spring and summer, this annual grows in thin, rocky soil, often competing with non-native annual grasses. To distinguish it from other *Amsinckia* species, look for one wide and three narrow calyx lobes. The specific name describes the repetitive, geometric pattern on the tiny fruit, which is visible only with magnification. **Plant height to 4 ft.; leaves alternate, unlobed, margins smooth; flower clusters showy; flowers small, petals 5, partially fused; radial symmetry; orange, yellow**

Erysimum capitatum
BRASSICACEAE

Wallflower

Many communities; up to 14,400 ft.; native

This summer-blooming perennial herb often lines the roadsides of California and can be found in a variety of habitats, from sand dunes up into the alpine zone. Two varieties are recognized: the winged seed form, variety *capitatum*, grows at lower elevations, and variety *purshii* occurs above 5000 ft., with wingless seeds and variable flower colors. **Plant height to 2 ft.; leaves alternate, unlobed, margins toothed; petals showy, 4, free; radial symmetry; orange, yellow, pink**

Opuntia littoralis
CACTACEAE

Coastal Prickly-pear

Coastal sage scrub, chaparral, grasslands; 300–6500 ft.; native

This spring-blooming perennial is common in coastal areas, where it forms large patches up to 10 ft. across. Flower buds tend to be pink, and petals are often orange and yellow when the flower is open. The spines are yellow, and the edible red fruit makes this an important wildlife plant. The specific name means "growing by the sea." **Plant height to 3 ft.; leaves modified into spines; petals showy, many, free; radial symmetry; orange, yellow, pink**

Opuntia phaeacantha
CACTACEAE

Brown-spine Prickly-pear

Deserts; 1800–7800 ft.; native

Blooming in summer, this succulent is similar to Coastal Prickly-pear in its flower color, growth habit, and fruit color. Although their distributions overlap, Brown-spine Prickly-pear is more commonly found in deserts and mountains and has dark spines, whereas Coastal Prickly-pear has yellow spines and often grows in coastal sage scrub. The specific name means "dark spine." **Plant height to 3 ft.; leaves modified into spines; petals showy, many, free; radial symmetry; orange with red center**

Dudleya cymosa
CRASSULACEAE

Canyon Dudleya

Rocky outcrops, slopes, canyons; up to 8800 ft.; native

This gorgeous little plant has erect red stems and succulent, green-gray foliage. Impressively, eight subspecies have been described, mostly based on subtle leaf variation. The genus is named for William Russell Dudley, a former chairman of the botany department at Stanford University. It blooms in spring and summer. **Plant height 3–6 in.; leaves in basal rosette, unlobed, margins smooth; petals showy, 5, partially fused; radial symmetry; orange, red, yellow**

Lathyrus sulphureus
FABACEAE

Sulphur Pea

Forests, woodlands; up to 9400 ft.; native

Like many members of the pea family, this spring-blooming, vining perennial's terminal leaflet is a tendril that helps it scramble over other vegetation. The upper petal (banner) is broad and short. The flowers are usually orange, but the banner can sometimes be lighter with purple veins. Flowers tend to darken with age. **Plant stem length to 4 ft.; leaves alternate, pinnately compound, margins smooth; petals showy, 5, partially fused (keel); mirror symmetry; orange, yellow, white**

Chasmanthe floribunda
IRIDACEAE

African Flag

Disturbed coastal areas; up to 150 ft.; non-native

Blooming in spring, this perennial herb has up to 40 large, orange-red flowers per stalk and straplike leaves. This attractive species is a garden escapee from the Cape Province of South Africa, which, like California, has a Mediterranean climate. It forms large rhizomatous masses in the Bay Area and coastal regions to the south. **Plant height 2–7 ft.; leaves alternate, unlobed, margins smooth; petals showy, 5, partially fused; mirror symmetry; orange-red**

Calochortus kennedyi
LILIACEAE

Desert Mariposa Lily

Deserts, conifer forests; 1900–7200 ft.; native

The short stems of this spectacular spring-blooming perennial herb give added emphasis to the large, upright, cup-shaped flowers. The petals are usually a shade of orange to red, occasionally yellow, with a dark hairy area at the base. The sepals are much narrower than the petals, and the stamens are purple. Its blue-green leaves are short and curly. **Plant height 2–18 in.; leaves alternate, unlobed, margins smooth; petals showy, 3, free; radial symmetry; orange, red, yellow**

Lilium kelleyanum
LILIACEAE

Kelley's Lily

Conifer forests, wetlands; 7200–10,800 ft.; native

The pendant flowers of this summer-blooming perennial herb have a sweet fragrance and strongly reflexed petals. Growing in moist, shady areas, it is quite tall and has whorled to alternate leaves. It looks very similar to Humboldt Lily (*L. humboldtii*), which is found in drier habitats. Swallowtails are common visitors.

Plant height 2–7 ft.; leaves whorled, alternate above, unlobed, margins smooth; tepals showy, 6, free; radial symmetry; orange

Lilium pardalinum
LILIACEAE

Leopard Lily

Forests, wetlands; up to 6600 ft.; native

Blooming in spring, this perennial bulb forms dense colonies in wet habits and has whorled leaves. Five subspecies are recognized based on flower and pollen characters. The typical subspecies (var. *paradalinum*) has two-toned pendant flowers, darker tips, and strongly recurved petals. Wiggins' Lily (subsp. *wigginsii*) is found only in the Klamath Ranges and has spotted flowers.

Plant height 2–6 ft.; leaves whorled, alternate above, unlobed, margins smooth; tepals showy, 6, free; radial symmetry; orange

Lilium parvum
LILIACEAE

Sierra Tiger Lily

Conifer forests; 4600–9500 ft.; native

In summer, this perennial produces lots of flowers. It is similar to Leopard Lily, but has horizontal to ascending, rather than pendant, flowers. The petals open widely and are only slightly recurved. The blossoms are relatively small for a lily, hence the name *parvum*, which means "small" in Latin. It performs well in gardens. **Plant height 2–6 ft.; leaves whorled, unlobed; margins smooth; tepals showy, 6, free; radial symmetry; orange**

Abutilon palmeri
MALVACEAE

Palmer's Abutilon

Desert scrub, chaparral; 2000–2600 ft.; native

Although this spring-blooming subshrub or shrub is not common in natural settings, it is used extensively in gardens. Native to the deserts of Southwestern North America, its range barely extends into the peninsular areas of Southern California. Its large, orange flowers and velvety, silver-gray, heart-shaped leaves are attractive. **Plant height to 5 ft.; leaves alternate, basally lobed, margins toothed; petals showy, 5, free, filaments fused; radial symmetry; orange, yellow**

Sphaeralcea ambigua
MALVACEAE

Desert Mallow

Desert scrub, pinyon–juniper woodlands; up to 8200 ft; native

This spring-blooming subshrub is covered with dense hairs and has thick, three-lobed leaves. Common in the deserts of Southwestern North America, it grows on sandy flats and rocky slopes. Research indicates that more than half of the diet of the desert lizard, Common Chuckwalla (*Sauromalus ater*), consists of Desert Mallow. **Plant height to 3 ft.; leaves alternate, unlobed to lobed, margins wavy, toothed; petals showy, 5, free, filaments fused; radial symmetry; orange, pink**

Lysimachia arvensis
MYRSINACEAE

Scarlet Pimpernel

Disturbed areas, wetlands; up to 3300 ft.; nonnative

Blooming in spring and summer, the flowers of this low-growing annual stay closed on cloudy days when insect pollinators are not likely to visit. Native to the Old World, it has been used to treat persistent wounds. Analyses show that chemicals isolated from Scarlet Pimpernel have an inhibitory effect on certain herpes and polio viruses.

Plant height to 10 in.; leaves opposite, unlobed, margins smooth; flowers small, petals showy, 5, free; radial symmetry; orange with purple center

Eschscholzia californica
PAPAVERACEAE

California Poppy

Grasslands, roadsides, gravel bars, woodlands; up to 11,300 ft.; native

Massive displays of this spring-blooming annual make hillsides look as though they are on fire. This iconic species is California's state flower. It is in the same family as Opium Poppy (*Papaver somniferum*) but does not contain opium. It does, however, have reported pain-reducing properties, presumably because of the action of other alkaloids present in the plant. **Plant height to 2 ft.; leaves basal, dissected, margins smooth; petals showy, 4, free; radial symmetry; orange, yellow**

Papaver californicum
PAPAVERACEAE

Fire Poppy

Woodlands, chaparral; up to 4000 ft.; native

Populations of this fairly rare spring-blooming annual increase in abundance after fire; smoke acts as a trigger, causing seeds to germinate. The center of the flower is usually light green, and the female part has no style, in contrast to Wind Poppy, which looks similar but has a short style connecting the stigma to the ovary. **Plant height to 2 ft.; leaves in basal rosette, deeply lobed, margins toothed; petals showy, 4–5, free; radial symmetry; orange, red**

Papaver heterophyllum
PAPAVERACEAE

Wind Poppy

Woodlands, chaparral, grasslands; up to 4900 ft.; native

This delicate spring-blooming annual grows in shaded places along the coast and into Baja California. Its flower resembles those of Fire Poppy but has a dark purple center and crinkly petals. The female part of the flower has a short style connecting the stigma to the ovary. Wind Poppy was formerly known as *Stylomecon heterophylla*. **Plant height to 2 ft.; leaves in basal rosette, dissected, margins toothed; petals showy, usually 4, free; radial symmetry; orange, red**

Diplacus aurantiacus
PHRYMACEAE

Bush Monkeyflower

Chaparral, conifer forests, woodlands, rock outcrops; up to 2600 ft.; native

This shrub blooms from spring through summer. Distinguishing characteristics include deep green, sticky leaves with rolled-under margins. All monkeyflowers have an interesting pollination mechanism. Their two-lobed stigmas close rapidly after being touched, which is thought to increase cross pollination. **Plant height to 4 ft.; leaves opposite, unlobed, margins smooth or toothed; petals showy, 5, partially fused; mirror symmetry; orange, yellow, red**

Collomia grandiflora
POLEMONIACEAE

Grand Collomia

Conifer forests, woodlands, chaparral; 400–10,000 ft.; native

Blooming in spring and summer, this annual is easily recognized by its flower color, which is unusual for species in the phlox family. Also, look for the blue pollen emerging from the heads of the showy flowers atop a single, upright, or branching stem. Leaves can be lance-shaped or linear. **Plant height to 3 ft.; leaves alternate, unlobed, margins smooth or toothed; flower clusters showy; petals 5, partially fused; radial symmetry; orange, yellow**

Tropaeolum majus
TROPAEOLACEAE

Garden Nasturtium

Disturbed coastal areas; up to 1500 ft.; non-native

This attractive annual blooms from spring through fall. Native to the Andes, it has escaped cultivation and grows in disturbed areas. The plant has bright flowers and deep green, round leaves. Rich in vitamin C, its foliage has a peppery flavor. Confusingly, its common name, Nasturtium, is also a genus in the mustard family. **Plant height 3 ft., scrambling; leaves alternate, unlobed, margins smooth; petals showy, 5, free; mirror symmetry; orange, yellow**

YELLOW
FLOWERS

Agave deserti
AGAVACEAE

Desert Agave

Deserts; 1000–5000 ft.; native

This summer-blooming succulent is reminiscent of an asparagus stem on steroids. Its similarity to the vegetable is not a coincidence. Both agave and asparagus are included in the order Asparagales. The basal rosette is 2 ft. tall, whereas the flowering stalk can grow up to a foot a day, reaching great heights. **Plant height 8–13 ft.; leaves in basal rosette, unlobed, margins toothed; sepals showy, 6, partially fused; radial symmetry; yellow**

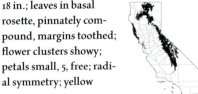

Cymopterus terebinthinus
APIACEAE

Turpentine Cymopterus

Rocky slopes and outcrops, river cobble, sandy deserts; 500–11,500 ft.; native

This perennial herb blooms in spring and early summer in open habitats. The genus name means "wavy wing," referring to the multiple wings on each dry fruit. The specific name, which means "resembling turpentine," refers to its strongly aromatic leaves. It is a host plant for Short-tailed Black Swallowtail larvae. **Plant height to 18 in.; leaves in basal rosette, pinnately compound, margins toothed; flower clusters showy; petals small, 5, free; radial symmetry; yellow**

Foeniculum vulgare
APIACEAE

Fennel

Disturbed areas; up to 5200 ft.; non-native

The aroma of the finely divided leaves of this perennial herb resembles licorice. Its large, flat umbels of yellowish flowers bloom in summer. It is classified as a noxious weed in California, where it can form dense stands that alter coastal wetlands and grasslands. It is a common food source for Anise Swallowtail larvae. **Plant height to 6 ft.; leaves alternate, dissected, margins smooth; flower clusters showy; petals small, 5, free; radial symmetry; yellow, pale green**

Lomatium utriculatum
APIACEAE

Common Lomatium

Grasslands, meadows, woodlands; up to 5000 ft.; native

This attractive, early spring–blooming perennial herb has showy clusters of tiny yellow flowers. Its wide leaf bases wrap around the stem. The genus name *Lomatium* is derived from the Greek word *loma*, which means "a lobe or flap" and references the prominent wings on the fruit. Butterflies and moths feed on its nectar. **Plant height 4–18 in.; leaves basal, dissected, margins smooth; flower clusters showy; petals small, 5, free; radial symmetry; yellow**

Sanicula bipinnata
APIACEAE

Poison Sanicle

Grasslands, woodlands; up to 3200 ft.; native

This spring-blooming perennial herb is endemic to California. Historically, its roots were used to treat snake bites. It may or may not be poisonous to humans. There are accounts of the leaves being eaten like a salad, though its common name leads one to think that eating it could be a bad idea. **Plant height 4–24 in.; leaves alternate, pinnately compound, margins toothed; flower clusters showy; petals small, 5, free; radial symmetry; yellow**

Sanicula crassicaulis
APIACEAE

Pacific Sanicle

Woodlands; up to 5000 ft.; native

The leaf of this perennial herb may grow up to 4 in. across, with a shape reminiscent of a mitten. Thick stems and branches support small, yellow, spherical flowerheads of up to a dozen tiny flowers in winter and early spring. Fruits have hooked prickles that will stick to socks and fur to accommodate dispersal. **Plant height to 5 ft.; leaves basal, lobed, margins toothed; flower clusters showy; petals small, 5, free; radial symmetry; yellow**

Asclepias subulata
APOCYNACEAE

Rush Milkweed

Deserts; up to 2300 ft.; native

This perennial herb blooms year-round. Clusters of striking flowers are borne at the ends of its succulent stems. It is dry-adapted and loses its leaves during periods of drought, during which it becomes a cluster of naked stems. Like all *Asclepias* species, it produces a milky sap and is a host plant of various butterfly species, including Monarchs. **Plant height 2–4 ft.; leaves opposite, unlobed, margins smooth; petals showy, 5, free; radial symmetry; yellow, white**

Lysichiton americanus
ARACEAE

Yellow Skunk Cabbage

Coastal wetlands; up to 4200 ft.; native

This perennial herb blooms from late winter through spring. When in bloom, it has a "skunky" odor that attracts pollinators. Flowers are produced in a spike (spadix), wrapped in a large, yellow bract (spathe). Basal leaves emerge with the flowers and continue to grow, overtopping the flower cluster. **Plant height to 4 ft.; leaves in basal rosette, unlobed, margins smooth; bract showy, 1; petals inconspicuous; yellow**

Baileya multiradiata
ASTERACEAE

Desert Marigold

Deserts; up to 5200 ft.; native

This annual to short-lived perennial herb has bright yellow flowers and is abundant in the Eastern Mojave Desert. The specific name, *multiradiata*, means "many-rayed." It can be distinguished from the many other yellow, sunflower-like desert flowers by its white-wooly foliage and two layers of ray petals. It blooms from spring through fall.

Plant height 1–2 ft.; leaves basal, alternate, lobed or unlobed; margins smooth; flowers small; flowerheads sunflower-like; radial symmetry; yellow

Balsamorhiza deltoidea
ASTERACEAE

Deltoid Balsamroot

Conifer forests, woodlands, chaparral; up to 7900 ft.; native

This stout perennial herb has cheerful flowerheads that bloom in spring and summer. Of the eight species of *Balsamorhiza* in California, two, including this species, have widely triangular (deltoid) leaves. Arrowleaf Balsamroot has densely hairy leaves, while Deltoid Balsamroot has sparsely hairy leaves.

Plant height 1–3 ft.; leaves in basal rosette, lobed at base, margins smooth or toothed; flowers small; flowerheads sunflower-like; radial symmetry; yellow

Balsamorhiza sagittata
ASTERACEAE

Arrowleaf Balsamroot

Deserts, conifer forests; 4500–8500 ft.; native

Flowering in spring and summer, this dramatic perennial herb has many yellow, sunflower-like flowerheads and a cluster of basal leaves that can be larger than a foot long. Elk, deer, pronghorn, and domestic livestock enjoy munching on the flowers and foliage. All parts of the plant have been eaten and/ or used medicinally by indigenous peoples. **Plant height 2 ft.; leaves in basal rosette, lobed at base, margins smooth; flowers small; flowerheads sunflower-like; radial symmetry; yellow**

Blennosperma nanum
ASTERACEAE

Yellow Carpet

Vernal pools; up to 4900 ft.; native

This annual of vernal pool habitats is among the first wildflowers to bloom in spring—a welcome sight. *Blennosperma* is Greek for "slimy seed" and refers to its fruits, which become slimy when wet. Variety *nanum* has white pollen, whereas variety *robustum* has yellow pollen and is restricted to two small areas in Mendocino and Marin counties. **Plant height to 5 in.; leaves basal, alternate, dissected, margins smooth; flowers small; flowerheads sunflower-like; radial symmetry; yellow**

Calycadenia truncata
ASTERACEAE

Rosin Weed

Conifer forests, woodlands, chaparral; 200–5200 ft.; native

One of ten *Calycadenia* species that occur in California, this rangy annual blooms in spring, summer, and fall. The relatively short (truncate) leaves have conspicuous glands at their tips. The genus name, *Calycadenia*, means "cup-gland" in Greek. Like other tarweeds, this species has a pungent aroma. **Plant height to 4 ft.; leaves alternate, unlobed, margins smooth or toothed; flowers small; flowerheads sunflower-like; radial symmetry; yellow**

Centromadia pungens
ASTERACEAE

Common Spikeweed

Wetlands, riparian, grasslands, woodland; up to 4000 ft.; native

The specific name, *pungens*, means "sharp or puncturing" and refers to the sharply pointed leaves that cover the plant. Of the two subspecies in California, subspecies *pungens* is the more wide-ranging, while subspecies *laevis* is restricted to the southwestern corner of the state and Northern Baja California. This annual herb blooms in summer and fall. **Plant height to 4 ft.; leaves alternate, opposite, unlobed to lobed, margins smooth; flowers small; flowerheads sunflower-like; radial symmetry; yellow**

Deinandra kelloggii
ASTERACEAE

Kellogg's Tarweed

Woodlands, grasslands; up to 4000 ft.; native

This upright annual has sticky-glandular hairs, an intense aroma, and many flowerheads. Like other tarweeds, it can flower when everything else is brown and dry, lending beauty to the parched landscape. Plants are self-sterile, meaning flowers are incapable of self-fertilization. It flowers from spring through fall. **Plant height 4–40 in.; leaves in basal rosette, unlobed to lobed; stem leaves alternate, margins smooth or toothed; flowers small; flowerheads sunflower-like; radial symmetry; yellow**

Encelia californica
ASTERACEAE

California Brittlebush

Chaparral; up to 2000 ft.; native

This shrub is found in frost-free areas in southwestern California. Green, diamond-shaped to oval leaves are smooth or barely hairy. Blooming in winter and spring, the large, generally solitary, sunflower-like flowerheads with brown-purple centers are attractive to butterflies and bees. It's a good garden plant, but it loses some of its leaves in summer. **Plant height 20–60 in.; leaves alternate, unlobed, margins smooth; flowers small; flowerheads showy, sunflower-like; radial symmetry; yellow with brown center**

Encelia farinosa
ASTERACEAE

Desert Brittlebush

Deserts; up to 5000 ft.; native

Silvery leaves bedeck this handsome, rounded shrub common in dry, sandy, or rocky areas in Southern California. Sunflower-like flowerheads cluster in bunches of three to nine at the ends of long, branched stalks. Reflective gray foliage keeps the plant cool. Stems are brittle, thus the common name. The stem sap has been used as incense. **Plant height 1–5 ft.; leaves alternate, unlobed, margins smooth; flowers small; flowerheads showy, sunflower-like; radial symmetry; yellow with brown center**

Enceliopsis covillei
ASTERACEAE

Panamint Daisy

Deserts; 1300–4100 ft.; native

Named for its similarity to species of *Encelia*, this rare, spring-blooming perennial herb is limited to a very small area in Death Valley National Park. Astute observers may recognize it on the logo of the California Native Plant Society. With its silvery leaves and huge, sunflower-like flowerheads, this iconic plant is unforgettable! **Plant height to 30 in.; leaves basal, unlobed, margins smooth; flowers small; flowerheads showy, sunflower-like; radial symmetry; yellow**

Ericameria linearifolia
ASTERACEAE

Narrow-leaf Goldenbush

Deserts, chaparral; up to 6600 ft.; native

Whereas most *Ericameria* species bloom in summer and fall, this highly branched shrub is covered with sunflower-like flowerheads in spring, striking a colorful note on the dry slopes and valleys where it grows. It produces huge, fluffy seedheads in the fall. The specific name, *linearifolia*, means "with narrow, parallel-sided leaves." Stems and leaves are sticky-glandular. **Plant height 16–60 in.; leaves alternate, unlobed, margins smooth; flowers small; flowerheads showy, sunflower-like; radial symmetry; yellow**

Eriophyllum confertiflorum
ASTERACEAE

Golden Yarrow

Conifer forests, woodlands, chaparral; up to 10,000 ft.; native

Blooming in spring and summer, the dense flower clusters of this species attract pollinators. Usually bearing four to six ray flowers per flowerhead, it can be either a shrub or a subshrub. The genus name, *Eriophyllum*, means "wooly leaf." It is common in dry areas mostly away from the immediate coast—unlike Seaside Wooly Sunflower, which is generally coastal. **Plant height 8–28 in.; leaves alternate, deeply lobed, margins toothed; flowers small; flowerheads sunflower-like; radial symmetry; yellow**

Eriophyllum lanatum

ASTERACEAE

Common Wooly Sunflower

Many communities; up to 12,000 ft.; native

This species is common from the coast to the
alpine zone, especially in the northern half
of the state. Blooming in spring and summer,
flowerheads generally have eight or more ray
flowers. The species exhibits variable morphology and includes both perennial herbs
and subshrubs. It has eight named varieties
that intergrade. **Plant height** 4–40 in.; leaves
alternate, unlobed to dis-
sected, margins smooth;
flowers small; flower-
heads sunflower-like; ra-
dial symmetry; yellow

Eriophyllum staechadifolium

ASTERACEAE

Seaside Wooly Sunflower

Dunes, shrublands; up to 300 ft.; native

Common along the coast from the northern Channel Islands to Southern Oregon,
this densely branched subshrub blooms in
spring and summer, attracting a variety of
insects. Leaf margins curl under and leaves
become less hairy with time. Clustered flowerheads have six to nine ray flowers per head.
Plant height 1–5 ft.; leaves alternate, base
sometimes opposite,
unlobed to dissected,
margins smooth; flow-
ers small; flowerheads
sunflower-like; radial
symmetry; yellow

Eriophyllum wallacei
ASTERACEAE

Wallace's Wooly Daisy

Deserts; 100–7900 ft.; native

This densely wooly annual is common in open, sandy areas, where it can be prolific in rainy years from winter through summer. The numerous flowerheads are large relative to the plant, occasionally obscuring the foliage entirely—and each flowerhead is ringed with five to ten ray flowers. Sometimes the rays are creamy white. **Plant height to 6 in.; leaves alternate, sometimes op-posite, unlobed or lobed, margins smooth; flowers small; flowerheads sunflower-like; radial symmetry; yellow**

Geraea canescens
ASTERACEAE

Hairy Desert Sunflower

Deserts; up to 4300 ft.; native

In years with plentiful rainfall, spectacular displays of this annual create shimmering, golden drifts in low, sandy areas. Blooming in winter and spring, the large flowerheads produce copious nectar that attracts bees and butterflies. The foliage is soft-hairy, and the pointed involucre bracts (phyllaries) are white, shaggy, and hairy. **Plant height 4–30 in.; leaves basal, alter-nate, unlobed, margins smooth or toothed; flowers small; flowerheads sunflower-like; radial symmetry; yellow**

Grindelia camporum
ASTERACEAE

Gumweed

Wetlands, grasslands, roadsides; up to 4600 ft.; native

Blooming from spring through fall, these perennial herbs support large, heavy flowerheads on branch tips. Their buds exude a noticeable white, gummy sap. *Camporum* means "fields," which is where this species can often be found. Located below the petal-like ray flowers, the involucre bracts (phyllaries) coil backward. **Plant height 2–4 ft.; leaves basal, alternate, unlobed, margins smooth or toothed; flowers small; flowerheads sunflower-like; radial symmetry; yellow**

Helenium bigelovii
ASTERACEAE

Bigelow's Sneezeweed

Wetlands; up to 11,000 ft.; native

This summer-blooming perennial herb has spherical flowerheads with ray flowers around a ball-like central disk. People once believed that sneezing reduced congestion; sneezeweed pollen is highly irritating and was purposefully used to cause people to sneeze. The genus was named for Helen of Troy, the manifestation of ideal human beauty. **Plant height to 4 ft.; leaves basal, alternate, unlobed, margins smooth; flowers small; flowerheads showy, sunflower-like; radial symmetry; yellow**

Helianthella californica
ASTERACEAE

California Helianthella

Conifer forests, woodlands, chaparral; up to 8500 ft.; native

With sunflower-like flowerheads at the ends of long stems, this perennial herb blooms in spring and summer. The leaf margins lack teeth. Of the three varieties, variety *nevadensis* has the widest range, extending into Southern Oregon and Western Nevada. **Plant height 2 ft.; leaves basal, stem leaves alternate or opposite, unlobed, margins smooth; flowers small; flowerheads sunflower-like; radial symmetry; yellow**

Helianthus annuus
ASTERACEAE

Common Sunflower

Disturbed areas, grasslands; up to 6600 ft.; native

Common along roadsides throughout the state, this species' range extends to Eastern North America. Blooming in spring and summer, this robust annual has numerous, large flowerheads with encircling ray petals more than 1 in. long. Cultivated sunflowers that produce edible seeds and oil were domesticated from this species. **Plant height to 9 ft.; leaves alternate, sometimes opposite, unlobed, margins smooth or toothed; flowers small; flowerheads showy, sunflower-like; radial symmetry; yellow**

Helianthus gracilentus
ASTERACEAE

Slender Sunflower

Woodlands, chaparral; up to 6600 ft.; native

Blooming from spring through fall, this slender perennial herb is quite common after fires—especially in the southwestern part of the state. It has opposite leaves below and sometimes alternate leaves above. The ray flowers are up to 1 in. long. The specific name, *gracilentus*, means "slender," in reference to its growth form. **Plant height 2–7 ft.; leaves alternate, sometimes opposite, unlobed, margins smooth or toothed; flowerheads sunflower-like; radial symmetry; yellow**

Hemizonia congesta
ASTERACEAE

Hayfield Tarweed

Shrublands, grasslands; up to 5300 ft.; native

The only species in the genus *Hemizonia*, this annual herb blooms almost year-round and is morphologically variable. Six subspecies have been described; two are rare. Subspecies *lutescens* has yellow ray flowers, whereas the other subspecies have white ray flowers. Plants favor grassy areas and have a pungent aroma typical of the tarweeds. **Plant height 20–30 in.; leaves alternate, sometimes opposite, unlobed or lobed, margins smooth or toothed; flowerheads sunflower-like; radial symmetry; yellow, white**

Heterotheca grandiflora
ASTERACEAE

Telegraph Weed

Many communities, disturbed areas; up to 3600 ft.; native

The stem of this summer-blooming annual is tall and straight. Its leaves are attached closely to the stem, which gives way to a many-branched cluster of small, yellow, flowerheads. Originally, it occurred only in California (endemic), but it has become naturalized in other places, including Hawaii. Its common name hints at its tendency to spread. **Plant height to 5 ft.; leaves alternate, unlobed, margins toothed; flowers small; flowerheads sunflower-like, radial symmetry; yellow**

Heterotheca sessiliflora
ASTERACEAE

Golden Aster

Chaparral, grasslands; up to 7200 ft.; native

This perennial herb has aromatic, hairy, gray-green leaves. The yellow flowers emerge in late summer, and the lower leaves fall off to conserve water. Based on leaf characteristics, hairiness, and geography, four subspecies have been described. Subspecies vary dramatically and can be matlike or large with tall stems. **Plant height to 3 ft.; leaves alternate, unlobed, margins smooth; flowers small; flowerheads sunflower-like; radial symmetry; yellow**

Hulsea vestita
ASTERACEAE

Pumice Alpinegold

Open gravel, talus slopes, montane chaparral, pine forests, pinyon–juniper woodlands; 4300–12,800 ft.; native

This perennial herb favors well-drained, often volcanic soils, and blooms spring through fall. Flowerheads are glandular, and leaves are wooly. Leaf and flower characteristics have been used to describe six subspecies. Five are narrowly distributed and rare, found mostly in mountainous areas of Southern California. **Plant height to 2 ft.; leaves basal, alternate, unlobed, margins smooth or toothed; flowers small; flowerheads sunflower-like; radial symmetry; yellow, orange**

Lagophylla ramosissima
ASTERACEAE

Common Hareleaf

Grasslands, openings in scrub, woodlands, forests; up to 5900 ft.; native

Lagophylla means "hare-leaf." It probably refers to the early leaves on this annual, which are as soft as a rabbit's fur. Blooming in spring, summer, and fall, this member of the tarweed group can be difficult to observe in flower because its heads close up around noon. It grows in dry areas throughout Western North America. **Plant height to 3 ft.; leaves alternate, unlobed, margins smooth or toothed; flowers small; flowerheads sunflower-like; radial symmetry; yellow**

Lasthenia fremontii
ASTERACEAE

Fremont's Goldfields

Vernal pools; up to 2300 ft.; native

This spring-blooming annual creates golden carpets in vernal pools, depressions where water does not drain readily. The pools fill up in spring and they slowly evaporate as the weather heats up. Plants and animals that live in this special habitat must tolerate this shift from wet to dry, and many of them are rare. **Plant height to 14 in.; leaves alternate, unlobed to lobed, margins smooth; flowers small; flowerheads sunflower-like; radial symmetry; yellow**

Lasthenia gracilis
ASTERACEAE

Common Goldfields

Many communities; up to 5000 ft.; native

A harbinger of spring, this abundant annual favors open, grassy areas, where it forms masses of tiny, yellow flowerheads that can be seen from a distance. It is the most commonly encountered member of the genus. The genus name is derived from Lasthenia, an Athenian girl who disguised herself as a boy in order to study with Plato. **Plant height to 16 in.; leaves alternate, unlobed, margins smooth; flowers small; flowerheads sunflower-like; radial symmetry; yellow**

Layia platyglossa
ASTERACEAE

Tidy Tips

Chaparral, grasslands, woodlands; up to 6600 ft.; native

A true wildflower, this spring-blooming annual covers grassy fields with its fragrant flowers, especially during years with adequate rainfall. Flowerheads have yellow ray flowers with three-pointed, white tips. Leaves are rough and hairy. This little beauty is easy to grow and is a common component of native wildflower seed mixes. **Plant height to 2 ft.; leaves alternate, unlobed, margins smooth; flowers small; flowerheads sunflower-like; radial symmetry; yellow, white**

Leptosyne bigelovii
ASTERACEAE

Bigelow's Tickseed

Deserts, woodlands; 500–6600 ft.; native

This slender, hairless annual has numerous green to reddish leafless stems. The relatively large flowerheads appear in winter and spring, with ray flowers that are horizontal in their orientation when fully open, seeming to catch the sunlight. It is called tickseed because the shiny, black fruits resemble ticks. Until recently, it was included in the genus *Coreopsis*. **Plant height 4–12 in.; leaves basal, alternate, deeply lobed, margins smooth; flowers small; flowerheads sunflower-like; radial symmetry; yellow**

Leptosyne gigantea
ASTERACEAE

Giant Coreopsis

Coastal sage scrub, dunes; up to 1600 ft.; native

Another common name for this unusual-looking coastal plant could be Dr. Seuss Plant, because that name captures the whimsical appearance of this shrub. With its thick and fleshy trunk, highly divided leaves, and numerous flowerheads, it is one of a kind. Blooming in winter and spring, it creates a showy display in abundant rainfall years. **Plant height to 6 ft.; leaves alternate, dissected, margins smooth; flowers small; flowerheads sunflower-like; radial symmetry; yellow**

Madia elegans
ASTERACEAE

Common Madia

Conifer forests, woodlands, alpine; up to 11,200 ft.; native

One of the showier tarweeds, the large, often bicolored flowerheads on this annual seem to float in the air. The specific name means "elegant." This highly variable species blooms from spring through fall and attracts an array of pollinators. It grows in open, grassy places from Baja California to Washington and into Nevada. **Plant height to 8 ft.; leaves opposite, alternate, unlobed, margins smooth, sometimes toothed; flowerheads sunflower-like; radial symmetry; yellow, maroon**

Monolopia lanceolata
ASTERACEAE

Common Monolopia

Woodlands, chaparral, grasslands; 160–5300 ft.; native

This upright annual can create spectacular displays in abundant rainfall years in interior locations such as the Carrizo Plain in eastern San Luis Obispo County. The specific name, *lanceolata*, means "lance-like," referring to the shape of the leaves. The white-wooly hairs on the foliage help the plant retain moisture. It blooms in late winter and spring. **Plant height to 30 in.; leaves alternate, unlobed, margins wavy, toothed; flowers small; flowerheads sunflower-like; radial symmetry; yellow**

Packera cana
ASTERACEAE

Wooly Groundsel

Conifer forests, shrublands; 4000–11,500 ft.; native

Growing from Western North America east to Kansas, this locally abundant perennial herb prefers rocky areas, including crevices. The lower surface of its leaves is densely white-wooly, whereas the upper surface is less hairy. The leaves bear some resemblance to native buckwheats. Clusters of flowerheads attract pollinators. **Plant height to 30 in.; leaves in basal rosette, stem leaves alternate, unlobed, margins smooth or toothed; flowers small; flowerheads sunflower-like; radial symmetry; yellow**

Packera multilobata
ASTERACEAE

Lobeleaf Groundsel

Deserts, woodlands; 3600–11,300 ft.; native

Blooming in spring and summer, this perennial herb is abundant in sandy-rocky soils from the High Sierra east into the Great Basin. The specific name, *multilobata*, which means "many-lobed," refers to its leaves, which have three to six pairs of lobes. The flowerheads are usually sunflower-like, but occasionally an individual will be discoid (rayless). **Plant height 8–16 in.; leaves in basal rosette, stem leaves alternate, lobed, margins toothed; flowers small; flowerheads sunflower-like or discoid; radial symmetry; yellow**

Rudbeckia californica
ASTERACEAE

California Coneflower

Wetlands; 2600–8500 ft.; native

Blooming in summer, this perennial herb has a prominent conelike central disc. A ring of droopy yellow ray flowers surround the cone, which comprises hundreds of tiny disc flowers. Plants spread by underground stems (rhizomes), and the dry fruits are edible. **Plant height 2–6 ft.; leaves basal, stem leaves alternate, unlobed or lobed, margins coarsely toothed or smooth; flowers small; flowerheads sunflower-like; radial symmetry; yellow with brown center**

Senecio flaccidus
ASTERACEAE

Threadleaf Ragwort

Chaparral, woodlands, deserts; up to 6600 ft.; native

Covered with sunflower-like flowerheads, this openly branching shrub blooms in spring, summer, and fall. The desert form, *S. flaccidus* var. *monoensis*, generally has green, hairless foliage. More wide-ranging in California is variety *douglasii*, which does not occur in deserts and generally has blue-gray, hairy foliage. Both varieties grow in rocky areas. **Plant height 16–48 in.; leaves alternate, unlobed to lobed, margins smooth; flowers small; flowerheads sunflower-like; radial symmetry; yellow**

Senecio triangularis
ASTERACEAE

Arrowleaf Ragwort

Conifer forests, riparian; 330–10,800 ft.; native

This summer-blooming perennial herb is common in the Sierra, where it occurs on both sides of the crest. The specific name, *triangularis*, refers to the narrowly triangular to triangular leaves that get smaller in size as they ascend the stem. Mountain butterweed (*S. integerrimus*) is similar but has a basal rosette and grows in drier sites. **Plant height 20–50 in.; leaves alternate, unlobed, margins toothed; flowers small; flowerheads sunflower-like; radial symmetry; yellow**

Solidago velutina
ASTERACEAE

Velvety Goldenrod

Woodlands, grasslands; up to 8200 ft; native

Growing throughout Western North America, this perennial herb blooms in spring, summer, and fall. Plants spread by underground stems (rhizomes). The foliage can range from sparsely to densely short-hairy, and the leaves are often three-veined. Flowerheads are massed together in an elongated arrangement, which is attractive to insects. **Plant height to 5 ft.; leaves alternate, unlobed, margins toothed; flowers small; flowerheads sunflower-like; radial symmetry; yellow**

Syntrichopappus fremontii
ASTERACEAE

Fremont's Gold

Deserts; 2000–8200 ft.; native

This wooly, spring-blooming annual is similar to Wallace's Wooly Daisy but has only five to eight rayflowers, versus eight or more. It grows throughout the Southwestern deserts of North America. It is one of only two species in the genus; the other, *S. lemmonii*, has white ray flowers and is a rare Southern California species. **Plant height to 4 in.; leaves alternate, unlobed to lobed, margins rolled under; flowers small; flowerheads sunflower-like; radial symmetry; yellow**

Venegasia carpesioides
ASTERACEAE

Canyon Sunflower

Chaparral, woodlands; up to 3300 ft.; native

This is the only species in the genus *Venegasia*. Occurring south to Baja California, this upright, many-branched shrub prefers moist, wooded areas. Bedecked with sunflower-type flowerheads in winter, spring, and summer, this fast-growing plant can be recognized by its lush, almost tropical appearance, making it a good garden specimen. **Plant height 20–60 in.; leaves alternate, unlobed, margins smooth or toothed; flowers small; flowerheads sunflower-like; radial symmetry; yellow**

Wyethia angustifolia
ASTERACEAE

California Compass Plant

Grasslands; up to 6700 ft.; native

This wide-ranging perennial herb has lance-shaped, roughly hairy leaves. The plant forms colonies that expand via thick underground stems (rhizomes). The specific name, *angustifolia*, means "narrow-leaved." Its comomon name came about because people believed its leaves were oriented to point north and south. **Plant height 12–35 in.; leaves basal, alternate, unlobed, margins smooth; flowers small; flowerheads sunflower-like; radial symmetry; yellow**

Wyethia mollis
ASTERACEAE

Wooly Mule's Ears

Conifer forests; 3000–11,000 ft.; native

Often abundant in montane areas in California—and extending into Oregon and Nevada—this arresting perennial herb creates picturesque scenes when in full bloom. The soft, gray-green leaves resemble mule's ears. With age, however, the foliage often becomes smooth and hairless. It blooms from spring to summer in open areas, meadows, and dry, rocky slopes. **Plant height 12–20 in.; leaves basal, alternate, unlobed, margins smooth; flowers small; flowerheads sunflower-like; radial symmetry; yellow**

Achyrachaena mollis
ASTERACEAE

Blow Wives

Grasslands; up to 4000 ft.; native

The fruits of this spring-blooming annual form beautiful balls of white, star-topped fruits. The showy parts are actually white scales that aid in fruit dispersal. Soft, velvety leaves resemble fingers ready to throw the seeds to the wind. The ray flowers are short and inconspicuous and age from yellow to orange-red. **Plant height to 1 ft.; leaves alternate, unlobed, margins smooth; fruits white; flowers small; flowerheads sunflower-like; radial symmetry; yellow, orange**

Agoseris grandiflora
ASTERACEAE

Giant Mountain Dandelion

Grasslands, woodlands; up to 6600 ft.; native

This perennial herb is among the largest species of *Agoseris* in California. It blooms in late spring. These tall plants have unbranched, hairy stems, and leaves have pointed lobes. The seedhead is gigantic, up to 4 in. wide. Seeds have feathery hairs that help them catch the wind. Its range extends from British Columbia to Utah. **Plant height to 3 ft.; leaves in basal rosette, lobed to unlobed, margins smooth or toothed; flowers small; flowerheads dandelion-like; radial symmetry; yellow**

Anisocoma acaulis
ASTERACEAE

Scale Bud

Deserts; up to 8500 ft.; native

In a year with ample rain, this spring-blooming annual can blanket dry slopes and sandy washes in color. Single, large flowerheads sit on leafless stalks (scapes) above rosettes of gray-green leaves. The bracts (phyllaries) below the flowerheads have distinct red spots and are scale-like, hence the common name. Plants exude milky sap. **Plant height to 8 in.; leaves basal, lobed, margins toothed; flowers small; flowerheads dandelion-like; radial symmetry; yellow**

Helminthotheca echioides
ASTERACEAE

Bristly Ox-tongue

Disturbed areas; up to 3400 ft.; non-native

This annual has white, warty bumps and bristles on its leaves. Blooming in summer and fall, large, dandelion-like flowers sit a top erect, branched stems. Like all *Helminthotheca* species, the flowerhead bracts (phyllaries) are quite large. Native to the Mediterranean Basin, it has naturalized across North America. **Plant height to 6 ft.; leaves alternate, unlobed, margins smooth; flowers small; flowerheads dandelion-like; radial symmetry; yellow**

Hypochaeris glabra
ASTERACEAE

Smooth Cat's Ear

Disturbed areas, grasslands; up to 5400 ft.; non-native

This common, spring-blooming annual is widespread throughout non-desert areas of the state. It resembles the lawn weed, dandelion. Like dandelions, it has milky sap, many straplike petals (ligules), and fluffy seedheads. The basal leaf rosettes on these invasive plants can smother small native annuals in sensitive habitats. **Plant height to 2 ft.; leaves in basal rosette, unlobed to shallowly lobed, margins smooth or toothed; flowers small; flowerheads dandelion-like; radial symmetry; yellow**

Lactuca serriola
ASTERACEAE

Prickly Lettuce

Disturbed areas; up to 8900 ft.; non-native

Blooming from spring through fall, this coarse annual is related to edible lettuce. Native to Europe, this traveler has made itself at home in vacant lots and along roadsides throughout North America. It is quite prickly, and its flowerheads are scattered among the spreading branches. Its leaves have milky sap and clasping bases. **Plant height 2–10 ft.; leaves basal, alternate, lobed to unlobed, margins toothed; flowers small; flowerheads dandelion-like; radial symmetry; yellow**

Malacothrix californica
ASTERACEAE

California Desert Dandelion

Coastal sage scrub, grasslands, deserts; up to 1700 ft.; native

This spring-blooming annual creates showy displays in years with adequate rainfall. Leaves are long-hairy at the base. Single, oversized, dandelion-like flowerheads sit atop its long, leafless stalks. Each flowerhead has numerous flowers with many straplike petals (ligules), the outermost of which often have red markings on their undersides. **Plant height to 18 in.; leaves basal, lobed, margins smooth; flowers small; flowerheads dandelion-like; radial symmetry; yellow, white**

Malacothrix glabrata
ASTERACEAE

Smooth Desert Dandelion

Deserts, foothill woodlands; up to 6600 ft.;
native

Like California Desert Dandelion, this
spring-blooming annual can be prolific in wet
years throughout Southwestern North America. It occurs in coarse soils in openings, often
between shrubs. It has leafy stems and lacks
red markings on the undersides of the straplike petals (ligules). **Plant height to 20 in.;**
leaves basal, alternate,
lobed, margins smooth;
flowers small; flower-
heads dandelion-like;
radial symmetry;
yellow, white

Microseris nutans
ASTERACEAE

Nodding Microseris

Conifer forests, shrublands; 3300–11,200 ft.;
native

All members of this genus have milky sap.
In addition, *Microseris* species generally have
drooping, or nodding, flower buds; *nutans*
means "nodding." The flower stalks straight-
en out before blooming. This dandelion-like
perennial herb blooms in spring and summer
and develops fluffy seedheads. **Plant height
4–28 in.;** leaves in basal
rosette, stem leaves alternate, unlobed to lobed,
margins smooth; flow-
ers small; flowerheads
dandelion-like; radial
symmetry; yellow

Sonchus asper
ASTERACEAE

Spiny Sowthistle

Disturbed areas; up to 6200 ft.; non-native

This coarse-looking annual with spiny leaves can bloom throughout the year. Its hollow, upright, fleshy stems are often tinged red, as are the leaf midribs. The flowerheads in bud have a distinctive, squat, dome shape, like the head of garlic. In fruit, the seedheads resemble those of small dandelions. **Plant height to 4 ft.; leaves basal, alternate, unlobed, margins toothed, almost lobed; flowers small; flowerheads dandelion-like; radial symmetry; yellow**

Taraxacum officinale
ASTERACEAE

Common Dandelion

Disturbed areas; up to 10,800 ft.; non-native

The familiar flowerhead of this perennial plant is composed of roughly 100 bright yellow, straplike, ligulate flowers. If pollinated, inflorescences develop into a lovely, 2-inch-wide, spherical seedhead with long-beaked, wind-dispersed fruits. The leaves have deep, ragged lobes that point back toward the base of the leaf. Its preferred habitat is your lawn. **Plant height to 1 ft.; leaves basal, lobed, margins smooth; flowers small; radial symmetry; yellow**

Tragopogon dubius
ASTERACEAE

Yellow Salsify

Disturbed areas; up to 8900 ft.; non-native

Blooming in spring and summer, Yellow Salsify has large flowerheads that open like starbursts, before noon. It is most easily recognized by its huge, tan-colored, globular seedheads, which are up to 3 in. wide. It can be either an annual or a perennial. A similar species, Purple Salsify (*T. porrifolius*), has purple flowerheads that open around noon. **Plant height 12–40 in.; leaves alternate, unlobed, margins smooth; flowers small; flowerheads dandelion-like; radial symmetry; yellow**

Uropappus lindleyi
ASTERACEAE

Silver Puffs

Conifer forests, woodlands, chaparral; up to 7800 ft.; native

The small, upright flowerheads on this spring-blooming annual are unobtrusive when growing in grasslands. In fruit, however, the plants are noticeable from a distance—with spherical seedheads of shimmering, silvery, bristle-tipped scales black fruits (achenes). Leaves are narrow, often with downward-pointing lobes. **Plant height to 2 ft.; leaves basal, alternate, unlobed to lobed, margins smooth; flowers small, dandelion-like; radial symmetry; seedheads showy, white; petals yellow**

Bebbia juncea
ASTERACEAE

Sweetbush

Deserts; up to 5000 ft.; native

An important food source for Desert Tortoise, this rounded shrub has a minimalist appearance, with narrow, sticklike stems and leaves that quickly fall off. Perhaps the powerful aroma of these plants beckons tortoises to enjoy a tasty meal. Curly yellow style branches emerge from each tiny flower. It blooms in spring and summer. **Plant height 2–5 ft.; leaves opposite, unlobed to lobed, margins smooth; flowerheads discoid; flowers small; radial symmetry; yellow**

Bidens frondosa
ASTERACEAE

Sticktight

Wetlands, disturbed areas; up to 6900 ft.; native

Blooming in summer and fall, this weedy annual is native to North America but has naturalized in other parts of the world. It tolerates high light intensity and disturbed, saturated soils. The common name refers to the barbed fruits that easily attach to passersby. **Plant height 2–4 ft.; leaves opposite, pinnately compound; margins toothed; flowerheads discoid or with a few ray flowers; flowers small; radial symmetry; yellow**

Brickellia californica
ASTERACEAE

California Brickellbush

Chaparral, conifer forests, woodlands; up to 8900 ft.; native

This highly branched, fragrant shrub occurs throughout many Western states. In California, it is tolerant of a wide range of conditions, including coastal, desert, and mountain habitats. It is immediately recognizable by its spade-shaped leaves and yellow flowers. Blooming in summer and fall, its stigma lobes are visible atop flowerheads. **Plant height 2–6 ft.; leaves alternate, opposite, unlobed, margins toothed; flowerheads discoid; flowers small; radial symmetry; yellow, green**

Centaurea solstitialis
ASTERACEAE

Yellow Star-thistle

Disturbed grasslands, woodlands; up to 4300 ft.; non-native

Native to southern Europe, this spiny-headed annual is highly invasive in rangelands and is classified as a noxious weed. Incredibly, a single plant can shed almost 75,000 seeds! So far, efforts to keep this species in check by releasing seed predators from its native habitat have been only mildly successful. It blooms from spring through fall. **Plant height 4–40 in.; leaves basal, alternate, unlobed to dissected, margins smooth; flowerheads discoid; flowers small; radial symmetry; yellow**

Chaenactis glabriuscula
ASTERACEAE

Yellow Pincushion

Chaparral, conifer forests, woodlands; up to 7500 ft.; native

Blooming from winter through summer, this annual can create beautiful displays in years with ample rain. It has erect stems covered in cobwebby hairs. The flowerhead has two kinds of flowers: the inner flowers have small and equal-sized lobes (radial symmetry), whereas the flowers on the edge of the flowerhead have longer petal lobes on one side (mirror symmetry). **Plant height to 2 ft.; leaves basal, alternate, dissected, margins smooth; flowerheads discoid; flowers small; radial symmetry; yellow**

Chrysothamnus viscidiflorus
ASTERACEAE

Yellow Rabbitbrush

Deserts, conifer forests; 3000–13,100 ft.; native

This shrub occurs predominantly in the eastern part of the state up to the alpine zone and is highly variable throughout its range. Covered in glands that produce a sticky, odiferous resin, the leaves are often wavy and twisted. It blooms in summer and fall. Its copious flowerheads are an important late-season resource for pollinating insects. **Plant height to 5 ft.; leaves alternate, unlobed, margins wavy; flowerheads discoid; flowers small; radial symmetry; yellow**

Cotula coronopifolia
ASTERACEAE

Brass Buttons

Wetlands, many communities; up to 4000 ft.; non-native

Originally from South Africa, this perennial herb blooms most of the year and can be quite abundant locally. It can grow completely underwater for a period of time and tolerates salty soils. Leaf bases encircle the stem, sheathing it for a short distance. The hemispherical flowerheads that droop with age are made up of numerous tiny flowers. **Plant height 2–16 in.; leaves alternate, lobed to unlobed, margins smooth; flowerheads discoid; flowers small; radial symmetry; yellow**

Ericameria cuneata
ASTERACEAE

Cliff Goldenbush

Conifer forests; 2000–9200 ft.; native

This evergreen shrub with generally wedge- or spoon-shaped leaves grows in crevices and cliffs in granitic rock outcrops. In late summer and early fall, it is covered with starburst-like flowerheads. A rare form with large flowerheads, variety *macrocephala* ("large-headed"), is restricted to a small area in San Diego County. **Plant height to 3 ft.; leaves alternate, unlobed, margins smooth; flowerheads discoid; flowers small; radial symmetry; yellow**

Ericameria nauseosa
ASTERACEAE

Rubber Rabbitbrush

Deserts, conifer forests, woodlands; 200–12,000 ft.; native

Blooming in summer and early fall, this shrub is common throughout California and the arid West. It has light-colored, flexible stems covered in feltlike, matted hairs and narrow, threadlike leaves. The specific name, *nauseosa*, alludes to its odor, which has been described as resembling that of pineapple by some but is more often characterized as rubbery and nauseating. **Plant height to 9 ft.; leaves alternate, unlobed, margins smooth; flowerheads discoid; flowers small; radial symmetry; yellow**

Hazardia squarrosa
ASTERACEAE

Sawtooth Goldenbush

Chaparral, woodlands; up to 4300 ft.; native

This shrub occurs from Monterey south to Northern Baja California. Its thick, leathery leaves may or may not be sticky. Below the elongated flowerheads are green, backward-bending bracts (phyllaries). Each flowerhead contains nine to thirty disc flowers, but no ray flowers. It blooms in summer and fall. **Plant height 12–90 in.; leaves alternate, unlobed, margins smooth or toothed; flowerheads discoid; flowers small; radial symmetry; yellow**

Isocoma menziesii
ASTERACEAE

Menzies' Goldenbush

Coastal sage scrub, many communities; up to 4000 ft.; native

Attractive to insects, the flowerhead displays of this variable species can be open to densely clustered. It grows in sandy soils in both inland and coastal habitats. Blooming from late spring through fall, this shrub has multiple rows of bracts (phyllaries) surrounding each flowerhead. Flowerheads are filled with cylindrical flowers with protruding stigmas. **Plant height to 7 ft.; leaves alternate, unlobed; margins smooth or toothed; flowerheads discoid; flowers small; radial symmetry; yellow**

Lepidospartum squamatum
ASTERACEAE

Scalebroom

Chaparral, deserts; up to 6200 ft.; native

This rounded shrub with aromatic foliage blooms in summer and fall in sandy-gravelly areas. The genus is easily recognizable by its grooved stems. The leaves, which vary in shape and size and can resemble scales, and fall off the plant with age, giving it a broomlike appearance. *Lepidospartum* means "scale-broom." **Plant height to 10 ft.; leaves alternate, unlobed, margins smooth; flowerheads discoid; flowers small; radial symmetry; yellow**

Lessingia glandulifera
ASTERACEAE

Valley Lessingia

Chaparral, conifer forests, deserts; 200–7200 ft.; native

This spring- through fall-blooming annual prefers sandy soil. Of three varieties, one is considered rare. Plants can be hairless to densely hairy, and basal leaves often wither before flowering. Although the flowerheads lack ray flowers, the disc flowers around the periphery are enlarged and petaloid. Yellow, tacklike glands occur at the base of flowerheads. **Plant height to 16 in.; leaves basal, alternate, unlobed to lobed, margins smooth; flowerheads discoid; flowers small; radial symmetry; yellow**

Matricaria discoidea
ASTERACEAE

Pineapple Weed

Disturbed areas; up to 7400 ft.; native

This abundant annual has a sweet, pineapple-like aroma when crushed. The flowerheads, which can be used to make an herbal tea, lack straplike rays and are composed of numerous, tiny disc flowers. The specific name, *discoidea*, describes the disc-flower–only flowerheads. It blooms in winter through summer, and has naturalized in many countries. **Plant height to 1 ft.; leaves alternate, dissected, margins smooth; flowerheads discoid; flowers small; radial symmetry; yellow**

Peucephyllum schottii
ASTERACEAE

Schott's Pygmy Cedar

Deserts; up to 4600 ft.; native

This long-lived, rounded shrub blooms in winter and spring. The dense habit and narrow, dark green leaves lend it a conifer-like appearance; *Peucephyllum* means "fir leaf." Clearly, the flowers attract pollinators, including hawk moths. *Peucephyllum* is a monotypic genus, meaning it includes only one species. **Plant height to 10 ft.; leaves alternate, unlobed, margins smooth; flowerheads discoid; flowers small; radial symmetry; yellow**

Psathyrotes ramosissima
ASTERACEAE

Velvet Turtleback

Deserts; up to 4000 ft.; native

This sharply aromatic, spring-blooming species creates dense, mounded, tortoise-shaped domes in sandy areas such as washes. *Psathyrotes* means "brittle," which describes the stems and branches. The velvety leaves have many deeply incised veins. The yellow flowerheads create a sharp contrast with the pale gray foliage. It can be an annual or a perennial. **Plant height to 1 ft.; leaves basal, alternate, unlobed, margins toothed; flowerheads discoid; flowers small; radial symmetry; yellow**

Senecio vulgaris
ASTERACEAE

Common Groundsel

Disturbed areas; up to 4300 ft.; non-native

The name of this species might lead you to believe that this is a rude, unsophisticated plant, but in fact *vulgaris* means "common." This common annual has a long bloom period, from winter to summer. The flowerheads contain only tiny disc flowers. Involucre bracts are tipped black. The genus name, *Senecio*, means "old man," in reference to the white-hairy fruit. **Plant height 4–24 in.; leaves alternate, un-lobed, margins toothed; flowerheads discoid; flowers small; radial symmetry; yellow**

Tetradymia axillaris
ASTERACEAE

Longspine Horsebrush

Desert scrub, woodlands; 3800–7500 ft.; native

This spring- and summer-blooming shrub grows in dry areas throughout Southwestern North America and has densely hairy stems and primary leaves that turn into long, straight spines. The secondary leaves are in clusters. Two varieties are distinguished by their range, hairiness, and the length of their fruit hairs. **Plant height to 5 ft.; leaves alternate, unlobed, margins smooth; flowerheads discoid; flowers small; radial symmetry; yellow**

Tetradymia canescens
ASTERACEAE

Spineless Horsebrush

Deserts; 3300–11,200 ft.; native

Blooming in summer and fall, this shrub has clustered leaves similar to those of Longspine Horsebrush, but it blooms later and lacks spines. The specific name, *canescens*, describes the short, gray-white hairs that unevenly cover the foliage. It contains a liver toxin that causes a disease called "bighead" in sheep. **Plant height to 32 in.; leaves alternate, unlobed, margins smooth; flowerheads discoid; flowers small; radial symmetry; yellow**

Berberis aquifolium
BERBERIDACEAE

Oregon Grape

Chaparral; up to 9000 ft.; native

This spring-blooming shrub, the state flower of Oregon, has bright yellow flowers that develop into blue-black berries. Its wavy leaflets have very spiny margins. Though it is not a true grape, its berries can be used for jelly—however, because the berries contain berberine, which can harm fetuses, they should not be eaten by pregnant people. **Plant height to 7 ft.; leaves alternate, pinnately compound, margins wavy, toothed; petals showy, 6, free; radial symmetry; bright yellow**

Oreocarya confertiflora
BORAGINACEAE

Yellow-flowered Oreocarya

Deserts; 3500–11,000 ft.; native

Commonly found in dry, rocky soils, this perennial herb has yellow flowers that tend to fade to white with age. It was formerly included in the genus *Cryptantha* but was reclassified to the genus, *Oreocarya*. Blooming in spring and summer, its flowers attract bees, making important for pollinators. **Plant height to 18 in.; leaves in basal rosette, unlobed, margins smooth; flower clusters showy; petals 5, partially fused; radial symmetry; yellow, fading to white**

Barbarea orthoceras
BRASSICACEAE

American Yellowrocket

Riparian, woodlands; up to 14,000 ft.; native

This spring-blooming perennial herb has thick stems and long, upward-pointing fruits. This native of North America and Asia prefers wet, shaded areas. The specific name describes its fruits; *orthos* means "straight," and *keras* means "horn." It resembles Yellow Cress but has only one row of seeds per fruit instead of two. **Plant height to 2 ft.; leaves in basal rosette, stem leaves alternate, deeply lobed, margins smooth; flower clusters showy; petals 4, free; radial symmetry; yellow**

Brassica nigra
BRASSICACEAE

Black Mustard

Disturbed areas; up to 5000 ft.; non-native

This is the largest of the weedy European mustards that are considered invasive in California. With ample moisture, this annual can grow quite tall. It resembles Shortpod Mustard but is less hairy and has a slender pedicel where the fruit attaches to the stem. Black Mustard seed is one of the sources of commercial mustard seed. **Plant height to 8 ft.**; leaves in basal rosette, stem leaves alternate, pinnately lobed, margins toothed; flower clusters showy; flowers small, petals 4, free; radial symmetry; yellow

Brassica tournefortii
BRASSICACEAE

Sahara Mustard

Disturbed grasslands; up to 2600 ft.; non-native

Blooming from winter through summer, this annual invasive, weedy mustard has pale yellow flowers, with sepals that are often purple-tinged. It is highly branched and can resemble a mound of twigs, especially as the fruits mature. Roadsides, grasslands, and open areas of Southern California have become choked with this invader. **Plant height to 3 ft.**; basal rosette pinnately lobed, stem leaves unlobed, margins toothed; flower clusters showy; flowers small, petals 4, free; radial to semi-radial symmetry; light yellow

Descurainia pinnata
BRASSICACEAE

Western Tansy-Mustard

Deserts, conifer forests, chaparral; up to 10,300 ft.; native

This plant resembles a delicate feather-duster. *Pinnata* means "feathery," in reference to its dissected leaves. Like most mustards, its leaves are edible. In some parts of the world, its seeds are dried, ground, and mixed with cold water and other ingredients to make a nutritious drink. This annual blooms in spring and summer. **Plant height to 30 in.; leaves in basal rosette, stem leaves alternate, dissected, margins toothed; flower clusters showy; petals 4, free; radial symmetry; yellow**

Descurainia sophia
BRASSICACEAE

Flixweed

Deserts, disturbed areas; up to 9800 ft.; non-native

Blooming from spring through fall, this annual is similar to Western Tansy Mustard, with deep green, feathery leaves, but its fruits are shaped slightly differently. Native to Eurasia, this Old World species has been used as a diarrhea treatment and to dress wounds. It has become naturalized in many areas in California. **Plant height to 30 in.; basal rosette; stem leaves pinnately compound, leaflets dissected, margins smooth; flower clusters showy; petals 4, free; radial symmetry; yellow**

Draba oligosperma
BRASSICACEAE

Fewseed Draba

Alpine; 7500–14,000 ft.; native

This spring- and summer-blooming perennial herb can be quite abundant on alpine barrens and dry slopes in the Sierra Nevada. Like many high-elevation species, it has a tightly mounded habit. To hedge against the need for pollinators, this species is capable of asexual apomictic reproduction, meaning it can produce seed without pollen. **Plant height to 6 in.; leaves alternate, unlobed, margins smooth; petals showy, 4, free; radial symmetry; yellow**

Hirschfeldia incana
BRASSICACEAE

Shortpod Mustard

Disturbed areas; up to 6500 ft.; non-native

This annual is similar to Black Mustard but is covered in scruffy, white hairs. It has short, stubby pedicels and rocket-shaped fruit tips. It is a noxious weed that displaces native species. Blooming from spring through fall, it tolerates summer heat and can flower later than some other mustards. **Plant height 2–4 ft.; basal rosette, stem leaves alternate, pinnately lobed to unlobed, margins wavy to toothed; flower clusters showy; petals 4, free; radial symmetry; yellow**

Isatis tinctoria
BRASSICACEAE

Dyer's Woad

Disturbed areas, grasslands; up to 7200 ft.; non-native

This invasive, spring-blooming biennial grows a basal tuft of leaves in the first growing season and blooms in a cloud of small yellow flowers the next spring. Flowers mature to black, dangling seed pods. Stem leaves are arrowhead shaped. The name *tinctoria* refers to its history as a source of blue dye. **Plant height to 4 ft.; basal rosette, leaves unlobed, stem leaves lobed, margins smooth to wavy or toothed; flower cluster showy; petals 4, free; radial symmetry; yellow**

Lepidium flavum
BRASSICACEAE

Yellow Pepper Weed

Deserts, wetlands; 700–7600 ft.; native

This spring-blooming annual occurs in both wet and dry areas. Like all pepper weeds, it has small, short-lived flowers. Like most mustards, the fruits are needed to identify the species. It has rounded fruits (silicles) with two little horns. The specific name, *flavum*, is Latin for "very yellow," which describes the flowers. **Plant height to 14 in.; leaves alternate, unlobed, margins toothed; flowers small, petals showy, 4, free; radial symmetry; yellow**

Lepidium jaredii
BRASSICACEAE

Jared's Pepper Weed

Grasslands; 2900 ft.; native

This rare spring-blooming annual is similar to Yellow Pepper Weed but is much hairier, more upright and found in the Inner Coast Ranges in only 12 locations. One of those places is the Carrizo Plain. In a year with ample rain, portions of the entire valley seems to be covered with Jared's Pepper Weed. Rare species can be very abundant locally. **Plant height to 2.5 ft.; leaves alternate, unlobed, margins smooth; flowers small, petals showy, 4, free; radial symmetry; yellow, white**

Physaria kingii
BRASSICACEAE

King Bladderpod

Conifer forests, woodlands; 5100–12,300 ft.; native

This striking perennial herb grows in dry and rocky habitats. Three subspecies have been described. The rarest is subspecies *bernardina*, which is federally listed as endangered and found in fewer than 10 places, all within the Big Bear Valley area. Specific threats include development, mining, and recreational activities. It blooms in spring and summer. **Plant height 8 in.; leaves alternate, unlobed, margins smooth; flower clusters showy; petals 4, free; radial symmetry; yellow**

Rorippa curvisiliqua
BRASSICACEAE

Curvepod Yellow Cress

Conifer forests, woodlands, chaparral; up to 11,000 ft.; native

This species' thick seed pods tend to curve upward like an old hat rack. Blooming from summer into fall, it can be either an annual or a biennial. The genus name describes its habitat affinity; *roro* means "moist" and *ripa* means "riverbank" in Latin. The plant is edible and grows in moist areas throughout Western North America. **Plant height to 1 ft.; leaves basal rosette, lobed, dissected, margins toothed; petals showy, 4, free; radial symmetry; yellow**

Sisymbrium altissimum
BRASSICACEAE

Tumble Mustard

Disturbed areas; 4000–10,500 ft.; non-native

A common weed found in disturbed, moist soils, this annual has distinct horns on its outer sepals and wide flower stalks (pedicels). The plant is quite tall, earning it the specific name *altissimum*; *altus* means "high," and *issimmus* means "very much." Records indicate that it can be used to induce vomiting. It blooms in summer. **Plant height to 5 ft.; leaves basal rosette, lobed, dissected, margins toothed; petals showy, 4, free; radial symmetry; yellow**

Sisymbrium orientale
BRASSICACEAE

Indian Hedge Mustard

Disturbed areas; up to 4200 ft.; non-native

This annual herb blooms in spring and summer. It has an upright habit and is covered in soft hairs. In reference to its Asian origin, it was given its specific name *orientale* by Carl Linnaeus, the creator of the scientific naming system. It is considered native to Europe and North Africa but is a problematic weed in North America. **Plant height to 3 ft.; leaves alternate, basal lobes, margins toothed; petals showy, 4, free; radial symmetry; yellow**

Tropidocarpum gracile
BRASSICACEAE

Dobie Pod

Woodlands, grasslands; up to 6300 ft.; native

This common, diminutive annual grows in grasslands partially shaded habitats. Its distribution extends into Baja California. Blooming in spring, the flowers are small and short-lived. The plant is coated in rough hairs, and its fruits are long and slender. The specific name describes these fruits: *gracilis* means "slender" in Latin. **Plant height to 18 in.; leaves alternate, dissected, margins smooth; petals showy, 4, free; radial symmetry; yellow**

Ferocactus cylindraceus
CACTACEAE

California Barrel Cactus

Deserts; up to 5000 ft.; native

Given enough time, this spring-blooming succulent can grow massive barrels (stems) upwards of 6 ft. tall. New spines are straight and red, becoming curved and gray as they age. The sculptural beauty of this species threatens its own survival: it has been the target of poachers. It is further threatened by solar and wind energy development. **Plant height to 6 ft.; leaves modified into spines; petals showy, many, free; radial symmetry; yellow**

Opuntia ficus-indica
CACTACEAE

Mission Prickly-pear

Chaparral, grasslands; up to 1500 ft.; non-native

The fruits of this summer-blooming succulent are edible as they ripen from yellow to red. The species was brought to the state from Central Mexico, presumably as a food source. The stems (pads) have reduced spines and can be eaten raw, boiled, or sautéed—or even fermented into alcohol. **Plant height to 16 ft.; leaves modified into spines; petals showy, many, free; radial symmetry; yellow, light orange**

Crocanthemum scoparium
CISTACEAE

Peak Rush-rose

Conifer forests, chaparral; up to 4000 ft.; native

This delicate perennial herb is endemic to the California Floristic Province, occurring only in the parts of California and Mexico that have a Mediterranean climate. Two varieties have been described: variety *scoparium* is a shorter plant with spreading stems that occurs in coastal areas, and variety *vulgare* is taller, has erect stems, and is found inland. **Plant** height to 18 in.; leaves alternate, unlobed, margins smooth; petals showy, 5, free; radial symmetry; yellow

Cleomella obtusifolia
CLEOMACEAE

Mojave Stinkweed

Deserts; up to 5500 ft.; native

This annual herb is native to the Mojave Desert in California and Western Nevada, where it grows in sandy, alkaline soils. There is considerable variation in hairiness, leaf base size, and fruit shape. It blooms from spring into fall, and strange little horned seed pods are borne on long, drooping pedicels. **Plant** height to 3 ft.; leaves alternate, compound, 3 leaflets, margins smooth; petals showy, 4, free; radial symmetry; yellow

Peritoma arborea
CLEOMACEAE

Bladderpod

Deserts, chaparral; up to 6000 ft.; native

Showy yellow flowers give way to large, in-flated fruit throughout the year. Easy to grow with a wide flowering period, this subshrub is a good choice for pollinator gardens to attract bees and butterflies when other species are not in bloom. Unfortunately, its foliage does have a distinct odor, reminiscent of rotten peanut butter. **Plant height 1–6 ft.; leaves alternate, palmately compound, usually 3 leaflets, margins smooth; petals showy, 4, free; radial symmetry; yellow**

Dudleya farinosa
CRASSULACEAE

Bluff Lettuce

Chaparral; up to 1500 ft.; native

This summer-blooming succulent is one of 26 species in the genus, some of which have been affected by poaching. It is estimated that more than 100,000 plants, worth tens of millions of dollars, have been removed from the wild to sell to private collectors. CNPS has worked to strengthen laws so that poachers face increased consequences. **Plant height 4–8 in.; leaves in basal rosette, unlobed, margins smooth; petals showy, 5, partially fused; radial symmetry; stem pink; flower yellow**

Sedella pumila
CRASSULACEAE

Sierra Mock Stonecrop

Conifer forests, woodlands, riparian; up to 9000 ft.; native

This spring-blooming annual succulent occurs only in California and is relatively abundant in the areas around the Central Valley. It has a neat fruit type (pyxidium)—a seed capsule that splits open, and the top lifts off like the lid of a box. Its flowers have a noticeably musty odor. **Plant height 1–7 in.; leaves alternate, unlobed, margins smooth; petals showy, 5, free; radial symmetry; yellow**

Sedum obtusatum
CRASSULACEAE

Sierra Stonecrop

Rock outcrops and rocky slopes, alpine, often on granite; up to 13,500 ft.; native

As its common name suggests, this succulent is endemic to the Sierra Nevada. It was once thought to occur in the Cascade, Klamath, and Coast ranges, but these occurrences have all been reassigned to other *Sedum* species. Basal leaves are wedge-shaped, broader above the middle, flattened, and blunt or notched at the tips. **Plant height 1–8 in.; leaves in basal cluster, stem leaves alternate, unlobed, margins smooth; petals showy, 5, free; radial symmetry; yellow, orange**

Sedum spathulifolium
CRASSULACEAE

Broadleaf Stonecrop

Conifer forests, chaparral; up to 7500 ft.; native

Blooming in spring and summer, this succulent has unnaturally yellow flowers in colors reminiscent of a highlighter. It occurs throughout California but is more abundant in the north part of the state. It spreads via stolons, aboveground horizontal stems that root and produce new flattened rosettes. In gardens, it requires well-drained soil to avoid crown rot. **Plant height 1–8 in.; leaves in basal rosette, unlobed, margins smooth; petals showy, 5, free; radial symmetry; yellow**

Cucurbita foetidissima
CUCURBITACEAE

Stinky Gourd

Chaparral, grassland; up to 5600 ft.; native

This summer-blooming vining or prostrate perennial stinks! It can, in fact, be identified from a distance by its odor. In addition, the species can be recognized by its distinct triangular leaves, held perpendicular to the vining stem. It has many documented uses, including a variety of remedies to treat venereal disease. **Plant stem length to 20 ft.; leaves alternate, basally lobed, margins smooth; petals showy, 5, partially fused; radial symmetry; yellow, orange**

Cucurbita palmata
CUCURBITACEAE

Coyote Gourd

Deserts, coastal sage scrub; up to 4500 ft.; native

The flowers of this vining perennial are quite large, up to 3 in. Mammals, including coyotes, eat its bitter, fleshy fruit, which can be dark green to mottled yellow, though it is not palatable to humans. This spring- and summer-blooming species also occurs in parts of the Desert Southwest that receive monsoonal summer rains.

Plant stem length to 6 ft.; leaves alternate, lobed, margins toothed; petals showy, 5, partially fused; radial symmetry; yellow, orange

Acacia longifolia
FABACEAE

Sydney Golden Wattle

Disturbed areas; up to 500 ft.; non-native

Native to Australia, this hardy shrub is used as a fast-growing windscreen. It was brought to North America as an ornamental and has escaped cultivation; it now grows in coastal communities. The specific name refers to its long, straplike leaves, which are actually long flattened petioles (phyllodes), rather than typical leaf blades. The showiest parts of the flower are the stamens. **Plant height to 25 ft.; leaves alternate, unlobed, margins smooth; stamens showy, many, free; radial symmetry; pale yellow**

Acmispon glaber
FABACEAE

Deerweed

Chaparral; up to 5000 ft.; native

This spring- and summer-blooming perennial is common along trails and in open areas. Its wiry, erect stems often lose their leaves in the summer heat, when the plant resembles the head of a broom. Up to seven small flowers appear in clusters. Its specific name means "without hairs," in reference to the hairless stem. **Plant height 1–3 ft.; leaves alternate, pinnately compound, margins smooth; flower clusters showy; petals 5, partially fused (keel); mirror symmetry; yellow**

Acmispon strigosus
FABACEAE

Strigose Lotus

Many communities; up to 7600 ft.; native

Common in open, sunny areas, this annual forms low-growing mats. Spring flowers have red veins and are attached to the plant via pedicels. In the California Floristic Province, plants usually have short, stiff hairs and narrow leaves, whereas in the deserts, they tend to have fleshy wider leaves and white-gray hairs. **Prostrate stem length to 18 in.; leaves alternate, pinnately compound, margins smooth; flowers small, petals 5, partially fused (keel); mirror symmetry; yellow, aging to orange-red**

Acmispon wrangelianus
FABACEAE

Chilean Lotus

Conifer forests, woodlands, chaparral; up to 4900 ft.; native

This annual groundcover has small flowers and compound leaves with oval leaflets arranged in asymmetric groups of four. Chilean Lotus is not from Chile. It can be found in thin soils into Oregon and throughout Southwestern North America. It once was very common in areas now overrun with weeds and non-native grasses. **Prostrate stem length to 1 ft.; leaves alternate, palmately compound, margins smooth; flowers small, petals 5, partially fused (keel); mirror symmetry; yellow**

Cytisus scoparius
FABACEAE

Scotch Broom

Disturbed areas; up to 3300 ft.; non-native

This spring-blooming shrub has bright flowers and an angular, sparsely-leaved stem that resembles a star in cross section. A noxious weed, it was originally brought to California as an ornamental and now displaces native species in foothill and coastal habitats. Once established, it is very difficult to eliminate; seeds can remain dormant for 80 years. **Plant height 3–10 ft.; leaves alternate, compound, 3 leaflets, margins smooth; petals showy, 5, partially fused (keel); mirror symmetry; yellow**

Genista monspessulana
FABACEAE

French Broom

Disturbed areas; up to 3000 ft.; non-native

Native to the Mediterranean, this attractive garden escapee forms dense thickets that smother natives. The spring-blooming shrub has ridged stems that age to become rounded and are covered in silky, gold hairs. It is unpalatable to grazing animals and can stump sprout after a fire. A single plant can produce 8000 seeds in a season, and it is difficult to eradicate once established. **Plant height to 9 ft.; leaves alternate, compound, 3 leaflets, margins smooth; petals showy, 5, partially fused (keel); mirror symmetry; yellow**

Hosackia gracilis
FABACEAE

Harlequin Lotus

Coastal wetlands; up to 3700 ft.; native

This spring-blooming perennial herb has a distinctive flower color pattern. The larger petal (banner) is yellow or sometimes orange, while the smaller petals are pink. It is considered a rare plant in California and is thought to be a larval host for Lotus Blue, a coastal butterfly species that has not been documented since 1983. **Plant height to 18 in.; leaves alternate, pinnately compound, margins smooth; petals showy, 5, partially fused (keel); mirror symmetry; yellow, pink**

Hosackia oblongifolia
FABACEAE

Narrow-leaved Lotus

Wetlands; up to 9000 ft.; native

The flower of this perennial, summer-blooming herb has a colorful, yellow upper petal (banner), while the wing and keel petals are white. The genus was named after Dr. David Hosack, who started the first public garden in the United States in New York. He also tried, and failed, to save Alexander Hamilton after his duel with Aaron Burr. **Plant height to 2 ft.; leaves alternate, pinnately compound, margins smooth; petals showy, 5, partially fused (keel); mirror symmetry; yellow, white**

Lupinus arboreus
FABACEAE

Yellow Bush Lupine

Dunes, coastal areas; up to 300 ft.; native

Few plants are considered both native and invasive in the same state. This attractive and aggressive floriferous shrub is one of them. Blooming from late spring through summer, it is considered native in coastal habitats from the Bay Area south to San Luis Obispo County. Northward, it invades coastal dunes, smothering diverse native habitats. **Plant height to 7 ft.; leaves alternate, palmately compound, margins smooth; petals showy, 5, partially fused (keel); mirror symmetry; yellow, lavender**

Lupinus stiversii
FABACEAE

Harlequin Lupine

Conifer forests, woodlands; up to 6600 ft.; native

Harlequin Lupine is one of the most distinct species in the genus. The two-toned flower has a yellow upper petal (banner) and pink lower petals. Though some *Hosackia* species have similar flower color patterns, they have very different leaf shapes. All lupines have distinctive palmately compound leaves, whereas *Hosackia* species have pinnately compound leaves. **Plant height to 18 in.; leaves alternate, palmately compound, margins smooth; petals showy, 5, partially fused (keel); mirror symmetry; yellow, pink**

Medicago polymorpha
FABACEAE

Burclover

Disturbed areas; up to 5000 ft.; non-native

Blooming in spring, this annual is originally from Europe. It thrives in disturbed areas and has spread throughout the world. A common lawn weed, it has small, yellow flowers that develop into tenacious, spiral-shaped, barbed fruits that are picked up easily by passersby. You could have one in your sock right now. **Plant stem length 4–20 in.; leaves alternate, palmately compound, margins toothed; flowers small, petals 5, partially fused (keel); mirror symmetry; yellow**

Melilotus indicus
FABACEAE

Sour Clover

Disturbed areas; up to 5600 ft.; non-native

Originally from Northern Africa, Europe, and Asia, this rangy annual has naturalized throughout much of the world. Leaflet margins are sharply toothed. Blooming in spring, the tiny yellow flowers atop erect stems form showy clusters. Yellow Sweetclover (*M. officinalis*) is a similar but slightly larger plant. **Plant height to 2 ft.; leaves alternate, compound, 3 leaflets, margins toothed; flower clusters showy; petals 5, partially fused (keel); mirror symmetry; yellow**

Parkinsonia florida
FABACEAE

Blue Palo Verde

Deserts; up to 3400 ft.; native

Admittedly, this tree is not a wildflower in the classic sense. It does, however, have very showy flowers that bloom in spring, and it is used extensively as an ornamental throughout California. Some hybrids produce massive displays for much of the year. It is a great choice for drought tolerant pollinator gardens with space for a small tree. **Plant height to 25 ft.; leaves alternate, pinnately compound, margins smooth; petals showy, 5, free; mirror symmetry; yellow**

Senna armata
FABACEAE

Desert Senna

Deserts; up to 6200 ft.; native

This shrub blooms in spring and summer and grows in sandy, rocky desert washes. After the leaf emerges, its leaflets drop off quickly, leaving a spiny tip. The grooved stems have pointy tips. During the bloom period, the plant is covered in showy, bright yellow, sometimes salmon-colored flowers that attract bumble bees. **Plant height to 3 ft.; leaves alternate, pinnately compound, margins smooth; petals showy, 5, free; mirror symmetry; yellow**

Spartium junceum
FABACEAE

Spanish Broom

Disturbed areas; up to 3000 ft.; non-native

The thick, round, succulent stems of this attractive perennial are photosynthetic, which is a common adaptation to dry, Mediterranean environments. Like most brooms, it was originally an ornamental and escaped cultivation. It was also planted along highways to prevent erosion. A single plant can produce a heroic number of seeds, up to 10,000 per season. **Plant height to 14 ft.; leaves alternate, unlobed, margins smooth; petals showy, 5, partially fused (keel); mirror symmetry; yellow**

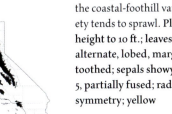

Trifolium dubium
FABACEAE

Little Hop Clover

Disturbed areas, grasslands; up to 1600 ft.; non-native

This spring-blooming annual has yellow flowers that droop with age and turn brown. Its leaf shape is reminiscent of a shamrock. A similar non-native yellow clover, Hop Clover (*T. aureum*), has generally more than 20 flowers per head, while this species has fewer flowers. Though small, these plants can displace native species. **Plant height to 10 in.; leaves alternate, compound, 3 leaflets, margins toothed; flower clusters showy; petals small, 5, partially fused (keel); mirror symmetry; yellow, aging to brown**

Ribes aureum
GROSSULARIACEAE

Golden Currant

Conifer forests, woodlands, riparian; up to 10,100 ft.; native

This shrub has a spicy fragrance reminiscent of cloves or vanilla. New growth is sticky and spineless. The bright green foliage can have a rubbery texture. Blooming in spring, the flowers have long tubes and form clusters that attract hummingbirds. The mountain variety of this species has an upright habit, whereas the coastal-foothill variety tends to sprawl. **Plant height to 10 ft.; leaves alternate, lobed, margins toothed; sepals showy, 5, partially fused; radial symmetry; yellow**

Ribes montigenum
GROSSULARIACEAE

Mountain Gooseberry

Conifer forests, alpine; up to 14,300 ft.; native

Blooming in summer, the flowers' large, usually lighter colored sepals are more obvious than the tiny, deep red petals, giving the overall impression of pink flowers. The shrub has bristly glandular hairs on its leaves. Within the genus, the spiny species are known as gooseberries, whereas the spineless species are considered currants. **Plant height to 3 ft.; leaves alternate, lobed, margins toothed; sepals showy, 5, partially fused; radial symmetry; yellow, pink, red, white**

Emmenanthe penduliflora
HYDROPHYLLACEAE

Whispering Bells

Grasslands, shrublands; up to 7000 ft.; native

This annual tends to germinate in abundance after a fire. Blooming in spring and summer, the flowers are yellow with petals that persist as the fruit develops. After the flowers have withered, their dry, papery corollas make a distinctive rustling sound in the breeze. It has a medicinal aroma. **Plant height to 2.5 ft.; leaves alternate, pinnately lobed, margins smooth; flower clusters showy; petals small, 5, partially fused; radial symmetry; yellow, fading to white**

Hypericum anagalloides
HYPERICACEAE

Tinker's Penny

Wetlands, riparian, conifer forests, woodlands; up to 10,600 ft.; native

This summer-blooming herb grows in wet soils and has glandular leaves. It can be annual or perennial and can tolerate being submerged. In former times, a tinker traveled from house to house, mending metal utensils. The delicate flowers may be reminiscent of the splatter made by molten tin on the floor of a tinker's workshop. **Plant height to 10 in.; leaves opposite, unlobed, margins smooth; petals showy, 5, free; radial symmetry; yellow**

Hypericum scouleri
HYPERICACEAE

Scouler's St. Johns Wort

Wet meadows, riparian, conifer forests, chaparral; 4000–7500 ft.; native

This summer-blooming perennial herb is found throughout Western North America, usually in wet areas. The plant is slender with short, elliptic leaves. Black glands appear along the petal and sepal margins. It is similar to the noxious European weed *H. perforatum*, which is larger, has reddish stems, and is found in disturbed areas. **Plant height 1–2 ft.; leaves opposite, unlobed, margins smooth; petals showy, 5, free; radial symmetry; yellow**

Sisyrinchium californicum
IRIDACEAE

Yellow-eyed Grass

Wetlands, coastal shrublands; up to 2000 ft.; native

This delicate perennial herb has star-shaped flowers that adorn somewhat flattened, winged stems. The grasslike leaves form tidy clumps. The flower parts are in sets of three, which is typical of monocots. The species is coastal and not abundant or common. However, it is commonly grown in nurseries and gardens. **Plant height to 1 ft.; leaves alternate, unlobed, margins smooth; tepals showy, 6, free; radial symmetry; yellow**

Calochortus amabilis
LILIACEAE

Diogenes' Lantern

Woodlands, shrublands; 300–3300 ft.; native

This spring-blooming perennial herb is similar to White Globe Lily but shorter, and its nodding flower globes have a more triangular shape. The petals are edged in short, thick hairs, and the pointed sepals are longer than the petals. A similar species, Mount Diablo Fairy-lantern (*C. pulchellus*), occurs only on and around Mount Diablo in Northern California. **Plant height 4–20 in.; leaves alternate, unlobed, margins smooth; petals showy, 3, free; radial symmetry; yellow**

Calochortus clavatus
LILIACEAE

Clubhair Mariposa Lily

Grasslands; up to 5900 ft.; native

Blooming in spring and early summer, the flowers of this perennial herb are large, upright cups. It is similar to Gold Nuggets (*C. luteus*), but its stems can zigzag and its stamens are often reddish purple. A round, hairy patch of club-shaped hairs appears on the inner petal surface. **Plant height to 3 ft.; leaves alternate, unlobed, margins smooth; petals showy, 3, free; radial symmetry; yellow**

Calochortus luteus
LILIACEAE

Gold Nuggets

Grasslands; up to 2300 ft.; native

This spring-flowering perennial herb has upright flowers on straight stems. Flowers are saucer- or cup-shaped, with yellow petals that often have brown markings. A crescent-shaped band of crowded, short hairs apears near the petal base, in contrast to the round, hairy patch on Clubhair Mariposa Lily petals. **Plant height to 30 in.; leaves alternate, unlobed, margins smooth; petals showy, 3, free; radial symmetry; yellow**

Calochortus monophyllus
LILIACEAE

Yellow Star Tulip

Woodlands; 1300–4000 ft.; native

This diminutive perennial herb blooms from spring to early summer with several upright, deep yellow flowers that are shaped like very open tulips. Petals are densely hairy on the inside and may have a red spot near the base. The fruits are nodding, and the thick, strap-like, narrow leaves are bluish green. **Plant height to 8 in.; leaves alternate, unlobed, margins smooth; petals showy, 3, free; radial symmetry; yellow**

Limnanthes douglasii
LIMNANTHACEAE

Common Meadowfoam

Many communities, wetlands; up to 3300 ft.; native

This low-growing annual can be abundant in vernal pools and meadows. In California, five subspecies have been described based on variation in flower form and color. The petals can be white with yellow veins, yellow with white tips, or completely yellow. *Limne* means "a marsh" and *anthos* means "a flower," which accurately describes the species. **Plant height to 18 in.; leaves alternate, pinnately compound, margins toothed; petals showy, 5, free; radial symmetry; yellow, white**

Mentzelia affinis
LOASACEAE

Yellow Comet

Deserts, woodlands; up to 4000 ft.; native

This small, spring-blooming annual has up to 30 stamens. The ovary is inferior, meaning that the flower parts are attached above it. Veatch's Blazing Star (*M. veatchiana*) is similar in size, flower shape, and distribution, but it has divided leaves instead of Yellow Comet's entire to barely lobed leaves. It is native to the deserts of the Southwest. **Plant height to 2 ft.; leaves alternate, unlobed to minutely lobed, margins minutely toothed; petals showy, 5, free; radial symmetry; yellow**

Mentzelia dispersa
LOASACEAE

Scattered Blazing Star

Conifer forests, woodlands, chaparral; 3000–10,200 ft.; native

Growing in sandy soil or on rocky slopes, this summer-blooming annual is native to Western North America. Its stems bear hairy flower clusters with shiny, iridescent petals. A study found that germination of this species increases significantly in response to smoke treatments, highlighting the importance of fire in its life history. **Plant height to 20 in.; leaves alternate, lobed or unlobed, margins toothed or smooth; petals showy, 5, free; radial symmetry; yellow**

Mentzelia laevicaulis
LOASACEAE

Giant Blazing Star

Roadcuts, conifer forest openings, woodlands, chaparral; up to 9500 ft.; native

This perennial herb has a smooth, white stem, reminiscent of ivory or bone. Its huge flowers have many stamens and last through the heat of summer into fall, well after most wildflowers have set seed. If you are tempted to pick the flowers for a summer bouquet, do so with caution: the plant is covered with barbed hairs. **Plant height to 3 ft.; leaves alternate, unlobed, margins toothed; petals showy, 5, free; radial symmetry; yellow**

Fremontodendron californicum
MALVACEAE

California Flannelbush

Chaparral, conifer forests; up to 7600 ft.; native

This spring-blooming shrub is not a wildflower in the classic sense, but the floral display of a single plant can be as showy as a meadow full of spring ephemerals. Its large flowers attract pollinators. Even squirrels could be considered pollinators—Western Gray Squirrels have been spotted drinking the nectar from the flowers. **Plant height 8–18 ft.; leaves alternate, lobed, margins smooth; petals showy, 5, free, filaments fused; radial symmetry; yellow, orange**

Proboscidea althaeifolia
MARTYNIACEAE

Desert Unicorn Plant

Deserts; up to 3300 ft.; native

The distribution of this species in California is limited, but it is common throughout the deserts of the Southwest. This perennial grows in sandy places and blooms during the heat of summer. Leaves are covered in sticky hairs. The fruit dries into a claw shape, and it almost literally grabs passersby. **Plant height to 10 in., trailing to 3 ft.; leaves alternate, lobed, margins wavy; petals showy, 5, fused; mirror symmetry; yellow, orange**

Abronia latifolia
NYCTAGINACEAE

Coastal Sand Verbena

Dunes; up to 330 ft.; native

This floriferous, beach-dwelling, fleshy perennial herb blooms from spring through fall. It has round leaves and sticky glandular hairs that get coated in sand. It is thought that the sand layer makes the plant resistant to herbivory (animals that feed on plants). It is the only coastal *Abronia* species with yellow flowers; others have red or pink flowers. **Plant height to 5 in.; leaves opposite, unlobed, margins smooth; sepals showy, 5, partially fused; radial symmetry; yellow**

Nuphar polysepala
NYMPHAEACEAE

Rocky Mountain Pond-lily

Aquatic; up to 8200 ft; native

This spring- and summer-blooming perennial is fully aquatic and grows in ponds and streams in Western North America. Its roots are anchored to the bottom, and its large, heart-shaped leaves float on the surface. The large, yellow sepals are petal-like, whereas the true petals are small. The flowers have an unreal quality, as though they were carved from wax. **Plant height to 6 ft.; leaves alternate, basally lobed, margins smooth; sepals showy, many, free; radial symmetry; yellow**

Camissonia campestris
ONAGRACEAE

Mojave Suncup

Deserts, grasslands; up to 6600 ft.; native

This spring-blooming annual has wispy, hairless white stems with leaves that are long and narrow. The flower has reflexed sepals and subtle red dots at the base of the petals. Its prominent spherical stigma extends beyond the anthers. The specific name means "of the open plains," appropriate for a species that grows in open flats. **Plant height to 10 in.; leaves alternate, unlobed, margins finely toothed; flowers small, petals showy, 4, free; radial symmetry; yellow, fading to pink**

Camissonia strigulosa
ONAGRACEAE

Sandy Soil Suncup

Dunes, grasslands, deserts; up to 6900 ft.; native

This spring-blooming annual has wiry, arching stems and narrow leaves with minute teeth on the margins. The flower buds nod and the sepals are reflexed. Bright yellow flowers turn orange as they age. The specific name, *strigulosa*, means "thin" and refers to the short, appressed (lying flat) hairs on the stems. **Plant height to 20 in.; leaves alternate, unlobed, margins subtly toothed; flowers small, petals showy, 4, free; radial symmetry; yellow, fading to pink**

Camissoniopsis cheiranthifolia
ONAGRACEAE

Beach Suncup

Coastal dunes, beaches; up to 330 ft.; native

This short-lived perennial's bloom period lasts from winter through summer. When it blooms, the beach turns golden. It creeps along the ground, forming huge mats. The plant is covered in silvery hairs and has coiled fruits. As with all dune species, habitat loss as a result of recreation and development is a looming threat. **Plant height to 6 in., spreading up to 4 ft.; leaves basal rosette, unlobed, margins smooth; flowers small, petals showy, 4, free; radial symmetry; yellow**

Camissoniopsis pallida
ONAGRACEAE

Pale Yellow Suncup

Deserts; up to 5900 ft.; native

This annual blooms from spring through summer and has a particular growth pattern. Low rosettes of lance-shaped leaves give rise to creeping shoots that produce additional rosettes. The foliage is dark gray-green and hairy, and the flowering stems are short. Its distribution outside California includes desert areas of Arizona and Nevada. **Plant height to 6 in.; leaves basal rosette, unlobed, margins smooth; flowers small, petals showy, 4, free; radial symmetry; yellow**

Chylismia brevipes
ONAGRACEAE

Golden Suncup

Deserts; up to 5900 ft.; native

This spring-blooming species is an annual or a short-lived perennial. It is found throughout the deserts of Southwestern North America. The hairy, erect flowering stems grow from rosettes of leaves that can be simple or compound, with distinct leaflets. Flower clusters develop from nodding buds. As plants age, their leaves become weirdly mottled. **Plant height to 20 in.; leaves basal rosette, variable, margins toothed; flower clusters showy; petals 4, free; radial symmetry; yellow**

Chylismia cardiophylla
ONAGRACEAE

Heart-leaf Suncup

Deserts; up to 4600 ft.; native

This spring-blooming herb grows in sandy and rocky areas in Southwestern North America. Unsurprisingly, given its name, it has heart-shaped leaves. It can be either a single, erect flowering stem more typical of an annual, or a multistemmed, bushy perennial. The bright yellow flowers age to orange. **Plant height to 2.5 ft.; leaves basal and alternate, basally lobed, margins toothed; flower clusters showy; petals 4, free; radial symmetry; yellow**

Eulobus californicus
ONAGRACEAE

California Primrose

Chaparral, woodlands, grasslands; up to 4300 ft.; native

This spring-blooming annual begins as a flat rosette of blotchy, gray-green leaves with ragged lobes. Plants become hairless and the red-spotted, yellow flower petals turn pink as they age. The species looks a lot like a weedy mustard, but unlike a mustard, it has nodding buds, an inferior ovary, and a globose (spherical) stigma. **Plant height 2–5 ft.; leaves in basal rosette, stem leaves alternate, lobed, margins toothed; petals showy, 4, free; radial symmetry; yellow**

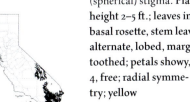

Ludwigia peploides
ONAGRACEAE

Marsh Purslane

Lakeshores, streambanks, seasonal wetlands; up to 3000 ft.; non-native

This perennial herb blooms in early summer through fall. It has glossy, hairless leaves and clawed petals that narrow at the base. Most likely it is native to Central and South America, but has become naturalized throughout the world. In some places, it is a serious wetland weed, floating, creeping, or forming large mats. **Plant stem length up to 6 ft.; leaves alternate, clustered, unlobed, margins smooth; petals showy, 4, free; radial symmetry; yellow**

Oenothera elata
ONAGRACEAE

Tall Evening Primrose

Many communities, wetlands; up to 9200 ft.; native

This biennial herb flowers prolifically throughout the hottest parts of summer. It is a robust, hairy plant with stout, erect stems and large leaves. The flower buds nod prior to opening and become erect as they open in the evenings. Hawk moths are its main pollinators. **Plant height to 6 ft.; leaves in basal rosette, stem leaves alternate, unlobed, margins smooth or toothed; petals showy, 4, free; radial symmetry; yellow**

Oenothera xylocarpa
ONAGRACEAE

Woodyfruit Evening Primrose

Conifer forests; 7200–10,200 ft.; native

This summer-blooming perennial herb produces a flat, basal rosette of hairy, gray-green leaves from a thick tap root. The large flowers are borne on a very short stem and intermingle with the leaves of the rosette. The bright yellow petals fade to pink as they age. The specific name, *xylocarpa*, means "woody fruit." **Plant height to 6 in.; leaves in basal rosette, unlobed or basally lobed, margins toothed; petals showy, 4, free; radial symmetry; yellow**

Tetrapteron graciliflorum
ONAGRACEAE

Hill Suncup

Woodlands, grasslands; up to 2600 ft.; native

The nodding buds of this spring-blooming annual become small flowers that intermingle with the foliage. Like all *Tetrapteron* species, it has an unusual four-winged fruit with a persistent style. This species is hairy with a short stem and long, linear leaves. Its distribution extends into Southern Oregon. **Plant height to 10 in.; leaves in basal rosette, unlobed, margins smooth; flowers small, petals showy, 4, free; radial symmetry; yellow**

Aphyllon fasciculatum
OROBANCHACEAE

Clustered Orobanche

Deserts, shrublands, conifer forests; up to 10,800 ft.; native

This parasitic perennial herb blooms from spring through summer. A cluster of stems pops out of the ground, each topped by a tubular flower. The plant does not have true leaves. It is completely parasitic and does not produce its own food through photosynthesis. Instead, it invades the roots of neighbor plants to obtain nutrients. **Plant height to 8 in.; leaves absent; flower clusters showy; petals 5, partially fused; mirror symmetry; yellow**

Parentucellia viscosa
OROBANCHACEAE

Yellow Glandweed

Riparian, grasslands, woodlands, disturbed areas; up to 2300 ft.; non-native

This summer-blooming annual has erect, unbranched stems. The plant is covered with glandular, sticky hairs and bright flowers. Originally from Europe, this hemiparasite has invaded many continents, including Western North America. In California, it parasitizes members of the pea family and grasses, displacing native vegetation. **Plant height to 30 in.; leaves opposite, alternate, unlobed, margins toothed; flower clusters showy; petals 5, partially fused; mirror symmetry; yellow**

Pedicularis semibarbata
OROBANCHACEAE

Pinewoods Lousewort

Conifer forests; 4900–11,500 ft.; native

This summer-blooming perennial herb occurs in California and Nevada. Its long, fernlike leaves often have dark purplish pigments that provide sun protection. Shrouded in leafy bracts, its flowers have hairy sepals. *Pediculus* means "louse," and the genus name comes from a bygone belief that cattle and people could be infected with lice after eating it. **Plant height to 8 in.; leaves in basal rosette, dissected, margins toothed; flower clusters showy; petals 5, partially fused; mirror symmetry; yellow**

Triphysaria eriantha
OROBANCHACEAE

Butter-and-Eggs

Woodlands, grasslands; up to 5200 ft.; native

The blossoms of this delicate annual can be quite prolific, forming eye-catching displays in spring. Its foliage is often purple-tinged. *Triphysaria* is a Greek word that means "three bladders." The flowers have three pouch-shaped lower petals and long, hairy tubes. The plant parasitizes the roots of other plants to obtain nutrients. **Plant height to 14 in.; leaves alternate, lobed, margins smooth; flower clusters showy; petals 5, partially fused; mirror symmetry; yellow**

Oxalis pes-caprae
OXALIDACEAE

Bermuda Buttercup

Disturbed areas; up to 2700 ft.; non-native

This mounding perennial herb blooms from
winter through early summer. It has distinct
clover-like leaves with three heart-shaped
leaflets, often with purple spots. Originally
from South Africa, it escaped cultivation and
is considered a noxious weed. It grows from
deeply buried bulbs, making it very difficult
to eradicate once established. **Plant height to
8 in.; leaves basal rosette,
compound, margins
smooth; petals showy,
5, free; radial symme-
try; yellow**

Dendromecon rigida
PAPAVERACEAE

Bush Poppy

Chaparral, foothill woodlands; up to 6200 ft.;
native

Blooming in late winter through spring, solitary flowers are abundant and lose their
sepals early as the petals open. This species
is common in recently burned areas before it
gets shaded out. It has long, rigid white stems,
hence its specific name, *rigida*. The genus
name means "tree poppy," though this is a
multi-stemmed shrub.
**Plant height to 10 ft.;
leaves alternate, unlobed,
margins finely toothed;
petals showy, 4, free; radial symmetry; yellow**

Ehrendorferia chrysantha
PAPAVERACEAE

Golden Eardrops

Conifer forests, woodlands, chaparral; up to 7500 ft.; native

This summer-blooming perennial herb has twice compound, powdery gray leaves. Similar to *Dicentra* species, the flower's outer petals curve back. Golden Eardrops can be found in dry, shrubby habitats into Baja California. The seeds germinate in response to fire; periodic, low-intensity fires are necessary to maintain populations. **Plant height to 5 ft.; leaves alternate, dissected, margins toothed; flower clusters showy; petals 4, partially fused; mirror symmetry; yellow**

Eschscholzia caespitosa
PAPAVERACEAE

Tufted Poppy

Woodlands, chaparral, grasslands; up to 5900 ft.; native

This annual blooms in spring and summer. Plants grow in leafy clumps, are hairless, and have erect buds. It is similar to the larger California Poppy but usually has yellow instead of orange petals. In addition, Tufted Poppy lacks the wide, flattened ring of tissue (torus) that separates the petals from the stem on California Poppy. **Plant height to 1 ft.; leaves in basal rosette, dissected, margins smooth; petals showy, 4, free; radial symmetry; yellow, orange**

Eschscholzia minutiflora
PAPAVERACEAE

Coville's Poppy

Deserts; up to 8500 ft.; native

This spring-blooming annual is found throughout Southwestern North America. It has distinctly droopy flower buds that become erect as the flowers open. The differences among the species of western poppies are subtle. Coville's Poppy has a distinctive receptacle shape: just before the petals attach to the receptacle, it constricts inward. **Plant height to 1 ft.; leaves in basal rosette, dissected, margins smooth; petals showy, 4, free; radial symmetry; yellow, orange**

Platystemon californicus
PAPAVERACEAE

Cream Cups

Woodlands, chaparral, grasslands; up to 3300 ft.; native

In the spring, this hairy annual forms attractive displays of yellow and white flowers throughout Western North America. It is the only species in the genus. Its stigma is highly divided into six lobes. Historically, many varieties have been recognized, but evaluation of geography and morphology does not support them. **Plant height to 1 ft.; leaves in basal rosette, unlobed, margins smooth; petals showy, 6, free; radial symmetry; yellow with white patterns**

Diplacus brevipes
PHRYMACEAE

Wide-throat Monkeyflower

Chaparral, conifer forests; up to 7200 ft.; native

This annual blooms in spring and summer in open areas following fire or other disturbance. This robust plant is covered in sticky hairs. *Brevis* means "short" and describes the plant's short, fat flower tube. The calyx lobes are uneven, which helps distinguish it from other closely related species. Until recently, it was included in the genus *Mimulus*. **Plant height 3–30 in.; leaves opposite, unlobed, margins smooth; petals showy, 5, partially fused; mirror symmetry; yellow**

Erythranthe bicolor
PHRYMACEAE

Yellow and White Monkeyflower

Conifer forests, woodlands, chaparral; 1200–2100 ft.; native

This spring-blooming annual is endemic to California. It has striking two-toned flowers, with white upper lobes and yellow lower lobes with red freckles. The pointed lobes are all the same length, or the upper lobes may be longer than the lower. **Plant height 2–10 in.; leaves opposite, unlobed, margins minutely toothed; petals showy, 5, partially fused; mirror symmetry; yellow, white**

Erythranthe floribunda
PHRYMACEAE

Many-flowered Monkeyflower

Conifer forests, woodlands, chaparral; up to 8200 ft; native

This annual herb blooms from spring through summer in wet areas throughout Western North America. Its glandular hairs make it feel slimy. It creeps along the ground or uses other plants for support. Flowers are tiny, and the pointy calyx lobes are equal in length. Like all *Erythranthe* species in California, it was formerly included in the genus *Mimulus*. **Plant height 1–6 in.; leaves opposite, unlobed, margins toothed; petals showy, 5, partially fused; mirror symmetry; yellow**

Erythranthe guttata
PHRYMACEAE

Seep Monkeyflower

Many communities, riparian; up to 8200 ft; native

This common spring-bloomer is a perennial herb. All monkeyflowers were in the genus *Mimulus* until DNA evidence prompted their reclassification into two main groups. Monkeyflowers that have prominent flower stalks (pedicels) are now included in the genus *Erythranthe*, whereas those with pedicels absent or shorter than the calyx are in the genus *Diplacus*. **Plant height 4–10 in.; leaves opposite, basal leaves lobed, margins toothed; petals showy, 5, partially fused; mirror symmetry; yellow**

Erythranthe tilingii
PHRYMACEAE

Tiling's Monkeyflower

Seeps, streambanks, wet meadows; 4600–11,200 ft.; native

This mostly hairless, summer-blooming perennial herb is found growing along streams and in wet meadows throughout Western North America. Its calyx lobes are unequal and it has filamentous, mat-forming underground stems (rhizomes). Seep Monkeyflower is similar, but it has thicker rhizomes. Digging up the rhizomes is not recommended. **Plant height 1–14 in.; leaves opposite, unlobed, margins toothed; petals showy, 5, partially fused; mirror symmetry; yellow**

Mimetanthe pilosa
PHRYMACEAE

False Monkeyflower

Conifer forests, woodlands, chaparral; up to 8500 ft.; native

This annual herb blooms from spring through fall. It occurs throughout Western North America. Its unequal calyx lobes are about half the length of the small flower. The foliage is lime-green. It has an upright growth form, soft hairs, and resembles Many-flowered Monkeyflower, but it has no slimy glands. **Plant height 1–14 in.; leaves opposite, unlobed, margins smooth; flowers small, petals showy, 5, partially fused; mirror symmetry; yellow**

Antirrhinum filipes
PLANTAGINACEAE

Tangled Snapdragon

Deserts; up to 5400 ft.; native

This spring-blooming annual has thin, mostly hairless, twining stems. The maroon-spotted flowers are borne singly on long stalks (pedicels), which are like tendrils and help the plant climb on other species for support and protection. Although it is common throughout Southwestern North America, its sparse foliage can be difficult to spot. **Plant height to 2 ft.; leaves alternate, unlobed, margins smooth; petals showy, 5, partially fused; mirror symmetry; yellow**

Antirrhinum mohavea
PLANTAGINACEAE

Golden Desert Snapdragon

Deserts; up to 6100 ft.; native

This hairy, spring-blooming perennial herb has an upright growth form. Until very recently, Ghost Flower and this species were the only members of the genus *Mohavea*. The reclassification is based on DNA evidence. Most other *Antirrhinum* species have four fertile stamens, whereas these have two fertile stamens and two sterile staminodes. **Plant height to 8 ft.; leaves alternate, unlobed, margins smooth; petals showy, 5, partially fused; mirror symmetry; yellow**

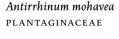

Keckiella antirrhinoides
PLANTAGINACEAE

Snapdragon Penstemon

Shrublands, woodlands; up to 3600 ft.; native

The range of this spring-blooming shrub extends into Arizona and Baja California. The flower has four fertile stamens and a hairy infertile stamen (staminode) that sits on the lower petals. This showy species has fragrant flowers that attract pollinators and make it a great garden addition. It loses its leaves completely in the winter. **Plant height 1–8 ft.; leaves opposite, unlobed, margins smooth; petals showy, 5, partially fused; mirror symmetry; yellow**

Keckiella lemmonii
PLANTAGINACEAE

Lemmon's Keckiella

Conifer and mixed forests, chaparral, woodlands; up to 6900 ft.; native

This summer-blooming shrub extends barely into Oregon. It is similar to Bush Beardtongue, with subtle differences in flower characteristics. The hairy, sterile stamen emerges from the flower along its lower lip. The plant resprouts from the base if top-killed by fire. The genus was named for David D. Keck, a botanist from Riverside, California.

Plant height 2–5 ft.; leaves opposite, unlobed, margins toothed infrequently; flower clusters showy; petals 5, partially fused; mirror symmetry; yellow, orange, pink

Kickxia spuria
PLANTAGINACEAE

Fluellin

Disturbed open areas; up to 2000 ft.;
non-native

The spurred flowers of this weedy, creeping perennial bloom from winter through
summer. It has purple upper petals and
lime-yellow lower petals. It is native to Europe and Asia and can be found along trails
in California. A similar species, Sharp-leaved
Fluellin (*K. elatine*), has lobed leaf bases and
is slightly more common.
**Plant height to 2 ft.;
leaves alternate, unlobed
or basally lobed, margins
smooth; flowers small,
petals showy, 5, partially
fused; mirror symmetry;
yellow-green, red**

Leptosiphon chrysanthus
POLEMONIACEAE

Golden Linanthus

Deserts, woodlands; up to 6600 ft.; native

The specific name, *chrysanthus*, means "with
golden flowers," though only one of the two
subspecies has yellow flowers; subspecies *de-
corus* has white flowers with maroon throats.
Although their ranges overlap, mixed yellow and white–flowered populations are not
found. This annual blooms in spring. **Plant
height to 6 in.; leaves opposite, lobed, margins smooth; petals
showy, 5, partially fused;
radial symmetry; yellow**

Navarretia breweri
POLEMONIACEAE

Brewer's Navarretia

Open wet areas, meadows, streamsides; 3300–10,100 ft.; native

This diminutive annual with needle-like leaves is punctuated by tiny yellow flowers in summer. Favoring moist areas in otherwise dry habitats, in a year with adequate rainfall, these prickly plants can be quite plentiful, often becoming dense and "bushy." The species is found throughout Western North America. **Plant height 1–3 in.; leaves alternate, lobed, margins toothed; flowers tiny, petals 5, partially fused; radial symmetry; yellow**

Eriogonum inflatum
POLYGONACEAE

Desert Trumpet

Deserts; up to 5900 ft.; native

Common in sandy and gravelly areas throughout the Southwestern states and into Mexico, this unusual-looking perennial herb blooms all year. Generally, it is distinguished by its upright, blue-green, noticeably inflated stems—a normal condition for the plant that is not caused by gall-forming insects. Pipes have been fashioned from the hollow, dried stems. **Plant height to 3 ft.; leaves basal, unlobed, margins smooth; flower clusters small; tepals 6, free; radial symmetry; yellow**

Eriogonum pusillum
POLYGONACEAE

Yellow Turbans

Desert woodlands; up to 8500 ft.; native

The specific name, *pusillum*, means "small, weak." This dainty annual is common in sandy areas in the Mojave Desert and Great Basin. Blooming in winter, spring, and summer, the structure that contains the flowers (involucre), as well as the tiny flowers themselves, are covered in glandular, sticky hairs. Its small basal leaves are wooly-hairy. **Plant height to 1 ft.; leaves basal, unlobed, margins smooth; flower clusters small; tepals 6, free; radial symmetry; yellow, red**

Eriogonum umbellatum
POLYGONACEAE

Sulphur Buckwheat

Conifer forests, deserts, woodlands; 300–11,800 ft.; native

This highly diverse species currently has 41 recognized varieties—25 of them occur in California, and 7 are rare. Growing from the low desert to the alpine zone, plants can be low-growing perennial herbs, subshrubs, or shrubs. The flower clusters appear from spring to fall. The cup-shaped involucre has long, recurved lobes.

Plant height to 4 ft.; leaves basal, unlobed, margins smooth; flower clusters showy; tepals 6, free; radial symmetry; yellow, red, white

Ranunculus californicus
RANUNCULACEAE

California Buttercup

Many communities, wetlands; up to 6600 ft; native

This spring-blooming perennial herb grows in sunny, open areas in the Pacific Coast states. It has iridescent flowers in long-branched clusters, each flower borne singly on a long pedicel. Leaves are deeply divided into three lobes. *Ranunculus* is Latin for "little frog," and you may well find frogs in the moist meadows and streams where buttercups grow. **Plant height to 2 ft.; leaves basal, alternate, lobed to dissected, margins toothed; petals showy, 9–17, free; radial symmetry; yellow**

Ranunculus eschscholtzii
RANUNCULACEAE

Eschscholtz's Buttercup

Open rocky slopes, meadows; 3000-13,100 ft.; native

This little montane to alpine gem blooms in summer along rocky ridges. The flowers of this perennial herb are quite large for a buttercup, up to 1 in., with many stamens. It occurs throughout Western North America. Five varieties are recognized based mostly on variation in leaf characteristics. Three varieties are found in California. **Plant height 2–10 in.; leaves basal, alternate, lobed, margins toothed; petals showy, 5–8, free; radial symmetry; yellow**

Coleogyne ramosissima
ROSACEAE

Blackbrush

Deserts; 2000–6500 ft.; native

Thorny and aromatic, Blackbrush grows in dense thickets in the deserts of Southern California. Adapted specifically to harsh desert conditions, the shrub's leaves are drought-deciduous, and it blooms only after a heavy spring rain. The flower's four showy sepals are partially fused at the base. Often the flower is petalless, which is very unusual for a member of the rose family. **Plant height 5–7 ft.; leaves opposite, unlobed, margins smooth; sepals showy, 4; radial symmetry; yellow**

Dasiphora fruticosa
ROSACEAE

Shrubby Cinquefoil

Conifer forests; 6500–11,800 ft.; native

Blooming in summer, this circumboreal shrub has distinctive saucer-shaped flowers at its branch tips. The branches are densely covered with small, pinnately compound leaves and coated with fine, silky hairs. A common sight in the High Sierra, Shrubby Cinquefoil also occurs in the Klamath and Warner mountains. **Plant height to 3 ft.; leaves alternate, pinnately compound, margins smooth; petals showy, 5, partially fused; radial symmetry; yellow**

Geum macrophyllum
ROSACEAE

Large-leaved Avens

Conifer forests, wet meadows; 3200–10,500 ft.; native

The small flowers of this spring-blooming perennial herb resemble cinquefoils, but its fruits are very different. Each flower's pistil has an elongated, bristly style that ends in a tiny hook, so that the cluster of pistils in the center of each flower resembles a pincushion. The terminal leaflet is significantly larger than the other leaflets and is lobed. **Plant height to 3.5 ft.; leaves basal, pinnately compound, margins toothed; flowers small, petals showy, 5, free; radial symmetry; yellow**

Ivesia gordonii
ROSACEAE

Alpine Ivesia

Alpine; 6000–11,500 ft.; native

Also known as Gordon's Mousetail, this perennial herb has densely compact, overlapping leaflets. It grows in rocky outcrops on the highest mountain peaks. Blooming in spring and summer, flowers appear in dense clusters on long stalks, perched above the plant like little satellite dishes hoping to attract alpine pollinators. **Plant height 2–8 in.; leaves basal, pinnately compound, margins smooth; flower clusters showy; petals 5, free; radial symmetry; yellow**

Ivesia lycopodioides
ROSACEAE

Clubmoss Ivesia

Alpine; 9000–13,000 ft.; native

Growing in crevices of rock ledges in the highest peaks of the Sierra, Inyo, and White mountains, this summer-blooming perennial herb ekes out an existence under very difficult conditions. For the few months when temperatures enable reproduction and photosynthesis, this plant stores up sugars to last the rest of the year while it is dormant. **Plant height** 2–6 in.; leaves basal, pinnately compound, margins smooth; flower clusters showy; flowers small, petals 5, free; radial symmetry; yellow

Potentilla gracilis
ROSACEAE

Slender Cinquefoil

Conifer forests, riparian; up to 11,500 ft.; native

In summer, native bees are attracted to the ultraviolet pattern on the notched petals of this perennial herb. In French, *Cinquefoil* literally means "foliage of five." Each palmately compound, hand-like leaf has at least five leaflets. With five varieties in the mountains of California, most can be found growing in moist meadows, streambanks, and open forests. **Plant height** 1–3 ft.; leaves basal, palmately compound, margins toothed; petals showy, 5, free; radial symmetry; yellow

Verbascum thapsus
SCROPHULARIACEAE

Wooly Mullein

Disturbed areas; up to 8000 ft.; non-native

Blooming in summer, this invasive biennial grows a rosette of large, fuzzy leaves in the first year. In the second growing season, a long flower stalk emerges from the rosette. It sets thousands of seeds and then dies. The seeds of this problematic species can remain viable in the soil for more than 100 years! **Plant height 1–6 ft.; leaves basal rosette, unlobed, margins smooth; flower clusters showy; petals 5, partially fused; +- radial symmetry; yellow**

Nicotiana glauca
SOLANACEAE

Tree Tobacco

Disturbed areas; up to 3500 ft.; non-native

Blooming in spring and summer, this shrub was brought from South America by Spanish missionaries. Tree Tobacco is considered invasive in California and in many other places. All parts of the plant contain an extremely poisonous alkaloid (anabasine). Interestingly, it has been used medicinally and in ceremonies by indigenous peoples who know how to use it safely. **Plant height 6–18 ft.; leaves alternate, unlobed, margins smooth; petals showy, 5, fused; radial symmetry; yellow**

Physalis crassifolia
SOLANACEAE

Thick-leaved Ground Cherry

Coastal sage scrub, deserts; up to 4300 ft.; native

Native to Southwest deserts, this perennial herb or subshrub is adapted to arid conditions and grows in rocky, dry washes as well as coastal sagebrush scrub. It is easily identified by its thick and leathery leaves, glandular hairs, and fruits with papery tomatillo-like persistent sepals. The fruits are edible, but the sepals are not. It blooms in spring. **Plant height to 2.5 ft.; leaves alternate, unlobed, margins smooth or wavy; petals showy, 5, fused; radial symmetry; yellow**

Bloomeria crocea
THEMIDACEAE

Common Goldenstar

Chaparral; up to 5600 ft.; native

This spring-blooming perennial herb can transform a grassy hillside into a floral fireworks display. The lobes of the petals spread abruptly, and 10–35 flowers occur in an umbel atop each stem. On the underside of each tepal is a brown midvein stripe. It was named after early San Francisco botanist H. G. Bloomer— what a great name for a botanist! **Plant height 2–24 in.; leaves basal, unlobed, margins smooth; tepals showy, 6, free; radial symmetry; yellow**

Triteleia ixioides
THEMIDACEAE

Prettyface

Conifer forests, woodlands, wetlands; up to 10,000 ft.; native

Often hiding in fading grassy areas in late spring, this perennial resembles little yellow sunbursts among the background foliage. The tepals often have dark stripes on the undersides. The stamens are unequal and appear among forked appendages. Blooming in late spring and summer, its distribution extends into Southwest Oregon, the northern extent of the California Floristic Province. **Plant height 6–9 in.; leaves basal, unlobed, margins smooth; tepals showy, 6, partially fused; radial symmetry; yellow**

Viola douglasii
VIOLACEAE

Golden Violet

Vernally moist flats and grasslands; up to 7500 ft.; native

Blooming from late winter to early summer, this violet has bright yellow petals tinged with purple streaks in the throat that guide pollinators to the nectar within. The leaves can be either deeply divided or compound, which is relatively unusual for a violet. Violets are not just pretty; their flowers are edible too. **Plant height to 8 in.; leaves basal, dissected, margins smooth; petals showy, 5, free; mirror symmetry; yellow**

Viola pedunculata
VIOLACEAE

Johnny Jump-up

Grasslands, chaparral, oak woodlands; up to 5000 ft.; native

A harbinger of spring, this little perennial blooms in winter and early spring. Flowers have purple streaks that guide bees toward the nectar within, and the upper petals are purple on the backside. Flower stalks are up to 8 in. tall. Many species of fritillary butterflies visit violets. This species is host to the federally endangered Callipe Sil-verspot butterfly. **Plant height to 15 in.; leaves alternate, unlobed, margins toothed; petals showy, 5, free; mirror symmetry; yellow-orange**

Viola purpurea
VIOLACEAE

Goosefoot Violet

Shrublands and forests, rocky slopes; 700–9500 ft.; native

As with all violets, this species' upper petal has an elongated base (spur) that produces nectar for pollinators. The upper petals are purple on the reverse side. The leaves are shaped like goose feet, hence the common name. The specific name, *purpurea*, refers to the leaves' purple undersides. This small perennial herb blooms in late spring and summer. **Plant height 1–6 in.; leaves basal, un-lobed, margins toothed; petals showy, 5, free; mir-ror symmetry; yellow**

Larrea tridentata
ZYGOPHYLLACEAE

Creosote Bush

Deserts; up to 3300 ft.; native

This spring-blooming shrub is a dominant species in the deserts of Southwestern North America. Following rain, the air is filled with its pungent, sweet, smoky odor. It tends to be evenly spaced across the landscape, and this is no accident—the species produces a chemical that inhibits the root growth of neighboring plants, including other Creosote Bushes. **Plant height to 8 ft.; leaves opposite, unlobed, margins smooth; fruits wooly white; petals showy, 5, free; radial symmetry; yellow**

Tribulus terrestris
ZYGOPHYLLACEAE

Puncture Vine

Disturbed areas; up to 3300 ft.; non-native

Most know this invasive by its fruits, which can puncture shoes and bicycle tires. It is sometimes called caltrop, named for a medieval weapon with sharp spines that are arranged so that however it's thrown on the ground, one spike always points upward. Tiny blooms on this prostrate annual appear in summer and fall. It is toxic to livestock. **Plant stem length 1–36 in.; leaves opposite, pinnately compound, margins smooth; flowers small, petals 5, free; radial symmetry; yellow**

GLOSSARY

achene small, dry fruit with a single seed and a thin fruit wall that does not split open, typical of the buttercup family

alkali flat an area with sparse vegetation that has high concentrations of evaporated alkali minerals (carbonates) in the soil

alkaline basic, having a high pH

alpine an area above the treeline; a high-elevation vegetation type dominated by tough, low-growing herbaceous perennials and subshrubs

alternate leaf an arrangement that occurs when each node has only one leaf

annual herb a plant that completes its life cycle (germinates, flowers, sets seed, and dies) within a single year or growing season

anther the male part of the flower that produces pollen

apomictic a type of asexual reproduction whereby a seed is produced from an unfertilized ovule

appendage any supplemental structure of a flower or other plant part

aquatic related to water; a plant that grows fully or partially submerged in water

ascending positioned upward at an angle

axil the angle between the main stem and a leaf or lateral shoot

banner uppermost and usually largest petal of the typical pea flower (subfamily Papilionoideae)

basal located at the lower part of a structure near the ground (the base) or an attachment point

beak an elongated, pointed structure (found in some flowers or fruits)

berry a fleshy fruit that has many seeds

biennial referring to two years; a herbaceous plant that completes its life cycle (germinates, flowers, sets seed, and dies) in two years or growing seasons

bilateral (mirror) symmetry one side reflects the other along a single plane of symmetry

biradial symmetry exactly two planes of symmetry at right angles; American Yellowrocket (*Barbarea orthoceras*) has biradial symmetry

bisexual flower a flower that has both male and femal parts, also called a perfect flower

bract a leaf that is located immediately below a flower or flower cluster and is often smaller than a vegetative leaf

bristle long, stiff hairs usually forming a bunch

bud a structure located at a node or shoot tip that contains a dormant meristem and often produces a new shoot or flower

bulb an underground storage structure that consists of a short shoot with swollen storage leaves

burl a swelling at the junction of stem and roots that contains dormant buds that can sprout after the stem is cut or burned; present in some manzanitas

buzz pollination a type of pollination in wthich a bee (usually a bumble bee) vibrates its wings at a particular frequency after landing on a flower, causing the pollen to shoot out of the anther onto the bee's body; the pollen is then inadvertently used to fertilize the next flower the bee visits

calcicole a plant that grows in alkaline, high pH, limestone-rich soils

calcifuge a plant that cannot tolerate growing in alkaline, high pH, limestone-rich soils

California Floristic Province an area of Western North America that experiences a Mediterranean climate; located primarily in California, but also includes small portions of Nevada, Oregon, and Baja California, Mexico

calyx (pl., calyces) all of the sepals in a flower

capsule a dry fruit that splits open at maturity to release its seeds

carpel (pistil) the female part of the flower composed of a stigma, style, and ovary; carpels often develop into fruits

catkin a slender, drooping cluster of wind-pollinated, unisexual flowers

caudex (pl., caudices) a short, usually thick and woody stem at or beneath ground level

cauline located along the stem; usually refers to leaves

chaparral a vegetation type typical of Mediterranean climates, composed of an overstory of drought-tolerant, evergreen, large, dense, and sturdy shrubs and sometimes an understory of subshrubs, grasses, and forbs

chlorophyll a green pigment in leaves (and sometimes stems) that absorbs light during photosynthesis

ciliate describes a fringe of generally straight hairs along a margin

circumboreal describes plants that grow in the high latitudes in northern parts of the Northern Hemisphere

circumscissile dehiscence a process in which the top of the dry fruit pops off like a cap and releases seeds

clasping partially or completely surrounding the stem; usually describing a leaf

clawed petal petal with a narrowed base and expanded blade at the tip

cleistogamous describes flowers that never open; they are pollinated by pollen from within the flower

coastal sage scrub a vegetation type composed of an overstory of drought-deciduous, relatively short shrubs, often including Coastal Sagebrush (*Artemisia californica*) and often with an understory of subshrubs, grasses, and forbs

complete flower a flower that has all possible whorls, including sepals, petals, anthers, and carpels

composite a member of the sunflower family with a flowerhead containing many individual flowers

compound divided into multiple parts

compound leaf the leaf blade is divided into segments all the way to the midvein (rachis) into multiple leaflike parts, or leaflets

cone the reproductive structure of a conifer composed of modified leaves on a short shoot that bear seeds or pollen

conifer a plant that produces seeds and pollen in cones, instead of flowers, such as a pine tree

conifer forest a broad vegetation classification that is dominated by cone-bearing trees, often with an understory of shrubs, grasses, and forb

corm a rounded underground storage structure made up of stem tissues and covered in small, papery modified leaves

corolla collectively all of the petals in a flower

crown the upper parts of a tree, including branches and leaves; or the accessory tissue on top of an ovary

deciduous a structure (typically leaves) that dies and falls off naturally in the fall; or a plant that loses its leaves seasonally in response to cold or drought

decumbent describes a plant or part of a plant that is positioned on the ground, curving upward near the tips

decurrent a structure that is attached to the stem for an extended length—for example, a decurrent leaf base

dehiscent describes a structure that splits open at maturity to release its contents, such as anthers releasing pollen or fruits releasing seed

deltoid triangular with equal sides

dentate a leaf margin with sharp, toothed projections that generally point to the side, rather than toward the tip

desert an area that receives less than 10 in. of rain annually (in California, the three deserts are the Mojave, the Sonoran, and the Great Basin); or a broadly defined vegetation type that is usually treeless and is composed of tough shrubs and a sparse understory of forbs, subshrubs, and grasses

determinate defines a structure that does not continue growing indefinitely, such as a leaf

dioecious a plant species that has either male or female flowers, but not both, on an individual plant

disc flower in the sunflower family, flowers that have radially symmetric, tubular short corollas

discoid head in the sunflower family, a floral arrangement comprising only disc flowers—for example, Coyote Brush or Coastal Sagebrush flower clusters

dispersal spreading away from a source

dissected deeply divided into many segments; dissected leaves are technically simple (not compound) but are so highly divided that it can be difficult to determine whether the blade connects back to the midvein—for example, Yarrow (*Achillea millefolium*) has dissected leaves

disturbed an area where the habitat has been modified, often by human activity; a vegetation type composed of weedy species, often non-native, that tend to thrive in modified soils

dominant a species that is common in a vegetation type and helps define it

dormant having extremely low physiological activity, not actively growing

drought-deciduous a strategy whereby a plant sheds its leaves in response to drought conditions

dunes a landform composed of wind or water-driven sand, which typically contains a vegetation type composed primarily of low-growing perennial herbs with deep roots that anchor the plant despite the shifting substrate

elliptic an elongated circle, widest at the middle and tapering equally on both ends

endemic naturally occuring and found only within a defined area; a California endemic occurs naturally only in California and nowhere else

entire a simple, unlobed leaf with smooth (untoothed) margins

erect oriented vertically, perpendicular to the ground

evergreen a plant with leaves that remain on the plant for an entire year; the leaves do not fall the plant off en masse

extinct no longer occurring anywhere in the world

extirpated no longer occurring in a specific geographic location, but still may be found elsewhere in the world

family a classification category of plants and animals consisting of one or more genera; plants in the same family usually have similar characteristics that unite them

fascicle a tight cluster or bundle, used to describe groups of flowers, leaves, stems, or roots

fell-field a slope in high-latitude or high-elevation areas composed of rocky substrate with sparse vegetation

fern a non-flowering vascular plant that reproduces by spores

fertilization the joining of male (sperm) and female cell (ovule) in an ovary to form a new embryo

filament the threadlike, usually slender part of a stamen that connects the anther to the receptacle

fire-following plant a plant species that grows more abundantly after a fire or requires fire for germination

flower a plant reproductive structure that typically includes sepals, petals, stamens, and carpels arranged along a short shoot; it develops into a fruit containing seeds following pollination and fertilization

flowerhead a dense cluster of flowers that lack internode elongation; heads in the sunflower family often have disc flowers surrounded by a ring of ray flowers, so that the head looks like a single large flower

foliage the entire vegetative (not reproductive) parts of a plant

follicle a dry dehiscent fruit that splits along a single side at maturity

forb a non-woody, herbaceous flowering plant, either annual or perennial, and not including grasses and grass allies (e.g., sedges and rushes)

foundational species a species that has in important ecological role in a habitat or community

fruit a ripened ovary containing one or more seeds; fruits may be fleshy or dry

gall irregular plant tissue growth that develops after being invaded by wasps or other pathogens

genus (pl., genera) a classification of biological diversity that includes one or more species and represents a lineage with unifying characteristics; the first part of a scientific name is the genus name

glabrous free from trichomes, hairless

gland a small structure on the plant surface that produces a fluid that is usually sticky

glaucous a waxy coating that makes plant surfaces look white and feel chalky

glochid minute barbed hairs that may surround the spine of a cactus, they are technically prickles

grasslands a vegetation type composed primarily of low-growing monocots in the grass family; in popular usage, grasslands often also contain non-grasses as well

habit the typical appearance or manner of growth of a plant—for example, herb, shrub, tree, vine

habitat the natural setting of a plant or animal, including both biotic (living) factors such as associated species, and abiotic (physical) factors such as soil chemistry, climate, and topography

haustoria specialized root structures that parasitic plants use to tap into the roots of host plants to acquire carbohydrates

hemiparasite a plant that takes some of its food from a host plant via root attachments, but also makes some of its own food via photosynthesis

herb an annual or perennial that does not produce wood or bark

herbaceous not having woody stems; includes plants that are annuals, biennials, and non-woody perennials

horticulture the science and art of growing plants in a garden setting

hybrid the offspring of two different species, subspecies, or varieties

inferior ovary an ovary that is attached below the flower parts, which are attached to the top of the ovary; inferior ovaries are less common than superior ovaries

inflorescence a cluster of flowers and associated plant parts, including stems, bracts, and pedicels

intergrade to transition from one form to another gradually; or an individual that is intermediate in form

internode a stem segment located between nodes

introduced species a species that is established outside its native range as a direct or indirect result of human activity

invasive species a non-native species that tends to reproduce and spread in natural areas, often displacing native species and altering the species composition of an area

involucre bracts that surround a dense flower cluster

keel the lower petal of the typical pea/legume flower (subfamily Papilionoideae/Faboideae), which is boat shaped and composed of two fused petals

lateral shoot a shoot that comes off of a main stem, originating from a lateral bud at a node

leaf a vegetative structure composed of a petiole and blade that is attached to the stem at a node; the primary site of food production and transpiration in most plants

leaf blade the flat, usually photosynthetic portion of a leaf or leaflet; also called a lamina

leaflet a leaflike segment of a compound leaf

legume a dry dehiscent fruit that usually splits along two seams at maturity; an alternate name for a member of the pea family (Fabaceae)

life form describes growth form (habit) and life cycle of a plant—for example annual, biennial, perennial herb, annual vine, shrub, tree

ligulate (ray) flowers in the sunflower family, flowers whose petals are fused into one long, showy, straplike petal

ligulate head in the sunflower family, a flowerhead that only has ray flowers, such as a dandelion

ligule a narrow, strap-shaped part of a plant

lobe a portion of a leaf, petal, or other structure that projects beyond the main structure

margin the edge of a structure, often the leaf

meristem an area of tissue where cell division takes place

midvein the central vein of a leaf

mirror (bilateral) symmetry a shape in which one side reflects the other along a single plane of symmetry

monocot a lineage of flowering plants that has several unifying characteristics, including a single seed leaf (cotyledon), flower parts in sets of three, and parallel leaf venation

monoecious a plant in which separate male and female flowers occur on the same individual

morphology structure or form

mycoheterotroph a plant that obtains its carbohydrates via a root association with soil fungus

native species a species that is indigenous to a region, whose presence is not the result of human introduction

naturalized a non-native species that is able to reproduce successfully in natural areas

nectary a gland, usually near the base of a flower petal, that secretes nectar

node an area on a plant stem where a leaf, lateral bud, or shoot originates

noxious weed a non-native species that proliferates and causes harm to other species or habitats; plants that are particularly problematic are often classified as noxious weeds by governmental agencies

nutlet a four-seeded indehiscent fruit common in the borage and mint families

oak woodland a vegetation type dominated by oak trees (*Quercus* spp.) and woody shrubs

oblong a shape that is longer than it is wide, with the longer sides nearly parallel to one another

opposite oriented across from another; opposite leaves arise from the same node along a stem

ovary the female flower part (carpel) that contains ovules; it develops into a fruit

ovate egg-shaped, wider toward the base than toward the tip

ovule the structure within the ovary that develops into a seed after fertilization

palmate radiating from a common point, similar to spreading fingers on a hand; used to describe compound or lobed leaves

panicle a loose, many-branched inflorescence (flower cluster)

parasite an organism that physically attaches to another to obtain food, water, or nutrients

pedicel the stalk of an individual flower or fruit

pendent hanging or drooping from a point of attachment

perennial a plant that lives for more than one growing season or year

perfect flower a single flower that has both male and female parts; also referred to as hermaphroditic

perianth referring to all of the sepals and petals of a flower; the term is often used when the sepals and petals are not easily distinguishable

petal the flower organ that is usually colorful and functions to attract pollinators

petiole the part of the leaf that connects the blade to the stem

photosynthesis the process by which plants with chlorophyll use the energy from the sun to make sugars from carbon dioxide and water

phyllaries bracts that subtend a group of flowers (inflorescence bracts)

phyllotaxy the arrangement of leaves along a stem (alternate, opposite, or whorled)

pinnate having parts arranged on both sides of a central axis, resembling a feather; a leaf can be pinnately compound or simple and pinnately lobed

pistil (carpel) the female part of the flower comprising a stigma, style, and ovary

pollen a small, usually three-celled structure produced by anthers that contains plant sperm; when pollen lands on the stigma of a flower, a pollen tube delivers the sperm to an ovule

pollination occurs when pollen from an anther (male part) is transferred to the stigma (female part)

prickle a sharp projection derived from the bark or the epidermis (outer layer) of a plant

prostrate lying on the ground

raceme a flower cluster that has individual flowers attached to a main axis (rachis) via pedicels

rachis the central axis of a compound leaf, visible between the leaflets; also, the axis of a flower cluster

radial symmetry symmetry around a central axis where three or more planes of reflection exist

radiate head in the sunflower family, a head that has disc flowers in the center surrounded by ray (ligulate) flowers

range the geographic area in which a plant species occurs

ray (ligulate) flowers in the sunflower family, flowers whose petals are fused into one long, showy, straplike petal

receptacle stem tissue where flower parts attach

resin a water insoluble, thick liquid produced by some plants; it is thought to be involved in healing wounds, preserving water, and deterring herbivory

rhizome an underground stem that can produce roots and shoots

riparian related to streams or rivers; also a vegetation type that grows along moving water courses that is composed of trees, shrubs, grasses, and forbs

rosette a shoot with short internodes that produces a cluster of leaves near the ground

scientific name a two-part name that includes the genus name and specific epithet (name)

seed a fertilized, mature ovule that has a seed coat and usually contains the plant embryo and storage tissue

seed bank the collection of seeds in the soil that can germinate under favorable conditions

sepal the often leaflike structures of a flower located below the petals

sessile without a stalk; a sessile leaf does not have a petiole

shoot apical meristem the area of tissue at the tip of a shoot where cell division happens

short shoot a shoot that lacks visible internode elongation

shrub a woody perennial that is smaller than a tree, generally lacks a main axis, and has multiple shoots

silicle a dry dehiscent fruit that has a relatively equal length to width ratio, typical of the mustard family

silique a dry dehiscent fruit that is much longer than wide, typical of the mustard family

simple leaf the leaf blade is not separated to the midrib, though it can be lobed or even dissected

sinus the open area between lobes of a leaf or petal

sp. abbreviation used for a single species when the name of the species is not known; for example, *Calystegia* sp. refers to one species

species a classification level comprising related plants that share common characteristics and are capable of interbreeding and producing viable offspring

specific epithet (name) the second part of an organism's scientific name

spike a flower cluster in which the flowers are attached directly to the main axis (no pedicels)

spine a modified leaf or leaf part that is sharp and pointed

spp. abbreviation used when referring to multiple species in a genus; for example, *Calystegia* spp. refers to multiple species within the genus *Calystegia*

spur a modified petal or sepal that is slender and usually contains nectar at the base

stamen a male plant part composed of a filament and a pollen-producing anther

staminode an infertile stamen

stem the main axis of a plant or one of its lateral branches

sterile not capable of reproduction

stigma the part of the carpel (pistil) that captures pollen, located at the tip of a style

stipule a modified leaf base that is leaflike or scale-like

stolon An aboveground stem that spreads horizontally and can grow new roots and stems—for example, strawberries (*Fragaria* spp.) spread via stolons

style the often long, narrow part of the carpel (pistil) that connects the stigma to the ovary

subshrub a woody perennial that is smaller than a shrub

subsp. abbreviation for subspecies

subspecies a classification level used to describe geographic or morphological variation with a species

succulent a fleshy plant whose tissues have water-holding properties; usually a perennial

superblooms a flowering event that happens when precipitation and temperature cause floriferous herbs to germinate and bloom en masse

superior ovary an ovary that is attached above the flower parts; more typical than an inferior ovary

temperate mid-latitude areas with relatively mild temperatures year-round

tendril a coiling, slender, threadlike structure used by vines to attach to another plant for support; usually composed of modified leaves or leaflets

tepal a sepal or petal; a term typical used when the sepals and petals are similar in color and shape

thorn a shoot that has been modified to become woody and sharp

throat the opening of a flower that has a floral tube; often it has patterns that guide pollinators towards a nectar reward

tooth a small, often sharp projection on the edge of a leaf

tree a tall, woody plant with generally a single main axis

trichomes plant hairs—single-celled, multi-celled, or glandular epidermal outgrowths that cover a plant's surface

trifoliate a compound leaf with three leaflets

tuber a short, fleshy underground stem that stores water or food—a potato is a tuber

twig a young shoot of a woody plant representing the current season's growth

umbel a flower cluster in which the individual flower stalks rise from a single point, similar to the spokes inside an umbrella

understory a vegetation layer that grows beneath a taller vegetation layer

unisexual having fertile reproductive parts of only one sex

unlobed a simple leaf that has a uniform shape without subdivisions; an unlobed leaf can have toothed margins

variety a classification level used to describe variation with a species; it describes a variation that is more subtle than the variation that would be described by a subspecies

vegetative any part of the plant that is not reproductive ; the leaves, stem, and roots

vein the canal-like tissue in a leaf, stem, or root that transports water, nutrients, and waste products

venation the pattern made by the veins of a leaf

vernal pools a habitat that is characterized by ponded water during the spring rainy season that evaporates over the course of a season; vernal pools host a vegetation type composed largely of herbs that are adapted to this specialized habitat

vine a plant that requires another plant or structure for support; vines often use tendrils to attach to a supporing structure

wash an intermittent stream bed that transports water for only part of the year

wetland a vegetation type associated with lakes, ponds, and estuaries, which is usually dominated by herbaceous perennials, grasses, and subshrubs

whorl a set of organs (leaves, petals, or stamens) arranged concentrically around the stem; three or more leaves connected to one node is considered a whorled leaf arrangement

wildflower an annual or herbaceous perennial that has noticeable, attractive flowers

wings the middle two petals of the typical pea flower (subfamily Papilionoideae), which often hide or partially hide the keel

woodland a vegetation type with dominant overstory hardwood tree species, a middle canopy of shrubs, and a variable understory composed of subshrubs, grass, and forbs

xeric very dry, in reference to a habitat or environment

SOURCES AND RESOURCES

BOOKS

Allen, R. L., and F. M. Roberts Jr. 2013. *Wildflowers of Orange County and the Santa Ana Mountains*. Laguna Beach, CA: Laguna Wilderness Press.

Baldwin, B. G., et al. 2012. *The Jepson Manual: Vascular Plants of California*. Berkeley, CA: University of California Press.

Barbour, M. G., et al. 1993. *California's Changing Landscape: Diversity and Conservation of California Vegetation*. Sacramento, CA: California Native Plant Society.

Blackwell, L. 2021. *Wildflowers of the Sierra Nevada and the Central Valley*. Auburn, WA: Lone Pine Publishing.

Coleman, R. A. 2002. *The Wild Orchids of California*. Ithaca, NY: Cornell University Press.

DeCamp, K., et al. 2021. *Wildflowers of California's Klamath Mountains*. Kneeland, CA: Backcountry Press.

Faber, P. M., ed. 2005. *California's Wild Gardens: A Guide to Favorite Botanical Sites*. Berkeley, CA: University of California Press.

Hastings, M. S., and J. M. DiTomaso. 1996. Fire Controls Yellow Starthistle (*Centaurea solstitialis*) in California Grasslands. Proceedings of the California Exotic Pest Plant Council Symposium.

Kauffmann, M. E., et al. 2015. *Field Guide to Manzanitas: California, North America, and Mexico*. Kneeland, CA: Backcountry Press.

Keator, G. 1994. *Complete Garden Guide to the Native Shrubs of California*. San Francisco: Chronicle Books.

Mackay, P. 2013. *Mojave Desert Wildflowers: A Field Guide to Wildflowers, Trees, and Shrubs of the Mojave Desert*. Lanham, MD: Falcon Guides.

Muir, J., 1894. "The Bee-Pastures" in *The Mountains of California*, pp. 336–381. New York: De Vinne Press.

Munz, P. A. 2004. *Introduction to California Spring Wildflowers of the Foothills, Valleys, and Coast*. Berkeley, CA: University of California Press.

Ornduff, R., et al. 2003. *Introduction to California Plant Life*. Berkeley, CA: University of California Press.

Redbud Chapter, California Native Plant Society. 2008. *Wildflowers of Nevada and Placer Counties, California*. Sacramento, CA: CNPS Press.

Ritter, M. 2018. *California Plants: A Guide to Our Iconic Flora*. San Luis Obispo, CA: Pacific Street Publishing.

Simpson, M. G. 2010. *Plant Systematics*. Burlington, MA: Academic Press.

Stearn, W. T. 1973. *Botanical Latin*. Devon, U.K.: Newton Abbot.

Thoreau, H. D. 1992. *The Writings of Henry David Thoreau*, Volume IV. Princeton, NJ: Princeton University Press.

Turland, N. J., et al. 2018. International Code of Nomenclature for algae, fungi, and plants (Shenzhen Code) adopted by the Nineteenth International Botanical Congress Shenzhen, China, July 2017. Glashütten, Germany: Koeltz Botanical Books.

JOURNAL ARTICLES

Amoros, M., et al. 1987. In vitro antiviral activity of a saponin from *Anagallis arvensis*, Primulaceae, against herpes simplex virus and poliovirus. *Antiviral Research* 8(1): 13–25.

Benesh, D. L., and W. J. Elisens. 1999. Morphological variation in *Malacothamnus fasciculatus* (Torrey & A. Gray) E. Greene (Malvaceae) and related species. *Madrono*: 142–152.

Brown, M. J. F., and K. G. Human. 1997. Effects of harvester ants on plant species distribution and abundance in a serpentine grassland. *Oecologia* 112(2): 237–243.

Donaldson, J. R., and R. G. Cates. 2004. Screening for anticancer agents from Sonoran desert plants: A chemical ecology approach. *Pharmaceutical Biology* 42(7): 478–487.

Eastwood, A. 1938. The wild flower gardens of San Francisco in the 1890s. *Leaflets of Western Botany* 4(6): 153–156.

Fausto, J. A., Jr., et al. 2001. Reproductive assurance and the evolutionary ecology of self-pollination in *Clarkia xantiana* (Onagraceae). *American Journal of Botany* 88(10): 1794–1800.

George, S., et al. 2009. Genetic diversity of the endangered and narrow endemic *Piperia yadonii* (Orchidaceae) assessed with ISSR polymorphisms. *American Journal of Botany* 96(11): 2022–2030.

Gray-Lee, R., and J. Lee. 2020. Molecular mechanisms of *Dicentra formosa's* analgesic effect. *Medicine in Drug Discovery* 8: 100061.

Hannan, G. L. 1982. Correlation of morphological variation in *Platystemon californicus* (Papaveraceae) with flower color and geography. *Systematic Botany*: 35–47.

Hansen, R. M. 1974. Dietary of the chuckwalla, *Sauromalus obesus*, determined by dung analysis. *Herpetologica*: 120–123.

Heisey, R. M., and C. Delwiche. 1984. Phytotoxic volatiles from *Trichostema lanceolatum* (Labiatae). *American Journal of Botany* 71(6): 821–828.

Jain, S., et al. 2016. Screening North American plant extracts in vitro against *Trypanosoma brucei* for discovery of new anti-trypanosomal drug leads. *BMC Complementary and Alternative Medicine* 16(1): 1–6.

Jennings, W. B., and K. H. Berry. 2015. Desert tortoises (*Gopherus agassizii*) are selective herbivores that track the flowering phenology of their preferred food plants. *PLOS One* 10(1): e0116716.

Kadereit, J. W., et al. 1997. The phylogeny of *Papaver* s.l. (Papaveraceae): Polyphyly or monophyly? *Plant Systematics and Evolution* 204(1): 75–98.

Keeley, J. E., et al. 2005. Seed germination of Sierra Nevada postfire chaparral species. *Madrono* 52(3): 175–181.

Kofron, C. P., et al. 2021. Camatta Canyon amole *Hooveria purpurea* var. *reducta* (Agavaceae): a threatened plant in La Panza Range, San Luis Obispo County, California. *Bulletin, Southern California Academy of Sciences* 120(1): 26–48.

Konstantinos, F., and R. Heun. 2020. The effects of *Rhodiola rosea* supplementation on depression, anxiety and mood—systematic review. *Global Psychiatry* 3(1): 72–82.

Lin, Q., et al. 2021. A new carnivorous plant lineage (*Triantha*) with a unique sticky-inflorescence trap. *Proceedings of the National Academy of Sciences* 118(33): e2022724118.

Lin, R. C. and M. D. Rausher. 2021. R2R3-MYB genes control petal pigmentation patterning in *Clarkia gracilis* ssp. *sonomensis* (Onagraceae). *New Phytologist* 229(2): 1147–1162.

Loizzo, M. R., et al. 2007. In vitro angiotensin converting enzyme inhibiting activity of *Salsola oppositifolia* Desf., *Salsola soda* L. and

Salsola tragus L. *Natural Product Research* 21(9): 846–851.

Oyama, R. K., and D. A. Baum. 2004. Phylogenetic relationships of North American *Antirrhinum* (Veronicaceae). *American Journal of Botany* 91(6): 918–925.

Pandey, M., et al. 2013. A narrowly endemic photosynthetic orchid is non-specific in its mycorrhizal associations. *Molecular Ecology* 22(8): 2341–2354.

Preston, R. E. 2011. *Brodiaea matsonii* (Asparagaceae: Brodiaeoideae) a new species from Shasta County, California. *Madrono* 57(4): 261–267.

Preston, R. E. 2013. A revision of *Brodiaea coronaria* (Asparagaceae: Brodiaeoideae): morphometric analysis and recognition of new and emended taxa. *Systematic Botany* 38(4): 1012–1028.

Sorrie, B. A. 1990. *Myosurus minimus* (Ranunculaceae) in New England with notes on flower morphology. *Rhodora* 92(870): 103–104.

Taguchi, N., et al. 2020. *Eriodictyon angustifolium* extract, but not *Eriodictyon californicum* extract, reduces human hair greying. *International Journal of Cosmetic Science* 42(4): 336–345.

Thompson, J. N., et al. 2013. Diversification through multitrait evolution in a coevolving interaction. *Proceedings of the National Academy of Sciences of the United States of America* 110(28): 11487–11492.

Wang, Y., et al. 2020. Kin recognition in the parasitic plant *Triphysaria versicolor* is mediated through root exudates. *Frontiers in Plant Science* 11: 560–682.

Wiesenborn, W. D. 2020. Pollen transport to *Lycium cooperi* (Solanaceae) flowers by flies and moths. *Western North American Naturalist* 80(3): 359–368.

WEBSITES

The American Southwest (americansouthwest .net) is a guide to the national parks, national monuments, and natural landscapes of the U.S. Southwest.

CalFlora (calflora.org) is a data conglomerate that amasses descriptive, location, and habitat information on California's plants. It also links to CalPhotos, which is an extensive database of plant photography managed by University of California, Berkeley. In fact, we used these resources to help find photographers for this book.

The California Invasive Plant Council (calipc.org) maintains an inventory of and information about non-native plants that have invaded natural areas in California.

California Natural Diversity Database (wildlife .ca.gov/Data/CNDDB) accesses an inventory of the status and locations of rare plants and animals in California based on GIS-mapped location data.

The California Plant Names (calflora.net) website has a huge amount of information about the Latin and Greek meanings and derivations of California plant names. It is written by Michael L. Charters, a photographer and California naturalist extraordinaire.

CalScape (calscape.org) is a database of native plant information maintained by the California Native Plant Society and designed to help gardeners save water and improve the environment by planting site-appropriate native plants.

Celebrating Wildflowers (fs.usda.gov/ managingland/wildflowers) is a U.S. Forest Service page that provides information about wildflowers and where to find them in forests and grasslands.

Consortium of California Herbaria (cch2.org/ portal) is a website and database that enables you to search for plant location information that is based on herbarium collections. Species distribution maps for this book are based on CCH data.

The Cooperative Extension Service (cespubs .uaf.edu/publications) database provides access to articles published by the University of Alaska Fairbanks, Cooperative Extension Service.

DesertUSA Wildflowers (desertusa.com/stories/ desertusas-wildflower-guide) enables people to post where and when desert wildflowers are in bloom.

Edible Wild Foods (ediblewildfood.com) provides information about foraging and how to prepare foraged foods.

Elkhorn Slough Coastal Training Program Factsheets (elkhornsloughctp.org/factsheet) provide detailed information about the endangered species found in Elkhorn Slough.

Fire Effects Information System (feis-crs.org/feis) is an online collection of reviews of the scientific literature about fire effects on plants, animals, and vegetation communities in the United States.

Flora of North America (beta.floranorthamerica .org) has information on the names, taxonomic relationships, distributions, and morphological characteristics of all plants native and naturalized found in North America north of Mexico.

Global Biodiversity Information Facility (gbif.org), an open access database, aggregates biological information from all over the world. Collection information used for mapping non-native species was accessed via this database.

iNaturalist (www.inaturalist.org) is a joint initiative of the California Academy of Sciences and the National Geographic Society that uses software originally developed for facial recognition to identify plants and animals. The iNaturalist phone app invites the community to be involved in photographing, tracking, and participaing in natural science–oriented activities.

Invasive.org (invasive.org) is a repository of information about invasive species of North America that is affiliated with University of Georgia–Center for Invasive Species and Ecosystem Health, USDA Animal and Plant Health Inspection Service, USDA Forest Service, USDA Identification Technology Program, and USDA National Institute of Food and Agriculture.

Jepson eflora (ucjeps.berkeley.edu/eflora) is the online version of *The Jepson Manual*. The taxonomy and plant names in this book follow *The Jepson Manual*. The eflora is freely available and updated regularly.

Lady Bird Johnson Wildflowercenter (wildflower.org) has is a database of native plants for North America run by the University of Texas at Austin.

Native American Ethnobotany (naeb.brit.org) is a database of plants used as drugs, foods, dyes, fibers, and more, by native peoples of North America, hosted by the Center at University of Michigan.

Nature at Hand (natureathand.com/sgmplants) is a wonderful native plant resource for Southern California made by Cliff and Gabi McLean that includes a guide to the Plants of the San Gabriel Mountains.

PlantID.net (plantid.net/Home.aspx) is a plant identification website produced by Bruce Homer-Smith, which tells stories about California plants using photo essays. Use it to generate illustrated, annotated, searchable plant lists for your local park.

PLANTS Database (plants.sc.egov.usda .gov/home) is a USDA-administered database that provides standardized information about plants of the United States and its territories.

Poisonous Plant Research: Logan, UT (ars.
usda.gov/pacific-west-area/logan-ut/poi-
sonous-plant-research/docs) is a USDA
page that provides documents and bibli-
ographies related to poisonous plants of
Western North America.

Rare Plant Inventory (rareplants.cnps.org) is
an Inventory of Rare and Endangered Plants
of California curated by the California Native Plant Society based on records from the
California Natural Diversity Database and
current research.

Theodore Payne Foundation Wildflower Hotline
(theodorepayne.org/learn/wildflower-hotline)
offers weekly recorded wildflower reports,
narrated by Emmy Award–winning actor Joe
Spano.

PHOTO CREDITS

Matthew Below, pg. 78 (left), 264 (right)

Matt Berger, pg. 3, 7 (row 2: third, fourth), 8 (row 3: fifth), 9 (row 1: fourth; row 2: fifth; row 3: third), 10 (row 1: fifth), 12 (row 2: first), 14 (row 1: fifth), 16 (row 1: fourth), 17 (row 1: second; row 4: second), 18 (row 2: fourth), 20 (row 1: fourth; row 4: first), 21 (row 2: third; row 3: first; row 4: first), 23 (row 4: first), 25 (row 1: fourth; row 3: first), 26 (row 1: first), 27 (row 1: fifth), 29 (row 2: first), 29 (row 2: first), 30 (row 1: third; row 4: second, third), 31 (row 1: third), 32 (row 3: second), 33 (row 3: third, fourth; row 4: first, thirdo, 34 (row 1: first; row 2: second), 117, 139 (left), 141 (left), 150 (right), 155 (left), 156 (right), 163 (right, inset), 168 (left), 178 (left, inset), 180 (right), 190 (right), 193 (right), 196 (right), 212 (right), 226 (left), 267 (left), 269 (left), 397 (left), 308 (right), 315 (left), 317 (left, inset), 331 (right), 332 (right), 358 (left, inset), 359 (left), 360 (left), 364 (right and inset), 370 (left and right), 376 (left), 377 (left, inset), 390 (left), 415 (right), 420 (left), 429 (right), 437 (right), 441 (left), 443 (left, inset; right), 450 (left), 454 (right, inset), 475 (left), 509 (right), 516 (left), 517 (left, inset), 523 (left), 526 (left), 528 (left), 540 (right, inset), 551 (right), 556 (left), 558 (right and inset), 565 (left), 569 (left; right, inset),

Jeff Bisbee, pg. 55 (left), 61, 67 (right), 101 (left), 184 (right)

Robert Martin Case, pg. 7 (row 2: fifth), 11 (row 1: first), 12 (row 1: fifth; row 4: first), 13 (row 2: fifth), 15 (row 1: second; row 3: fourth), 18 (row 2: third), 19 (row 1: third), 28 (row 3: fifth), 32 (row 1: second), 34 (row 1: third), 64, 115 (right), 129 (left), 130 (right), 131, 158 (right), 186 (left), 201 (right), 207 (left), 219 (right), 242 (left), 251 (left, inset), 277 (left), 279 (right), 313 (left), 316 (right), 319 (left), 450 (right, inset),

Christopher J. Collier, pg. 292 (right)

Patrick Crooks, pg. 6 (row 1: fifth), 17, (row 1: first), 100 (right), 115 (right, inset), 306 (right, inset), 449 (right and inset), 460 (left, inset),

John T. Doyen, pg. 6 (row 1: fourth), 12 (row 2: third), 14 (row 3: first), 21 (row 4: fourth), 22 (row 1: third), 25 (row 2: third), 27 (row 2: fifth; row 3: first), 28 (row 1: second), 113 (right, inset), 114 (left, inset), 118 (left, inset), 123 (right, inset), 129 (left, inset), 137 (left), 154 (right, inset), 182 (left, inset), 193 (right, inset), 205 (right), 213 (left), 216 (right), 222 (right, inset), 225 (right, inset), 242 (left, inset), 243 (left, inset), 260 (left and right insets), 277 (right), 294 (left, inset), 369 (right and inset), 387 (left, inset), 418 (left), 436 (left), 438 (left, inset), 444 (left), 464 (right and inset), 484 (left), 496 (right and inset), 521 (right), 557 (right),

Tawnee Dupuis, pg. 339 (left)

Aaron Echols, pg. 7 (row 1: second, fourth), 8 (row 2: first), 11 (row 4: second), 14 (row 3: first; row 4: fourth), 20 (row 1: third; row 2: second), 24 (row 1: first), 25 (row 1: second), 26 (row 2: third), 27 (row 3: second), 30 (row 2: third), 114

(left), 127 (left and right insets), 145 (right), 152 (left), 153 (left), 159 (right), 167 (right, inset), 176 (right), 182 (right), 198 (left), 235 (right), 237 (right), 246 (left, inset), 247 (right), 250 (left), 253 (right, inset), 266 (left; right, inset), 287 (left, inset), 319 (right), 323 (right, inset), 342 (right), 347 (left), 357 (left and inset), 360 (right and inset), 393 (right, inset), 400 (left), 427 (right), 453 (right), 464 (left inset), 476 (right), 484 (right, inset), 485 (left and right), 494 (left), 497 (right and inset), 501 (right, inset), 507 (right), 514 (right), 515 (right), 519 (left), 526 (left, inset), 533 (right), 540 (right), 546 (right), 553 (left), 567 (right)

Ann L. Elliott, pg. 468 (right)

Julie M. Evens, pg. 65

Susan Fawcett, pg. 14 (row 4: third), 30 (row 4: fourth), 32 (row 3: third), 139 (right and inset), 140 (left), 197 (left), 306 (right), 310 (left), 434 (left), 435 (right), 481 (right), 502 (left), 520 (left), 545 (left),

Sherrie Felton, pg. 139 (right and inset), 140 (left), 306 (right)

John Game, pg. 6, (row 3: second, fifth), 7 (row 3: first), 8 (row 2: fifth), 9 (row 1: fifth), 10 (row 5: first), 11 (row 3: second), 13 (row 1: first), 14 (row 1: second), 16 (row 4: third), 17 (row 2: second; row 3: fourth), 18 (row 3: second), 22 (row 4: fifth), 23 (row 1: fourth; row 3: fourth), 24 (row 1: fifth; row 2: fifth), 27 (row 4: third), 29 (row 1: fourth), 32 (row 1: fourth), 34 (row 2: first), 123 (left), 129 (right), 133 (left), 135 (right), 153 (left, inset), 172 (right and inset), 173 (left, inset), 199 (left and inset), 202 (left and inset), 203 (right), 204 (left and inset), 205 (right, inset), 206 (left), 209 (right), 210 (left), 220 (left, 221 (right), 229 (right), 230 (right and inset), 231 (left), 232 (right), 233 (left; right, inset), 238 (left), 240 (right and inset), 252 (left), 254 (left), 261 (right), 266 (left, inset), 271 (right), 275 (right), 285 (left), 288 (right), 291 (right), 296 (left), 297 (right), 300 (left), 303 (right), 308 (left), 313 (right), 318 (right), 320 (left), 333 (left), 334 (right and inset), 339 (right), 352 (left), 353 (left), 359 (right), 354 (left), 368 (left), 378 (right), 396 (left), 398 (left), 402 (left), 407 (right), 413 (right), 417 (left), 421 (right), 423 (left), 424 (left and inset), 426 (left), 428 (right), 432 (right), 434 (right), 446 (left), 448 (right), 451 (left), 459 (right), 465 (right), 468 (left), 479 (left and inset), 485 (left, inset), 486 (left), 489 (right and inset), 499 (left), 509 (left), 516 (right), 530 (left), 537 (left), 538 (left and inset), 552 (left), 554 (left), 566 (right),

David Greenberger, pg. 4 (bottom left), 5 (bottom left), 7 (row 3: second; row 4: fifth), 8 (row 2: third; row 3: third; row 4: first, second, fourth), 9 (row 1: first; row 3: second), 10 (row 1: second, fourth; row 2: third; row 3: fourth; row 4: fourth), 11 (row 1: fourth, fifth; row 3: first, fourth; row 4: third, fifth), 12 (row 1: first; row 4: third–fifth), 13 (row 2: third; row 3: second, third, fifth; row 4: second), 14 (row 1: third; row 3: fourth, fifth; row 4: first), 15 (row 1: third; row 2: fourth; row 3: fifth), 16 (row 2: third; row 4: second), 17 (row 2: fourth; row 3: second; row 4: first, fifth), 20 (row 1: first; row 2: third; row 4: second), 21 (row 2: fifth), 23 (row 2: first; row 4: third–fifth), 24 (row 1: third, fourth; row 2: third, fourth), 24 (row 1: first; row 3: second), 29 (row 1: second, fifth; row 4: fifth), 30 (row 2: first), 31 (row 4: third), 32 (row 1: first; row 2: first; row 4: third, fourth), 33 (row 1: second; row 2: third, fourth), 34 (row 2: third), 125 (eft), 133 (right), 158 (left), 172 (left), 173 (left, right), 187 (right), 195 (left), 198 (right), 210 (insets), 215 (right, inset), 228 (right, inset), 230 (right), 244 (right, inset), 247 (left), 254 (right), 256 (left), 257 (left), 270 (right), 276 (right), 284 (left), 288 (right), 289 (right), 292 (left, inset), 326 (left), 340 (right), 344 (left), 356 (left), 363 (right, inset), 372 (right), 376 (right), 390 (right), 394 (left), 402 (right), 405 (left, inset; right), 432 (left, inset), 480 (left), 506 (right), 535 (right), 539 (left), 549 (left), 554 (right inset), 559 (right), 561 (right),

Devlin Gandy, pg. 305 (right), 374 (right), 428 (left), 458 (right), 460 (left), 487 (right), 522 (right)

Kean S. Goh, pg. 110 (right)

Terrence Gosliner, pg. 24 (row 4: fifth), 80 (right), 148 (right)

Ken Hickman, pg. 15 (row 3: third), 18 (row 2: fifth), 111 (right), 138 (left), 145 (left), 154 (left), 174 (right), 227 (left), 345 (left), 412 (right), 479 (right), 539 (right)

David A. Hofmann, pg. 126 (right, inset)

Mary Hunter, pg. 8 (row 4: third), 17 (row 1: third), 321 (right), 345 (right, inset), 406 (right)

Ingramphoto.com ©Stephen Ingram, pg. 4 (top), 6 (row 2: second; row 3: third), 8 (row 1: first), 10 (row 1: first), 11 (row 2: third), 12 (row 1: third; row 2: second, fifth), 13 (row 4: first), 16 (row 4: fifth), 17 (row 1: fourth; row 3: first; row 4: third), 18 (row 3: fifth; row 4: second), 19 (row 1: second, fourth; row 3: fourth), 20 (row 4: fifth), 22 (row 1: second; row 2: fourth, fifth), 23 (row 2: first), 24 (row 3: first, second), 25 (row 1: fifth; row 4: fifth), 26 (row 2: first), 27 (row 1: fourth; row 2: fourth; row 4: first), 28 (row 1: first; row 2: third), 29 (row 2: third), 32 (row 2: fourth; row 3: fifth), 33 (row 4: fourth), 34 (row 1: second fifth; row 2: fourth), 35, 43 (right), 44, 54, 57, 107 (right), 117 (left, inset), 120 (right), 123 (left, inset), 134 (left), 135 (left), 147 (left), 185 (right), 188 (left, inset), 192 (left), 207 (right), 213 (right), 217 (right, inset), 218 (right), 219 (left, inset), 231 (right), 237 (left), 241 (left), 248 (left), 249 (left), 274, 278 (left), 280 (left), 281 (left), 294 (left), 305 (left), 309 (left), 312 (left), 314 (left), 315 (right), 322 (right, inset), 325 (right), 336 (left, inset), 337 (right), 338 (right), 340 (left), 346 (left), 350 (left), 355 (left), 356 (right), 357 (right), 365, 366 (left), 367 (left), 377 (right), 378 (left), 386 (right and inset), 391 (left), 393 (right), 400 (right), 404 (left), 407 (left, inset), 408 (left), 409 (left), 415 (left), 418 (left and inset), 419, 425 (right), 426 (left, inset), 430 (left), 440 (left), 447 (right), 449 (left), 457, 458 (left), 460 (right and inset), 461 (left), 462 (right), 463 (left, inset), 467 (left), 470 (left), 474 (left), 478 (left), 481 (left), 483 (right), 489 (left), 490

(right), 491 (left), 492 (right), 500 (right), 506 (left), 510 (right), 511 (left), 512 (left), 515 (left), 517 (left), 522 (left), 540 (left), 541 (left), 544 (right), 547 (left), 555 (left, inset), 556 (right), 562 (left, inset; right), 564 (left and inset; right), 566 (left), 569 (left, inset), 570

Nicholas Jensen, pg. 9 (row 1: third), 11 (row 4: first), 12 (row 3: first), 18 (row 1: fourth), 19 (row 3: first), 21 (row 1: third; row 2: fourth), 23 (row 2: fourth), 24 (row 2: second), 26 (row 1: fifth), 28 (row 2: fifth), 38, 40, 53 (left), 56, 63, 67 (left), 69, 71, 99, 116 (right), 163 (left), 170 (left), 214 (left), 217 (right), 223 (right), 224 (left), 241 (right), 287 (right, inset), 294 (right), 304 (right), 325 (right), 328 (right), 336 (right), 341 (left), 343 (left, inset), 350 (left, inset), 363 (left), 366 (left), 379 (left), 380 (right), 392 (right), 405 (left), 407 (left), 422 (right), 446 (right), 452 (right), 465 (left), 470 (right), 475 (right), 478 (left), 482 (right), 490 (left), 498 (right), 517 (left), 543 (right),

Julie Ann Kierstead, pg. 22 (row 3: fifth), 302 (right), 524 (left), 532 (right and inset)

Ira Koroleva, pg. 524 (right)

Neal Kramer, pg. 6 (row 1: second), 10 (row 1: third), 13 (row 3: first), 14 (row 4: second), 15 (row 2: third; row 3: second), 18 (row 3: third), 20 (row 3: first), 118 (left), 143 (right), 151 (right, inset), 176 (left, inset), 178 (right), 180 (left), 183 (left), 189 (right, inset), 243 (left), 245 (left), 247 (left, inset), 251 (right, inset), 258 (right), 265 (left, inset), 276 (left), 336 (right, inset), 345 (right), 352 (right), 363 (left, inset), 389 (left), 431 (left), 448 (left), 473 (left), 497 (left), 515 (right, inset), 525 (left), 527 (right), 543 (left), 544 (left), 557 (right, inset),

Tony Kurz, pg. 33 (row 1: fourth), 122 (right), 286 (left, inset), 287 (left), 303 (left), 326 (right), 351 (right), 354 (left), 372 (left), 397 (right), 568 (right)

Laura Lovett, pg. p. 16 (row 1: second), 331 (left), 403 (right)

Steve Matson, pg. 6 (row 1: first, fourth; row 2 first, third–fifth; row 3: fourth), 7 (row 1: first, third; row 2: first; row 4: first), 8 (row 1: first), 9 (row 2: second, fourth; row 4: first, second, fifth), 10 (row 2: first, fourth, fifth; row 3: second, third), 11 (row 2: first; row 3: first, fifth), 12 (row 1: second, fourth; row 2: fourth; row 4: second), 13 (row 1: second; row 2: fourth; row 3: fourth; row 5, fifth), 14 (row 1: first, fourth; row 2: third, fourth; row 3 first, second), 15 (row 1: fifth; row 2: first), 16 (row 2: fourth; row 3: fifth; row 4: first), 17 (row 4: fourth), 18 (row 3: first, fourth), 19 (row 1: first; row 2), 20 (row 2: fourth; row 3: fifth), 21 (row 3: third; row 4 second), 22 (row 1: fifth; row 2: first, third; row 3 second; row 4: second), 23 (row 1: first; row 3 first, fifth), 24 (row 1: second; row 2: first; row 4: fourth), 25 (row 2: fourth, fifth; row 3: fifth; row 4: second, fourth), 26 (row 1: second, fourth; row 2: fifth; row 3: second, third), 27 (row 1: first; row 2: first), 28 (row 2: second; row 3: fourth), 29 (row 1: second, row 2: second; row 3: first, third, fourth; row 4: first), 30 (row 1: first, second;

row 2: fourth, fifth; row 3: first, third, fourth), 31 (row 1: first; row 2: second, fifth; row 3: second; row 4: second, fourth), 32 (row 1: third), 33 (row 2: second, fourth; tow 3, fifth), 34 (row 1: fourth; row 2: first, fifth), 78 (right), 103 (right), 110 (right), 113 (left), 116 (left and inset), 119 (right), 120 (left and inset), 121 (left, inset; right and inset), 124 (right, inset), 125 (right), 127 (right), 132, 136 (right, inset), 138 (left, inset), 144 (left), 146 (insets), 151 (right), 156 (left), 157 (right), 161 (left), 162, 163 (left, inset, right), 164 (left; right, inset), 166 (left), 167 (left, right), 174 (left), 175 (left), 177 (right), 179 (left), 180 (left, inset), 182 (right, inset), 183 (left, inset), 193 (left), 196 (left, inset), 200 (right), 206 (right), 211 (left), 215 (right), 218 (left, inset), 227 (right), 228 (left, inset), 229 (left, inset), 233 (right), 234 (right, inset), 238 (right), 239 (left), 243 (right), 248 (right), 252 (right and inset), 258 (left and inset), 259 (left, inset), 260 (left; right, inset), 261 (left), 269 (right), 272 (left), 278 (right), 279 (left), 281 (right), 287 (right), 289 (left, inset), 290 (right), 293 (right), 295 (right, inset), 299 (left), 300 (right and inset), 304 (left), 320 (right), 323 (right), 331 (right, inset), 334 (right, inset), 342 (left), 343 (left), 358 (left), 362 (left, inset), 376 (left, inset), 381 (left), 388 (right), 394 (left, inset), 395 (right), 403 (left), 408 (right), 414 (right, inset), 421 (left), 429 (left), 431 (right, inset), 432 (left), 440 (right and inset), 441 (left, inset), 452 (left and inset), 453 (left), 456, 458 (left, inset), 461 (right), 469 (right), 470 (left), 493 (right), 496 (left; right, inset), 499 (right), 502 (left, inset; right), 507 (left, inset), 526 (left, inset), 518 (right), 519 (right and inset), 526 (right), 530 (right, inset), 534 (insets), 542 (right), 543 (left, inset), 553 (right), 559 (right, inset), 562 (left), 564 (right, inset), 565 (left, inset)

Jason Matthias Mills, pg. 208 (left)

Len Mazur, pg. 101 (right), 106 (right), 183 (right), 184 (left), 188 (left), 542 (left), 563 (right)

Maureen McHale, pg. 28 (row 4: fourth), 32 (row 2: third; row 4: fifth), 127 (left), 565 (right)

Gabi McLean, pg. 5 (top, left), 7 (row 3: third), 10 (row 3: fifth; row 4: second, third, fifth), 17 (row 3: third), 18 (row 2: first), 20 (row 3: second), 21 (row 2: first), 22 (row 4: first), 24 (row 3: fifth), 25 (row 2: first), 26 (row 3: first), 27 (row 4: second), 28 (row 4: third), 30 (row 3: second), 31 (row 1: fourth; row 2: fourth; row 3: third, fifth), 41, 104 (left), 107 (left and inset), 112 (right), 113 (right), 115 (left, inset), 118 (right), 119 (left), 120 (right, inset), 134 (right and inset), 139 (left, inset), 140 (right and inset), 144 (right), 151 (left), 152 (left, inset), 166 (right), 169, 171 (left), 184 (left, inset), 190 (left), 194 (left), 196 (left), 197 (right), 200 (left), 222 (right), 224 (right and inset), 226 (right), 235 (left), 253 (left), 255 (right), 286 (right and inset), 299 (right), 311 (right, inset), 318 (left and inset), 327 (left), 329 (left and inset), 330 (left), 335 (right and inset), 347 (right), 387 (right), 397 (left), 428 (left, inset), 431 (right), 436 (right and inset), 444 (right), 455 (left and inset), 462 (left), 467 (right), 477 (right, inset), 482 (right, inset), 492 (left), 493 (left), 498 (left), 503 (left), 504 (left), 507 (right, inset), 510 (left), 524 (right, inset), 529 (left), 531 (left), 532 (left and inset), 545 (right and inset)

Cliff McLean, 202 (right, inset), 226 (right, inset), 286 (left), 484 (left, inset), 514 (left and inset)

L. Maynard Moe, pg. 11 (row 1: third), 188 (right), 204 (right), 323 (right), 330 (right), 375 (right), 447 (left), 463 (left), 555 (left)

Graham Montgomery, pg. 141 (right), 246 (left), 295 (right), 297 (left), 298 (left), 322 (right), 433 (right and inset)

Keir Morse, pg. 7 (row 2: second; row 3: fourth, fifth), 9 (row 2: third; row 3: fifth), 13 (row 1: fourth, fifth), 14 (row 4: fifth), 15 (row 3: first), 16 (row 1: third, fifth), 21 (row 2: second), 22 (row 3: third), 29 (row 2: fourth), 31 (row 3: fourth), 33 (row 4: fifth), 114 (left, inset), 128 (right), 129 (right, inset), 136 (left, inset), 137 (right), 143 (left, inset), 147 (right), 153 (right, inset), 168 (right), 177 (left), 181 (right and inset), 189 (right), 191 (right), 202 (right), 216 (left), 223 (left), 228 (left), 229 (left), 238 (right, inset), 239 (right, inset), 240 (left), 245 (left, inset), 259 (left, inset), 262 (left), 267 (right, inset), 275 (left), 283 (right), 284 (right), 314 (right and inset), 317 (left), 334 (left), 375 (left, inset), 395 (left), 406 (left), 477 (left), 495 (right), 505 (right), 513 (right), 518 (left), 531 (right and inset), 551 (left), 557 (left), 563 (left),

Caroline Murray, pg. 53 (right), 143 (left), 584

David Lincoln Nelson, MD, pg. 108 (right)

Dylan Neubauer, pg. 20 (row 1: second), 105 (left), 411 (right)

Gary Nored, pg. 59

Dan Noreen, pg. 27 (row 3: fifth), 29 (row 1: third), 121 (left), 239 (right), 267 (right), 283 (left), 373 (left), 387 (left), 471 (left, inset), 480 (right), 529 (left), 534 (right)

Amy Patten, pg. 82, 100 (left), 103 (left), 108 (left)

Katy Pye, pg. 8 (row 3: first), 11 (row 3: third), 18 (row 1: second), 22 (row 4: fourth), 23 (row 4: second), 25 (row 4: third), 31 (row 2: third), 32 (row 2: second, fifth; row 3: first), 112 (left), 152 (right), 205 (left), 220 (right), 307 (right), 362 (right), 369 (left), 398 (right), 410 (left), 445 (right), 467 (left), 528 (right), 541 (right), 542 (left, inset)

Gina Radieve, 55 (right)

Casey H. Richart, pg. 502 (right, inset)

Lynn Robertson, pg. 14 (row 3: third), 262 (left and inset)

©Jake Ruygt 2009, pg. 106 (left)

John O. Sawyer, Jr., pg. 66

Aaron Schusteff, pg. 18 (row 4: fourth), 124 (left), 161 (right), 215 (right), 273, 280 (right), 332 (left), 399 (left), 417 (right), 442 (left),

Vernon Smith, pg. 5 (top, right), 9 (row 1: second; row 3: first, fourth; row 4: third), 10 (row 2: second), 11 (row 1: second), 12 (row 3: second, third), 16 (row 2: fifth; row 3: first, second, fourth), 18 (row 4: first), 19 (row 1: fifth), 20 (row 1: fifth; row 4: fourth), 21 (row 1: fourth, fifth), 23 (row 1: third; row 2: third; row 3: third) 24 (row 3: third; row 4: third), 26 (row 1: third), 28 (row 1: fourth; row 3:

second; row 4: fifth), 29 (row 1: first; row 2: fifth; row 4: fourth), 31 (row 4: fifth), 32 (row 4: second), 33 (row 3: second), 123 (right), 126 (right), 128 (left), 136 (right), 37 (left, inset), 144 (left, inset), 149, 153 (right), 160 (left), 164 (left, inset), 165 (left), 170 (right), 175 (right), 179 (right, inset), 181 (left), 182 (left), 183 (right), 184 (right, inset), 185 (left), 186 (right), 194 (right), 195 (right), 203 (left), 211 (right), 212 (left), 217 (left), 218 (left), 220 (right, inset), 221 (right), 223 (left, inset), 225 (right), 242 (left), 250 (left, inset; right and inset), 251 (left), 259 (right), 262 (right), 263 (right), 264 (left, inset), 265 (right), 268 (right), 270 (left), 282 (right), 290 (right, inset), 291 (left), 292 (left), 293 (left and inset), 321 (left), 324, 328 (left), 329 (right), 337 (right), 338 (left), 341 (right), 344 (right), 346 (right), 350 (right), 354 (right), 358 (right), 369 (left, inset), 371 (left and inset), 374 (left), 381 (right), 388 (left), 389 (right), 396 (right), 397 (right, inset), 399 (right), 410 (right), 411 (left), 412 (left, inset), 413 (left), 414 (right), 422 (left), 423 (right), 424 (right), 425 (left), 426 (right), 435 (left), 438 (left), 442 (right), 451 (right), 454 (left), 455 (right), 471 (right), 472 (right), 476 (left; right, inset), 483 (right), 484 (right), 485 (right, inset), 486 (right), 495 (right, inset), 496 (left, inset), 501 (left, right), 511 (right), 521 (left), 527 (left), 536 (right), 537 (right), 538 (right), 547 (right), 549 (right), 550 (right), 558 (left)

Morgan Stickrod, pg. 4 (bottom, right), 8 (row 2: second, fourth), 9 (row 2: first; row 4: fourth), 10 (row 3: first), 11 (row 2: second, fourth), 13 (row 1: third; row 2: first, second), 14 (row 2: first, second), 15 (row 1: fourth; row 2: second), 16 (row 2: second; row 3: third; row 4: fourth), 17 (row 1: fifth; row 2: fifth), 18 (row 1: first, third, fifth; row 4: third), 19 (row 3: third, fifth), 21 (row 1: second; row 3: fourth; row 4: fifth), 22 (row 2: second; row 3: first, fourth), 23 (row 2: second), 24 (row 4: first, second), 25 (row 1: third; row 2: second; row 4: first), 26 (row 2: fourth), 27 (row 2: third), 28 (row 1: fifth; row 2: fourth; row 3: first; row 4: first, second), 29 (row 3: fifth), 30 (row 1: fifth; row 2: second; row 4: fifth), 31 (row 1: fifth; row 2: first; row 3: first), 32 (row 1: fifth; row 5, first), 33 (row 1: first, fifth; row 3: first), 100 (row 1: fifth), 102 (right), 124 (right), 139 (left), 142 (right), 146 (left), 155 (right), 157 (left), 159 (left), 164 (right), 187 (left), 191 (left, inset), 192 (right), 207 (left, inset), 210 (right), 222 (left), 234, (left, right), 236 (right), 240 (left, inset), 244 (right), 246 (right and inset), 253 (right), 257 (right, inset), 264 (left), 268 (left), 272 (right), 289 (left), 290 (left), 296 (right), 301, 304 (right, inset), 309 (right, inset), 310 (right), 312 (right), 316 (left), 317 (right), 327 (left, inset), 335 (left), 348, 349, 351 (left), 353 (right), 359 (left, inset), 361 (left; right, inset), 362 (left), 363 (right), 379 (right and inset), 380 (left), 382 (right), 383 (right), 392 (left), 401 (left, right), 404 (right), 409 (right), 412 (left), 416, 420 (right), 426 (right), 433 (left), 437 (left), 438 (right), 439 (left), 445 (left), 459 (left), 463 (right), 464 (left), 466, 472 (left), 473 (right), 487 (left and inset), 488 (right), 494 (right), 498 (left, inset),

504 (left, inset; right), 505 (right), 506 (right, inset), 520 (right), 525 (right), 533 (left), 534 (left), 535 (left), 548, 552 (right), 554 (right), 560 (right), 561 (left)

Robert Sweatt, pg. 8 (row 3: second), 126 (left), 146 (right), 214 (right), 225 (left), 232 (left), 244 (left), 311 (right), 339 (left, inset), 377 (left), 385 (left), 559 (left)

Ron Vanderhoff, pg. 7 (row 4: second, third), 8 (row 3: fourth; row 4: fourth), 12 (row 3: fifth), 15 (row 1: first), 16 (row 1: first), 17 (row 3: fifth), 20 (row 3: third, fourth), 21 (row 3: fifth), 22 (row 1: first), 25 (row 3: third, fourth), 27 (row 1: second; row 2: second; row 3: third, fourth; row 4: fourth), 28 (row 3: third), 29 (row 4: third), 30 (row 1: fourth; row 3: fifth; row 4: first), 32 (row 3: fourth), 33 (row 4: second), 104 (right and inset), 122 (left), 133 (right, inset), 148 (left), 160 (right and inset), 179 (right), 189 (left), 191 (left), 198 (left, inset), 199 (right), 228 (right), 236 (left), 245 (right and inset), 256 (right and inset), 257 (right), 265 (left), 268 (left, inset), 282 (left, inset), 295 (left), 370 (left, inset), 375 (left), 380 (left, inset), 383 (left, inset), 384, 385 (right), 390 (right, inset), 396 (right, inset), 439 (left and inset), 442 (right, inset), 443 (left), 445 (left, inset), 454 (right), 471 (left), 482 (left), 503 (right, inset), 508 (right), 518 (right, inset), 520 (right, inset), 533 (right, inset), 546 (left and inset), 550 (left), 551 (right, inset), 568 (left)

Brad Winckelmann, pg. 560 (left)

Gary R. Zahm, pg. 488 (left)

CALPHOTOS

Creative Commons Attribution 3.0 Generic

Jean Pawek, pg. 114 (right), 115 (left), 249 (right)

FLICKR

Attribution 2.0 Generic

Paul Asman and Jill Lenoble, pg. 322 (left), 343 (right)

chuck b., pg. 367 (right)

Tim Berger, pg. 28 (row 2: first)

Evan Blaser, pg. 72

Mark Byzewski, pg. 23 (row 3: second)

Joyce Cory, pg. 368 (right)

Jitze Couperus, pg. 260 (right)

Dick Culbert, pg. 333 (right)

Dag Terje Filip Endresen, pg. 19 (row 3: second)

Tom Hillton, pg. 7 (row 4: fourth), 21 (row 3: second), 31 (row 1: second)

Jerry Kirkhart, pg. 257 (right, inset)

manuel m. v., pg. 24 (row 3: fourth)

Melissa McMasters, pg. 512 (right)

Pacific Southwest Forest Service, Region 5/Don Lepley, pg. 22 (row 4: third), 391 (right)

Harry Rose, pg. 503 (right)

John Rusk, pg. 26 (row 2: second), 453 (left, inset)
Katja Schulz, pg. 20 (row 2: fifth)
Wendell Smith, pg. 500 (left)
Forest and Kim Starr, pg. 8 (row 2: first), 13 (row 4: third)
Kevin Thiele, pg. 31 (row 4: first)
Amy Washuta, pg. 20 (row 4: third)
Andrey Zharkikh, pg. 8 (row 1: second), 188 (right, inset), 373 (right)

Attribution NoDerivs 2.0 Generic
Gertjan van Noord, pg. 386 (left), 450 (right)

Attribution ShareAlike 2.0 Generic
J Brew, pg. 23 (row 1: fifth),
Laura Camp, pg. 266 (right), 414 (left)
Aaron Carlson, pg. 176 (left)
Joe Decruyenaere, pg. 13 (row 4: fourth), 17 (row 2: first), 27 (row 1: third), 310 (left, inset), 327 (right), 401 (right, inset)
Bernard Dupont, pg. 569 (right)
Elaine with Grey Cats, pg. 142 (left)
Tracie Hall, pg. 138 (right)
Matt Lavin, pg. 208 (right), 248 (left, inset), 302 (left)
Vahe Martirosyan, pg. 22 (row 1: fourth)
Jim Morefield, pg. 336 (left), 508 (left)
Andreas Rockstein, pg. 11 (row 2: fifth), 29 (row 4: second), 208 (right, inset)
Ton Rulkens, pg. 6 (row 3: first), 122 (left, inset)
Lucy Wayland, pg. 18 (row 4: fifth)

CCO 1.0 Universal
Patrick Alexander, pg. 394 (right)

Creative Commons Attribution 2.0 Generic
Forest and Kim Starr, pg. 249 (right, inset)

Public Domain Dedication
Patrick Alexander, pg. 16 (row 2: first)

Public Domain Mark 1.0
Bureau of Land Management California-Kiska Media; pg. 81
NPS-Hannah Schwalbe, pg. 285 (right)
USGS Bee Inventory and Monitoring Lab, pg. 8 (row 1: fourth)

PIXABAY

Pixabay License
Kimberly Rotter; pg. 80 (left)

WIKIMEDIA

Attribution 3.0 Unported
Dcrjsr, pg. 491 (right)

Attribution ShareAlike 2.5 Generic
Stan Shebs, pg. 361 (right)

Attribution ShareAlike 3.0 Unported
Hans Hillewaert, pg. 371 (right)
Michal Klajban, pg. 536 (left)
©2009 Walter Siegmund, pg. 165 (right)

Attribution ShareAlike 4.0
Pelican Hill and South CDM by D Ramey Logan.jpg from Wikimedia Commons by D Ramey Logan, CC-BY-SA 4.0., pg. 73

Attribution ShareAlike 4.0 International
Zeynel Cebeci-Wikimedia Commons, pg. 361 (left, inset)
Michal Klajban, pg. 536 (left)
Stefan Lefnaer, pg. 171 (right)
Slimguy, pg. 171 (right, inset)
Kenraiz Krzysztof Ziarnek, pg. 530 (right)

Creative Commons Attribution 4.0 International
Dcrjsr, pg. 20 (left)

Public Domain
AnRo0002, pg. 17 (row 2: third), 311 (left)

Brodiaea elegans, 345
Brodiaea matsonii, 101
Brodiaea terrestris, 345
Brodiaea terrestris subsp. *kernensis*, 345
Brodiaea terrestris subsp. *terrestris*, 345
Brook Foam, 261
Broomrape, 93
Brown Bells, 123
Brown-eyes, 216
Brown-spine Prickly-pear, 460
Brown's Peony, 421
Bruneau Mariposa Lily, 203
Brussels sprouts, 87
Buckbean, 92, 211
Buckbrush, 61, 68, 244
Buckthorn, 95
Buckwheat, 68, 94
Bull Thistle, 359
Bumble Bee, 447
Bunchgrass, 63
Bur Chervil, 142
Burclover, 530
Burrobush, 112
Bush Anemone, 90
Bush Beardtongue, 227, 557
Bush Monkeyflower, 467
Bush Poppy, 550
Butcher's Broom, 95
Butter-and-Eggs, 549
Buttercup, 95
Butterfly Mariposa Lily, 204
Button-willow, 258

Cabbage, 87
Cacao Tree, 92
Cactus, 87–88
Cakile maritima, 362
Calandrinia breweri, 405
Calandrinia menziesii, 405
California Aphyllon, 324
California Barrel Cactus, 520
California Bedstraw, 128
California Bee Plant, 96, 454
California Blackberry, 257
California Bluebell, 305
California Brickellbush, 503

California Brittlebush, 477
California Buckeye, 95, 260
California Buckwheat, 236
California Buttercup, 561
California Butterwort, 66
California Chicory, 153
California Coffeeberry, 126
California Compass Plant, 494
California Condor, 81
California Coneflower, 491
California Corn Lily, 210
California Cottonrose, 157
California Desert Dandelion, 498, 499
California Dogface Butterfy, 293
California Evening Primrose, 218
California Everlasting, 158
California False Indigo, 293
California Fawn Lily, 205
California Flannelbush, 540
California Fuchsia, 414
California Goosefoot, 119
California Grape, 65, 131
California Ground-cone, 326
California Harebell, 290
California Hedge-nettle, 396
California Helianthella, 483
California Hemp, 295
California Jewelflower, 75, 98, 363
California Laurel, 67
California Loosestrife, 399
California Manroot, 182
California Milkweed, 148, 353
California Milkwort, 437
California Mountain Ash, 258
California Mugwort, 114
California Mustard, 166
California Peony, 421
California Pipevine, 87, 355
California Pitcherplant, 66, 96, 452
California Poppy, 75, 80, 94, 466, 551
California Prickly Phlox, 434
California Primrose, 545
California Rock Parsnip, 111, 145
California Sagebrush, 61
California Sandwort, 174

California Saxifrage, 264
California Scrub Oak, 61
California Skullcap, 200
California Spikenard, 87, 149
California Sweet Cicely, 146
California Sycamore, 65
California Valerian, 271
California Wild Rose, 449
California Yerba Santa, 61, 323
Calla Llily, 149
Calliandra californica, 381
Calliandra eriophylla, 381
Calocedrus decurrens, 68
Calochortus, 80–81, 82
Calochortus albus, 81, 201
Calochortus amabilis, 536
Calochortus bruneaunis, 203
Calochortus catalinae, 202
Calochortus clavatus, 537
Calochortus coeruleus, 320
Calochortus invenustus, 202
Calochortus kennedyi, 462
Calochortus leichtlinii, 203
Calochortus luteus, 537
Calochortus monophyllus, 91, 538
Calochortus plummerae, 397
Calochortus pulchellus, 536
Calochortus splendens, 321
Calochortus superbus, 203
Calochortus tiburonensis, 101
Calochortus tolmiei, 321
Calochortus venustus, 204
Caltha leptosepala, 241
Caltrop, 97, 569
Calycadenia truncata, 476
Calycanthus floridus, 367
Calycanthus occidentalis, 367
Calypso, 93
Calypso bulbosa, 416
Calyptridium monandrum, 405
Calyptridium monospermum, 405
Calyptridium umbellatum, 406
Calystegia, 88
Calystegia macrostegia, 178
Calystegia occidentalis, 178
Calystegia purpurata, 374
Calystegia stebbinsii, 102
Camassia leichtlinii, 275

Camatta Canyon Amole, 105
Camissonia campestris, 542
Camissonia strigulosa, 543
Camissoniopsis cheiranthifolia, 543
Camissoniopsis pallida, 544
Campanula scouleri, 172
Canbya candida, 224
Candy Flower, 212
Canyon Dudleya, 461
Canyon Live Oak, 65
Canyon Nemophila, 196
Canyon Sunflower, 494
Capsella bursa-pastoris, 164
Cardamine californica, 165
Cardamine oligosperma, 165
Cardinal Catchfly, 372
Cardoon, 282
Carduus pycnocephalus, 358
Carnation, 88
Carnegiea gigantea, 58
Carolina Allspice, 367
Carpenteria californica, 90
Carpobrotus chilensis, 350
Carpobrotus edulis, 350
Carrizo Plain National
  Monument, 75
Carrot, 86
Cascade Range, 55
Cassiope mertensiana, 185
Castilleja, 42, 93, 324
Castilleja applegatei, 418
Castilleja attenuata, 125
Castilleja densiflora, 324
Castilleja exserta, 42, 75, 325
Castilleja foliolosa, 418
Castilleja lemmonii, 325
Castilleja miniata, 419
Castilleja pilosa, 125
Castor Bean, 122
Catclaw Acacia, 191
Caulanthus amplexicaulis, 286
Caulanthus anceps, 166
Caulanthus californicus, 75, 98, 363
Caulanthus coulteri, 363
Caulanthus inflatus, 364
Caulanthus lasiophyllus, 166
Caulanthus major, 166
Cax Currant, 390

Ceanothus, 61, 68, 95
Ceanothus cuneatus, 244
Ceanothus integerrimus, 245
Ceanothus lemmonii, 342
Ceanothus leucodermis, 342
Celery, 86
Centaurea solstitialis, 402, 503
Central Valley, 53
Centromadia pungens, 476
Centromadia pungens subsp.
  laevis, 476
Centromadia pungens subsp.
  pungens, 476
Centrostegia thurberi, 233
Cephalanthera austiniae, 219
Cephalanthus, 95
Cephalanthus occidentalis, 258
Cercis occidentalis, 381
Cercocarpus betuloides, 247
Cercocarpus ledifolius, 248
Chaenactis douglasii, 155
Chaenactis fremontii, 156
Chaenactis glabriuscula, 504
Chaenactis xantiana, 156
Chalk Dudleya, 375
Chamaebatia, 68
Chamaebatia foliolosa, 248
Chamaebatiaria millefolium, 249
Chamerion angustifolium, 409
Chamise, 61, 79, 245, 246
Chaparral Bindweed, 178, 374
Chaparral Bush Mallow, 401
Chaparral Currant, 390
Chaparral Dodder, 180
Chaparral Gilia, 228
Chaparral Nightshade, 344
Chaparral Spaghetti, 88
chaparral vegetation, 61
Chaparral Whitethorn, 342
Chaparral Yucca, 86, 134
Charming Centaury, 387
Chasmanthe floribunda, 462
Checker Bloom, 403
Checkerspot Butterfly, 456
Cheesebush, 113
Cheese Weed, 208
Chenopodium album, 119
Chenopodium californicum, 119

Chia, 315
Chick Lupine, 382
Chicory, 281
Chilopsis linearis, 87, 361
Chimaphila umbellata, 377
Chinese Caps, 121
Chlorogalum angustifolium, 133
Chlorogalum pomeridianum, 133
Chloropyron maritimum, 222
Chorizanthe membranacea, 438
Chorizanthe polygonoides, 438
Chorizanthe polygonoides var.
  longispina, 438
Chorizanthe staticoides, 439
Chrysothamnus viscidiflorus, 504
Chuparosa, 350
Chylismia brevipes, 544
Chylismia cardiophylla, 545
Chylismia claviformis, 216
Cichorium intybus, 281
Cicuta douglasii, 145
Circaea alpina, 217
Cirsium fontinale var. *fontinale*,
  102
Cirsium occidentale, 359
Cirsium vulgare, 359
citrus, 95
Clare's Pogogyne, 64
Clarkia amoena, 410, 412
Clarkia concinna, 410
Clarkia gracilis, 411
Clarkia gracilis subsp. *gracilis*, 411
Clarkia gracilis subsp. *sonomensis*,
  411
Clarkia purpurea, 411
Clarkia rubicunda, 412
Clarkia speciosa, 412
Clarkia speciosa subsp.
  immaculata, 412
Clarkia springvillensis, 103
Clarkia unguiculata, 413
Clarkia xantiana, 413
Clarkia xantiana subsp.
  parviflora, 413
Clarkia xantiana subsp. *xantiana*,
  413
Clasping-leaf Wild Cabbage, 286
Claytonia, 92

Claytonia exigua, 211
Claytonia perfoliata, 212
Claytonia sibirica, 212
Clearwater Cat's Eyes, 160
Clematis, 65
Clematis, 65
Clematis ligusticifolia, 242
Cleomella obtusifolia, 521
Cleveland Sage, 314, 316
Cliff Aster, 152
Cliff Goldenbush, 505
Cliff Spurge, 189
Climbing Milkweed, 355
Clinopodium douglasii, 199
Clintonia andrewsiana, 397
Clintonia uniflora, 204
Clio Tiger Moth, 353
Clubhair Mariposa Lily, 537
Clubmoss Ivesia, 564
Clustered Orobanche, 548
Coastal California/Coast Ranges, 55–56
Coastal Cholla, 365
Coastal Prickly-pear, 460
Coastal Sagebrush, 113
Coastal Sand Verbena, 541
Coast Buckwheat, 439
Coast Range Bindweed, 78
Coast Redwood, 67
Coast Silktassel, 192
Cobweb Thistle, 359
Coffea arabica, 95
Cold Desert Phlox, 436
Coleogyne ramosissima, 562
Collinsia, 329
Collinsia corymbosa, 75, 103
Collinsia heterophylla, 328
Collinsia parryi, 329
Collinsia sparsiflora, 329
Collinsia tinctoria, 427
Collomia grandiflora, 468
Collomia heterophylla, 432
Collomia tinctoria, 432
Comandra Blister Rust, 177
Comandra umbellata, 88, 177
Common Bluecup, 291
Common Buckeye Caterpillar, 454

Common Chickweed, 176
Common Chuckwalla, 465
Common Cow Parsnip, 144
Common Dandelion, 500
Common Fishhook Cactus, 366
Common Flax, 91
Common Goldenstar, 566
Common Goldfields, 41, 75, 487
Common Groundsel, 510
Common Hareleaf, 486
Common Lomatium, 471
Common Madia, 489
Common Manzanita, 184
Common Meadowfoam, 538
Common Monolopia, 75, 490
common names, 45, 79–80
Common Pussypaws, 405
Common Sandaster, 277
Common Skullcap, 318
Common Snowberry, 369
Common Spikeweed, 476
Common Sunflower, 46, 483
Common Vetch, 302
Common Woodland Star, 263
Common Wooly Sunflower, 480
Condea, 310
Condea emoryi, 310
conifer forest vegetation, 67–68
Conium maculatum, 86, 143
Contra Costa Goldfields, 106
Convolvulus arvensis, 179
Corallorhiza maculata, 416
Corallorhiza striata, 417
Cordylanthus rigidus, 222
Cordylanthus rigidus subsp. *littoralis*, 222
Cordylanthus tenuis, 223
Cordylanthus tenuis subsp. *capillaris*, 223
Coreopsis, 488
Corethrogyne filaginifolia, 277
Coriander, 86
Cornus, 88
Cornus nuttallii, 180
Cornus sericea, 181
Corylus, 87
Corylus cornuta, 159
Cotoneaster pannosus, 249

Cottonwood, 64
Cotula coronopifolia, 505
Coulter's Matilija Poppy, 79, 80, 224
Coulter's Snapdragon, 226, 327
Coulter's Wild Cabbage, 363
Coville's Poppy, 224, 552
Coyote Brush, 61, 154
Coyote Gourd, 525
Coyote Mint, 312
Coyote Tobacco, 267
Cream Cups, 552
Creeping Sage, 317
Creeping Snowberry, 370
Creeping Wild Ginger, 356
Creosote Bush, 69, 97, 112, 569
Cressa truxillensis, 179
Crevice Alumroot, 262
Crocanthemum, 88
Crocanthemum scoparium, 521
Crocus, 91
Crossosoma, 89
Crossosoma bigelovii, 89, 181
Croton setiger, 121
Crown Brodiaea, 344, 345
Cryptantha, 512
Cryptantha flaccida, 160
Cryptantha intermedia, 160
Cryptantha pterocarya, 161
Cucumber, 89
Cucurbita foetidissima, 524
Cucurbita palmata, 525
Cultivated grape, 97
Curl-leaf Mountain Mahogany, 248
Curly Dock, 444
Currant, 68
Curvepod Yellow Cress, 518
Cuscuta, 88
Cuscuta californica, 180
Cushion Buckwheat, 237
Cutleaf Geranium, 389
Cylindropuntia bigelovii, 116
Cylindropuntia echinocarpa, 117
Cylindropuntia prolifera, 365
Cymopterus terebinthinus, 470
Cynara cardunculus, 282
Cynoglossum grande, 282

Cypripedium, 93
Cypripedium montanum, 220
Cytisus scoparius, 527

Dagger Pod, 287
Damasonium, 86
Damasonium californicum, 137
Dandelion, 87
Darlingtonia californica, 66, 96, 452
Darmera peltata, 453
Dasiphora fruticosa, 562
Datura wrightii, 265
Daucus carota, 143
Daucus pusillus, 144
Davidson's Beardtongue, 330
Davidson's Buckwheat, 235
Davidson's Bush-mallow, 107
Deerbrush, 245
Deer's Tongue, 193
Deerweed, 526
Deinandra kelloggii, 477
Delphinium cardinale, 448
Delphinium glaucum, 340
Delphinium hansenii, 242
Delphinium nudicaule, 448
Delphinium parryi, 341
Delphinium patens, 341
Deltoid Balsamroot, 474
Dendromecon rigida, 550
Dense False Gillyflower, 334
Dense-flower Paintbrush, 324
Denseflower Willowherb, 414
Descurainia pinnata, 514
Descurainia sophia, 514
Desert Agave, 470
Desert Almond, 255
Desert Bluebell, 305
Desert Brittlebush, 478
Desert Calico, 434
Desert Candle, 364
Desert Christmas Tree, 320
Desert Five-spot, 400
Desert Holly, 118
Desert Lavender, 310
Desert Lily, 134
Desert Mallow, 465
Desert Marigold, 474

Desert Mariposa Lily, 462
Desert Palafox, 360
Desert Peach, 449
Desert Pepperweed, 168
Desert Plantain, 227
deserts, 57–58
Desert Sage, 315
Desert Sand Verbena, 408
Desert Senna, 532
Desert Stingbush, 207
Desert Threadplant, 173
Desert Tortoise, 117, 217
Desert Trumpet, 559
Desert Unicorn Plant, 541
desert vegetation, 69
Desert Willow, 87, 361
Desert Wishbone Bush, 408
Devil's Lettuce, 459
Dianthus, 88
Dicentra formosa, 422
Dicentra uniflora, 422
Dichelostemma, 97
Dichelostemma volubile, 455
Dieteria canescens, 278
Digitalis purpurea, 427
Dill, 86
Diogenes' Lantern, 536
Diplacus, 94, 423
Diplacus aurantiacus, 467
Diplacus bigelovii, 423
Diplacus brevipes, 553
Diplacus douglasii, 423
Diplacus fremontii, 424
Diplacus kelloggii, 424
Diplacus layneae, 425
Diplacus mephiticus, 425
Dipterostemon, 97
Dipterostemon capitatus, 346
Distant Phacelia, 198, 306
Dobie Pod, 519
Dodder, 88
Dogbane, 86
Dogwood, 88–89
Dolores Campion, 372
Dot-seed Plantain, 227
Douglas' Aster, 280
Douglas Fir, 67, 68
Douglas Iris, 307

Douglas' Mesamint, 313
Douglas' Pincushion, 155
Douglas' Stichwort, 174
Doveweed, 121
Downingia, 292
Downingia cuspidata, 290
Downingia pulchella, 291
Downy Pincushion Plant, 338
Draba cuneifolia, 167
Draba oligosperma, 515
Draba verna, 167
Drosera, 66, 89
Drosera rotundifolia, 376
Drymocallis glandulosa, 250
Dudleya, 60, 374
Dudleya cymosa, 461
Dudleya densiflora, 104
Dudleya farinosa, 522
Dudleya lanceolata, 374
Dudleya pulverulenta, 375
Dudleya stolonifera, 104
dune vegetation, 66–67
Dwarf Brodiaea, 345
Dwarf Owl's Clover, 421
Dwarf White Milkvetch, 293
Dyer's Woad, 516

Eastwood's Fiddleneck, 458
Eastwood's Manzanita, 183
Echinocereus engelmannii, 365
Echinocereus mojavensis, 366
Echinocereus triglochidiatus, 366
Echium candicans, 283
education, 83
Eggplant, 96
Ehrendorferia chrysantha, 551
Ehretia, 89
Elderberry, 97
Eldorado Larkspur, 242
Elegant Clarkia, 413
Elephant's Head, 420
El Segundo Blue Butterfly, 237
Emmenanthe penduliflora, 534
Emory's Rock-daisy, 151
Encelia californica, 477
Encelia farinosa, 478
Enceliopsis covillei, 478
Enchanter's Nightshade, 217

Enemion occidentale, 243
Engelmann's Hedgehog Cactus, 365
Epilobium, 93, 415
Epilobium canum, 414
Epilobium densiflorum, 414
Epilobium obcordatum, 415
Epilobium siskiyouense, 415
Epipactis, 93
Epipactis gigantea, 417
Eremalche parryi, 400
Eremalche parryi subsp. *kernensis*, 400
Eremalche rotundifolia, 400
Eremogone congesta, 173
Eremothera boothii, 217
Eriastrum, 335
Eriastrum densifolium, 334
Eriastrum pluriflorum, 335
Eriastrum pluriflorum subsp. *pluriflorum*, 335
Eriastrum sapphirinum, 335
Eriastrum wilcoxii, 336
Ericameria cuneata, 505
Ericameria cuneata var. *macrocephala*, 505
Ericameria linearifolia, 479
Ericameria nauseosa, 506
Erigeron breweri, 278
Erigeron foliosus, 279
Erigeron glaucus, 279
Eriodictyon, 93, 320
Eriodictyon californicum, 61, 323
Eriodictyon parryi, 323
Eriodictyon trichocalyx, 215
Eriogonum, 60, 68, 94
Eriogonum angulosum, 234
Eriogonum baileyi, 234
Eriogonum callistum, 98
Eriogonum davidsonii, 235
Eriogonum elongatum, 235
Eriogonum fasciculatum, 236
Eriogonum inflatum, 559
Eriogonum latifolium, 439
Eriogonum lobbii, 440
Eriogonum maculatum, 440
Eriogonum nudum, 80, 236
Eriogonum ovalifolium, 237

Eriogonum parvifolium, 237
Eriogonum pusillum, 560
Eriogonum roseum, 441
Eriogonum saxatile, 238
Eriogonum spergulinum, 238
Eriogonum spergulinum var. *reddingianum*, 238
Eriogonum umbellatum, 560
Eriogonum wrightii, 239
Eriophyllum confertiflorum, 479
Eriophyllum lanatum, 480
Eriophyllum staechadifolium, 480
Eriophyllum wallacei, 481
Erodium, 90
Erodium botrys, 388
Erodium cicutarium, 388
Erodium texanum, 389
Eryngium castrense, 110
Erysimum capitatum, 459
Erysimum capitatum var. *capitatum*, 459
Erysimum capitatum var. *purshii*, 459
Erysimum teretifolium, 105
Erythranthe, 60, 94, 423, 426, 554
Erythranthe bicolor, 553
Erythranthe cardinalis, 426
Erythranthe floribunda, 554
Erythranthe guttata, 554
Erythranthe lewisii, 426
Erythranthe tilingii, 555
Erythronium californicum, 205
Erythronium purpurascens, 205
Eschscholtz's Buttercup, 561
Eschscholzia, 75
Eschscholzia caespitosa, 551
Eschscholzia californica, 75, 94, 466
Eschscholzia minutiflora, 552
Eucnide urens, 207
Eucrypta chrysanthemifolia, 196
Euphorbia, 89
Euphorbia albomarginata, 188
Euphorbia crenulata, 121
Euphorbia misera, 189
Eureka Dunes Evening Primrose, 107
European Honeybee, 236
European Licorice, 190

Evening Primrose, 93
Evening Snow, 231
Evergreen Huckleberry, 379
evolution, 82–83
Explorers' Gentian, 194, 303

Fagopyrum esculentum), 94
Fairy Mist, 443
Fairy Slipper, 416
Fallugia paradoxa, 250
False Asphodel, 97
False Hellebore, 92
False Lily of the Valley, 95
False Monkeyflower, 555
Fanleaf Crinklemat, 376
Farewell-to-clarkia, 410, 412
Farnsworth's Jewelflower, 288
Fendler's Meadow-rue, 126
Fennel, 86, 471
Fern Bush, 249
Ferocactus cylindraceus, 520
Fetid Adder's Tongue, 398
Few-flowered Collinsia, 329
Fewseed Draba, 515
Field Bindweed, 179
Figwort, 96
Firecracker Penstemon, 429
Fire Poppy, 466, 467
Fireweed, 409
Fivespot, 197
Flax, 91
Fleshy Porterella, 292
Flixweed, 514
Floerkea, 91
flower petals, 50–51
Fluellin, 558
Foeniculum vulgare, 471
Foothill Clover, 383
Foothill Jepsonia, 263
Foothill Penstemon, 331
Forestiera, 93
Fountain Thistle, 102
Fouquieria splendens, 58, 75, 386
Four O'clock, 93
Four-Wing Saltbush, 117
Foxglove, 427
Fragaria vesca, 251
Fragrant Bedstraw, 128

Fragrant Water-lily, 216
Frangula californica, 126
Frankenia, 90
Frankenia, 90
Frankenia salina, 387
Frasera, 90
Frasera albicaulis, 193
Frasera speciosa, 193
Fraxinus, 93
Freckled Milkvetch, 294
Freeway Iceplant, 350
Fremontodendron californicum, 540
Fremont Pincushion, 156
Fremont's Bush Mallow, 401
Fremont's Death Camas, 209
Fremont's Gold, 493
Fremont's Goldfields, 487
Fremont's Indigobush, 300
Fremont's Monkeyflower, 424
Fremont's Phacelia, 393
French Broom, 528
Fringe Cups, 454
Fringed Checkerbloom, 402
Fringed Onion, 275
Fritillaria affinis, 122
Fritillaria atropurpurea, 123
Fritillaria micrantha, 123
Fritillaria pinetorum, 123
Fritillaria pluriflora, 75
Fritillaria recurva, 91, 398
Fuchsia, 93
Fuchsia, 93
Fuchsia-flowered Gooseberry, 392
Funastrum cynanchoides, 355

Galium, 95
Galium angustifolium, 127
Galium aparine, 259
Galium californicum, 128
Galium triflorum, 128
Garden Nasturtium, 468
Garlic, 86
Garrya, 90
Garrya, 61
Garrya elliptica, 192
Gaultheria shallon, 61, 186
Gayophytum diffusum, 218
Genista monspessulana, 528

Gentian, 90
Gentiana, 90
Gentiana calycosa, 303
Gentiana newberryi, 194
Gentiana newberryi var. *tiogana*, 194
Gentianopsis, 90
Gentianopsis holopetala, 304
Gentianopsis simplex, 304
Geraea canescens, 481
Geranium, 90
Geranium dissectum, 389
Geum macrophyllum, 563
Ghost Flower, 226, 556
Giant Blazing Star, 540
Giant Coreopsis, 489
Giant Four O'clock, 409
Giant Mountain Dandelion, 496
Giant Sequoia, 68
Giant Wakerobin, 404
Giant Woolystar, 334
Gilia, 436
Gilia angelensis, 228
Gilia capitata, 336
Gilia stellata, 229
Gilia tricolor, 337
Ginseng, 87
Giraffe Head, 394
Githopsis specularioides, 291
Gladiolus, 91
Glycyrrhiza glabra, 190
Glycyrrhiza lepidota, 190
Golden Aster, 485
Golden Currant, 533
Golden Desert Snapdragon, 556
Golden Eardrops, 551
Golden Linanthus, 558
Golden Suncup, 544
Golden Violet, 567
Golden Yarrow, 479
Gold Nuggets, 537
Gooding Verbena, 347
Goodyera oblongifolia, 220
Gooseberry, 90
Goosefoot, 88
Goosefoot Violet, 568
Gopherus agassizii, 117, 217
Gourd, 89

Grand Collomia, 468
Granite Prickly Phlox, 231
Grape, 97
Grapefruit, 95
Grape Soda Lupine, 298
grassland vegetation, 62–64
Grayia spinosa, 120
Gray Pine, 62
Gray's Lovage, 145
Greasewood, 79–80
Great Basin Desert, 58
Great Camas, 275
Great Valley Coyote Thistle, 110
Great Valley Phacelia, 305
green flowers, 109–131
Greya Moth, 263
Greya suffusca, 146
Grindelia camporum, 482
Grinnell's Beardtongue, 429
Gumweed, 482
Gunsight Clarkia, 413
Gymnogyps californianus, 81
Gypsophila, 88

Hackelia micrantha, 283
Hairy Desert Sunflower, 481
Hairy Pink, 371
Hairy Yerba Santa, 215
Harlequin Lotus, 528
Harlequin Lupine, 42, 43, 530
Hartweg's Doll's-lily, 96, 269
Hartweg's Umbrellawort, 111
Harvest Brodiaea, 345
Hawk Moth, 93
Hayfield Tarweed, 484
Hazardia squarrosa, 506
Hazelnut, 87
Heart-leaf Milkweed, 354
Heart-leaf Suncup, 545
Heartleaf Twistflower, 287
Heart-leaved Keckiella, 428
Heather, 89
Helenium bigelovii, 483
Helianthella californica, 483
Helianthella californica var. *nevadensis*, 483
Helianthus annuus, 46, 483
Helianthus gracilentus, 484

Heliotrope, 90
Heliotropium curassavicum, 194
Helminthotheca, 497
Helminthotheca echioides, 497
Hemizonia congesta, 484
Hemp Dogbane, 148
Heracleum maximum, 144
Hesperocallis undulata, 134
Hesperolinon, 91
Hesperoyucca whipplei, 86, 134
Heterocodon rariflorum, 292
Heteromeles arbutifolia, 61, 251
Heterotheca grandiflora, 485
Heterotheca sessiliflora, 485
Heuchera, 96
Heuchera micrantha, 262
Heuchera rubescens, 453
Hibiscus, 92
Hibiscus denudatus, 401
Hibiscus lasiocarpos, 208
Hieracium albiflorum, 151
Hiker's Fringed Gentian, 304
Hill Suncup, 547
Himalayan Blackberry, 65, 256
Hirschfeldia incana, 515
Hoary Buckwheat, 238
Hoary Tansy-aster, 278
Hoita macrostachya, 295
Hollyleaf Redberry, 127
Holodiscus discolor, 252
Honey Mesquite, 191
Honeysuckle, 88
Hooded Lady's Tresses, 221
Hooveria purpurea var. reducta, 105
Hop Clover, 533
Hopsage, 120
Horkelia tridentata, 252
Horned Sea Rocket, 362
Hosackia, 530
Hosackia gracilis, 528
Hosackia oblongifolia, 529
Howell's Onion, 276
Huckleberry Oak, 61, 68
Hulsea heterochroma, 356
Hulsea vestita, 486
Humboldt Lily, 463
Hummingbird, 361, 368, 447, 533
Hummingbird Sage, 395

Hydrangea, 90
Hydrangea, 90
Hydrocotyle, 87
Hypericum anagalloides, 535
Hypericum perforatum, 90, 535
Hypericum scouleri, 535
Hypochaeris glabra, 497
Hyptis, 310

Iceplant, 86, 136
Imbricate Phacelia, 197
Incense Cedar, 68
Indian Hedge Mustard, 519
Innocence, 328
Inside Out Lily, 269
Ipomopsis aggregata, 433
Ipomopsis congesta, 229
Iris, 91
Iris, 91
Iris douglasiana, 307
Iris hartwegii, 308
Iris macrosiphon, 308
Iris missouriensis, 309
Isatis tinctoria, 516
Island Bindweed, 178
Isocoma menziesii, 507
Italian Thistle, 358, 361
Ivesia gordonii, 563
Ivesia lycopodioides, 564
Ivesia santolinoides, 253

Jacob's Ladder, 339
Jared's Pepper Weed, 75, 517
Jeffrey Pine, 62, 68
Jepsonia heterandra, 263
Jepson Prairie, 75
Johnny Jump-up, 568
Jojoba, 96, 130
Joshua Tree, 57, 69, 75, 80, 135
Joshua Tree National Park, 75
Juniper, 62, 69
Juniperus, 62, 69
Justicia californica, 350

Kale, 87
Kalmia, 378
Kalmia polifolia, 377
Keckiella antirrhinoides, 557

Keckiella breviflora, 227
Keckiella cordifolia, 428
Keckiella lemmonii, 557
Kelley's Lily, 463
Kelloggia galioides, 452
Kellogg's Monkeyflower, 424
Kellogg's Snapdragon, 327
Kellogg's Tarweed, 477
Kern Mallow, 400
Kickxia elatine, 558
Kickxia spuria, 558
King Bladderpod, 517
Klamath Mountains, 55
Knotweed, 94
Knotweed Spineflower, 438
Kopsiopsis strobilacea, 326
Krameria, 91
Krameria bicolor, 393
Krascheninnikovia lanata, 177

Lactuca serriola, 498
Lacy Phacelia, 306
Lagophylla ramosissima, 486
Laguna Beach Dudleya, 104
Laguna Mountains Jewelflower,
   170
Lamium amplexicaule, 394
Lanceleaf Dudleya, 374
Large-leaved Avens, 563
Larrea tridentata, 69, 97, 569
Lasthenia conjugens, 106
Lasthenia fremontii, 487
Lasthenia gracilis, 41, 75, 487
Lathyrus, 302
Lathyrus latifolius, 382
Lathyrus sulphureus, 461
Lathyrus vestitus, 295
Laurel Sumac, 61, 138
Lawrence's Goldfinch, 458
Layia glandulosa, 150
Layia munzii, 41
Layia platyglossa, 488
Layne's Monkeyflower, 425
Leafy Fleabane, 279
Leek, 86
Lemmon's Ceanothus, 342
Lemmon's Keckiella, 557
Lemmon's Mustard, 166

Lemmon's Paintbrush, 325
Lemon, 95
Lemonade Berry, 79, 139
Lennoa, 91
Leopard Lily, 463
Lepechinia calycina, 310
Lepidium flavum, 516
Lepidium fremontii, 168
Lepidium jaredii, 75, 517
Lepidium nitidum, 168
Lepidospartum squamatum, 507
Leptosiphon chrysanthus, 558
Leptosiphon ciliatus, 433
Leptosiphon liniflorus, 230
Leptosiphon parviflorus, 230
Leptosyne bigelovii, 488
Leptosyne gigantea, 489
Lessingia glandulifera, 508
Lewisia, 92
Lewisia nevadensis, 213
Lewisia pygmaea, 213
Lewisia rediviva, 214
Lewisia triphylla, 214
Lewis' Monkeyflower, 426
Ligusticum grayi, 145
Lilium, 91
Lilium humboldtii, 463
Lilium kelleyanum, 463
Lilium occidentale, 106
Lilium pardalinum, 463
Lilium pardalinum subsp.
  wigginsii, 463
Lilium parvum, 464
Lilium washingtonianum, 206
Lily, 91
Lime, 95
Limnanthes, 75, 91
Limnanthes alba, 91, 207
Limnanthes douglasii, 538
Limonium, 333
Limonium californicum, 333
Limonium sinuatum, 333, 439
Linanthus californicus, 434
Linanthus californicus subsp.
  californicus, 434
Linanthus dichotomus, 231
Linanthus parryae, 42, 337
Linanthus pungens, 231

Linnaea borealis, 92, 399
Linum, 91
Linum bienne, 322
Linum lewisii, 322
Linum usitatissimum, 91
Listera convallarioides, 124
Lithophragma affine, 263
Little Elephant's Head, 419, 420
Little Hop, 533
Little Western Bittercress, 165
Lizard's Tail, 96
Loasa, 92
Lobb's Buckwheat, 440
Lobeleaf Groundsel, 491
Lobelia, 88
Lobelia, 88
Lobularia maritima, 169
Lodgepole Pine, 68, 177
Loeseliastrum matthewsii, 434
Logfia filaginoides, 157
Lomatium californicum, 111
Lomatium dasycarpum, 145
Lomatium macrocarpum, 146
Lomatium mohavense, 145
Lomatium utriculatum, 471
Long-Beak Stork's Bill, 388
Longbeak Streptanthella, 116
Longspine Horsebrush, 510
Longspur Seablush, 456
Longstalk Clover, 385
Longstem Buckwheat, 235
Lonicera, 88
Lonicera ciliosa, 368
Lonicera hispidula, 368
Lonicera involucrata, 369
Loosestrife, 92
Lopseed, 94
Lotus Blue Butterfly, 528
Lotus purshianus, 189
Ludwigia peploides, 546
Lupine, 75
Lupinus, 75
Lupinus albifrons, 296
Lupinus arboreus, 529
Lupinus benthamii, 296
Lupinus bicolor, 297
Lupinus concinnus, 297
Lupinus excubitus, 298

Lupinus microcarpus, 382
Lupinus nanus, 298
Lupinus stiversii, 42, 530
Lupinus succulentus, 299
Lycium, 96
Lycium andersonii, 266
Lycium cooperi, 266
Lysichiton americanus, 473
Lysimachia, 92
Lysimachia arvensis, 465
Lysimachia latifolia, 92, 406
Lythrum, 92
Lythrum californicum, 399

Macloskey's Violet, 272
Madder, 95
Madia elegans, 489
Maianthemum, 95
Maianthemum stellatum, 259
Malacothamnus davidsonii, 107
Malacothamnus fasciculatus, 401
Malacothamnus fremontii, 401
Malacothrix californica, 498
Malacothrix glabrata, 75, 499
Malacothrix saxatilis, 152
Mallow, 92
Malosma laurina, 61, 138
Malva assurgentiflora, 402
Malva neglecta, 208
Mammillaria tetrancistra, 366
Many-flowered Monkeyflower,
  554, 555
Manzanita, 61, 68, 89
Maple, 64, 95
maps, 44
Marah fabacea, 182
Marah macrocarpa, 182
Mariposa Lily, 80–81
Marjoram, 91
Marrubium vulgare, 199
Marsh Grass-of-Parnassus, 225
Marsh Purslane, 546
Marsh Rosemary, 333
Matricaria discoidea, 508
Meadow Beardtongue, 331
Meadow Death Camas, 209
Meadowfoam, 75, 91
Meadow Stickseed, 283

Medicago polymorpha, 530
Medicago sativa, 299
Melilotus indicus, 531
Melilotus officinalis, 531
Melissa Blue Butterfly, 189
Melon, 89
Mentha spicata, 311
Mentzelia, 92
Mentzelia affinis, 539
Mentzelia dispersa, 539
Mentzelia laevicaulis, 540
Mentzelia veatchiana, 539
Menyanthes trifoliata, 92, 211
Menzies' Fiddleneck, 458
Menzies' Goldenbush, 507
Mertensia ciliata, 284
Mertensia ciliata var.
  stomatechoides, 285
Mesembryanthemum crystallinum,
  136
Micranthes californica, 264
Micranthes tolmiei, 264
Micropus californicus, 157
Microseris nutans, 499
Microsteris gracilis, 435
Milk Kelloggia, 452
Milk Maids, 165
Milk Thistle, 361
Milkvetch, 190, 380
Milkweed, 86, 148
Milkwort, 94
Milkwort Jewelflower, 289
Mimetanthe, 94
Mimetanthe pilosa, 555
Mimulus, 94, 423
Miner's Lettuce, 92, 212
Miniature Lupine, 297
Mint, 91
Minuartia californica, 174
Minuartia douglasii, 174
Mirabilis, 93
Mirabilis laevis, 408
Mirabilis multiflora, 409
Mission Bells, 122
Mission Blue Butterfly, 296
Mission Manzanita, 380
Mission Prickly-pear, 88, 520
Mitella, 454

Mock Orange, 90, 195
Modesty, 195
Mohavea, 556
Mojave Desert, 57
Mojave Indigobush, 300
Mojave Kingcup Cactus, 366
Mojave Lomatium, 145
Mojave Pincushion, 156
Mojave Stinkweed, 521
Mojave Suncup, 542
Mojave Woody Aster, 281
Mojave Yucca, 135
Monarch Butterfly, 353, 354, 394,
  473
Monardella breweri, 311
Monardella macrantha, 395
Monardella odoratissima, 312
Monardella villosa, 312
Monkshood, 340
Mono Lake Aliciella, 228
Monolopia lanceolata, 75, 490
Monument Plant, 193
Morning Glory, 88
Mosquito Bill, 446
Moth Combseed, 162
Mountain Butterweed, 492
Mountain Carpet Clover, 192
Mountain Coyote Mint, 312
Mountain Fringepod, 171
Mountain Gooseberry, 534
Mountain Hemlock, 68
Mountain Lady's Slipper, 220
Mountain Maple, 129
Mountain Misery, 68, 248
Mountain Pride, 430
Mountain Threadplant, 172
Mount Diablo Fairy-Lantern, 536
Mount Hood Pussypaws, 406
Mousetail, 243
Mousetail Ivesia, 253
Muilla maritima, 269
Mule Fat, 155
Mule's Ears, 68
Munz's Tidy Tips, 41
Muskroot, 97
Mustard, 68, 87
Myoporum laetum, 265
Myosotis laxa, 284

Myosurus minimus, 243
Myrica, 92
Myrsine, 92

Naked Buckwheat, 80, 236
Nama, 92–93
Nama, 93
Nama demissa, 407
Nama demissa var. *demissum*, 407
Narrowflower Flaxflower, 230
Narrow-leaf Goldenbush, 479
Narrowleaf Milkweed, 354
Narrowleaf Onion, 138
Narrowleaf Soap Plant, 133
Narrow-Leaved Bedstraw, 127
Narrow-leaved Lotus, 529
Nasturtium, 97, 169, 468
Nasturtium officinale, 169
Navarretia breweri, 559
Navarretia intertexta, 232
Navarretia leucocephala, 232
Navarretia pubescens, 338
Needle-leaf Navarretia, 232
Nemacladus montanus, 172
Nemacladus rubescens, 173
Nemophila heterophylla, 196
Nemophila maculata, 197
Nemophila menziesii, 304
Nemophila menziesii var.
  atomaria, 304
Nettle, 97
Nettle-leaf Giant Hyssop, 394
Nevada Lewisia, 213
Ngaio Tree, 265
Nicotiana attenuata, 267
Nicotiana glauca, 565
Nicotiana quadrivalvis, 267
Nightshade, 96, 217
Nodding Microseris, 499
Nolina, 95
Nolina parryi, 260
North Coast Dunes, 75
Northern Water-Plantain,
  136
Nuphar polysepala, 542
Nuttallanthus texanus, 330
Nuttall's Snapdragon, 327
Nymphaea odorata, 216

Oak, 62
Oceanspray, 252
Ocotillo, 58, 75, 386
Odontostomum, 269
Odontostomum hartwegii, 96, 269
Oemleria cerasiformis, 253
Oenothera, 93
Oenothera californica, 218
Oenothera californica subsp. *eurekensis*, 107
Oenothera deltoides, 219
Oenothera elata, 546
Oenothera xylocarpa, 547
Olive, 93
One-seeded Pussypaws, 405, 406
Onion, 86
Opium Poppy, 94, 466
Opuntia basilaris, 367
Opuntia ficus-indica, 88, 520
Opuntia littoralis, 460
Opuntia phaeacantha, 460
Orange, 95
orange flowers, 457–468
Orange Honeysuckle, 368
Orchid, 93
Oregano, 91
Oregon Checkerbloom, 404
Oregon Grape, 511
Oreocarya confertiflora, 512
Oreostemma alpigenum, 280
Orobanche, 93
Orthilia secunda, 186
Osmorhiza brachypoda, 146
Oso Berry, 253
Oxalis, 93
Oxalis californica, 67
Oxalis oregana, 326
Oxalis pes-caprae, 550
Oxyria digyna, 441
Oxytheca perfoliata, 442

Pacific Aster, 280
Pacific Bindweed, 374
Pacific Bleeding Heart, 422
Pacific Dogwood, 180
Pacific Hound's Tongue, 282, 362
Pacific Madrone, 67
Pacific Ninebark, 254

Pacific Onion, 353
Pacific Pea, 295
Pacific Rhododendron, 378
Pacific Sanicle, 472
Packera cana, 490
Packera multilobata, 491
Padre's Shooting Star, 445
Paeonia, 421
Paeonia brownii, 421
Paeonia californica, 421
Paintbrush, 93
Palafoxia arida, 360
Palafoxia arida var. *gigantea*, 360
Pale Face, 401
Pale Flax, 322
Pale Smartweed, 442
Pale Yellow Suncup, 544
Pallid Manzanita, 100
Palmer's Abutilon, 464
Panamint Daisy, 478
Panax ginseng, 87
Papaver californicum, 466
Papaver heterophyllum, 467
Papaver somniferum, 94, 466
Paperbag Bush, 318
Parentucellia viscosa, 548
Parish's Yampah, 147
Parkinsonia florida, 531
Parnasia, 94
Parnasia, 94
Parnassia palustris, 225
Parrot-head Paintbrush, 125
Parry's Beargrass, 260
Parry's Blue-eyed Mary, 329
Parry's Linanthus, 42, 43, 337
Parry's Mallow, 400
Parsnip, 86
Pea, 82, 89
Peach Thorn, 266
Peak Rush-rose, 521
Pearly Everlasting, 154
Pectiantia breweri, 129
Pectocarya penicillata, 161
Pectocarya setosa, 162
Pedicularis attollens, 419
Pedicularis densiflora, 420
Pedicularis groenlandica, 420
Pedicularis semibarbata, 549

Peninsula Onion, 352
Penstemon, 68
Penstemon, 60, 69, 428
Penstemon centranthifolius, 428
Penstemon davidsonii, 330
Penstemon davidsonii var. *davidsonii*, 330
Penstemon eatonii, 429
Penstemon grinnellii, 429
Penstemon heterophyllus, 331
Penstemon newberryi, 430
Penstemon rostriflorus, 430
Penstemon rydbergii, 331
Penstemon speciosus, 332
Penstemon spectabilis, 332
Peony, 93–94
Pepper, 96
Perennial Sweet Pea, 382
Perideridia parishii, 147
Perideridia parishii subsp. *latifolia*, 147
Perideridia parishii subsp. *parishii*, 147
Peritoma arborea, 88, 522
Perityle emoryi, 151
Persicaria lapathifolia, 442
Petasites frigidus, 152
Petrorhagia dubia, 371
Peucephyllum schottii, 509
Phacelia, 75
Phacelia, 75
Phacelia bicolor, 393
Phacelia campanularia, 305
Phacelia ciliata, 305
Phacelia distans, 306
Phacelia fremontii, 393
Phacelia imbricata, 197
Phacelia minor, 305
Phacelia ramosissima, 198
Phacelia tanacetifolia, 306
Phantom Orchid, 219
Philadelphus, 90
Philadelphus lewisii, 195
Phlox, 68, 94
Phlox diffusa, 233
Phlox speciosa, 435
Phlox stansburyi, 436
Phoenicaulis cheiranthoides, 287
Pholisma arenarium, 320
Pholisma sonorae, 376

Pholistoma auritum, 306
Pholistoma membranaceum, 198
photos, 44
Phyla nodiflora, 97, 271
Phyllodoce breweri, 378
Physalis crassifolia, 566
Physaria kingii, 517
Physocarpus capitatus, 254
Phytolacca americana, 94, 225
Picherplant, 95–96
Pieris, 378
Pine, 67
Pineapple Weed, 508
Pinewoods Fritillary, 123
Pinewoods Lousewort, 549
Pinguicula macroceras, 66
Pink, 88
Pink Alumroot, 453
Pink Fairy Duster, 78, 381
Pink Honeysuckle, 368
Pink Sand Verbena, 408
Pink Spineflower, 438
pink to red flowers, 349–456
Pinpoint Clover, 300
Pinus, 67
Pinus contorta, 68
Pinus jeffreyi, 68
Pinus lambertiana, 68
Pinus monophylla, 69
Pinus ponderosa, 68
Pinus sabiniana, 62
Pinyon, 69
Piperia unalascensis, 124
Piperia yadonii, 108
Pipevine, 87
Pipevine Swallowtail Butterfly, 355
Pipsissewa, 377
Pismo Clarkia, 412
Plagiobothrys arizonicus, 162
Plagiobothrys nothofulvus, 163
Plagiobothrys tenellus, 163
Plain Mariposa Lily, 202, 321
Plantago, 94
Plantago erecta, 227
Plantago ovata, 227
Plantain, 94
plant blueprint, 78–79
plant families, 45, 82, 84–97

plant identification, 45–46
plant morphology, 46–51
plant parts, 76–78
Platanthera dilatata, 221
Platanthera dilatata var. *leucostachys*, 221
Platanus racemosa, 65
Platystemon californicus, 552
Plectritis, 97
Plectritis ciliosa, 456
Pleiacanthus spinosus, 357
Pluchea odorata, 360
Pluchea sericea, 360
Plummer's Mariposa Lily, 397
Poa, 63
Pogogyne clareana, 64
Pogogyne douglasii, 313
Poison Angelica, 141
Poison Hemlock, 86, 143
Poison Ivy, 177
Poison Oak, 74, 86, 140
Poison Sanicle, 472
Pokeweed, 94
Polemonium eximium, 338
Polemonium occidentale, 339
Polemonium pulcherrimum, 339
Polemonium pulcherrimum var. *pulcherrimum*, 339
Polygala, 94
Polygala californica, 437
Polygala cornuta, 437
Polygonatum, 259
Polygonum, 94
Polygonum aviculare, 239
Polystichum, 67
Pomegranate, 92
Ponderosa Pine, 177
Poodle-dog Bush, 323
Poppy, 75, 94
Populus, 64
Porterella carnosula, 292
Potato, 96
Potentilla gracilis, 564
Prairie Flax, 322
Prettyface, 567
Prickly Lettuce, 498
Prickly Poppy, 223
Pride of Madeira, 283

Primrose, 95
Primula, 95
Primula clevelandii, 445
Primula hendersonii, 446
Primula jeffreyi, 446
Primula suffrutescens, 447
Proboscidea, 92
Proboscidea althaeifolia, 541
Prosopis glandulosa, 191
Prostrate Knotweed, 239
Prostrate Pigweed, 110
Prunella vulgaris, 313
Prunus andersonii, 449
Prunus emarginata, 254
Prunus fasciculata, 255
Prunus virginiana, 255
Psathyrotes ramosissima, 509
Pseudognaphalium californicum, 158
Pseudostellaria jamesiana, 175
Pseudotsuga menziesii, 67, 68
Psoralea, 295
Psorothamnus arborescens, 300
Psorothamnus fremontii, 300
Pterospora andromedea, 187
Pterostegia drymarioides, 443
Pumice Alpinegold, 486
Puncture Vine, 569
Purple False Gilia, 431
Purple Fawn Lily, 205
Purplemat, 407
Purple Mouse Ears, 423
Purple Needlegrass, 63
Purple Owl's Clover, 42, 44, 75, 325
Purple Salsify, 501
Purple Sanicle, 276
Purple Three-awn, 63
purple to blue flowers, 274–348
Purshia tridentata, 256
Pyrola picta, 187

Q-tips, 157
Queen Anne's Lace, 143, 144
Quercus, 62, 67
Quercus berberidifolia, 61
Quercus chrysolepis, 65
Quercus lobata, 65
Quercus vaccinifolia, 61, 68

Radish, 364
Rafinesquia californica, 153
Ragged Rockflower, 89, 181
Rainbow Iris, 308
Rancheria Clover, 300, 383
Ranger's Buttons, 141
Ranunculus aquatilis, 244
Ranunculus californicus, 561
Ranunculus eschscholtzii, 561
Raphanus sativus, 364
rare species, 41, 98–108
Ratany, 91
Rattlesnake Plantain, 220
Rattlesnake Sandmat, 188
Rattlesnake Weed, 144
Red Admiral Butterfly, 130
Red Baneberry, 240
Red Elderberry, 272
Red Fir, 68
Red Flowering Currant, 392
Red Larkspur, 448
Redmaids, 405
Red Monardella, 395
Red Osier Dogwood, 181
Redray Alpinegold, 356
Red Ribbons, 410
Red Sandspurry, 373
Red Sand Verbena, 407
Redshanks, 246
Red-skinned Onion, 352
Redspot Clarkia, 412
Red Triangles, 233
Redwood Ivy, 159
Redwood Sorrel, 67, 326
Rhamnus ilicifolia, 127
Rhodiola integrifolia, 375
Rhododendron, 378
Rhododendron macrophyllum, 378
Rhododendron occidentale, 188
Rhus aromatica, 139
Rhus integrifolia, 79, 139
Rhus ovata, 79, 140
Ribes, 68
Ribes aureum, 533
Ribes cereum, 390
Ribes malvaceum, 390

Ribes malvaceum var. *viridifolium*, 390
Ribes montigenum, 534
Ribes nevadense, 391
Ribes roezlii, 391
Ribes sanguineum, 392
Ribes speciosum, 392
Ricinus communis, 122
Rigid Bird's Beak, 222
riparian vegetation, 65–66
Rockfringe Willowherb, 415
Rock rose, 88
Rocky Mountain Pond-lily, 542
Romneya coulteri, 79, 224
Rorippa curvisiliqua, 518
Rosa, 95
Rosa californica, 449
Rosa woodsii, 450
Rose, 95
Rose Clover, 384
Rose Mallow, 208
Rose Meadowsweet, 451
Rose Spiraea, 451
Rosin Weed, 476
Rotala, 92
Rough Cocklebur, 115
Rough Hedge-nettle, 396
Roundhead Collinsia, 75, 103
Roundleaf Brook Foam, 262
Roundleaf Oxytheca, 442
Round-leaved Snowberry, 370
Round-leaved Sundew, 376
Royal Beardtongue, 332
Royal Mallow, 402
Rubber Rabbitbrush, 506
Rubus, 65, 68
Rubus armeniacus, 65, 256
Rubus parviflorus, 67, 257
Rubus spectabilis, 450
Rubus ursinus, 257
Ruby Chalice Clarkia, 412
Rudbeckia californica, 491
Rumex acetosella, 443
Rumex crispus, 444
Rumex hymenosepalus, 444
Rumex salicifolius, 445
Rush Milkweed, 473
Rush-rose, 88

Russian Thistle, 120
Rusty Popcorn Flower, 163

Sacapellote, 357
Sack Clover, 384
Sacred Datura, 265
Sacred Tobacco, 267
Sage, 91
Sagebrush, 87
Sagina decumbens, 175
Sagina decumbens subsp. *occidentalis*, 175
Sagittaria, 86
Sagittaria latifolia, 137
Saguaro, 58
Sahara Mustard, 513
Salal, 61, 186
Salix, 65
Salmonberry, 450
Salsola tragus, 120
Saltbush, 67
Saltcedar, 455
Salt Heliotrope, 194
Salt Marsh Bird's Beak, 222
Saltmarsh Fleabane, 360
Saltugilia splendens, 436
Salvia apiana, 200
Salvia carduacea, 314
Salvia clevelandii, 314
Salvia columbariae, 315
Salvia dorrii, 315
Salvia dorrii var. *pilosa*, 315
Salvia leucophylla, 316
Salvia mellifera, 316
Salvia pachyphylla, 317
Salvia sonomensis, 317
Salvia spathacea, 395
Sambucus, 97
Sambucus mexicana, 272
Sambucus racemosa, 272
San Bernardino Larkspur, 341
Sandfood, 376
Sand Fringepod, 170
Sand Verbena, 67, 75, 93
Sandweed, 164
Sandy Soil Suncup, 543
San Francisco Campion, 108

San Gabriel Mountains Live-forever, 104
Sanicula bipinnata, 472
Sanicula bipinnatifida, 276
Sanicula crassicaulis, 472
San Luis Purple Sage, 316
Santa Barbara Milkvetch, 190
Santa Catalina Mariposa Lily, 202
Santa Monica Mountains, 75
Sapphire Woolystar, 335
Sarcobatus vermiculatus, 80
Sarcodes sanguinea, 379
Saskatoon Serviceberry, 246
Sauromalus ater, 465
Sawtooth Goldenbush, 506
Saxifrage, 96
Scalebroom, 507
Scale Bud, 496
Scarlet Bugler, 428
Scarlet Fritillary, 398
Scarlet Gilia, 433
Scarlet Larkspur, 448
Scarlet Milkvetch, 380
Scarlet Monkeyflower, 426
Scarlet Paintbrush, 419
Scarlet Pimpernel, 465
Scattered Blazing Star, 539
Schott's Pygmy Cedar, 509
scientific names, 45, 80–81
Scoliopus bigelovii, 398
Scotch Broom, 527
Scouler's Harebell, 172
Scouler's St. Johns Wort, 535
Scrophularia californica, 96, 454
Scrub Oak, 61
Scutellaria californica, 200
Scutellaria mexicana, 318
Scutellaria tuberosa, 318
Scytheleaf Onion, 351
Seacliff Buckwheat, 237
Sea Muilla, 269
Seaside Fleabane, 279
Seaside Wooly Sunflower, 479, 480
Sea Thrift, 431
Sedella pumila, 523
Sedum, 523

Sedum obtusatum, 523
Sedum spathulifolium, 524
Seep Monkeyflower, 554, 555
Self-heal, 313
Senecio flaccidus, 492
Senecio flaccidus var. *douglasii*, 492
Senecio integerrimus, 492
Senecio triangularis, 492
Senecio vulgaris, 510
Senegalia greggii, 191
Senna armata, 532
Sequoiadendron giganteum, 68
Sequoia sempervirens, 67
Serpentine Spring-beauty, 211
Shadscale, 69
Sharp-leaved Cancer Wort, 558
Sheep Sorrel, 443
Shepherd's Purse, 164
Shieldplant, 289
Shining Pepperweed, 168
shoot apical meristem (SAM), 78
Shortpod Mustard, 513, 515
Short-tailed Black Swallowtail Butterfly, 470
Showy Penstemon, 332
Showy Phlox, 435
Shrubby Cinquefoil, 562
shrubland vegetation, 61
Sicklepod Rockcress, 286
Sidalcea diploscypha, 402
Sidalcea hartwegii, 403
Sidalcea malviflora, 403
Sidalcea oregana, 404
Sidalcea oregana subsp. *oregana*, 404
Sidalcea oregana subsp. *spicata*, 404
Sidebells Wintergreen, 186
Sierra Columbine, 241
Sierra Currant, 391
Sierra Gentian, 304
Sierra Gooseberry, 391
Sierra Larkspur, 340
Sierra Milkwort, 437
Sierra Mock Stonecrop, 523
Sierra Nevada, 54–55
Sierra Onion, 351
Sierra Primrose, 447

Sierra Shooting Star, 446
Sierra Stonecrop, 523
Sierra Tiger Lily, 464
Silene antirrhina, 176
Silene gallica, 371
Silene laciniata, 372
Silene verecunda, 372
Silene verecunda subsp. *verecunda*, 108
Silk Tassel, 61, 90
Silver Beachweed, 112
Silver Cholla, 117
Silverleaf Cotoneaster, 249
Silverleaf Nightshade, 343
Silver Lupine, 296
Silver Puffs, 501
Silybum marianum, 361
Simarouba, 96
Simmondsia chinensis, 96, 130
Single-leaf Pinyon, 69
Siskiyou Fireweed, 415
Sisymbrium altissimum, 518
Sisymbrium orientale, 519
Sisyrinchium bellum, 309
Sisyrinchium californicum, 536
Skunk Bush, 139
Skunky Monkeyflower, 425
Sky Lupine, 298
Sky Pilot, 338
Sleeping Combseed, 161
Sleepy Silene, 176
Slender Bird's Beak, 223
Slender Cinquefoil, 564
Slender Clarkia, 411
Slender Phlox, 435
Slender Popcorn Flower, 163
Slender Sunflower, 484
Slender Wild Cabbage, 166
Small-headed Clover, 385
Small Wire Lettuce, 358
Smith's Blue Butterfly, 439
Smokey Mariposa Lily, 203
Smooth Cat's Ear, 497
Smooth Desert Dandelion, 75, 499
Snake Lily, 455
Snapdragon Penstemon, 557
Snowberry, 88

Snowdrop Bush, 96, 268
Snow Plant, 379
Soapberry, 95
Solanum, 96
Solanum americanum, 268
Solanum elaeagnifolium, 343
Solanum xanti, 344
Solidago velutina, 493
Solomon's Seal, 259
Sonchus asper, 500
Sonoran Desert, 58
Sorbus californica, 258
Sour Clover, 531
Southern California Mountains., 56–57
Spanish Broom, 532
Spanish Lotus, 189
Spartium junceum, 532
Spearmint, 311
Spergularia macrotheca, 373
Spergularia rubra, 373
Sphaeralcea ambigua, 465
Spice Bush, 367
Spiderflower, 88
Spider Lupine, 296
Spineless Horsebrush, 511
Spiny Sowthistle, 500
Spiraea densiflora, 451
Spiraea douglasii, 451
Spiraea splendens, 451
Spiranthes romanzoffiana, 221
Splendid Mariposa Lily, 202, 321
Splendid Woodland Gilia, 436
Spotted Buckwheat, 440
Spotted Coral Root, 416
Spotted Fritillary, 123
Spotted Hideseed, 196
Spreading Groundsmoke, 218
Spreading Phlox, 233
Springbank Clover, 386
Spring Draba, 167
Springville Clarkia, 103
Spurge, 89
Spurry Buckwheat, 238
Squash, 89
Stachys albens, 201
Stachys bullata, 396
Stachys rigida, 396

Stachys rigida var. *quercetorum*, 396
Stachys rigida var. *rigida*, 396
Staining Collomia, 432
Star Gilia, 229
Starflower, 92, 406
Starry False Lily of the Valley, 259
Star Water-Plantain, 137
Statice, 333, 439
Stebbins's Morning Glory, 102
Steer's Head, 422
Stellaria media, 176
Stephanomeria exigua, 358
Sticktight, 502
Sticky Cinquefoil, 250
Sticky Sandspurry, 373
Stickywilly, 259
Stinging Nettle, 97, 130
Stinky Gourd, 524
Stipa pulchra, 63
St. John's Wort, 90
Stonecrop, 89
Storax, 96
Storax, 96
Stream Orchid, 417
Streamside Bluebells, 284
Streptanthella longirostris, 116
Streptanthus bernardinus, 170
Streptanthus cordatus, 287
Streptanthus farnsworthianus, 288
Streptanthus glandulosus, 288
Streptanthus polygaloides, 289
Streptanthus tortuosus, 289
Streptopus amplexifolius, 206
Strigose Lotus, 526
Striped Coral Root, 417
Stylomecon heterophylla, 467
Styrax redivivus, 96, 268
Sugar Bush, 79, 140
Sugar Pine, 68
Sugarstick, 183, 187
Sulphur Buckwheat, 560
Sulphur Creek Brodiaea, 101
Sulphur Pea, 461
Summer Coral Root, 417
Sundew, 66, 89
Sunflower, 42, 82, 87
Superb Mariposa Lily, 203

Sweet Alyssum, 169
Sweetbush, 502
Sweet Pea, 302
Swertia, 90
Sword Fern, 67
Sydney Golden Wattle, 525
Symphoricarpos, 88
Symphoricarpos albus, 369
Symphoricarpos mollis, 370
Symphoricarpos rotundifolius, 370
Symphyotrichum chilense, 280
Symphyotrichum subspicatum, 280
Syntrichopappus fremontii, 493
Syrphid Fly, 417

Table Mountain, 75
Tall Evening Primrose, 546
Tall Sock-destroyer, 142, 147
Tamarisk, 96
Tamarisk, 96
Tamarix ramosissima, 455
Tangled Snapdragon, 556
Taraxacum, 87
Taraxacum officinale, 500
Tauschia hartwegii, 111
Tecophilaea, 96
Teddybear Cholla, 116
Tehachapi Buckwheat, 98, 99
Tehachapi Woolystar, 335
Telegraph Weed, 485
Tellima grandiflora, 454
Tetradymia axillaris, 510
Tetradymia canescens, 511
Tetrapteron, 547
Tetrapteron graciliflorum, 547
Texas Stork's Bill, 389
Thalictrum fendleri, 126
Thamnosma montana, 343
Theobroma cacao),, 92
Thick-leaved Ground Cherry, 566
Thimbleberry, 67
Thistle Sage, 314, 315
Thorn Skeletonweed, 357
Threadleaf Ragwort, 492
threats, 70–73
Three Hearts, 307
Three-leaf Lewisia, 214
Three-tooth Horkelia, 252

Thysanocarpus curvipes, 170
Thysanocarpus laciniatus, 171
Tiburon Mariposa Lily, 101
Tidy Tips, 488
Tiling's Monkeyflower, 555
Tincture Plant, 427
Tinker's Penny, 535
Tiquilia, 89
Tiquilia plicata, 376
Tolmie's Saxifrage, 264
Tolmie Star-tulip, 320, 321
Tomato, 96
Tomcat Clover, 301
Toothed Calico Flower, 290
Torilis arvensis, 142, 147
Tower Mustard, 171
Toxicodendron, 86
Toxicodendron diversilobum, 74, 140
Toxicoscordion, 92
Toxicoscordion fremontii, 209
Toxicoscordion venenosus, 209
Toyon, 61, 251
Tragopogon dubius, 501
Tragopogon porrifolius, 501
Transmontane Sand Verbena, 215
Tree Tobacco, 565
Triantha occidentalis, 66, 270
Tribulus terrestris, 569
Tricardia watsonii, 307
Trichostema lanatum, 319
Trichostema lanceolatum, 319
Trientalis, 406
Trifolium albopurpureum, 383
Trifolium aureum, 533
Trifolium ciliolatum, 383
Trifolium depauperatum, 384
Trifolium dubium, 533
Trifolium gracilentum, 300
Trifolium hirtum, 384
Trifolium longipes, 385
Trifolium microcephalum, 385
Trifolium monanthum, 192
Trifolium variegatum, 301
Trifolium variegatum var. *geminiflorum*, 301
Trifolium variegatum var. *major*, 301

Trifolium variegatum var. *variegatum*, 301
Trifolium willdenovii, 301
Trifolium wormskioldii, 386
Trillium, 92, 404
Trillium chloropetalum, 404
Trillium ovatum, 209
Triphysaria, 421
Triphysaria eriantha, 549
Triphysaria pusilla, 421
Triteleia, 97
Triteleia hyacinthina, 270
Triteleia ixioides, 567
Triteleia laxa, 346
Tropaeolum, 97
Tropaeolum majus, 169, 468
Tropidocarpum gracile, 519
Trumpet Creeper, 87
Tsuga heterophylla, 67
Tsuga mertensiana, 68
Tuber Starwort, 175
Tufted Poppy, 551
Tumble Mustard, 518
Tundra Aster, 280
Turkey Tangle Fogfruit, 97, 271
Turkish Rugging, 439
Turpentine Broom, 343
Turpentine Cymopterus, 470
Turritis glabra, 171
Twinberry Honeysuckle, 369
Twincrest Onion, 351
Twinflower, 91–92, 399
Twisted Stalk, 206
Two-color Phacelia, 393
Typha latifolia, 66

Umbellularia californica, 67
Umbrella Plant, 453
Unicorn Plant, 92
Uropappus lindleyi, 501
Urtica, 97
Urtica dioica, 130
Utah Serviceberry, 247

Vaccinium ovatum, 379
Valerian, 97, 271
Valeriana, 97
Valeriana californica, 271

Valeriana officinalis, 271
Valley Calico Flower, 291
Valley Checkerbloom, 403
Valley Lessingia, 508
Valley Oak, 65
Valley Tassels, 125, 324
Vancouveria, 87
Vancouveria hexandra, 158
Vancouveria planipetala, 159
Variable-leaf Collomia, 432
Variable Linanthus, 230
Veatch's Blazing Star, 539
vegetation, 60–69
Velvet Turtleback, 509
Velvety Goldenrod, 493
Venegasia carpesioides, 494
Veratrum, 92
Veratrum californicum, 210
Verbascum thapsus, 565
Verbena, 97
Verbena, 97
Verbena gooddingii, 347
Verbena lasiostachys, 347
vernal pool vegetation, 64
Veronica americana, 333
Vetch, 302
Vicia, 302
Vicia americana, 302
Vicia sativa, 302
Vicia villosa, 303
Vinca major, 277
Vinegar weed, 319
Viola, 97
Viola, 97
Viola beckwithii, 348
Viola douglasii, 567
Viola macloskeyi, 272
Viola pedunculata, 568
Viola purpurea, 568
Vitis californica, 65, 131
Vitis vinifera, 97

Wallace's Wooly Daisy, 481, 493
Wallflower, 459
Wally Basket, 346
Wand Buckwheat, 441
Warrior's Plume, 420
Washington Lily, 206

Watercress, 169
Water Jacket, 266
Waterleaf, 90
Waterlily, 93
Water plantain, 86
Wavy-leaf Paintbrush, 418
Wavyleaf Soap Plant, 133
Weak-stem Cat's Eyes, 160
Wedgeleaf Draba, 167
West Coast Lady Butterfly, 403
Western Anemone, 240
Western Azalea, 188
Western Blue-eyed Grass, 309
Western Blue Flag, 309
Western Chokecherry, 255
Western False Asphodel, 66, 270
Western Gray Squirrel, 540
Western Hazelnut, 159
Western Hemlock, 67
Western Hound's Tongue, 362
Western Lily, 106
Western Moss Heather, 185
Western Pearl-flower, 292
Western Pearlwort, 175
Western Polemonium, 339
Western Redbud, 381
Western Roseroot, 375
Western Rue-anemone, 243
Western Tailed Blue butterfly, 190
Western Tansy-Mustard, 514
Western Thimbleberry, 257
Western Trillium, 209
Western Verbena, 347
Western Water Hemlock, 145
Western White Clematis, 242
wetland vegetation, 66
Whipplea modesta, 195
Whiskerbrush, 433
Whispering Bells, 534
White Bog Orchid, 221
White-daisy Tidy Tips, 150
White Fiesta Flower, 198
white flowers, 132–273
White Globe Lily, 81, 201, 536
White Goosefoot, 119
White Hawkweed, 151
Whitehead Navarretia, 232

White Horehound, 199
White Inside-out Flower, 158
Whiteleaf Manzanita, 185
White Marsh Marigold, 241
White Meadowfoam, 91, 207
White Rhatany, 393
White Sage, 200
Whitestem Frasera, 193
Whitestem Hedge-nettle, 201
Whitetip Clover, 301
White-veined Wintergreen, 187
White Water Buttercup, 244
Wide-throat Monkeyflower, 553
Wiggins' Lily, 463
Wilcox's Woolystar, 336
Wild Buckwheat, 94
Wild Cabbage, 87
Wild Cucumber, 182
wildflower viewing areas, 74–75
Wild Ginger, 87
Wild Hyacinth, 270
Wild Licorice, 190
Wild Radish, 364
Wild Rhubarb, 444
Wild Tarragon, 114
Willow, 65
Willow Dock, 445
Willowherb, 93
Windmill Pink, 371
Wind Poppy, 467
Winecup Clarkia, 411
Wing-nut Cat's Eyes, 161
Winter Fat, 177
Winter Vetch, 303
Wiry Snapdragon, 328
Woodbalm, 310
Woodland Pinedrops, 187
Woodland Strawberry, 251
woodland vegetation, 62
Woods' Rose, 450
Woodyfruit Evening Primrose, 547
Wooly Fruited Lomatium, 145
Wooly Paintbrush, 418
Wooly Bluecurls, 319
Wooly Groundsel, 490

Wooly Mule's Ears, 495
Wooly Mullein, 565
Woolypod Milkvetch, 294
Woolypod Milkweed, 79, 80, 148
Wyethia, 68
Wyethia angustifolia, 494
Wyethia mollis, 495

Xanthium strumarium, 115
Xerophyllum, 92
Xerophyllum tenax, 210
Xylococcus bicolor, 380
Xylorhiza tortifolia, 281

Yadon's Piperia, 108
Yarrow, 150
Yellow and White Monkeyflower, 553
Yellow Bush Lupine, 529
Yellow Carpet, 475
Yellow Comet, 539
Yellow-eyed Grass, 536
Yellow-flowered Oreocarya, 512
yellow flowers, 469–570
Yellow Glandweed, 548
Yellow Pepper Weed, 516
Yellow Pincushion, 504
Yellow Pine, 68
Yellow Rabbitbrush, 504
Yellow Salsify, 501
Yellow Skunk Cabbage, 473
Yellow Star-thistle, 402, 503
Yellow Star Tulip, 538
Yellow Sweetclover, 531
Yellow Turbans, 560
Yerba Buena, 199
Yerba Mansa, 261
Yucca, 86
Yucca brevifolia, 57, 80, 135
Yucca schidigera, 135

Zantedeschia aethiopica, 149
Zauschneria, 414
Zeltnera venusta, 387
Zerene eurydice, 293
Zig Zag Larkspur, 341

ABOUT THE AUTHORS

Sandra Namoff is a botanist and botany instructor. As an adjunct professor, she teaches biology classes and hopes to inspire the next generation of California botanists. She has also taught numerous botany workshops for the California Native Plant Society and other organizations. After completing her undergraduate degree in biology at Florida International University, she worked at Miami's Fairchild Tropical Botanic Garden as a research assistant for the Palm Biology Program. She then moved west to study plants in the genus *Calystegia* at California Botanic Garden/Claremont Graduate University. During her Ph.D. work, she traveled around California and became enamored with the flora. Her research interests include conservation genetics, systematics, and floristics. When not immersed in plant work, Sandy enjoys gardening, hiking, pottery, and growing houseplants, especially begonias.

John Game grew up in England and has liked plants since early childhood. In 1978, he came to California to pursue a career in molecular genetics at the Lawrence Berkeley National Laboratory. He developed a strong interest in Californian plants and plant photography. He became an active member of the California Native Plant Society and a research associate at the University of California Herbarium at Berkeley. Special interests include ferns, bryophytes, and the family Liliaceae, as well as plants of the Pacific Islands. He is currently on the board of directors for Calflora and is a research associate and fellow at the National Tropical Botanical Garden on Kauai in Hawaii.

Bruce Homer-Smith is the author of PlantID. net, a website that helps curious people identify and learn about California's wild plants. He's an active California Native Plant Society member in the Marin and Santa Clara chapters, where he collaborates with dozens of experts and photographers to write photo-rich stories about California plants for PlantID. net. Developing database skills he now uses to describe plants, he spent 30 years running Quartet Systems, a custom database developer. His team worked closely with small groups of experts at the University of California, the Catholic Church, and Alameda County to build beautiful systems. Bruce has recently developed a learning system for grasses that focuses on common grasses of the greater Bay Area.

Nick Jensen currently serves as the Conservation Program Director for the California Native Plant Society and is a fellow of the Switzer Foundation. In this position, he oversees the conservation work of staff and volunteer advocates statewide. Nick's work involves state and federal legislative advocacy, project-level work including presiding over litigation, participation in coalitions of environmental organizations, media relations, and supervising a team of talented conservation professionals. Nick earned his B.S. in environmental horticulture at UC Davis and completed his Ph.D. in botany at California Botanic Garden/Claremont Graduate University, where he produced the first Flora of Tejon Ranch and studied evolutionary patterns in perennial *Streptanthus* species (jewelflowers).

Julie Kierstead retired as forest botanist for the Shasta-Trinity National Forest after 30 years, from 1989 to 2019, conducting rare plant surveys and managing the botany program for this 2.2-million-acre federal property. She earned a B.S. in botany from Oregon State University and an M.S. in biology from Northern Arizona University. Her focus is on the Klamath Range flora of Northwest California, where she has published several new species, and she recently co-authored the book *Wildflowers of California's Klamath Mountains*. Julie is a California certified consulting botanist and currently serves on the Calflora board of directors and the California Native Plant Society's Rare Plant Program Committee.

Shawna Martinez is a professor emeritus in botany from Sierra College, where she spent 33 years teaching classes in forestry, biology, botany, and environmental science. She spent the earlier part of her career working for the U.S. Forest Service as a rare plant botanist. She has led many ecology-based field trips over the years for Sierra College, both locally and abroad. She also has spent time leading wildflower and naturalist hikes for the California Native Plant Society, other non-profits, and several local land trusts. She earned her B.S. degree from UC Davis in natural resource science and completed her M.S. in conservation biology and botany from Sacramento State University, which included a thesis on Giant Sequoia ecology. Shawna is an active gardener, hiker, nature enthusiast, and tree-hugger.

Dylan Neubauer is a self-taught, self-employed botanist based in Santa Cruz. For more than 20 years, she has conducted floristic and rare-plant surveys in the Santa Cruz Mountains and elsewhere in California. She is the author of the second edition of the *Checklist of the Vascular Plants of Santa Cruz County, California*, published in 2013 by the local chapter of the California Native Plant Society, and is currently working on a third edition. Dylan also edits botanically themed books, floras, and factsheets and is working on an annotated checklist for the Crooked Creek Station area of the White Mountains in Eastern California. She enjoys collecting and mounting her own herbarium specimens, especially from under-collected areas.

SIMPLE LEAVES

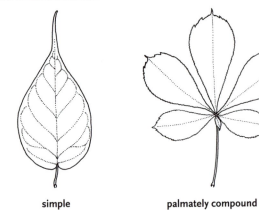
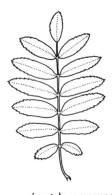

simple   palmately compound   pinnately compound

LEAF SHAPE

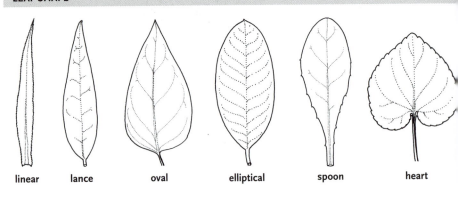

linear   lance   oval   elliptical   spoon   heart

LEAF MARGINS

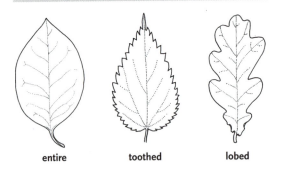

entire   toothed   lobed

LEAF ARRANGEMENT

alternate

INDEX

Abies magnifica, 68
Abronia, 67, 75, 93, 541
Abronia latifolia, 541
Abronia maritima, 407
Abronia turbinata, 215
Abronia umbellata, 407, 408
Abronia villosa, 408
Abutilon palmeri, 464
Acacia, 191
Acacia greggii, 191
Acacia longifolia, 525
Acanthus, 86
Acer, 64, 95
Acer glabrum, 129
Achillea millefolium, 150
Achlys, 87
Achyrachaena mollis, 495
Acmispon americanus, 189
Acmispon glaber, 526
Acmispon strigosus, 526
Acmispon wrangelianus, 527
Aconitum columbianum, 340
Aconitum columbianum subsp.
  viviparum, 340
Acourtia microcephala, 357
Actaea rubra, 240
Adelinia grandis, 282, 362
Adenocaulon bicolor, 153
Adenostoma fasciculatum, 61,
  79–80, 245
Adenostoma sparsifolium, 246
Adobe Lily, 75
Aesculus californica, 95, 260
African Flag, 462
Agarista, 378
Agastache urticifolia, 394
Agave, 86
Agave deserti, 470
Agoseris grandiflora, 496
Alaska Rein Orchid, 124
Alder, 64, 87
Alfalfa, 299
Aliciella monoensis, 228
Alisma triviale, 136
Alkali Seaheath, 387
Alkaliweed, 179

Allium, 86, 269, 351
Allium amplectens, 138
Allium bisceptrum, 351
Allium campanulatum, 351
Allium falcifolium, 351
Allium fimbriatum, 275
Allium haematochiton, 352
Allium howellii, 276
Allium peninsulare, 352
Allium validum, 353
Allophyllum divaricatum, 431
Allophyllum gilioides, 334
Allophyllum gilioides subsp.
  gilioides, 334
Allophyllum gilioides subsp.
  violaceum, 334
Allotropa virgata, 183
Alnus, 64, 87
Alpine Gentian, 194
Alpine Ivesia, 563
Alpine Lewisia, 213
Alpine Mountain Sorrel, 441
alpine vegetation, 68
Amaranth, 86
Amaranth, 86
Amaranthus albus, 110
Ambrosia chamissonis, 112
Ambrosia dumosa, 112
Ambrosia salsola, 113
Amelanchier alnifolia, 246
Amelanchier utahensis, 247
American Black Nightshade, 268
American Pokeweed, 94, 225
American Speedwell, 333
American Trailplant, 153
American Vetch, 302
American Yellowrocket, 512
Ammania, 92
Amorpha californica, 293
Amorpha fruticosa, 293
Amsinckia, 458, 459
Amsinckia eastwoodiae, 458
Amsinckia menziesii, 458
Amsinckia tessellata, 459
Anaphalis margaritacea, 154
Andersonglossum occidentale, 362

Andrew's Clintonia, 397
Anemone occidentalis, 240
Anemopsis californica, 261
Angelica capitellata, 141
Angelica lineariloba, 141
Angle-stem Buckwheat, 234
Anise Swallowtail Butterfly, 111,
  141, 145, 471
Anisocoma acaulis, 496
Anna's Hummingbird, 392
Antelope Bitterbrush, 256
Anthriscus caucalis, 142
Antirrhinum confertiflorum, 226
Antirrhinum coulterianum, 226
Antirrhinum filipes, 556
Antirrhinum kelloggii, 327
Antirrhinum mohavea, 556
Antirrhinum nuttallianum, 327
Antirrhinum vexillocalyculatum,
  328
Anza-Borrego Desert State
  Park, 75
Apache Plume, 250
Aphyllon californicum, 324
Aphyllon fasciculatum, 548
Apiastrum angustifolium, 142
Apocynum cannabinum, 148
Aquilegia formosa, 447
Aquilegia pubescens, 241
Aralia californica, 87, 149
Arbutus menziesii, 67
Arctic Sweet Coltsfoot, 152
Arctostaphylos, 61, 68, 89
Arctostaphylos glandulosa, 183
Arctostaphylos glauca, 184
Arctostaphylos manzanita, 184
Arctostaphylos manzanita subsp.
  glaucescens, 184
Arctostaphylos pallida, 100
Arctostaphylos viscida, 185
Arenaria, 173
Argemone munita, 223
Aristida purpurea, 63
Aristolochi, 87
Aristolochia californica, 87, 355
Arizona Popcorn Flower, 162

Armeria maritima, 431
Arrowleaf Balsamroot, 474, 475
Arrowleaf Ragwort, 492
Arrowweed, 360
Arroyo Lupine, 299
Artemisia, 87
Artemisia californica, 61, 113
Artemisia douglasiana, 114
Artemisia dracunculus, 114
Artemisia tridentata, 58, 61, 69, 115
Arum, 86–87
Asarum, 87
Asarum caudatum, 356
Asclepias, 86, 354
Asclepias californica, 353
Asclepias cordifolia, 354
Asclepias eriocarpa, 79, 148
Asclepias fascicularis, 354
Asclepias subulata, 473
Asian Ginseng, 87
Astragalus brauntonii, 100
Astragalus coccineus, 380
Astragalus didymocarpus, 293
Astragalus lentiginosus, 294
Astragalus purshii, 294
Astragalus trichopodus, 190
Asyneuma prenanthoides, 290
Athysanus pusillus, 164
Atriplex, 67
Atriplex canescens, 117
Atriplex confertifolia, 69
Atriplex hymenelytra, 118
Atriplex semibaccata, 118
Australian Saltbush, 118

Baby Blue Eyes, 304
Baby's Breath, 88
Baccharis pilularis, 61, 154
Baccharis salicifolia, 155
Baileya multiradiata, 474
Bailey's Buckwheat, 234
Bajada Lupine, 297
Baja Fairy Duster, 381
Bald Duskywing Butterfly, 189
Ballhead Ipomopsis, 229
Ballhead Sandwort, 173
Balsamorhiza, 474
Balsamorhiza deltoidea, 474

Balsamorhiza sagittata, 475
Barbarea orthoceras, 512
Barberry, 87
Bastard Sage, 239
Bastard Toadflax, 88, 177
Bayberry, 92
Bay Forget-me-not, 284
Beach Suncup, 543
Bead Lily, 204
Beaked Penstemon, 430
Beargrass, 95, 210
Bear Vally, 75
Beautiful Rockcress, 285
Beavertail Grass, 320
Beavertail Prickly-pear, 367
Bebbia juncea, 502
Beckwith's Violet, 348
Bellflower, 88
Ben Lomond Wallflower, 105
Berberis, 87
Berberis aquifolium, 511
Bermuda Buttercup, 550
Betula, 87
Bidens frondosa, 502
Bigberry Manzanita, 184
Bigelow's Monkeyflower, 423
Bigelow's Sneezeweed, 483
Bigelow's Tickseed, 488
Big-leaf Periwinkle, 277
Big Sagebrush, 58, 61, 69, 115
Bigseed Biscuitroot, 146
biogeography, 52–58
biological organization, 81–82
Birch, 87
Birch-leaf Mountain Mahogany, 247
Birdcage Evening Primrose, 219
Bird's-eye Gilia, 337
Bitter Cherry, 254
Bitter-root, 214
Blackberry, 65, 68
Black Elderberry, 272
Black Mustard, 513, 515
Black Sage, 316
Bladderpod, 88, 522
Blazing Star, 92
Blennosperma nanum, 475

Bloomeria crocea, 566
Blow Wives, 495
Blueberry, 89
Blue Dicks, 346
Blue Fiesta-flower, 306
Bluegrass, 63
Bluehead Gilia, 336
Blue Palo Verde, 531
Blue Sage, 317
Blue Toadflax, 330
Bluff Lettuce, 522
Boechera breweri, 285
Boechera breweri subsp. *shastaensis*, 285
Boechera pulchra, 285
Boechera sparsiflora, 286
Bogbean, 92
Bog Laurel, 377
Booth's Suncup, 217
Borage, 87
Bougainvillea, 93
Bowl-tube Iris, 308
Boykinia occidentalis, 261
Boykinia rotundifolia, 262
Branching Phacelia, 198
Brass Buttons, 505
Brassica nigra, 513
Brassica oleracea, 87
Brassica tournefortii, 513
Braunton's Milkvetch, 100
Brewer's Fleabane, 278
Brewer's Mitrewort, 129
Brewer's Monardella, 311
Brewer's Mountain Heather, 378
Brewer's Rockcress, 285
Brewers's Calandrinia, 405
Brewers's Navarretia, 559
Brickellia californica, 503
Bristly Jewelflower, 288
Bristly Ox-tongue, 497
Broadleaf Arrowhead, 137
Broadleaf Cattail, 66
Broadleaf Stonecrop, 524
Broad-Lipped Twayblade, 124
Broccoli, 87
Brodiaea, 96–97
Brodiaea, 97
Brodiaea coronaria, 344